Christianity
and Monasticism
in Aswan and Nubia

Christianity and Monasticism in Aswan and Nubia

Edited by
Gawdat Gabra and Hany N. Takla

The American University in Cairo Press
Cairo   New York

Dar el Kutub No. 14559/15
ISBN 978 977 416 764 5

Dar el Kutub Cataloging-in-Publication Data

Gabra, Gawdat
        Christianity and Monasticism in Aswan and Nubia/Gawdat Gabra, Hany Takla.—
Cairo: The American University in Cairo Press, 2016
        p.   cm.
        ISBN: 978 977 416 764 5
        Coptic Church——History
        Coptic Monasticism and religious order—Egypt
        I. Takla, Hany (jt. Author)
        276. 2301

1 2 3 4 5   20 19 18 17 16

Designed by Jon W. Stoy
Printed in Egypt

Contents

List of Illustrations   ix
Contributors   xiii
Foreword   xvii
Introduction   xix

Language and Literature
1. Coptic Ostraca from Hagr Edfu   1
   Anke Ilona Blöbaum
2. Imagining Macedonius, the First Bishop of Philae   9
   James E. Goehring
3. Apa Hadra (Hidra) in the *Difnar*   21
   Nashaat Mekhaiel
4. Christianity on Philae   27
   Samuel Moawad
5. The Indexing of Manuscripts of the Monastery
   of the Great Saint Pachomius in Edfu   39
   Fr. Angelous el-Naqlouny
6. The Beginnings of Christianity in Nubia   47
   Siegfried G. Richter
7. A Foreshadowing of the Desert Spirituality in Ancient Nubia
   and Upper Egypt   55
   Ashraf Alexandre Sadek

8. Contested Frontiers: Southern Egypt and Northern Nubia,
    AD 300–1500: The Evidence of the Inscriptions   63
    Jacques van der Vliet
9. The Veneration of Saints in Aswan and Nubia   79
    Youhanna Nessim Youssef

Art, Archaeology, and Material Culture

10. Dayr al-Kubbaniya: Review of the Documentation
    on the 'Isisberg' Monastery   93
    Renate Dekker
11. The Development of the Church at Dayr Anba Hadra:
    A Study of the Plasterwork and Dated Inscriptions   105
    Renate Dekker
12. An Updated Plan of the Church at Dayr Qubbat al-Hawa   117
    Renate Dekker
13. The Christian Wall Paintings from the Temple of Isis
    at Aswan Revisited   137
    Jitse H.F. Dijkstra and Gertrud J.M. van Loon
14. Monastic Life in Makuria   157
    Włodzimierz Godlewski
15. Christian Aswan in the Modern Era and the History
    of Its Cathedral   175
    Metropolitan Hedra
16. The Word and the Flesh   187
    Karel C. Innemée
17. The Ascension Scene in the Apse of the Church at
    Dayr Qubbat al-Hawwa: A Comparative Study   201
    Mary Kupelian
18. The Nubian Marble Object Preserved in Dayr al-Suryan
    in Wadi al-Natrun   213
    Bishop Martyros
19. The Digital 3D Virtual Reconstruction of the Monastic
    Church, Qubbat al-Hawa   221
    Howard Middleton-Jones
20. Christian Objects in the Aswan and Nubia Museums   231
    Atif Naguib
21. Sources for the Study of Late Antique and Early Medieval
    Hagr Edfu   237
    Elisabeth R. O'Connell

22. Christianity in Kom Ombo   249
    Adel F. Sadek
23. Identification of the Monastery of the Nubians in
    Wadi al-Natrun   257
    Fr. Bigoul al-Suriany
24. Monneret de Villard (1881–1954) and Nubia   265
    Fr. Awad Wadi

Preservation
25. The Conservation of the Mural Paintings of
    St. Hatre Monastery   271
    Ashraf Nageh

Abbreviations   281

Bibliography   283

Illustrations

Figure

1.1	Writing exercise: grouped lines and isolated words	3
1.2	Writing exercise: isolated letters and syllables	4
1.3	Writing exercise: isolated letters, syllables, set phrases, and book-hand	5
4.1	The First Cataract area in Late Antiquity	27
4.2	Plan of the Island of Philae	35
10.1	'Isisberg' Monastery: view from the north	94
10.2	'Isisberg' Monastery: view from the east	95
10.3	'Isisberg' Monastery: plan of the monastery	95
10.4	'Isisberg' Monastery: view from the south	96
10.5	'Isisberg' Monastery: the Virgin and a saint	100
11.1	Dayr Anba Hadra: plasterwork in the *khurus*	108
11.2	Dayr Anba Hadra: the sanctuary, to the north of the niche	109
11.3	Dayr Anba Hadra: the sanctuary, to the south of the niche	109
11.4	Dayr Anba Hadra: the western niche	110
11.5	Dayr Anba Hadra: Christ flanked by bowing angels	111
11.6	Dayr Anba Hadra: the 'hidden' cave wall	112
12.1	Dayr Qubbat al-Hawa: view of the church	119
12.2	Dayr Qubbat al-Hawa: plan of the church	121
12.3	Dayr Qubbat al-Hawa: the sanctuary	122
12.4	Dayr Qubbat al-Hawa: updated plan of the church	123
12.5	Dayr Qubbat al-Hawa: the staircase in the northern aisle	124
12.6	Dayr Qubbat al-Hawa: painting of three figures	129
12.7	Dayr Qubbat al-Hawa: painting of two monks	130
12.8	Dayr Qubbat al-Hawa: figurative graffito of a praying monk	130
12.9	Dayr Qubbat al-Hawa: recently discovered painting	131

12.10   Dayr Qubbat al-Hawa: painting   131
12.11   Dayr Qubbat al-Hawa: recently discovered *dipinto*   133
13.1   Topographical map with areas investigated during the first six
        campaigns of the Swiss–Egyptian mission   138
13.2   The temple of Isis at Aswan   139
13.3   Key map to the temple of Isis at Aswan with a tentative
        reconstruction of (parts of) the church   139
13.4   Temple of Isis at Aswan: plans of the south face of the
        northern pillar and the north face of the southern pillar with
        the graffiti and the (approximate) position of the wall paintings   142
13.5   Temple of Isis at Aswan: wall painting on the south face of the
        northern pillar   143
13.6   Temple of Isis at Aswan: wall painting on the north face of the
        southern pillar   144
13.7   Bawit, Chapel III, north wall: David in King Saul's armor   145
13.8   Sohag, Red Monastery, Church of Anba Bishai, northern conch of the
        sanctuary   147
13.9   Bawit, Chapel XVIII, niche in east wall: the Virgin Mary accompanied
        by archangels   147
14.1   Apa Amone. Cathedral of Paulos, Pachoras (Faras)   158
14.2   Pachoras. The hermitage of Theophilos; plan and walls with
        localization of the texts   161
14.3   Qasr al-Wizz. Plan of the early monastery   164
14.4   Dongola. Kom H. Monastic Church   168
14.5   Dongola. Kom H. Building S, hermitage and chapel of Anna By   169
14.6   Dongola. Kom H. Building S, graffiti   170
14.7   Dongola. Kom H. The chapel over bishops' tombs   171
15.1   Aswan Cathedral: Somers Clarke memorial   181
15.2   Aswan Cathedral exterior   183
15.3   Aswan Cathedral at night   183
15.4   Aswan Cathedral interior   184
15.5   Aswan Cathedral: archangel doors   185
16.1   Apse from cell 6 in Bawit   191
16.2   Northern semi-dome, Epiphany, Dayr al-Suryan   193
16.3   Nativity from Abdalla Nirqi, Central Church   195
16.4   Nativity from the Cathedral of Faras   195
16.5   Southern semi-dome, Christ Enthroned between four evangelists,
        Red Monastery, Sohag   196
16.6   Cross-theophany from Abdalla Nirqi, Central Church   197
16.7   Apse with double composition, Qubbat al-Hawa   198
17.1   The western apse in the northern church at Dayr Qubbat al-Hawa   205
17.2   The northern wall showing saints with a square halo at Dayr
        Qubbat al-Hawa   205
17.3   The Ascension in the western semi-dome of the nave in the Church
        of al-Adra at Dayr al-Suryan   206

17.4   The Ascension scene, the Sanctuary of Benjamin, Dayr Abu Maqar,
       in Wadi al-Natrun   208
17.5   The central apse in the Chapel of al-Adra in Dayr Abu Sayfayn,
       a mixture of Ascension and Christ in Majesty   209
17.6   Christ Enthroned in Majesty, flanked by two angels, Dayr Anba
       Hadra at Aswan   210
18.1   Marble tray with the inscription of King Giorgios IV from the
       Monastery of the Syrians in Wadi al-Natrun   214
18.2   Back of the tray of King Giorgios IV   214
18.3   The monasteries of the area of St. John the Little, including
       the Monastery of (Nubians?) and the Monastery of St. Pshoi
       (Anba Bishoi), as well as Dayr al-Suryan   218
19.1   Overall view of the site of Qubbat al-Hawa from the Nile   222
19.2   Qubbat al-Hawa: west apse with the bust of Christ and angels   223
19.3   Qubbat al-Hawa: revised floor plan   224
19.4   Qubbat al-Hawa: initial reconstruction model   225
19.5   Qubbat al-Hawa: initial reconstruction model showing the
       location of the apse with paintings and staircase   226
20.1   Wooden Coptic cross from Gebel Adda   235
20.2   Kohl stick from Sabagura, tenth century   235
20.3   Pottery bowls used in the prayer for the anointing of the sick   236
20.4   Pottery tray from Elephantine decorated with a fish, tenth century 236
21.1   Quickbird satellite image of the Edfu region   237
21.2   Topographical map of Hagr Edfu (2011) with Areas indicated   241
21.3   Hagr Edfu: plan of architecture in Area 2a–b   242
21.4   Hagr Edfu: facsimile of painted cross in Tomb D, Area 2a   243
21.5   Hagr Edfu: ostracon from Area 2a   244
21.6   Hagr Edfu: frontispiece of the Martyrdom of St. Mercurius   246
22.1   Ombos viewed from the Nile   249
22.2   Plan of the column bases forming the church in the Ptolemaic
       temple at Kom Ombo   251
22.3   Copper chalice with inscriptions from Kom Ombo   252
22.4   Iron cross with inscriptions from Kom Ombo   253
22.5   Kom Ombo: copper chandelier ornamented with crosses, with
       places to hold oil lamps   253
22.6   Kom Ombo: wooden weight box with carved cross on the cover   254
25.1   St. Hatre Monastery: apse of the main church, in 1927 (above) and
       in 2010 (below)   272
25.2   St. Hatre Monastery: location of the monastery   273
25.3   St. Hatre Monastery: ground floor plan, showing the location of
       the wall paintings   274
25.4   St. Hatre Monastery: first floor and the keep plan, showing the
       locations of the wall paintings   275
25.5   Composition of the wall-painting layers in St. Hatre monastery   276

Contributors

Anke Ilona Blöbaum is a research assistant at the Institute for Egyptology and Coptology of Münster, specializing in Ancient Egyptian and Coptic language and literature. She is currently working on a publication of the Coptic ostraca found at Hagr Edfu.

Renate Dekker studied Coptology at Leiden University and wrote her MPhil thesis on the "Encomium on Bishop Pesynthios of Coptos." She is currently working on her PhD, on the subject of the episcopal authority of Theban bishops in late antiquity, and on the publication of Dayr Qubbat al-Hawa.

Jitse H.F. Dijkstra is associate professor of classics at the University of Ottawa. He has published widely on Late Antique Egypt, in particular the monograph *Philae and the End of Ancient Egyptian Religion* (2008). Since 2001, he has been a member of the joint Swiss–Egyptian archaeological mission at Aswan.

Gawdat Gabra is the former director of the Coptic Museum, Cairo, a member of the board of the Society of Coptic Archaeology, and chief editor of the St. Mark Foundation for Coptic History Studies. He is the author, coauthor, and editor of numerous books related to the literary and material culture of Egyptian Christianity. He has taught at American and Egyptian universities. He is currently a visiting professor of Coptic Studies at Claremont Graduate University, California.

Włodzimierz Godlewski is professor of archaeology at Warsaw University. He directs the Polish Center in Cairo excavations in Naqlun and in Old Dongola in Sudan. He is the author of several publications on archaeology and the history of Christian Nubia and Egypt.

James E. Goehring is professor of religion at the University of Mary Washington in Fredericksburg, Virginia. He is the author of *Ascetics, Society, and the Desert: Studies* *in Early Egyptian Monasticism* (1999) and coeditor of *The World of Early Egyptian Christianity* (2007).

Metropolitan Hedra obtained a bachelor's degree in agriculture science from Alexandria University in 1962. In 1970 he joined the Monastery of the Syrians (Dayr al-Suryan). Pope Shenouda III ordained him Bishop of Aswan in 1975 and Metropolitan in 2006. He built the Cathedral of the Archangel Michael in Aswan, the second largest cathedral in Egypt.

Karel Innemée is an affiliated fellow at the faculty of Archaeology, Leiden University (Netherlands). He is the project director of the Leiden Wadi al-Natrun project, which includes excavation at Dayr al-Baramus, survey at the site of Dayr Abu Maqar, and conservation work at Dayr al-Surian.

Mary Kupelian is a lecturer in the Faculty of Tourism and Hotel Management, Helwan University. In June 2010, she was awarded a PhD in Tourism Guidance; her dissertation was on "Art and Archaeology in Egypt in the Byzantine Era" under the joint supervision of Helwan University and Leiden University (Netherlands). Her research interests include Coptic monastic wall paintings and the Armenian heritage in Egypt.

Bishop Martyros is General Bishop in the Coptic Orthodox Church in Cairo. He was formerly the hegumen of the Syrian Monastery in Wadi al-Natrun. He is a frequent contributor to international conferences of Coptology. He has authored multiple books on Coptic monasticism in Wadi al-Natrun.

Nashaat Mekhaiel is a researcher at the University of Münster. He holds a PhD from the University of Münster on the subject of the Coptic *Difnar*. He is the author of a number of articles on this subject.

Howard Middleton-Jones is an archaeologist with a special interest in the Coptic period in Egypt. He teaches Coptic Studies modules for the part-time Humanities degree and the Department of Continuing Adult Education at Swansea University, Wales, UK. He is also the originator and author of the Coptic Multi-Media Database project.

Samuel Moawad is a Coptologist and researcher at the Institute for New Testament Textual Research at the University of Münster (Germany), specializing in Coptic and Copto-Arabic literature.

Ashraf Nageh is a specialist conservator of wall paintings and building materials at the Supreme Council of Antiquities in Egypt. He is a member of the French mission in Bawit and the Dutch mission in Hammam Faroun. He holds a doctorate from Cairo University and participates in various restoration projects.

Atif Naguib is the director of the Museum of Aswan. He holds a PhD from the Higher Institute of Coptic Studies, Cairo, on the subject of the Coptic Church and Nubia.

He is the coauthor of *Tarikh al-masihiya wa 'atharuha fi Aswan wa-l-Nuba* (History of Christianity and Its Monuments in Aswan and Nubia, 2003).

Fr. Angelous el-Naqlouny is a monk in the Monastery of the Archangel Michael in Naqada. He is working on the surveying and cataloguing of manuscripts of Christian Egypt within the diocese.

Elisabeth R. O'Connell is curator of Roman and Late Antique Egypt in the Department of Ancient Egypt and Sudan in the British Museum. She is co-director (with W.V. Davies) of the British Museum Expedition to Hagr Edfu and a member of the Italian mission to Antinoopolis.

Siegfried G. Richter is Special Professor at the Institute of Egyptology and Coptology at the University of Münster, and research associate of the North Rhine–Westphalian Academy of Science and Humanities at the Institute for New Testament Textual Research, Münster. He has taught Coptic and Oriental studies in Münster, Bonn, and Munich and is the author of several books and articles on history, culture, and religion in late antique Egypt and Nubia.

Adel Sadek is a lecturer at the Institute of Coptic Studies, Anba Ruways, Cairo. For many years he participated in the restoration of manuscripts of the Coptic Patriarchate and many monasteries. He has authored a number of books in Arabic about the history and heritage of several Coptic dioceses. He is currently a member of the editorial board of *Bulletin of Rakoti: Spotlight on Coptic Studies*, published in Arabic in Alexandria.

Ashraf Alexandre Sadek is professor of Egyptology and biblical archaeology at the University of Limoges in France, as well as professor in Coptic Orthodox faculties in Egypt and Europe, and in the Coptic Institute of Higher Studies in Cairo. A one-time inspector for Egypt's Department of Antiquities, he is the author of books on the history of religion and on Egyptian philology, including the first Hieroglyphics–French dictionary, in collaboration with Yvonne Bonnamy. For thirty-six years he has been the editor of the journal *Le monde copte*, which has published thirty-four volumes dedicated to Coptic culture.

Fr. Bigoul al-Suriany is a Coptic monk and scholar, and curator of manuscripts at the library of the Syrian Monastery in Wadi al-Natrun, responsible for the monastery's conservation, restoration, and excavation projects. He is the author of several books on Coptic history.

Hany N. Takla is founding president of the St. Shenouda the Archimandrite Coptic Society, director of the St. Shenouda Center for Coptic Studies, Coptic language instructor at the Pope Shenouda III Theological College in Los Angeles, and a member of the board of trustees for the St. Mark Coptic Cultural Center in Cairo. He is currently a Coptic language lecturer at the University of California, Los Angeles (UCLA).

Jacques van der Vliet is senior lecturer in Coptology at Leiden University, and Extraordinary Professor of Egyptology and Coptology at Radboud University, Nijmegen, the Netherlands. He is a member of the Polish archaeological mission in Naqlun, and participates in various epigraphical and papyrological projects.

Gertrud J.M. van Loon is a researcher at KU Leuven University (Belgium). Her research interests include painting, iconography and iconology, and early monasticism. She is currently working in Middle Egypt, documenting monastic sites in pharaonic quarries and tombs.

Fr. Awad Wadi is a Franciscan friar and, since 1986, researcher in the Franciscan Oriental Christian Studies in Cairo. He teaches patrology in the Coptic Catholic Seminary and in the Theological Institute in Cairo. He is the author of many articles and books in the field of Christian Arabic heritage.

Youhanna Nessim Youssef is senior research associate at the Centre for Early Christian Studies, Australian Catholic University. He is currently editing the Coptic and Copto-Arabic corpus of Severus of Antioch, and is the author of several books and articles on Coptic literature, history, liturgy, art, and Christian Arabic studies.

Foreword

Fawzy Estafanous

THIS IS THE FIFTH volume of the series *Christianity and Monasticism in Egypt*. It contains the essays presented at the fifth international symposium of the St. Mark Foundation for Coptic History Studies and the St. Shenouda the Archimandrite Coptic Society. The symposium was held from January 31 to February 4, 2010 in a beautiful spot near the Monastery of St. Hadra, west of Aswan. In addition to a number of Egyptians, the invited contributors, who represent a variety of academic disciplines, came from Australia, England, France, Germany, the Netherlands, Poland, and the United States. Their valuable contributions show the richness of the Christian heritage in this southernmost part of Egypt including "Egyptian Nubia." Taken together, these contributions cover many aspects of Coptic civilization and Christian Nubian culture as well. Moreover, they reflect the strong relations between the Coptic Church and the Nubian Church during the late antique and medieval periods. Heartfelt thanks are due to all the scholars for traveling long distances to participate in the symposium and for enriching the volume with their contributions. We are looking forward to our next symposium, "Christianity and Monasticism in Middle Egypt," which will be held in Dayr al-Muharraq from the fourth to the eighth of February, 2013.

As we progress toward covering Christianity and monasticism in the remaining regions of Egypt, I remember in deep gratitude the unforgettable love of His Holiness the late Pope Shenouda III, whose unparalleled support for the St. Mark Foundation has greatly encouraged all its activities in general and these symposia in particular. His Holiness showed great interest in welcoming scholars in his residence before the beginning of each symposium and encouraged them to devote more research to Coptic monasticism. Needless to say, Pope Shenouda was once a monk, and he was convinced that when monasticism in the Egyptian deserts is strong, then Christianity and the Coptic Church are strong. Therefore, he repopulated many of the abandoned monasteries and encouraged them to be cultural centers and to receive visitors.

I would like to give special thanks to His Eminence Metropolitan Hedra for hosting the symposium in the new residences in such a fantastic area. My thanks are due to Mr. Michael Kamel and his wife for their great efforts before and during the symposium in every respect. I thank Mr. Megala Habib for the preparatory work for the symposium in Aswan.

I am indebted to Sherif Doss and Shahira Loza for their unfailing support. As always, I thank the organizers of the symposium: Faheem Wassef and Niveen Ramzy. A special thank-you goes to Hoda Garas who finalized contacts with the contributors.

Fawzy Estafanous, President
The St. Mark Foundation for Coptic History Studies

Introduction

Gawdat Gabra and Hany N. Takla

WITH TWO EXCEPTIONS, the chapters in this volume originated as papers presented to the international symposium "Christianity and Monasticism in Aswan and Nubia" organized by the St. Mark Foundation for Coptic History Studies and the St. Shenouda the Archimandrite Coptic Society. The symposium was held from 31 January to 4 February 2010 in the new residences that the Coptic Orthodox diocese of Aswan built near the Monastery of St. Hadra on the west bank of the Nile.

The contributors to the symposium, and other scholars who were not able to come to Aswan, were invited to cover the Christian heritage in the region extending from Edfu in the north to the Egyptian–Sudanese frontier in the south. Today the governorate of Aswan and—ecclesiastically—the Coptic Orthodox diocese of Aswan administer this very region. However, geographical or political terms such as Lower Nubia, Upper Nubia, Egyptian Nubia, and Sudanese Nubia do not represent ethnic distinctions. Although Christian Nubia is in many respects, especially ethnically and linguistically, independent and different from Christian Egypt, there is no doubt that one has to research Christian Egypt when dealing with most of the aspects of Christianity in Nubia. This fact is clearly evident in a number of chapters, in particular the contributions of Jacques van der Vliet, "Contested Frontiers: Southern Egypt and Northern Nubia, AD

300–1500: The Evidence of the Inscriptions"; Włodzimierz Godlewski, "Monastic Life in Makuria"; and Karel C. Innemée, "The Word and the Flesh." This applies also to the chapters related to early Christianity in Nubia—Siegfried G. Richter, "The Beginnings of Christianity in Nubia"; James E. Goehring, "Imagining Macedonius, the First Bishop of Philae"; and Samuel Moawad, "Christianity on Philae"—as well as the chapter of Youhanna Nessim Youssef on the veneration of saints in Aswan and Nubia. Relations between Christian Nubia and Wadi al-Natrun are discussed by Bishop Martyros, "The Nubian Marble Object Preserved in Dayr al-Suryan in Wadi al-Natrun," and Fr. Bigoul al-Suriany, "Identification of the Monastery of the Nubians in Wadi al-Natrun." Atif Naguib describes several Christian objects in the Aswan and Nubia Museums that originate from Abdalla Nirqi, Sakinya, Qasr al-Wizz, Gebel Adda, Sabagura, Wadi al-Sebua, Aswan, and Elephantine. Fr. Wadi Awad highlights the invaluable studies of Monneret de Villard (1881–1954) on Christian Nubia, the majority of which are based on archaeological expeditions.

During late antique and medieval times the 'borderlands' of northern Nubia and southern Egypt comprised the area of Aswan in addition to Philae, where the 'frontier' was sometimes moved southward or northward. Important Christian monuments of that region have been thoroughly investigated by Jitse H.F. Dijkstra and Gertrud J.M. van Loon, "The Christian Wall Paintings from the Temple of Isis at Aswan Revisited," and Renate Dekker, "Dayr al-Kubbaniya," "Dayr Anba Hadra," and "Dayr Qubbat al-Hawa." Ashraf Nageh explains how to conserve the deteriorating wall paintings of Dayr Anba Hadra. While Mary Kupelian makes the Ascension scene in the apse of the church at Dayr Qubbat al-Hawa the object of an intensive study, Howard Middleton-Jones demonstrates the advantages of the digital reconstruction project, which he accomplished in that significant church. Nashaat Mekhaiel explains the importance of the *Difnar* text on St. Hadra, Bishop of Aswan.

Adel F. Sadek introduces Christianity in Kom Ombo, which lies twenty-five miles north of Aswan, focusing on the metal liturgical objects discovered there. Hagr Edfu is the northernmost site covered by contributors to the symposium. Elisabeth R. O'Connell explores Christianity at that site in late antique and early medieval times using the results of the British Museum mission, which started work there in 2000, as well as the information from medieval manuscripts found in the site. Anke Ilona Blöbaum introduces the Coptic ostraca of Hagr Edfu that were discovered in 1981.

Fr. Angelous el-Naqlouny describes the new manuscripts of the monastery of St. Pachomius at Hagr Edfu, which was resettled in 1975.

Metropolitan Hedra summarizes the history of Christianity in modern times in the diocese of Aswan and tells the story of the second largest Coptic Orthodox cathedral in Egypt.

It is evident that the volume lacks chapters on a number of important sites, such as Qasr Ibrim and Elephantine, and on significant topics, including the Christian pottery in the area of Aswan and the tombstones of the Monastery of St. Hadra. This is due either to the withdrawal of some scholars only a few months before the symposium or the inability of others, who presented their papers, to submit them for publication. Therefore, after covering the regions of Middle Egypt, Cairo and the Delta, and the Egyptian deserts, we hope to dedicate a symposium to the sites and subjects that were not covered in the series "Christianity and Monasticism in Egypt." This will be followed by a general index of all the published volumes.

Our heartfelt thanks are due, first and foremost, to the symposium participants for their travel to Aswan and for their valuable contributions. We would like to express our special thanks to His Eminence Metropolitan Hedra for hosting the symposium. Our thanks are due to Dr. Fawzy Estafanous, President of the St. Mark Foundation, for his great efforts in supporting research on Christianity and monasticism in Egypt. Finally, we would like to express our thanks to the American University in Cairo Press for their interest and professionalism in publishing the proceedings of the symposia on Christianity and Monasticism in Egypt, and especially to Mark Linz, former director; Nigel Fletcher-Jones, present director; Neil Hewison, associate director for editorial programs; Nadia Naqib, managing editor; Johanna Baboukis, project editor; and Cait Hawkins, for her tireless work in copyediting this volume.

1 Coptic Ostraca from Hagr Edfu

Anke Ilona Blöbaum

WHILE THE GREEK AND COPTIC documentary texts of late antique Tell Edfu are well represented in the scientific discourse,[1] very little information is known about comparable material from Hagr Edfu. In fact, a number of Greek and Coptic ostraca have been located in Hagr Edfu as well.

In the year 1941, a number of Coptic and Greek ostraca were found near the ruins surrounding the nineteenth-century church. Unfortunately they were never published and their whereabouts remains unknown (Fakhry 1947: 47; Gabra 1985: 11; 1991: 1200; Effland 1999: 25).

Forty years later, during an excavation conducted by the inspector of Edfu at that time, Mohamed Ibrahim, another large number of ostraca were discovered at the site. They were found near the northern wall of the modern monastery, Dayr Anba Bakhum (Monastery of St. Pachomius). These ostraca were previously mentioned by Gawdat Gabra (1985: 12; 1991: 1200), Andreas Effland (1999: 29), Anne Boud'hors (1999: 4), and Elisabeth O'Connell (Davies and O'Connell 2009: 56f.; 2011: 106). They are currently the focus of an editing project associated with the Institute of Egyptology and Coptology at the University of Münster, Germany.[2]

The following short overview of the material is based on the photographic documentation undertaken in the year 1981 during the excavation.[3] The corpus consists of approximately 180 ostraca. Ten of them are inscribed on recto and verso. As most of the material is broken

1

into pieces, the number of fragments is accordingly higher. It is possible
to join several fragments. The size of the ostraca and state of preservation
of the texts differ greatly, from tiny fragments measuring not more than
three centimeters in height and width, with only a few words or even
letters, to completely preserved ostraca measuring more than twenty centimeters in height or width. Most of the texts are Coptic, only two (or
possibly three) ostraca are Greek without a doubt;[4] due to their state of
preservation, the language and script of approximately a dozen other
pieces are difficult to assess.

The types of hands vary. They show a whole spectrum from inexperienced hands to very skillful writing using ligatures. So far, it has been
possible to assign only two ostraca to the same (unnamed) scribe with
confidence. Unfortunately, only set phrases of the beginning of a letter are
preserved on both fragments.

Indeed, most of the texts are letters (for issues of letters and genre, see
Choat 2006). Only a few pieces do not belong to this genre. Phraseol-
ogy and titles clearly set the corpus into a probable monastic context. It
seems to be the correspondence of a relatively small community of monks
or people related to a monastery and a settlement located nearby (cf.
Boud'hors 1999: 4; Davies and O'Connell 2009: 56). This differs from the
mainly economic and administrative character of the Greek and Coptic
documentary texts from Tell Edfu (Boud'hours 1999a: 4).

The dialect is mainly Sahidic. Particular dialectal forms can be related
to the variations of the language in the Coptic texts of Tell Edfu (cf. Bacot
2009: 5ff.). Personal names, like Abraham, Victor, Jacob, Dios, or Kollu-
thos, find parallels in the epigraphic evidence of Hagr Edfu (O'Connell
in Davies and O'Connell 2009: 56), and in the Greek and Coptic texts
of Tell Edfu (cf. Bacot 2009: 198ff.; Remondon 1953: 225ff.). But this
common Onomasticon gives no further results. Specific persons or places
are not identified yet. The subjects of the letters deal mainly with personal
concerns, mostly in connection with requests. Difficulties and questions
concerning, for example, payment, rent, and delivery of goods such as
bread, oil, clothing, and papyrus are described.

As mentioned above, most of the texts contain letters, or rather letter
fragments. Only a few texts do not belong to this group. Three of them
form a small unit of their own because they all belong in a context of education and writing practice (for Greek school text, see Cribiore 1996; for
Coptic, see Cribiore 1999).

There are at least three other ostraca that could possibly also be classified as writing exercises, because the hands seem unskillful and inexperienced, and the orthography is incorrect. But in each case the preserved text is characteristic of a letter, thus making it difficult to decide whether it could be an exercise for a letter or a real letter written by a scribe lacking experience. Without additional clues, I prefer to omit these texts in the following presentation.

1. Fragment of a writing exercise: grouped lines and isolated words[5]

The first exercise is written on a small fragment of pottery (h: 8 cm, w: 7.5 cm). The left margin of the ostracon is incomplete. Parts of four lines are preserved. Three of them consist of groups formed by vertical and horizontal lines (ll. 1, 2, and 4) and the third of two single words. The sherd was reused: in the upper half, two text groupings have been rubbed out. One part (between lines 1 and 2 on the right) was left blank. The group in line 2 and the beginning of line 3 are written over the other cleaned part. In all probability this was done by the same student.

The hand is very unskilled. The groups of lines seem to form rows

Fig. 1.1. Writing exercise: grouped lines and isolated words (D. Johannes)

of the letter ⲡ, but a closer look reveals that it is more a general exercise of writing horizontal and vertical lines than practice of isolated letters. In each case a long continuous horizontal line on the top is combined with three to six vertical lines. Maybe this was a first step of practice before starting to write isolated letters. But the student skipped this next step. Instead of isolated letters, the writer attempted two words: ⲁⲛⲟⲕ and ⲁⲛⲁⲛ (l. 3). The letter ⲁ, in particular, shows a lack of practice. In one case the student had to rewrite the letter twice. Obviously this is an exercise of a writer who has just started to learn.

2. Ostracon with writing exercise: isolated letters and syllables

The second ostracon with a writing exercise seems almost completely preserved (h: ca. 8 cm, w: ca. 6.5 cm). Only the right margin is probably incomplete. The edges are worn and at the upper left a small part of the surface is damaged. The hand is more skillful than the one in figure 1.1, but still gives the impression of inexperience. It is very difficult to recognize any structure or pattern in the text, or, rather, the scrawl, because the student wrote several times on the sherd without first making erasures. As a result, the upper part is not very clear or legible. At least eight lines can be recognized. Three of them were probably written first, the five others over them. It is also possible that a fragment of a non-practice ostracon was reused. Because the whole text in every discernible layer was obviously written by the same hand, this option is not very plausible. The more legible traces give the impression of a student's exercise of isolated letters, with a special focus on ⲝ, and probably also syllables. In the last two lines, for example, ⲕⲁ ⲝⲁ ⲥⲁ (?), and ⲝⲉ ⲡⲉ ϭ[ⲉ] (?) are recognizable.

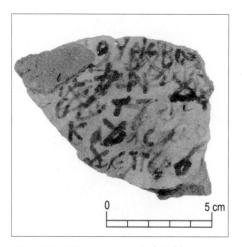

Fig. 1.2. Writing exercise: isolated letters and syllables (D. Johannes)

3. Ostracon with writing exercise: isolated letters, syllables, set phrases, and book-hand

The last of the three writing exercises is an almost completely preserved ostracon (h: ca. 19 cm, w: ca. 11 cm) that shows four different types of training. The hand is very skillful and practiced. Unfortunately the text was rubbed out, so that only some of the content is recognizable. These traces can be divided into four different parts. The first part consists of eleven or twelve lines, most of which were damaged by the cleaning. The words ⲁⲗⲗⲁ and ϥ︦ⲝⲱ ⲙ︦ⲙ[ⲟⲥ] give the impression that the writer had worked on formulating a letter. It is also possible that he reused an ostracon with an old letter for his exercise. In any çase, it is clear that all the text was written by the same hand. Thus its identification as an exercise is more probable.[6] The second part is located below the first. Consisting of three lines, it shows an exercise of a book-hand. The text does not make much sense but this could be because of the damage. Apparently the scribe was concentrating more on forming particular letters, and he did this quite successfully, forming a regular and light book-hand with a wavy character. The empty space on the right side, below the lines and sometimes even between the lines, was used to work on particular letters. Different types of є are visible on the upper part; farther down he focused on ⲱ and ⲱ. This constitutes the third part. Finally, in the fourth part below the last line of the book-hand, he practiced syllables. The text reads ⲟⲱⲱ and ⲱⲱ. This is no longer the work of a student, but of someone who would like to improve his handwriting.

Each of these three ostraca shows a different level of practice and education, giving the impression of a developed system of education and writing practice in the context of the settlement or

Fig. 1.3. Writing exercise: isolated letters, syllables, set phrases, and book-hand (D. Johannes)

a probable monastery. This is supported by the great number and different types of hands appearing in the material. Besides, one of the writers is known by his name, Kyros, as one text (No. 81.004) names ⲕⲩⲣⲟⲥ ⲡⲥⲁϩ within a list of different persons.

Further research on the texts will need to be focused on the organization and relation of the community in the settlement of late antique Hagr Edfu as well as its relation to the town of Tell Edfu. Finally, the question about the chronological dimension of the material arises. This point is still unsettled.

The manuscripts connected with Hagr Edfu date to the tenth to eleventh century AD (Gabra 1985: 9f.). Whereas the Greek and Coptic texts from Tell Edfu have been dated to the seventh century AD (Bacot 2009: 2), late antique ceramics found in Hagr Edfu (area 3) give a range dating from the sixth to the ninth century AD (Davies and O'Connell 2009: 55).

So far, not much information has been found in the texts that can help to date the material, with the exception of the use of set phrases attested from the Theban region and dating to the seventh and eighth centuries AD (Davies and O'Connell 2009: 56, referring to Biedenkopf-Ziehner 1983; for epistolary formulae in early Coptic letters, see Choat 2007 and 2010). Although an adaptation of a systematic paleographic method for Coptic manuscripts as well as for documentary texts is a desideratum in general (Layton 1985; Boud'hors 2006: 106; for a scientific paleography of Coptic with a particular focus on the early documentary material, see Gardner and Choat 2004), features of the book-hand in the last of the presented texts may provide further clues for dating. Monika Hasitzka (1990: 16) and recently Karl-Heinz Brune (2005: 35; 2010: 39) have pointed out that the dating of writing exercises is extremely difficult due to the fact that we are dealing with unskilled hands. Nevertheless, while I appreciate that there are not many paleographic features in text number 3, above, that can help to date it with certainty, I believe that the evidence of the light and wavy character of this book-hand exercise may suggest a date around the eighth century AD. This is supported by three exercises of a similar book-hand that Monika Hasitzka considered to date from the eighth and ninth centuries AD.[7] Further research on the ostraca of Hagr Edfu is required in order to confirm this assumption.

Notes

1   Cf. Crum 1925; Remondon 1953; Gascou 1979; Palme 1986; MacCoull 1988; Fournet and Gascou 1998; Heurtel 1998; Boud'hors 1999; Gascou 1999; Łukaszewicz 1999; Mossakowska 1999; Kruit and Worp 2002; Bacot 2006, 2007, 2008, 2009.

2   The project is kindly supported by a fellowship of the Brigitte and Martin Krause Foundation. The first copy and translation are based mainly on the photographic documentation made in 1981. I am grateful to Gawdat Gabra who not only gave me a set of the pictures but initiated this project in the first place. The corpus is stored in the Elkab magazine, and I am grateful to Vivian Davies and Elisabeth O'Connell who gave me the opportunity to work with the British Museum Expedition in Hagr Edfu and in the Elkab magazine. During the 2010 season it was possible to collate approximately half of the material. The continuation of this work was originally planned for the following season. Due to the political situation in Egypt during spring 2011, this work had to be postponed and was continued in spring 2012. During this season another group of about 380 ostraca

were located in the Elkab Magazine, which can be unmistakably attributed to
Hagr Edfu by physical joints with the whole material.

3 I am deeply grateful to Elisabeth O'Connell for her support, her essential remarks
   and comments on this paper, and revising my English. All of the remaining faults
   are my own responsibility.

4 Four fragments belong together and could be assembled. Judging by the ware and
   the hand, it is most probable that one of the remaining Greek fragments belongs to
   this text, too.

5 Due to the fact that I had the opportunity to collate only one (no. 1) of the three
   original objects, I have not been able to give the exact dimensions or describe the
   pottery. Further, I decided not to give a facsimile that could only be called preliminary but to reduce my contribution to a description of the texts in the present
   context. A full publication of the corpus is planned for 2012.

6 Another suggestion is that the rubbing out of text could be part of the student's
   training. I am grateful to Ludwig D. Morenz for providing this idea in the discussion
   after a presentation of these texts during the second day of "Egyptology in North
   Rhine-Westphalia" (Cologne, 18 November 2010).

7 Hasitzka 1990: 230 (No. 293: O.Berlin P 9427, eighth–ninth century AD); 225 (No.
   285: O.Vindob K539, eighth century AD); and 226–27 (No. 287: O.Vindob K 187,
   eighth century AD).

2

Imagining Macedonius, the First Bishop of Philae

James E. Goehring

As TIM VIVIAN OBSERVED in the introduction to his English translation of *The Histories of the Monks of Upper Egypt and the Life of Onnophrius*, the modern study of monasticism in Egypt, if it treats Aswan (Syene) and Philae at all, tends to relegate them to the borderlands. Histories dependent on the usual sources of early Egyptian monasticism (*Apophthegmata Patrum, Lausiac History, History of the Monks in Egypt*, and *Life of Pachomius*) produce maps that reach no farther south than the monasteries of the Pachomian federation, the southernmost of which was located at Sne (Latopolis), modern-day Esna. When Aswan and Philae do appear, they frame the lower edge of the map, "dangerously close to the borders of the known world" (Vivian 1993: 54–55). The pattern reflects, in fact, the nature of the surviving sources, which likely reflects in turn the general situation in fourth-century Egypt. Aswan and Philae, while important in Egyptian history, occupied the borderlands, the outer limits of the reach of Egyptian and then Roman imperial power. Their status as the outer edge became even more pronounced in AD 298 when Diocletian withdrew from the Dodekaschoinos back to the First Cataract. Aswan, with the associated island of Elephantine, replaced Hiera Sykaminos as the southernmost town in Roman Egypt. Philae, slightly farther south, was retained as an important cult center, guarded by a military camp stationed on the east bank of the Nile.[1]

Borderlands identify the location of contact between those inside and those outside of a politically defined body, in this case the Roman Empire, and more specifically Roman Egypt. Borderlands fashion their own political and social world, defined by the interaction between peoples across the frontier. The Roman administration had thus to deal with a frontier where the indigenous Nubian population, the Noubades, and the Blemmyes impinged upon and interacted with the empire (Dijkstra 2008: 131–73). Access to the cult sites on Philae, for example, was granted to the 'outsiders' and one can only speculate as to how deeply such interaction impacted the social and religious world of the frontier. More significant for my purposes, borderlands, by their very nature, remain peripheral to the center, not only spatially, but also, as viewed from the center, politically, economically, culturally, and intellectually. The political, cultural, and intellectual pull of the empire directed its population's gaze toward the center, which in the case of Egypt meant northward toward Alexandria and thence across the Mediterranean toward Rome and Constantinople. As with gravity, the pull remained weakest in the borderlands, and the very nature of the phenomenon relegated them to relative obscurity. When one turns toward the center, one turns one's back to the borderlands.[2]

While the nature of the borderlands garners some attention in the sources, as one might expect, information is generally limited and historical reconstructions necessarily require considerable speculation. Archaeological evidence and a few brief references in ecclesiastical sources supply relatively concrete points of contact around which one can begin to reconstruct the story of Christianity's emergence and growth in the area, but they offer in themselves little in the sense of an actual story. For the latter, one is often dependent on later hagiographic accounts whose participation in the totalizing discourse of Coptic Christianity renders their use in reconstructing the historical periods they purport to describe suspect at best. While the authors of such texts likely had some form of access to the actual events they describe, their survival as historical facts carries little weight in the literary project. Their inclusion depends on their having been conformed to the prevailing ideology and reconfigured in terms of its purpose and need. The resulting discourse subsumes history into ideology, fashioning the story of Christianity's expansion as a form of manifest destiny. History and ideology become so intertwined as to make their separation impossible, though that does not stop scholars from trying. Indeed we must try, for without the use of such sources, numerous figures, important places, and significant periods in Christian history become little more than disembodied names, inscriptions, and stones.[3]

The figure of Macedonius, the first Christian bishop of Philae (ca. AD 330–50), offers an interesting case in point.[4] In a list of the bishops who subscribed to the Council of Serdica in AD 343, Athanasius names a certain Macedonius seventieth in a list of ninety-four bishops of Egypt.[5] Were we dependent on this reference alone, Macedonius would virtually disappear alongside the numerous other named bishops about whom we know little or nothing. Athanasius does not even include their individual sees, which means that we cannot even be sure that this Macedonius was the bishop of Philae.[6] The entertaining stories of Macedonius of Philae recounted in the Coptic *Life of Aaron*, however, offer a possible link, which draws the name out from the list by embodying it in narrative.[7] While the stories put clothes on the man, so to speak, the tendentious nature of the evidence leaves the historian to struggle with the enigma of a historical figure clothed in imaginative, romantic legend. While the legend certainly offers important information on the religious sensitivities of the text's author and his times, the question of what it can reliably tell us about the historical Macedonius is much less clear. Since, however, it is all that historians have, they are compelled either to grapple with the enigma or concede that the stories are legendary, return to Athanasius's list, and admit that all we really have in the case of the historical Macedonius is a name.

The Coptic *Life of Aaron*[8] survives in complete form in but a single paper manuscript copied in AD 992 by a certain Zokrator, archdeacon of the church of Esna, and donated to the Monastery *(topos)* of Apa Aaron in Edfu. A few fragments of a second manuscript preserved among the cartonnage of other manuscripts from Edfu date to the sixth or seventh century, which coupled with internal evidence indicates a sixth-to-seventh-century date for the original composition (Dijkstra 2008: 227–31). Attributed to a certain Paphnutius,[9] the *Life of Aaron* divides literarily into three distinct sections. The first reports Paphnutius's journey to a monastic community near Syene where Apa Pseleusius regales him with stories about various ascetic holy men (§§1–25); the second section records his visit to the old ascetic Apa Isaac on an island in the First Cataract, where he hears the stories of the bishops of Philae, including those of Macedonius (§§26–85); and the final section records the life and miracles of Apa Aaron as told by Apa Isaac (§§86–140). The hagiographic nature of these stories is unmistakable. They form an ideological discourse on the Christian conquest of Egypt in which the conversion of the famous cult center of Philae marks the final stage. It underscores Christianity's ultimate success through the elimination of paganism in its last stronghold at the edges of civilization.[10]

When Paphnutius turns in section two to the account of Macedonius, he reports that his evidence came from stories passed down orally over three generations, a fact that suggests even in its current literary setting ample opportunity for the emerging discourse of Coptic Christianity to do its work on historical memory. Paphnutius heard the stories from the old monk, Apa Isaac, who had heard them from his holy father, Apa Aaron, who in turn had heard them from the blessed bishop Apa Macedonius himself.[11] The account revolves around Macedonius's killing of the holy falcon in the temple at Philae during the priest's absence and the aftermath of that act. It leads inexorably through a series of secondary accounts to the conversion of all of the island's inhabitants.[12] Cleverly crafted, the story carries its reader through the miraculous conversion of the island, establishing the inevitability of Christianity's success, and, in the process, affirming and undergirding the reader's faith.[13]

The author introduces Macedonius as an orthodox Christian who, on a trip south as "governor *(pagarchē)* over these cities," visited the island of Philae, where he discovers that the local Christians suffer under the island's dominant pagan population.[14] Upon a subsequent trip to Alexandria to meet with a military commander *(stratēlatēs),* he reports the situation to the archbishop Athanasius and asks him to ordain a bishop to minister to the Christians on the island. Recognizing Macedonius's abilities and personal involvement in the situation, Athanasius convinces him to accept the post and ordains him as the first bishop of Philae.[15]

Returning to the island, Macedonius distributes his belongings to the needy and then notices people going into a temple to worship a sacred falcon held in a cage.[16] Shortly thereafter, when the temple's priest, Aristos, is away on business, Macedonius, using the deceit of wanting to offer a sacrifice to the falcon, acquires access to it through the priest's two sons who had been left in charge. Once inside the temple, he removes the falcon from its cage, chops off its head, and throws it into the fire kindled for the sacrifice. Macedonius's act naturally horrifies the priest's sons, who flee to the desert for fear of their father's reaction. The priest eventually returns, discovers what has transpired, and learns the identity of the offender from an old woman, who describes Macedonius as "the law-breaking monk." Angered, the priest vows that if he finds Macedonius, he will kill him.[17]

Warned of the threat by a fellow believer, Macedonius "arose and proceeded north to a place called 'the valley' (ⲡⲓⲁ). He dwelt there, supplicating God through fasting and frequent night vigils."[18] A resulting vision leads Macedonius to the priest's two sons, who had withdrawn some three miles into the desert, where they were weak from lack of food and water. They, having experienced a parallel vision, place themselves in the bishop's hands and return to live with him in "the valley."[19] Once there, Macedonius baptizes them, gives them the Christian names of Mark and Isaiah, and administers the Eucharist to them. They in turn ask him to shave their heads (tonsure them) so that they can serve him. Macedonius complies, making Mark a priest and Isaiah a deacon.[20]

The account then proceeds to the conversion of Aristos, Mark's and Isaiah's father, the temple's priest. When Aristos learns of the miraculous healing of a Nubian's camel by Macedonius and Isaiah, he immediately goes to "the valley" to see them.[21] After an exchange with the bishop, the priest asks to be baptized. Macedonius initially refuses, sending the priest back to the city to attend to his affairs and build a church. The priest obeys, returns to the city, puts his house in order, and gives away everything he owns. He then sends word to Macedonius, informing him of his actions and asking the bishop to come to the city. Macedonius complies and, together with Mark, gathers everyone into the church, where he proceeds to baptize first the priest and then the entire population of the city.[22]

To complete the literary circle, Macedonius next remembers the old woman who had informed the priest of his killing of the falcon and whom in response he had cursed so that "her tongue became like iron and remained motionless until God's gift was revealed."[23] He requests that the woman be brought to him and heals her, which in turn leads to her conversion and baptism. Then, after seven days, Macedonius leaves the city and returns to "the valley."[24] The story ends with an account of his death on the morning of the eighth of Amshir (14 February), the arrival of the people from the city to mourn his loss, and his burial "in a manner befitting his rank" outside his abode in "the valley."[25]

The author has fashioned the story of Macedonius as a literary whole, the individual episodes effectively linked together to create an interconnected narrative. The miracle story of the healing of the Nubian's camel, for example, offers the occasion to reunite the pagan priest and his sons who had fled to the desert, which leads in turn to the priest's own conversion. The priest's conversion results in the conversion of the entire city,

which culminates in the conversion of the old woman whom Macedonius
had cursed earlier in the story. Her conversion effectively ties the end of
the story back to the beginning. Macedonius's introduction and his ordination by Athanasius, which begins the account, and his death and burial,
which end it, serve as bookends enclosing the tale.[26] The legend formulates
the conversion of the whole of pre-Christian Philae as a miraculous work
wrought through Macedonius by the power of God channeled to him
through the Alexandrian archbishop Athanasius. The discourse participates
in the centralization of religious authority in the person of Athanasius,
from whom it permeates to the borderlands, confounds all opposition,
and unifies Egypt in the orthodox faith. It is totalizing in that it not only
shapes the memory of the past, but in the process "naturalize[s] a cultural and social construction, representing an artificial world as if it were
simply given or inevitable" (Mitchell 1994: 2; cf. Goehring 2005: 146). The
artificial world fashioned in the legend enforces a particular ideological
construction on the past, which makes the construction both inevitable
and foundational for the present. Shaped by and in the present, it emerges
as the background, a reality "simply given or inevitable" against which the
present is understood and defined.

In recognizing the legendary character of the story, historians have
tended to focus their methodological debate on the evidence of pre-Christian religious practice and its undoing contained in the text. The debate
centers on what can and cannot be garnered from the account of Macedonius's slaughter of the sacred falcon with respect to its cult in the middle of
the fourth century, the information it offers on local religion in the area,
and the processes whereby the island of Philae became Christian.[27] There
appears to be consensus that while the evidence supports the continuing
existence of the falcon cult into the first half of the fourth century, the
specific story of Macedonius's killing of the bird "can probably better be
regarded as an explanation to a sixth-century audience of how the first
bishop of Philae made the island Christian" (Dijkstra 2008: 211; cf. Frankfurter 1998: 109–11; 2006: 25–26) The debate intensifies, however, when
the question becomes the degree to which one can read such legendary
accounts in terms of the 'persistence of authentic memory' associated with
a particular place, and use such memories to explore localized religion and
its transitional moves toward Christianity. David Frankfurter, for example,
applies a sophisticated methodology to such sources in an effort to uncover
evidence of local Egyptian religion. "Saints' lives," he argues, "can preserve

local memories of a particular sort: religious topography, religious gestures, and occasionally the outlines of social patterns. They do not tell us *when* something happened or the inner details or ideas of a religious system they oppose; but they do reflect sensibilities and attitudes towards places, people, and even images" (Frankfurter 2006: 37). In response, Jacques van der Vliet contends that such compositions offer little if anything with respect to the historical facts they purport to describe. They represent rather creative pieces designed to "legitimize and explain a new Christian landscape. . . . The stories about the conversion of the landscape as told in the *Life* [*of Aaron*] are not about historical facts, but about the actual present landscape. Rather than documenting historical processes, they are themselves part of the historical process that constructs and reconstructs the Christian land-scape" (Van der Vliet 2006: 51). In a similar vein and more directly against Frankfurter's claims, Peter van Minnen contends that "Egyptian hagiogra-phy does not build on authentic memory of what happened in the fourth century, but amounts to an imaginative explanation-after-the-fact" (Van Minnen 2006: 57). The thrust of the latter two comments suggests that the drawn portrait or created landscape of the text, in so far as it incorporates elements from the past like the falcon episode, draws them into the author's present in such a way as to eviscerate them of their historical value with respect to the time and setting in which the author places them in his nar-rative. They function rather as props in the author's creative imagination, which, while they may draw in some fashion from memories of the past, have little to do with the actual reality of the past at the time and in the place the author sets them.

My interest in this essay, however, lies not in the specifics of the debate with respect to the falcon cult in early fourth-century Philae and what it might or might not tell us with respect to the process of Christianiza-tion. However fascinating and important that debate might be, I want to address here the implications of the methodological insights generated by it on the other components of the story. In particular, I would suggest that if we embrace the notion of the falcon episode as an imaginative explanation-after-the-fact, as I think we must,[28] then it is logically incum-bent on us to entertain the same methodological challenge with respect to other episodes and elements in the work. In particular here, I would draw attention to the author's portrayal of monasticism in early- to mid-fourth-century Philae. If in fact the account of the falcon cult in the *Life of Aaron* represents a "historical process that constructs and reconstructs the Christian landscape" as opposed to anything approaching an authentic memory, then must we not consider the likelihood that the same process conformed the memory of Macedonius to the expectations of the author's contemporary Christian landscape, grafting a monastic life onto his character as an "imaginative explanation-after-the-fact"? The literary legend draws not only forward from the pre-Christian past to fashion its creative memory of the fourth century, but also backward from the author's present to shape that memory in terms of the then current Christian discourse. Macedonius's monastic bona fides serves to authenticate his status and authority in terms that make sense within the Christian landscape of the author's own day.

When one turns from the more fanciful episodes of the narrative, namely, Macedonius's killing of the sacred falcon and its aftermath, the miraculous healing of the Nubian's camel, and the cursing and healing of the old woman, to the more mundane elements, namely, his secular rank, appointment as bishop, and ensuing monastic life, it is easy enough to imagine that the latter are somehow less legendary and thus more historical. Such assumptions falter, however, when one recognizes the anachronistic nature of the author's identification of Macedonius as "pagarch," a title that does not occur in this sense until the reign of Anastasius I (491–518).[29] While one may assume that Macedonius came from the ranks of the elite, as was the common pattern for bishops in fourth-century Egypt,[30] the author's hand in shaping his protagonist's specific credentials is evident. One suspects that he likewise made the bishop conform to the later, more dominant monastic image of the episcopacy.

Within the *Life of Aaron*, the following references in chronological order connect Macedonius to the ascetic life: (1) upon his appointment as bishop, he distributes his belongings to those in need; (2) the old woman who accuses him to the temple priest identifies him as "that law-breaking monk"; (3) as a result of the threat to his life, he flees north to a place called "the valley," where he entreats God through fasting and night vigils, and where the priest's two sons eventually join him; (4) his abode ("the valley") is in an area where Nubians live and where inhabitants from Philae occasionally pass by (that is, it is not in Philae); (5) he sends the converted priest to the city from his abode in "the valley" and likewise travels himself from his dwelling to the city and returns; and finally, (6) the people of the city go out to his dwelling in "the valley" to bury him. The author clearly imagines Macedonius as a monastic, a person who embraces the ascetic life as part and parcel of the life of a bishop and who, in good monastic fashion, withdraws from the city he has been ordained to serve into the desert.

When one situates the account of Macedonius within its broader literary context, however, it becomes clear that in the imagination of the author his life could be no other. In the story of Macedonius alone, those whom he converts, namely the temple priest and his two sons, similarly take up the ascetic life as a constituent element of conversion. The priest's two sons initially flee some three miles into the desert to escape their father's wrath, where Macedonius eventually finds and converts them. They then return with him to his dwelling place in "the valley," where he tonsures them and ordains them as priest and deacon, and where they remain living together with him. Macedonius functions here as the founder of a monastery whose ascetic ability draws others to him. In the case of the priest who converts after his sons, we learn only that he, like Macedonius earlier, gave away everything he owned as part of his conversion process. While the text does not specify his subsequent abode, the ascetic nature of his conversion suggests his association with Macedonius's monastery.

The construction of Macedonius's ascetic life fits naturally into the author's broader account of the bishops of Philae. When the entourage arrives in Alexandria for Mark's ordination as Macedonius's successor, they learn that Athanasius had withdrawn from the city to a small monastery in search of solitude.[31] Macedonius's monastic orientation, like his episcopal authority, appears to originate with Athanasius. After his ordination and return south, Mark continues to reside outside of Philae, presumably in "the valley," whence he proceeds to the city when needed.[32] Upon his death, his brother Isaiah, who succeeds him, similarly withdraws from the city to his own abode, again presumably in "the valley," and enters the city only on special occasions.[33] Upon Isaiah's death, the people forcibly seize the monk Pseleusius, the first episcopal candidate explicitly identified as a monk, and take him to Alexandria to be ordained.[34] The pattern is clear. For the author, to be a bishop is to be a monk. The ascetic life gives authority and stature to the office. The identification begins with the archbishop himself, who is found residing in a small monastery outside the city. His ordination of Macedonius as bishop thrusts the latter into the ascetic life, which in turn leads to a "monastic" expansion in "the valley," from whence the next two bishops come. In the author's literary history, the conversion of Philae occurs through a miraculous process that conforms the beginning to the end. The monk-bishop is in place from the start, ordained as such by Athanasius. He in turn establishes a monastic center in "the valley" from which through him the power of God enters the city and converts it *in toto* to Christianity.

The classic monastic paradigm of the bishop-monk, promoted by Athanasius in the fourth century, became the general pattern in Egypt in the fifth century (Brakke 1995: 99). While it is thus certainly possible that Macedonius became a monastic bishop (Dijkstra 2008: 261), the literary nature of the *Life of Aaron* with its unified portrayal of the monk-bishop raises serious doubts with respect to its historical veracity. The weight of the evidence suggests that the author, writing in the sixth to seventh century, constructed an imaginary history of Philae's fourth-century conversion by telescoping elements forward from the more distant past and backward from the present to create a fourth-century world that both participates in and naturalizes the totalizing discourse of Coptic Christianity. In his sixth- to seventh-century world, the monk-bishop represented the current custom to which he in his imagination conformed his portrayal of Macedonius and his followers. The portrayal of Macedonius thus participates in the "imaginary explanation-after-the-fact" of Philae's conversion, and supports in the process the current power structure. For the sixth- to seventh-century audience, the story establishes continuity with the past, gives the strength of tradition to the present, and thereby empowers it to shape the future. As such the monk-bishop Macedonius in the *Life of Aaron* offers greater access to the imagination of the author and the ecclesiastical worldview of his day than to the historical bishop Macedonius. In the end, the only certainty with respect to the latter remains his presence in a list of bishops who attended the Council of Serdica in AD 343.[35]

Notes

1   On the history of this area in late antiquity, see Dijkstra 2008: 23–36; see also Dijkstra 2002, 2004, and 2007a. His 2008 volume, in particular, gathers all of the known evidence and offers valuable insights into its interpretation.

2   It is interesting to note that the Pachomian monastic federation added only one monastery (Phnoum at Latopolis) upriver or south of its original foundation at Tabennesi. All remaining additions moved downriver toward Alexandria, ending with the monastery of Metanoia on Canopus.

3   Such sources, of course, tell their own story, through which one gains access to their authors' worlds. For an insightful discussion, see Papaconstantinou 2006: 65–86.

4   Macedonius of Philae does not appear in the *Coptic Encyclopedia*.

5   Athanasius, *Apol. sec.* 49.3; Dijkstra 2008: 55–56.

6   Dijkstra (2008: 255–69) offers the most thorough analysis of the evidence to date. While he favors the identification of the Macedonius mentioned in Athanasius's list

with the first bishop of Philae, he notes that the Coptic *Life of Aaron* "shows us the perspective of a later Christian community about its formative period."

7 Budge (1915) has published the Coptic text (432–95) with an English translation (948–1011). Vivian (1993) supplies an English translation. I will refer to the text using both the folio numbers recorded in Budge, which Vivian includes in his margins, and Vivian's section numbers.

8 Also referred to as the *Histories of the Monks of the Egyptian Desert* (Budge 1915) and the *Histories of the Monks of Upper Egypt* (Vivian 1993).

9 On the common name Paphnutius and the various figures who bore it, see Vivian 1993: 42–50.

10 Dijkstra (2008: 267) notes that the conversion story is an "invented tradition" that "has to be seen not as an accurate description of a historical event, but as a story that has a message to convey."

11 *Life of Aaron* 11b (Vivian §28). The text interweaves first- and third-person narrative.

12 The account of Macedonius appears on ff. 12a–23b (Vivian §§29–54).

13 On the unity of the *Life of Aaron*, see Dijkstra 2008: 245.

14 *Life of Aaron* 12a (Vivian §29); for a good translation, see Dijkstra 2008: 255.

15 *Life of Aaron* 12b (Vivian §30).

16 On the cage, see Dijkstra 2002: 7–10.

17 *Life of Aaron* ff. 13a–15a (Vivian §§31–36); Vivian's translation.

18 *Life of Aaron* f. 15a (Vivian §36); my translation.

19 Literally "the place where he lived"; *Life of Aaron* f. 17a.

20 *Life of Aaron* ff. 15a–18a (Vivian §§37–43).

21 *Life of Aaron* ff. 18a–20a (Vivian §§44–48). The text does not name "the valley," but states only that the priest "went to the place where the bishop and his sons were."

22 *Life of Aaron* ff. 20a–22a (Vivian §§48–52). The text appears confused at this point, since the baptism occurs between the bishop's sending of the priest to the city and his own subsequent journey there after Aristos had set his house in order. The plot seems to require the inversion of the order of pages 21a and 21b, though the pagination as recorded in Budge (1915: 453–54) indicates the present order.

23 *Life of Aaron* f. 15a (Vivian §36); my translation.

24 *Life of Aaron* f. 23a (Vivian §53); again the text does not specifically name "the valley," referring to his abode.

25 *Life of Aaron* f. 23b (Vivian §54); again, "the valley" is not specifically named.

26 See above, n. 13.

27 The debate becomes clear in the articles by David Frankfurter, Jacques van der Vliet, and Peter van Minnen published together in Dijkstra and van Dijk 2006; material from the *Life of Aaron* also appears in Frankfurter 1998: 68, 282–83 and Brakke 2006: 236.

28 I am not convinced, however, that to do so automatically precludes any sense of the author's creative imagination having drawn in some fashion on authentic memories. To what extent we can knowingly distinguish them is another question.

29 *Life of Aaron* f. 12a (Vivian §29); Dijkstra 2008: 231, 261–62.

30 Bagnall 1993: 285, 292; Martin 1996: 653–59; Dijkstra 2008: 261. The subsequent mention of Macedonius's return to Alexandria to meet with a military commander *(stratēlatēs)* leads Dijkstra to suggest he had a military function (262).

31 *Life of Aaron* f. 25a (Vivian §57).
32 *Life of Aaron* f. 32b (Vivian §73).
33 *Life of Aaron* f. 34a (Vivian §77).
34 *Life of Aaron* ff. 34b–35a (Vivian §79).
35 This does not question the existence of a monastery called "the valley" north of
    Philae or another identified as "the (hill) top" near Syene (Dijkstra 2008: 250), but
    only the linkage of the former to Macedonius. One suspects that local bishops were
    at some point subsequently drawn from the monasteries, which established the pat-
    tern to which Macedonius was conformed.

3 Apa Hadra (Hidra) in the *Difnar*

Nashaat Mekhaiel

THE COPTS REMEMBER during the church year many saints who are important for the way their church sees itself and with whom the faithful can
identify. Among them are famous personalities such as the abbot Shenoute
(7 Abib) and the patriarchs Athanasius (7 Basans) and Cyril (3 Abib), as
well as saints whose reputation is limited locally and has spread primarily
within a narrower environment. To the latter belongs Apa Hadra (Hidra),
one of the bishops of Aswan in the fourth century, to whom a monastery
was dedicated in the vicinity of Aswan. This is now known under the name
of the Monastery of St. Simeon (Gabra 1988: 91f.). His sphere of influence
is limited to the region of Aswan, where he has acquired great significance.
All subsequent bishops of Aswan and the surrounding area were consecrated with the name Hadra (or Hidra/Hedra). However, the fact that
Hadra is venerated in the liturgy of the Coptic Church throughout Egypt
shows that he has won a permanent place in the canon of saints and is celebrated in all parts of Egypt.

The liturgical compilation of the Copts, known as the *Difnar*, contains
many hymns that are worthy of close investigation. It is difficult to make
a selection and probably the hymn to Apa Hadra would not be one of the
first to be chosen. It stands out first of all by its brevity: with sixteen stanzas
it is one of the shortest of all Coptic hymns.[1] In the present case, however,
interest was determined by the theme of the symposium. Because of the

21

brevity of the hymn we certainly would not expect to find in the *Difnar*—
in contrast to the *Synaxarion*—any outline of his biography, as is sometimes
found in hymns for other saints. The following presentation will therefore
describe the picture of Hadra that is drawn in the *Difnar*, that is, what
aspects are placed in the foreground to present the person of Hadra to the
believers. It should be noted that the ancient believers could be expected
to possess certain information about the saint already. A hymn of this type
should not be misunderstood as a sort of sung biographical article whose
purpose is to provide information, but should be considered an apostrophe
from the faithful.[2] In the case of Hadra, who is remembered on 12 Kiyahk,
the first part of the song melody Adam and the entire song melody Batos
are devoted to the saint. The two parts differ in their mode of singing and
probably derive from different sources.

The Adam melody begins with a *makarismos*, in which Apa Hadra is
described as a bearer of the Spirit (ⲡⲓⲡ̅ⲛ̅ⲁ̅ⲧⲟⲫⲟⲣⲟⲥ, fol. 146r, 5) and righteous (ⲡⲓⲣⲱⲙⲓ ⲛ̇ⲇⲓⲕⲉⲟⲥ, fol. 146r, 6). These common epithets are the only
ones used for Apa Hadra in the Adam section, and they are explained in
the subsequent stanzas. The first epithet draws on the metaphor of a sports
competition that is found in the Pauline letters.[3] This idea of running in a
race is popular in the hymns of the *Difnar* that deal with martyrs.[4] Running stands for the torture suffered by the martyrs; in the current example,
it stands for the efforts made by Apa Hadra until he became bishop. Thus it
is indicated that he achieved his goal of a godly life, which he has pursued
consistently. Such a life is characterized through the practical realization of
the virtues (ⲛⲓⲡⲟⲗⲏⲧⲓⲁ̇, fol. 146r, 12)[5] and a focus on God (in the form of
persistence in prayer, ⲛⲓⲡⲣⲟⲥⲉⲩⲭⲏ ϧⲉⲛⲟⲩϩⲩⲡⲟⲙⲟⲛⲏ, fol. 146r, 13–14).
In both of these efforts, Apa Hadra has distinguished himself so that he has
become a shining example (ⲧⲩⲡⲟⲥ, fol. 146r, 11), an example right up to
the present day. This reference draws the listeners in. The last sentences in
the Adam melody allude to the parable of the money left in trust.[6] Here
two aspects are relevant: first, the fact that Apa Hadra is in the service of
God, that is, he has surrendered to Him completely; second, that he has
met God's expectations and accomplished the task for which the Lord has
chosen him. This thought leads to the prediction that promises Apa Hadra
the joy of the Lord. His worldly merits open the way to the perpetual joy
that is promised to him. It should be noted that Apa Hadra is addressed
consistently in the second person: first by the author/editor of the hymn,
then by the faithful who sing or speak the words, then finally by God

Himself, who calls Apa Hadra to Himself at the end of his life. Also remarkable in this section is the number of expressions that derive from Greek
words.[7] This may be mere coincidence, but could also be interpreted with
great caution as an indication of a Greek original.

In the Batos melody, Apa Hadra takes up almost twice as much space as
in the Adam melody. Although one also cannot speak here of a biography
of the saint, as in other hymns,[8] traces are nevertheless recognizable. At
the beginning of the Batos melody, we find the frequent theme of humility, in which the speaker/singer degrades his own person and also praises
the exalted person who is the subject of the hymn. This creates a gap
between the singer and the subject of the song, and, furthermore, gives the
first opportunity to introduce the saint. As in the Adam melody, the attri-
butes ΠΙΔΙΚΕΟC ('the righteous'; fol. 147r, 10) and ΜΑΚΑΡΙΟC ('blessed'; fol.
147r, 11) occur, which are certainly not very specific. More definite is the
expression ΠΙΝΟΜΟΘΕΤΗC ΕΘΟΥΑΒ ΜΠΙϢΛΟΛ ΤΗΡϤ ΝΝΙΜΟΝΑΧΟC ('the
holy lawgiver of the whole group of monks'; fol. 147r, 13–14). It is clear
that this phrase is addressed to the head of a monastic community the saint
has formed, who follow the rules given by him. This aspect can be understood as a heading in which the main feat is emphasized. It shows Hadra's
life by faith. Inspired by the reading of the Gospels, Hadra understands
the word of Christ and follows it. Furthermore, the rules of other leading
monks give him guidance, and he stands in their tradition by receiving
their blessing: ΑΠΟΥΠΝΑ ΚΩΒ ΕΧΩϤ ('their spirit multiplied over him';
fol. 147v, 12) shows that Apa Hadra has surpassed his predecessor. Therefore
he can be compared with Moses and Elijah, the prophets par excellence.
Love and devotion to everyone (ΑϤϢΩΠΙ ϧΕΝΤΜΕΤΜΑΙΟΝ ΝΕΜΠΙΜΕΙ
ΝΟΥΟΝ ΝΙΒΕΝ; fol. 147v, 14–148r, 1) are the points on which Apa Hadra
can be compared with the famous prophets. What matters is that he passes
on his attitude through preaching and his exemplary behavior, because he
inspires the same behavior in his children (ΝΑϤΧΟϧΧΕϧ ΝΝΕϤϢΗΡΙ; fol.
148r, 7). Those who are faint-hearted and distressed, in particular, he fills
with courage impelled by his love for people, which is presented to him
by Jesus (ϧΕΝΤΕϤΑΓΑΠΗ ΕΤΧΗΚ ΕΒΟΛ ϧΙΤΕΝΠΕΝϬ͞C Ι͞Η͞C Π͞Χ͞C; fol.
148r, 13–148v, 1). At the end of the hymn there is a change, as the saint
is addressed directly. The change from third to second person is sudden,
which is typical of the hymns of the *Difnar*. Just as at the end of the Adam
section, the saint is invited to receive his heavenly reward for his worldly
achievements, namely, to enter into heaven.

The Adam melody does not present a logical sequence of thoughts, but instead joins statements together to add up to a glorification of the saint in a descriptive form. In the Batos melody, on the other hand, can be seen at least some structure based on the following sequence: 1) attestation of humility with the introduction of the saint; 2) pious life on the basis of gospel and monastic rules; 3) comparison with Moses and Elijah; 4) shining example and help to the faithful; 5) reward in heaven. The hymn is very general *in toto*, for no specific information about Apa Hadra is given. His name could be replaced by that of any other excellent monk-father with impunity. Any geographical or temporal setting is missing; other people are not mentioned. From the *Life of Apa Hadra* and the entry in the *Synaxarion*, we know that he was located in Aswan and the holy Poemen was his teacher (Gabra 1988: 93). Furthermore, he was ordained by Patriarch Theophilos as bishop and died under Emperor Theodosius.

It is amazing that in the *Difnar* the episcopate of Apa Hadra is entirely concealed. Has this important detail perhaps been omitted in the revision of the texts? It is hard to accept that an editor could have been so neglectful. Or could it have been not so important to the author/editor that Apa Hadra was a bishop? In fact, it is also striking that the description of Apa Hadra in the *Synaxarion* focuses on the representation of his character and work as a holy monk. In contrast, the bishop Apa Hadra recedes into the background. The *Synaxarion* does mention the episcopate, emphasizing two aspects: on the one hand, his skills that make him so fit for the task of bishop; on the other hand, his unwillingness to be consecrated as bishop because he was absorbed in monastic life. It is therefore conceivable that the faithful have thought of Apa Hadra primarily as a monk and not as a bishop.

The object of the hymnographer was to depict Apa Hadra's charitable nature and his closeness to his fellow human beings. These characteristics spring from his virtuous, ascetic life that he has inherited from the monastic fathers and have nothing to do with his consecration as bishop. The hymn also points to Apa Hadra's resemblance to the prophets, not to his episcopate, as the quality that brings about a special connection with other people. They are referred to as his children (ⲚⲈϥϢⲎⲣⲓ; fol. 148r, 7), in accordance with the expression in the hymns for the faithful who turn to a monk-father.[9] In contrast, for bishops the image of the shepherd and his sheep often occurs.[10] And the expression ⲚⲀϥⲈⲣⲯⲀⲐⲓⲬⲓⲚ (fol. 148r, 9), behind which lies the Greek verb κατηχειν, is not a technical term for the sermon of a bishop, but (unlike in the Greek) a general term for 'to instruct, to preach.'[11] On the other hand, the texts of many other hymns argue against a deliberate concealment of the episcopate, mentioning particularly for monk-fathers that they were often appointed as bishops against their will. Should we finally assume that the author or editor of the hymn was not aware of the episcopate of Apa Hadra? Could the text, to which the hymn in the *Difnar* goes back, perhaps have been written when Apa Hadra was not yet bishop? Since he was consecrated during the reign of Theodosius and probably died in AD 395, his ordination must have taken place between 385 and 395 (Gabra 1988: 94). In this case, the original text would have been written within the lifetime of the saint, and undergone no revision at a later date. We would also have great evidence of a very early source for a hymn, in which Apa Hadra in his role as monk-father is placed at the center in general terms.

This rather short and, within the multitude of the texts in the *Difnar*, inconspicuous hymn is unimportant as a source for the person of Apa Hadra, but it does provide a valuable clue in connection with the question of the compilation of the *Difnar*.[12]

Notes

1 Not all of the stanzas even deal with Apa Hadra; some of them mention other saints. The sixteen stanzas come to little more than five pages in the oldest known manuscript, a fourteenth-century one from St. Antony's Monastery, while other hymns take up from seven to ten pages.
2 Not without reason, in many hymns the faithful seem to be in a dialogue with the saint.
3 1 Cor 9:24; 2 Tim 4:7; Heb 12:1.
4 See, for example, "The Dormition of the Holy Simeon Stylites from Antiochia" (29 Basans; fol. 105v, 11).
5 ΠΟΛΗΤΙΑ in the plural refers to virtuous life, as in the Batos melody of this hymn (fol. 147v, 10). Almost synonymous with this is ΑΡΕΤΗ (at the beginning of the song, melody Batos, fol. 147r, 10).
6 See Mt 25:14–30, esp. 21, 23, and 25.
7 The Greek words and expressions are: ΜΑΚΑΡΙΟC (fol. 146r, 3), ΠΝΑΤΟΦΟΡΟC (fol. 146r, 5), ΔΙΚΕΟC (fol. 146r, 6), ΚΑΛΩC (three times: fol. 146r, 7; 146r, 18; 146r, 20), CΤΑΤΙΟΝ (fol. 146r, 8), ΤΥΠΟC (fol. 164r, 11), ΠΟΛΗΤΙΑ (fol. 146r, 12), ΠΡΟCΕΥΧΗ (fol. 146r, 13), ΖΥΠΟΜΟΝΗ (fol. 146r, 14), ΠΙCΤΟC (fol. 146r, 15), and ΕΠΙΤΗ (fol. 146v, 3).
8 See, for example, "The Martyrdom of St. John of Senhout" (8 Basans; fol. 30v, 5–32r, 3), "The Martyrdom of St. Apa Hor of Soriakos" (12 Abib; fol. 44v, 8–48r, 1), and "The Dormition of the Holy Empress Helena" (9 Basans; fol. 34r, 5–37r, 9).
9 Another such example is found in the hymn "God performed a great miracle in the town of Alexandria" (14 Misra; fol. 154r, 5).

10 For example, in the hymns for "The Memory of the Holy Paphnutius, the Bishop"
    (11 Basans; fol. 45v, 6) and "The Dormition of Lazarus, the brother of Martha and
    Mary, after he had become bishop of Kypros" (27 Basans; fol. 102r, 3).
11 Another example is "The Martyrdom of the Holy Abu Kir, John, of the Virgin and
    her mother" (6 Amshir; fol. 145r, 5).
12 I examined this question myself in detail in my dissertation (Mekhaiel 2009a).

4 Christianity on Philae

Samuel Moawad

PHILAE (COPTIC: Ⲡⲓⲗⲁⲕ, Ⲡⲓⲗⲁⲕ︦ϩ; Arabic: Bilaq) is a small island in the Nile River about four miles south of Aswan at the southern end of the First Cataract. It is 460 meters long and 150 meters wide. It was the most famous place of pilgrimage devoted to the Egyptian goddess Isis in the late period (732–30 BC) (Winter 1982: 1022; Richter 2002: 115; Dijkstra 2008: 249). The origin of the name is unknown. According to the Byzantine historian Procopius (ca. 500–ca. 562) in chapter 19 of the first book of his *Persian Wars,* written in 550/551, the name Philae is derived from the Greek word φίλαι, meaning 'friends' (Eide et al. 1998: 1190 [Greek text], 1191 [English translation]). He argues that the emperor Diocletian (284–305) gave this name to the island because he allowed the Blemmyes to practice their religion there and

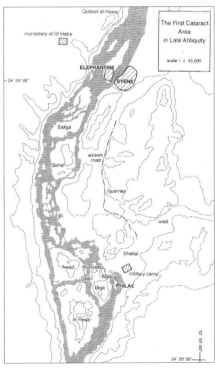

Fig. 4.1. The First Cataract area in Late Antiquity

27

thus made peace with them. However, references to the island with this name are found in Greek and Latin literature before Diocletian (Dijkstra 2008: 142–43). A possible etymology is the demotic form *pr-jw-rq* (Richter 2002: 115).[1]

Although the literary sources report that Christianity first spread to the island of Philae during the patriarchate of Athanasius of Alexandria (328–73), as is mentioned below, the acts of the martyrs written in Coptic mention Philae several times as the southern border of Egypt (Timm 1984–92: 1:392–93, n. 3, p. 398). The martyrdom of Eusebius, for example, reports that Diocletian commanded that everyone, from Rome to Philae of the Nubians (ⲓⲥⲭⲉⲛ ⲧⲣⲱⲙⲁⲛⲓⲁ ϣⲁ ⲡⲓⲗⲁⲕϩ ⲛ̄ⲧⲉ ⲛⲓⲉⲑⲁⲩϣ), should sacrifice to the gods (Hyvernat 1977: 23). The martyrdom of Piroou and Athom, likewise, mentions that the emperors Diocletian and Maximian appointed governors everywhere in Egypt, from Alexandria to Philae (ⲓⲥⲭⲉⲛ ⲣⲁⲕⲟⲧ̄ ϣⲁ ⲡⲓⲗⲁⲕϩ), to persecute Christians (Hyvernat 1977: 135). However, these texts do not offer any information about Philae itself or about Christianity on it.

The Bishops of Philae

The exact beginning of Christianity on Philae is uncertain. Eutychius, the Melchite patriarch of Alexandria in the tenth century, mentions in his Arabic *Annales* a certain Eusebius "bishop of the city of Philae" *(usquf madinat fila)* as an adherent of Arius (Cheikho 1906: 1:125). Eutychius's testimony, which is not attested in any other source, is a mistake. His Eusebius of Philae is none other than Eusebius of Pamphylia, in the south of Asia Minor (Timm 1984–92: 1:399, n. 9; Richter 2002: 118; Dijkstra 2008: 55).

The main source for the origin of the Diocese of Philae is the *Life of Aaron*, a literary Coptic source transmitted in a paper manuscript from the last quarter of the tenth century and preserved now in the British Library (Or. 7029) (Layton 1987: 196–99 (Nr. 163); Budge 1915: lvi–lix). According to its colophon, the manuscript was donated to the *topos* (monastery) of Apa Aaron in Hagr Edfu (ⲡⲧⲟⲟⲩ ⲛ̄ⲧⲃⲱ) (Gabra 1985: 9–10, 14) by an unnamed deacon (van Lantschoot 1929: 197–200 (nr. CXIII); Layton 1987: 198).[2] The Coptic text was published with an English translation by Wallis Budge in 1915 under the title *Histories of the Monks in the Egyptian Desert* (Budge 1915: 432–502). A better translation was made by Tim Vivian in 1993 (Vivian 1993: 71–141). An Italian translation was published by Campagnano and Orlandi in 1984 (Campagnano and Orlandi 1984: 67–125). In addition, there are three unpublished papyrus fragments preserved in the same library (Or. 7558), which offer parallel texts to the *Life of Aaron* (Layton 1987: 172–73 [Nr. 150]). Although the text itself mentions a certain Paphnutius as the author, it is still hard to identify this person since Paphnutius was a common name among Egyptian Christians in late antiquity (Vivian 1993: 42–50).[3] Both the manuscript and the fragments were probably used for liturgical purposes, since MS Or. 7029 (fol. 57r–60v) contains the lessons for the Feast of Apa Aaron. The original of the *Life of Aaron* may have been written between 491 and 700 in imitation of the style and the framework of the well-known *Historia Monachorum* (Vivian 1993: 42–54; Dijkstra 2008: 225–52).

Although the *Life of Aaron* is a literary and not a historical source, and therefore contains some legendary accounts, the historical events narrated in it seem to be authenticable and some of them are confirmed by other undisputable sources as discussed below (Timm 1984–92: 1:393).

According to this literary work, which narrates the biographies of some monks from Aswan and its environs, the first bishop of Philae was Macedonius. At an unspecified date in the first half of the fourth century he became a governor near Philae. Unfortunately, the place of his governorship is a lacuna in the manuscript. After he asked for a church where he could participate in the Eucharist, Macedonius was told that a certain member of the clergy from Aswan used to come to Philae and celebrate the Eucharist for the few Christians there. Macedonius visited Archbishop Athanasius and told him the whole account. Athanasius consecrated Macedonius as the first bishop of Philae.[4]

Fortunately, the *Life of Aaron* is not the only source that mentions Macedonius. According to the *Apologia Secunda* of Athanasius, the Council of Serdica held in 343 was attended by ninety-four Egyptian bishops, including Macedonius.[5]

The *Life of Aaron* narrates how Macedonius went to the temple on Philae where a falcon was worshiped and convinced the two sons of the temple priest that he would like to sacrifice to their idol. While they were preparing the offerings, Macedonius chopped off the head of the falcon and burned it. The two sons tore their clothes and escaped to the desert for fear of their father and the people of the island.[6] A few days later, Macedonius saw in a vision a man standing, with two sons kneeling before him. On the next day a voice commanded him to look for the "chosen vessels." After a long walk he found the priest's sons half dead after six days without eating and drinking. They accompanied him to the place where he lived and received baptism there. Macedonius gave them new names, Mark and Isaiah, and later ordained Mark as a priest and his brother Isaiah as a deacon.[7]

Although it is not explicitly mentioned in the *Life of Aaron* that Bishop Macedonius was a monk, there are some hints in this literary text, as James Goehring has observed,[8] that Macedonius lived a solitary life in the valley, where he "entreated God through fasting and frequent night vigils."[9] It seems that he founded there a kind of monastic community where he and others practiced a monastic way of life. In the *Life of Aaron*, Macedonius is described by an old pagan woman as a "law-breaking monk."[10] It is also reported that the sons of the pagan priest wanted to imitate him and asked him to tonsure them: "They were observing his manner of prayer and way of life and monastic routine. . . . Mark said, 'My holy father, we want you to shave the hair from our heads so we can serve you.' And he shaved their heads, and they obeyed him in everything."[11] This shaving of the head was a usual practice among new Coptic monks as a sign of dedicating their life to God in the monastic life.[12]

The *Life of Aaron* mentions Mark as the second bishop of Philae. He was consecrated by Athanasius in Alexandria.[13] While the *Life of Aaron* dedicates long and detailed passages to the ordination of Mark and his return to Philae, it reports very briefly on his episcopal career and omits some things that other sources report. For example, according to the *Historia Arianorum* written by Athanasius of Alexandria in 358, the same Mark was exiled with five other Egyptian bishops to the Siwa Oasis in the western desert.[14] Mark of Philae is also mentioned explicitly in Athanasius's *Synodal Letter to the People of Antioch*, written in 362.[15]

Bishop Mark of Philae would have officiated at his post until 368 or shortly before this date. He was succeeded by Isaiah, as Athanasius's Festal Letter 41 in the year 369 attests (Coquin 1984: 146 [fol. 8r]). According to the *Life of Aaron*, Isaiah was the biological brother of his predecessor, Mark. He was ordained a deacon by Macedonius and later a priest by his brother Mark at the command of Archbishop Athanasius, who prophesied that Isaiah would succeed his brother in the episcopate. Isaiah was elected by the people of Philae, and he was ordained as bishop of Philae by Athanasius himself in Alexandria. Just as in the case of Mark, very little is reported on the episcopal activities of Isaiah.[16] He lived in solitude like his predecessors and did not go into the city except on great feast days. He "was a good man and a benevolent man, and greatly loved. The rich [listened to his counsel and gave to the poor]." Apart from this, nothing is known about him.[17]

Isaiah was succeeded by a monk named Psoulousia, or Pseleusias, who is mentioned only in the *Life of Aaron*.[18] Here it is mentioned explicitly that the new bishop of Philae was a monk. The election of Coptic bishops from among the monks became usual in the fourth century and a rule before the end of the fifth century (Muyser 1944: 134; Krause 1981: 58b; Brakke 1998: 99). The account of the *Life of Aaron* concerning the election of Psoulousia and his ordination in Alexandria is very similar to those of his predecessors. The significant difference is that since Psoulousia was a monk and held no clerical office, he would have been ordained first as a deacon and then as a priest before being consecrated as a bishop.[19] Although the name of the patriarch who consecrated Psoulousia is not mentioned, it is very likely that it was Timothy I of Alexandria (380–84), because immediately after the consecration of Psoulousia the *Life of Aaron* reports the death of Patriarch Timothy and the election of Theophilos as his successor. The same source narrates that Bishop Psoulousia traveled to Alexandria to congratulate Patriarch Theophilos on his consecration as archbishop of Alexandria: "Now it happened that after these things Abba Timothy went to his rest and Abba Theophilos sat on the Episcopal throne. And all the bishops went to Alexandria to pay their respects to him. Now the holy man Abba Pseleusias also went."[20] This would have happened in about 385.

The *Life of Aaron* ends with the death of Aaron during the episcopate of Psoulousia, whose successor is unknown. Here the Christian inscriptions found at Philae provide precious information that helps us to expand the episcopal list of Philae. Two inscriptions dated to 449/450 or 464/465 mention Bishop Daniel, who renovated a part of a quay wall on Philae (Munier 1938: 47; Dijkstra 2008: 56–58).

With Bishop Theodore our knowledge about Christianity on Philae flourishes. He probably served as bishop between 525 and 577. According to the *Church History* of John of Ephesus (507–86), Theodore was consecrated as bishop of Philae by Patriarch Timothy III (517–35). When Patriarch Theodosius I (535–67), Timothy's successor, died, Bishop Theodore had spent fifty years in the episcopate.[21] He transformed the Isis temple on Philae into a church dedicated to St. Stephen, as the inscriptions there attest (Dijkstra 2008: 221–22). It is perhaps to be expected that Theodore would be involved in the first Christian mission to Nubia because Philae was the nearest see to Noubadia. And, in fact, according to John of Ephesus, Theodore of Philae accompanied a priest from Constantinople called Julian to Noubadia to Christianize the people there. That probably happened shortly after the official closure of the temple of Isis between 535 and 537. After two years, Julian left the Noubades in the hands of Theodore, who kept in contact with them. In 569 Noubadia became an independent diocese with its own bishop, Longinus.[22] The last thing John of Ephesus reports on Bishop Theodore of Philae is that two Syrian bishops were sent to Theodore and Longinus to consult them concerning Paul of Antioch and whether he could be accepted again into the church after his fall.[23]

An undated tombstone that probably comes from Philae mentions Bishop Pousi of Philae, who may have been the successor of Theodore and the first abbot of the Monastery of St. Hatre (Dayr Anba Hadra) near Philae (Richter 2002: 119–21; Dijkstra 2008: 325).

Another inscription found on Philae dated to 17 December 752 mentions the second year of the episcopate of Bishop Severus (Richter 2002: 121; Dijkstra 2008: 320). However, it is not certain whether this Severus was a bishop of Philae in the eighth century.

The colophon of the manuscript Or. 7024, preserved in the British Library and dated to 987, mentions a certain Nicodemus, bishop of Edfu, Thebes, and Philae. However, the name of Nicodemus is not mentioned in the colophon itself but in a reader's note with the date AM 750, that is, AD 1033/1034 (Layton 1987: 188–90 (Nr. 159); Winlock and Crum 1926: 1:107, n. 1; Gabra 1985: 13; Budge 1913: l–lvi and plate lviii opposite p. 176; Munier 1938: 48). The same evidence thus proves that Philae lost its status as an independent diocese no later than the eleventh century and became a part of the neighboring bishoprics. Furthermore, some Copto-Arabic manuscripts list Philae among the Egyptian dioceses in the fourteenth century (Munier 1943: 51).

The Churches on the Island of Philae

Because of the erection of the Aswan Dam in 1902 and later the High Dam between 1960 and 1971, the island of Philae now lies under water. From 1972 to 1980, UNESCO sponsored a project to save the archaeological monuments of Philae. Most of the ancient Egyptian buildings were transported to the neighboring island of Agilkia that lies about eight hundred meters northwest of Philae. Unfortunately, some Christian monuments were not saved and are now under water (Winter 1982: 1022–25; Grossmann 2002: 461; Richter 2002: 115; Dijkstra 2008: 38–39).

In the nineteenth century, the island of Philae was covered with mud-brick houses from the late antique and Arab periods. In 1895–96 the island was cleaned and renovated by the British officer Henry Lyons with the assistance of the German Egyptologist Ludwig Borchardt. Lyons prepared a map of the monuments on the island that is still used in modern studies (Dijkstra 2008: 315–16).

On Philae there were six, or possibly seven, churches, depending on how the Imhotep temple is counted. Most of the churches on Philae cannot be dated exactly, particularly those that were built before the sixth century. However, it is possible to date them roughly. The churches of Philae can also be divided into two categories: the churches that were erected outside the temples, and the ancient Egyptian temples that were transformed into churches after their 'symbolic' closure in 535–37.

The first category includes the so-called East Church and West Church. Both of them lie in the northern part of the island of Philae behind the temple of Isis. It is probable that these two churches are the oldest on Philae. According to the *Life of Aaron* we know that the Eucharist used to be celebrated by a priest who came from Aswan before Philae became an independent diocese.[24] The same source speaks in some instances about the seating or the enthroning of the new bishop in the church.[25] In addition, the petition of Bishop Appion of Syene (Aswan), who mentions "God's holy churches at Philae," attests that there was more than one church on Philae before the middle of the fifth century (Eide et al. 1998: 1138–41; Dijkstra 2008: 357–58). These facts lead us to assume that there was a church on the island in the fourth century.

The location of the East and West churches far from the temple's complex makes it possible that they or older buildings in the same area are the oldest churches on Philae. Because of the large size of the asymmetric four-nave East Church, it is reasonable to think that it functioned as the episcopal church of Philae. It can be dated to the end of the sixth century or the beginning of the seventh century. The West Church, which is also lost under water, was built in a simpler style and was smaller than the East Church. It was a provincial church with a three-nave naos and tripartite sanctuary. Some of its building blocks were taken from the nearby temple of Harendots. This supports the assumption that the West Church cannot be dated before the official closure of the temples between 535 and 537, and more probably to the second half of the sixth century. The inscription found in the street to the west of this church is dated to the year 752 and mentions the establishing of "the *topos* of the lady of us all, the holy Theotokos Mary on Philae." Whether this inscription refers to the

West Church remains unclear, and whether we should identify the date of the erection of the West Church with the date of this inscription is also uncertain. However, the West Church could have been a renovation or a rebuilding of an older church dedicated to the Virgin Mary (Grossmann 2002: 461–65; Richter 2002: 125–28; Dijkstra 2008: 316–22).

The second category includes four or five churches. The most important is the church in the Isis temple dedicated to St. Stephen. The transformation of this temple to a church probably happened immediately or shortly after the closure of the temples in 535/537 by Narses in the reign of Justinian (527–65). The inscriptions in the church mention Bishop Theodore (ca. 525–77) who founded it (Richter 2002: 124–27; Dijkstra 2008: 221–22, 306–15). In addition, there are three or four other churches that had previously been used, in whole or in part, as temples. The church in the temple of Arensnuphi and the church in the temple of Hathor are dated after 535/537. The church in front of the temple of Caesar Augustus is dated to the seventh or eighth century. According to Lyons, there are some Christian traces in the temple of Imhotep, such as some painted saints' figures and an inscription in the northern room of the temple. From the style of construction, it appears that this space could not have been used as a church to celebrate the mass, but just as a chapel for individual prayers (Richter 2002: 125–27).

The *History of Churches and Monasteries*, written between 1160 and 1349 and attributed to Abu al-Makarim and others, mentions that there are two churches on Philae, dedicated to the Archangel Michael and Patriarch Athanasius respectively (Evetts and Butler 1895: 131 [Arabic text], 283 [English translation]). However, it is not clear whether these churches were still in use at that time.

Paganism and Christianity on Philae

In the Late Period (ca. 715–332 BC) Philae became the most important pilgrimage site for the goddess Isis. The temple of Isis was erected by Ptolemy II (285–246 BC) and completed later by Ptolemy VIII (170–163, 145–116 BC).

Christianity expanded throughout Egypt gradually. Despite the Edict of Milan in the year 313 that tolerated Christianity in the Roman Empire, Christianity in Egypt remained a religion of the minority until the death of Constantine the Great in 337, and Christians did not become a majority before the end of the fourth century (Hussey 1966: 42–44; Martin 2001: 110). The situation in the area of the First Cataract was no different. In

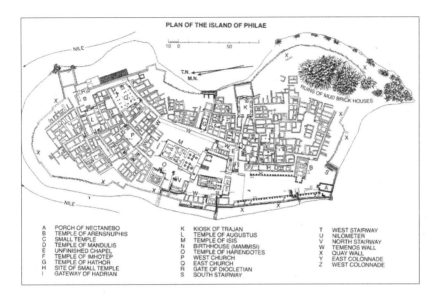

Fig. 4.2. Plan of the Island of Philae

the fifth century, there is evidence that the bishops in and around Aswan gained, in addition to their religious authority, secular power as well. Sometime between 425 and 450, Appion, the bishop of Aswan and Elephantine, sent a petition to the emperors Theodosius II (408–50) and Valentinian III (425–55) complaining about the attacks of the Blemmyes and the Noubades against the churches in his diocese and asking them to put the military garrison that was stationed near his diocese under his own command, just as the troops stationed on Philae were under the command of its bishop (Eide et al. 1998: 1138–41; Dijkstra 2008: 51–52, 357–58).

According to the Byzantine official and historian Procopius, the emperor Justinian (527–65) sent his military general Narses to put an end to the ancient Egyptian cults on Philae and to destroy the temples there (Eide et al. 1998: 1190 [Greek text], 1191 [English translation]). This must have happened between 535 and 537. Modern scholars have relied on Procopius's statement and considered the cult of Isis to be the last ancient Egyptian cult that survived in Christian Egypt until that date. However, a closer view and an exact analysis of the demotic and Greek inscriptions found at Philae give us enough reasons to doubt Procopius's statement, or at least to interpret his words in a different way. We are indebted to the

recent and brilliant study by Jitse Dijkstra (2008), who was able to disprove
this theory and prove that the temple at that date did not actually function
any more and the closure of the temple by the command of Justinian was
actually symbolic or official. Dijkstra did not limit himself to studying the
inscriptions found at or in the temple, but he took into consideration their
placement, their distance from the sanctuary of the temple, their language,
and the nature of their writers (Dijkstra 2008: 175–97). The last hieroglyphic inscription, as well as the last demotic one, in Ancient Egypt are
both found at Philae and date to 394 and 452 respectively. The last Greek
inscription at Philae is dated to 456/457 and was incised by the priest of
the Isis temple. All other datable Greek inscriptions after 457 are Christian
in style. The inscriptions by pilgrims to the ancient Egyptian cults became
fewer, and most of the inscriptions, including the last one from 456/457,
were made by the priestly family that served in the temple of Isis. After
that date we have no traces on Philae of visited cults or surviving cults
on the island. Thus the words of Procopius should be understood as Byzantine propaganda and the destruction of the temples on Philae merely
constituted a symbolic closure. In addition, the temples that, according to
Procopius, had been destroyed were reused and transformed into Christian
churches (Dijkstra 2008: 175–218, 355). Dijkstra concludes that "the commonly accepted picture that the Ancient Egyptian cults, and hence Ancient
Egyptian religion as an institution, came to an end in 535–537 needs to be
discarded" (Dijkstra 2008: 218).

Whether the closure of the temples of Philae affected the otherwise
peaceful relations with the Nubians who were allowed by the emperor
Diocletian to practice their religion on Philae is not known. In the archive
of Dioscorus of Aphrodite (Kum Ishqaw), there is a petition written by
Dioscorus himself to the governor of the Thebaid that can be dated to
the year 567. The petition includes an accusation against a man whose
name is not mentioned and who is "making his own life and deeds evil,
setting aside the taught Christian worship and religion, and consecrat-
ing shrines with demons and wooden statues." Moreover, it seems that
this man contacted a group of the Blemmyes and offered them help in
regaining their places of worship. The same person plundered houses and,
with the help of his gang, he forced the inhabitants to pay taxes to him.
Although the petition does not mention where these events occurred,
the only place that could be considered is the island of Philae (Dijkstra
2008: 1–11, 351–54). Unfortunately, it is not clear to what extent the

Blemmyes were involved in this matter and how the governor of the Thebaid reacted to the petition of Dioscorus.

Philae in the Writings of Muslim Historians

Some Muslim historians and geographers mention Philae under its Arabic name, Bilaq. In his *Muruj al-Dhahab*, al-Mas'udi (d. 957) mentions the island with a large number of inhabitants and a mosque. On both banks of the Nile opposite of the island, says al-Mas'udi, there were many palm trees ('Abd al-Hamid 1973: 2:21–22). About five centuries later al-Maqrizi (d. 1441) repeats the description of al-Mas'udi and adds that Philae is the strongest fortress of the Muslims and a big town where the palms grow (and not on the shore as al-Mas'udi wrote) (Zaynahum and al-Sharqawi 1998: 1:558). However, the descriptions of al-Mas'udi, and in particular of al-Maqrizi, suit the town opposite the island better than the island itself (Ramzi 1994: 2/4:218). The witness of the *History of Churches and Monasteries* supports this fact when it states that the Muslims possess, opposite to Philae, a strong lofty fortress also called Philae (Evetts and Butler 1895: 127 [Arabic text], 274–75 [English translation]). This is probably the reason for the confusion by Muslim historians.

Yaqut al-Hamawi (d. 1226) mentions Philae very briefly in his *Mu'jam al-Buldan* as the southernmost town *(balad)* in Upper Egypt and the border between Egypt and Nubia (Yaqut al-Hamawi 1977: 1:478a). Whether he means the island itself or the town opposite remains unclear.

Other Muslim geographers, such as Muhammad ibn 'Abd al-Mun'im al-Himiari (eighth/ninth century) in *al-Rawd al-Mi'tar* ('Abbas 1984: 176a) and al-Idrisi (d. 1165) in *Nuzhat al-Mushtaq* (Cerulli et al. 1970–84: 1:38–39) mention a certain Bilak. However, on the basis of their description it cannot be Philae but another place with the same name located near present-day Khartoum in Sudan (Ramzi 1994: 2/4:219–20).

Notes

1   Westendorf (1977: 77, 478) mentions the etymology p3 iw rk and the demotic form p3-(ij-)lk with a possible translation: 'The Island of the End (Die Insel des Endes).'

2   In his project *Corpus dei Manoscritti Copti Letterari* (CMCL), Tito Orlandi gives this manuscript the siglum MERC.AF.

3   O'Leary (1937a: 219–20) identifies this Paphnutius with Paphnutius the Hermit who was a disciple of St. Antony and later the successor of Isidor as the priest of Scetis. However, it remains an assumption that lacks any evidence.

4   *Life of Aaron* §§29–30 (Budge 1915: 443–44; Vivian 1993: 85–87).

5   Athanasius, *Apologia Secunda* §49.3 (ed. Opitz 1935–41: 130 (no. 218), English
    translation Schaff and Wace 1994: 2.4:127).
6   *Life of Aaron* §§31–32 (Budge 1915: 445–46; Vivian 1993: 87–88).
7   *Life of Aaron* §§37–43 (Budge 1915: 447–50; Vivian 1993: 89–92).
8   See his contribution "Imagining Macedonius, the First Bishop of Philae" in this
    volume.
9   *Life of Aaron* §§37 (Budge 1915: 447; Vivian 1993: 89).
10 *Life of Aaron* §§35 (Budge 1915: 446; Vivian 1993: 88).
11 *Life of Aaron* §§43 (Budge 1915: 450; Vivian 1993: 92).
12 See, for example, the *Panegyric on Macarius of Tkōou* IX.7 (Sahidic version ed.
    Johnson 1980: 1:77, English translation 2:59; Arabic version ed. Moawad 2010: 89,
    German translation 132).
13 *Life of Aaron* §§55–61, 69–74 (Budge 1915: 456–59, 462–66; Vivian 1993: 98–101,
    105–108).
14 Athanasius, *Historia Arianorum* §72.2 (ed. Opitz 1935–41: 2.1:222, English transla-
    tion Schaff and Wace 1994: 2.4:297).
15 Athanasius, *Synodal Letter to the People of Antioch* §10 (Migne, *Patrologia Graeca* 26,
    808, English translation Schaff and Wace 1994: 2.4:486); Munier 1943: 8.
16 *Life of Aaron* §§31–33, 37–43, 69, 73, 75–78 (Budge 1915: 445–46, 447–50, 463,
    465–67; Vivian 1993: 87–88, 89–92, 105, 108–10).
17 *Life of Aaron* §§77–78 (Budge 1915: 467; Vivian 1993: 110).
18 *Life of Aaron* §§79–85 (Budge 1915: 467–71; Vivian 1993: 110–14).
19 *Life of Aaron* §§81 (Budge 1915: 468; Vivian 1993: 112).
20 *Life of Aaron* §83 (Budge 1915: 469–70; Vivian 1993: 113).
21 John of Ephesus, *Church History* 4.9.4 (ed. Brooks 1935: 189; English translation in
    Payne Smith 1860: 259; German translation in Richter 2002: 50).
22 John of Ephesus, *Church History* 4.7.6, 4.8.1, 4.9.4, 4.49.1 (ed. Brooks 1935: 186–
    87, 189, 233–34; English translation in Payne Smith 1860: 255–56, 259, 315–16;
    German translation in Richter 2002: 48–51); Dijkstra 2008: 282–304.
23 John of Ephesus, *Church History* 4.10 (ed. Brooks 1935: 189–90; English transla-
    tion in Payne Smith 1860: 259–60).
24 *Life of Aaron* §29 (Budge 1915: 444; Vivian 1993: 86).
25 *Life of Aaron* §§72, 77, 82 (Budge 1915: 465, 467, 469; Vivian 1993: 107, 109–10,
    112–13).

5 The Indexing of Manuscripts of the Monastery of the Great Saint Pachomius in Edfu

Father Angelous el-Naqlouny

Introduction[1]

THE ABANDONED MONASTERY of Saint Pachomius at Hagr Edfu (Gabra 1991; Timm 1985: 1148–57) was rebuilt by Bishop Hidra and reoccupied in 1975, hence the manuscripts are very recent (Meinardus 1999: 245; 2002: 185). In this catalog, I have adopted the same system that was used in my previous article (el-Naqlouny 2010). Our presentation was inspired by the Simaika Catalogue (Simaika and 'Abd al-Masih 1939). Most of the manuscripts are liturgical except for one containing hagiographical texts relating to monks and saints, mainly from Upper Egypt.

The Catalog

Serial #	Call Number	Description
1	1 Liturgy	Lectionary for Holy Week from Palm Sunday to the Feast of the Resurrection The manuscript is in Bohairic Coptic with an Arabic introduction and dated Thursday 30 Amshir AM 1628 (AD 1912) Another date of copying the manuscript was given as 15 Tuba AM 1638 (AD 1922). The scribe is Bakhum Soliman Daoud Hanna from the family of Ezab El Masry in the Monastery of St. Shenoute the

		Archimandrite, a new *waqf* (religious endowment). 267 folios; 20 lines; 35.3 x 29 cm (text: 25 x 16 cm). Western paper with a watermark: shield containing an image of the moon. Black ink with red rubrics and dots within some of the characters. Coptic numbers. Illuminations include a cross miniature at the beginning, and ornamental page headers and capitals. Some marginalia notes by the scribe. Colophon includes the date of completion of the manuscript. Binding is yellowish-red leather with embossed ornaments and broken locks, measuring 36.2 x 25.6 cm.
2	2 Liturgy	Lectionary of the feasts of the saints Bohairic Coptic with Arabic rubrics. Undated but probably twentieth century. The scribe is Mikhail 'Abd al-Masih Qudsi Yuhanna al-Baghl. The manuscript needs restoration. We notice several hands. 111 folios; 17 lines; 32.3 x 22 cm (text: 22 x 14 cm). Western paper with a watermark: three crescents (Tre Lune). Black ink with red rubrics and dots within some of the characters. Unnumbered. Illuminations include ornamental page headers in blacks and capitals. No endowment or colophon. Binding lost.
3	3 Liturgy	Rites of Sundays of Kiyahk, and the Nativity and Epiphany feasts. Doxologies for the month of Kiyahk, the Ode of Kiyahk, some Upper Egyptian saints such as Pesynthios of Coptus, Pachomius and Theodore his disciple, Matthew the Poor (or the Potter), Palamon the teacher of St. Pachomius, St. Bedaba, and Andrew his disciple. Bohairic Coptic with a parallel Arabic column, with some folios in Bohairic or Arabic only. Many authors but the only name found is that of Pope Mark VIII, the 108th patriarch (AD 1796–1809). Not dated but probably from the nineteenth and twentieth centuries. No scribe name. The manuscript needs much restoration. Has different hands. 218 folios; Bohairic–Arabic 24 lines, Bohairic 22 lines, Arabic 16 lines; 33 x 23 cm (text: Bohairic–Arabic 25 x 16 cm, Bohairic 24 x16 cm, Arabic 24 x 13 cm). Western paper with a watermark: AC with Tre Lune. Black ink with red rubrics and dots within some of the characters. Coptic numbers on verso. Illuminations include ornamental page headers and capitals. No endowment or colophon. Modern binding from 2006 by one of the monks in the monastery, measuring 34 x 24.5 cm.

4	4 Liturgy	Rites of Lent and Holy Week, and some Praises for the month of Kiyahk Bohairic Coptic with some Arabic. Undated but probably twentieth century. The manuscript needs much restoration. Has different hands. 390 pages; 13 lines; 21.5 x 16 cm (text: 17 x 11 cm). Western paper with no visible watermark. Black ink with some blue pencil *(kobya)* rubrics. Arabic numbers on top center of every page. No endowment, illuminations, scribe name, or colophon. Binding is cardboard, measuring 21 x 16 cm.
5	1 Homilies	A collection of lives of the Holy Fathers: St. Ba'isa (Paese), St. Onophrius, St. Isaac the Priest of Cells, St. Theodora, St. Epiphanius of Cyprus, St. Ammonios the Hermit, St. Martyrianus of Palestine, St. Mary the Copt, St. Poemen the Hermit, St. Latsoon from al-Bahnasa (Oxyrhynchos), St. Paphnutius the Bishop, St. Sylvanus the Monk, St. Praxia the Virgin, St. Sarapamon priest of the Monastery of St. John, St. Marina the Nun, St. Shenoute the Archimandrite, St. Pshoi, St. Besarion the Monk, St. Zosima the Priest, St. Macarius the Alexandrian, St. Isaac disciple of St. Apollo, St. Moses the Black, St. George companion of St. Abraam; and homilies on the Judgment of Adam and salvation by St. John the Little, a homily by St. Shenoute the Archimandrite, and a homily on the Judgment of the Righteous by St. Basil the Great. Arabic. Undated, probably from the twentieth century. The manuscript needs much restoration. 214 folios; 11 lines; 21.8 x 15 cm (text: 17 x 10 cm). Western paper with no visible watermark. Black ink. Unnumbered. No endowment, illuminations, scribe name, or colophon. Binding is mutilated leather with cardboard, measuring 21.5 x 15 cm.
6	5 Liturgy	Rite of Baptism Arabic, dated 13 April AD 1971 (5 Barmuda AM 1687). Dedication date 18 June AD 1976 (12 Ba'una AM 1692). The scribe and sponsor is the late monk Maximus al-Bakhomy. The endowment is to the monastery of St. Pachomius. 66 folios; 13 lines; 33.5 x 24.3 cm (text: 26.5 x 16 cm). Modern paper with no visible watermark. Black ink with red rubrics. Unnumbered. No illuminations. Colophon includes the above dates and the scribe name. Cardboard binding, measuring 34.2 x 25 cm.

| 7 | 6 Liturgy | Lectionary and Rite of Holy Week Part 1 (Sunday–Wednesday), containing a historical introduction taken from the printed text.
Arabic. Dated Wednesday 10 November AD 1971 (30 Baba AM 1668). The scribe and sponsor is the late monk Maximus al-Bakhoumy. The endowment is to the monastery of St. Pachomius. 217 folios; 12 lines; 36 x 29.5 cm (text: 27 x 16 cm). Modern paper with no visible watermark. Black ink with some brown, red, and green. Unnumbered. Illuminations include ornamental page headers at beginning of each day heading and capitals.
Colophon: "The first section of the Holy Pascha book was completed, followed by the second section by God's will, on Wednesday 10 November 1971, which is 30 Baba 1668 according to the Coptic Calendar of Martyrs. Dear Lord, please reward the efforts of those who helped the Kingdom of Heaven. This book is named after Saint Pachomius, the father of the community belonging to Edfu, the Western desert. Bless your servant the scribe of this book, the humble sinner who am not worthy to be called by name because of the greatness of my sins and trespasses, and I ask for the intercessions of the great Virgin Mary and Saint Pachomius. Amen."
Binding is modern brown leather with locks, measuring 37 x 28 cm. |
| 8 | 7 Liturgy | Lectionary and Rite of Holy Week Part 2 (Thursday–Easter Sunday), containing a historical introduction taken from the printed text and a sermon by St. Shenoute the Archimandrite.
Arabic. Dated Friday 24 March AD 1972 (15 Baramhat AM 1669). The scribe and sponsor is the late monk Maximus al-Bakhoumy. The endowment is to the monastery of St. Pachomius. 250 folios; 17 lines; 35.8 x 25 cm (text: 27 x 17 cm). Modern paper with no visible watermark. Black ink with rubrics in red, or red and green. Unnumbered. Illuminations include ornamental page headers at beginning of each day heading and Coptic cross as well as capitals.
Colophon (1): "The first section of the Holy Pascha book was completed, followed by the second section by God's will, on Wednesday 10 November 1971, which is |

		30 Baba 1668 according to the Coptic Calendar of Martyrs. Dear Lord, please reward the efforts of those who helped the Kingdom of Heaven. This book is named after Saint Pachomius, the father of the community belonging to Edfu, the Western desert. Bless your servant the scribe of this book, the humble sinner who am not worthy to be called by name because of the greatness of my sins and trespasses and I ask for the intercessions of the great Virgin Mary and Saint Pachomius. Amen." A note from a reader states that the scribe of the manuscript is the Man of God, the monk-priest Maximus al-Bakhoumy, who passed away early on Sunday 3 Abib 1704 AM (10 July AD 1988). Colophon (2): "This book is eternally in God's name, and the monastery of Saint Pachomius in the Western mountain of Edfu. Whoever takes this book for himself from its rightful place in this monastery, let God's wrath fall upon him in this life and for eternity. Dear Lord, please reward the efforts of those who helped the Kingdom of Heaven. This book was completed on Friday 15 Baramhat 1669 according to the Coptic Calendar of Martyrs, which is 24 March AD 1972." Binding is modern brown leather with locks, measuring 37.3 x 28 cm.
9	8 Liturgy	Part of the Lectionary of Lent from the offering of incense Arabic (?). Fragment of one folio.

Summary

1. A number of the manuscripts are without dates, scribes, and endowments. It is therefore not known whether they belong to a church or to the Monastery of St. Pachomius. They all appear to be of modern date and probably date from the end of the nineteenth century or the beginning of the twentieth century to the second half of the twentieth century.
2. The oldest manuscript among them is suggested by the researcher to date back to the eighteenth to nineteenth century because it does not differ in its writing or paper from manuscripts of that period.
3. The latest manuscript dates to AD 1972. It was copied by one of the monks of the Monastery of St. Pachomius.
4. There are also some abstracts from an apocryphal book(?) titled "The Judgment of Adam and the Sign of Salvation" in Manuscript 5 (1 Homilies).

Recommendations of the Researcher

1. Since the number of manuscripts is small, the researcher believes that they should be preserved by restoration and proper storage.
2. Manuscripts should not be collected from other churches and monasteries because they are the private possessions of the places in which they are found and are used in prayers and for religious purposes.
3. A committee should be formed in the Coptic Orthodox Church, specializing in the preservation of the Coptic heritage. It should include specialists in this field from all the different monasteries and dioceses.

Appendix 1:
Names of Churches and Monasteries in the Manuscripts

Monastery of the Great St. Shenoute Archimandrite	Manuscript 1	1 Liturgy
Monastery of the Great St. Pachomius, Father of the community in the western mountain of Edfu	Manuscript 6 Manuscript 7 Manuscript 8	5 Liturgy 6 Liturgy 7 Liturgy
Church of the Virgin Mary in Edfu, east of the lake	Manuscript 1	1 Liturgy

Appendix 2:
Names of Popes, Bishops, and Priests in the Manuscripts

Pope Mark VIII, the 108th patriarch	Manuscript 3	3 Liturgy
Monk-priest Maximus al-Bakhoumy	Manuscript 6 Manuscript 7 Manuscript 8	5 Liturgy 6 Liturgy 7 Liturgy

Appendix 3:
Names of Towns/Villages in the Manuscripts

Azzab al-Masry	Manuscript 1	1 Liturgy
Azzab al-Nassara	Manuscript 1	1 Liturgy
Edfu	Manuscript 1 Manuscript 6 Manuscript 7	1 Liturgy 5 Liturgy 6 Liturgy

Appendix 4:
Names of Scribes in the Manuscripts

Bakhum Soliman Daoud Hanna	Manuscript 1	1 Liturgy
Mikhail 'Abd al-Masih Qudsi Yuhanna al-Baghl	Manuscript 2	2 Liturgy
Monk-priest Maximus al-Bakhoumy	Manuscript 6 Manuscript 7 Manuscript 8	5 Liturgy 6 Liturgy 7 Liturgy

Appendix 5:
Watermarks

Profile of a moon inside a shield	Manuscript 1	1 Liturgy
Three moons (Tre Lune)	Manuscript 2 Manuscript 3	2 Liturgy 3 Liturgy
English Letters: AC	Manuscript 3	3 Liturgy

Appendix 6:
Titles of the Manuscripts

Readings of Holy Pascha	Manuscript 1	1 Liturgy
Katamares Feasts of Saints	Manuscript 2	2 Liturgy
Readings of Kiyahk, Praises of the Christmas Feast and Baptism Feast, Doxologies of Angels and Saints, Parts of the Ode of Kiyahk, Glorification of Saints, Praises, Expositions of the Nativity Kiyahk and the Feast of Epiphany, Psalis of Batos and Adam for the whole year	Manuscript 3	3 Liturgy
Yearly Praise, some Kiyakh hymns, some of the collections of Psalis for Holy Lent.	Manuscript 4	4 Liturgy
St. Ba'isa, St. Abnofar (Onophrius), St. Isaac 'Priest of Cells *(Qalali)*,' St. Theodora, St. Epiphanius Bishop of Cyprus, St. Ammonios 'al-Motawahed,' St. Martyrianus from Palestine, St. Mary the Coptic, St. Poemen 'al-Motawahed,' St. Latsoon from al-Bahnasa	Manuscript 5	1 Homilies

(Oxyrhynchos), St. Paphnutius the bishop, St. Silvanus the monk, St. Praxia the Virgin, St. Sarapamon the priest of the Monastery of St. John, St. Marina the nun, St. Shenoute Archimandrite, St. Pshoi Light of the Desert, St. Besarion the worshiper, St. Zosima the priest, St. Macarius the Alexandrian, St. Isaac the disciple of St. Apollo, St. Moses the Black, St. Georgy companion of Anba Abraam, the Judgment of Adam and the Sign of Salvation by St. John the Little, the sermon of St. Shenouda Archimandrite, the sermon on the Judgment of the Righteous by St. Basil the Great		
The Rite of Baptism: the blessing of baptismal water, untying of the girdle, cursing of the devil, absolution of the woman, and the three great prayers	Manuscript 6	5 Liturgy
Lectionary of Holy Week from Palm Sunday to Wednesday of Holy Pascha week	Manuscript 7	6 Liturgy
Readings of Holy Thursday, Good Friday, the Eve of Bright Saturday, Prime of Bright Saturday, the Mass of Bright Saturday and Easter Eve	Manuscript 8	7 Liturgy
Prayer said during Prime, raising of incense during Holy Lent. Part of a paper	Manuscript 9	8 Liturgy

Appendix 7:
The Endowments

Manuscript 1	1 Liturgy	Church of the Virgin Mary, east of the lake, Edfu
Manuscript 6	5 Liturgy	Monastery of Saint Pachomius, Hagr Edfu
Manuscript 7	6 Liturgy	Monastery of Saint Pachomius, Hagr Edfu
Manuscript 8	7 Liturgy	Monastery of Saint Pachomius, Hagr Edfu

Notes

1   Many thanks to Dr. Youhanna Nessim Youssef for his kind help in rereading my text.

6 The Beginnings of Christianity in Nubia

Siegfried G. Richter

THE TERRITORY OF NUBIA extends over an area between the First Cataract in the north and the region of Khartoum in the south. The Red Sea marks the eastern border; the desert forms a natural boundary in the west. Depending on the use of 'Nubia' in its historical sense or as a geographical term, the definition diversifies. Some studies would set the southern boundary in the area of the Fourth or the Fifth Cataract.[1] In the sixth century, Nubia was divided politically into three kingdoms—Noubadia in the north, Makuria in the middle, and Alodia in the south.

From its beginning, the investigation of Nubia was connected to research in Egypt. Like scientific research in its northern neighbor, it started with the Napoleonic expedition, which marked the birth of modern Egyptology. The Egyptologist Karl Richard Lepsius reached Nubia in December 1843 and traveled as far south as Khartoum. The publication of the monumental work, *Denkmäler aus Aegypten und Aethiopien*, in the years from 1849 to 1859 offered a systematic investigation of monuments and inscriptions. Further archaeological investigation was mostly connected with the construction and enlargement of the dam at Aswan. The old dam was finished in the year 1902. In the years 1912 and 1934 the dam was built up higher, preceded by archaeological campaigns to conserve antiquities. A first campaign took place in the years 1907 to 1911, and a second one in the years 1929 to 1934.[2]

Research into Christian Nubia has its first milestone with the work of Ugo Monneret de Villard, *Storia della Nubia Cristiana*, published four years after the end of the second campaign in 1938. The next step was marked by the globally known Nubia Campaign, started after a request by the Egyptian and Sudanese governments in 1959. The results definitely changed our knowledge about the Christian heritage of Nubia. Not only the international public, but also archaeologists with their home grounds in different academic fields, such as Egyptology or prehistoric and proto-historic archaeology, were surprised by the results. The amount of ecclesiastical remains and the quality of objects, like the famous wall-paintings of Faras (Michałowski 1974), established Nubia in the lineup of countries with a highly developed Christian culture.

On the one hand, such 'salvage archaeology' has the advantage of making it clear that archaeological campaigns do in fact have to be carried out from time to time. Teams of specialists from several countries and international material support led to a large number of excavations and surveys. On the other hand, under salvage conditions, time is limited. During the investigations into the cathedral of Faras, for instance, there was not much time for the excavators to deal with the layers of the oldest church there, the Mud Church, which was built in the mid-sixth century (See Adams 1965: no. 68; Michałowski 1967: 48–53; Grossmann 1971: 331–35; Godlewski 1992: 282f.). A lot of other places, which were only objects of survey, are lost in the water.

Ongoing archaeological campaigns such as in Banganarti (near Old Dongola), which started over ten years ago, or the older ones in Old Dongola present new discoveries year after year (Żurawski 2007, 2008; Jakobielski 2008). Nubia should be labeled as El Dorado, a gold mine or the blessed land for today's archaeologists of Christianity, since totally new church complexes with several stages of development, paintings, inscriptions, objects of daily use, and so on have been found. Especially in the first decade of this millennium, several new discoveries and publications of older investigations have enlarged our knowledge of the Christian era in Nubia.[3]

The number of sources about the process of Christianization is limited and can roughly be divided into archaeological and philological ones. The restriction of available data is not only the reason for wide gaps in our historical knowledge, but leads also to several possibilities for interpreting the data. In the case of the archaeological witnesses for early Christian influences on Nubian ground in the fifth century, the limited number of sources and their exact dating is still a problem. The difficulty of getting reliable facts depends also on the interpretation of the finds, which depends on the background of the interpreter. Furthermore, the number of archaeological and literary sources that provide information about the process of Christianization are very different from area to area. While a lot of information concerns the conversion of Noubadia, less is available for Makuria and Alodia. However, even for the north of Nubia many questions and details remain open. Because of different social and geological structures, the development in Nubia cannot be compared with that in Egypt in detail, but it is a fact that the process of Christianization took place later. According to archaeological finds, some Christian evidence can be dated back to the second half of the fifth century in the northern region of Nubia (see Edwards 2001). The Christians started to build churches in the second half of the sixth century—the century from which the look of the land was determined more and more by Christian culture. It seems that the sixth century in Nubia is comparable to the end of the fourth century in Egypt and the Roman Empire as a whole, when Christianity became the dominant religion. In Nubia itself the development has to be considered from kingdom to kingdom and area to area. In the south, in the area of Alodia, "it must be considered that many areas may have remained pagan, or only superficially Christianised, during the medieval period" (Edwards 2001: 95).

The fifth-century sources provide little information about the diffusion and the character of the faith. Christianity was accepted, but the sources for such observations are not numerous. There exists no certain evidence for organized Christian communities, bishoprics, churches, or monasteries in the fifth century. For this reason it is very difficult to argue for a strong process of Christianization before the sixth century; it really remains a postulate rather than an assertion with its source in historical facts.[4] Besides the impossibility of estimating the percentage of Christians, it is also an unanswered question whether Christian signs, such as some famous items discovered at the tombs of Ballana, must be evidence for Christian faith on Nubian soil. Can a man who uses the Christian cross only for magical purposes be counted as a Christian? Is the discovery of such crosses in a funeral context actual evidence for believers of the Christian faith? This question is not as theoretical as it may seem at first view. The stories involving missionaries, transmitted in Old Nubian, include tales about Christian monks who were able to heal animals by using the sign of the cross, and how astonished the Nubian people were at this (Richter 2002: 122f.).

We must also keep in mind that there is evidence for the practice of pagan cults in Nubia during the fourth and fifth centuries. One example is provided by an inscription in Tafa, which is datable to the second half of the fourth century (Eide et al. 1998: 1132–34 no. 312; Raven 1996: 47f.). At Thebes, Olympiodorus, writing in Greek between 407 and 425, does not mention Christians, but his report includes reference to pagan cults in Talmis for the year 423 (Eide et al. 1998: 1126–28 no. 309; Richter 2002: 140; Dijkstra 2008: 154).[5] And in the mid-fifth century, 452/453, one article in a peace treaty gives Blemmyes and Noubades permission to take the statue of Isis of Philae to their own country (Eide et al. 1998: 1153–58 no. 318; Dijkstra 2008: 143–46).

To sum it up, the following sources are the most important for early Christianity in Nubia.[6]

First of all there is the story about the conversion of an official at the court of the *kandake*, the queen of the Ethiopians, in the New Testament (Acts 8:26–39), that is, in the first century AD in Palestine, but there is no mention of him returning to his homeland in Africa. Furthermore, there is no archaeological or textual evidence for the existence of Jewish-Christian communities in Nubia itself until the fifth century. For this reason it is possible that this incident served only to illustrate the expansion of the Christian faith to the far reaches of the world, with Ethiopia as a suitably remote area.[7]

It is likely that the bishoprics and churches attested to in the fourth century in Egypt could well have exercised influence on Nubia. At that time, Nubia's neighbor to the south, Aksum, was also Christianized. Trade and caravans could have been instrumental in spreading the Christian faith and ideas, enabling Nubians to come into contact with Christianity. It is likely that centers of trade like the port city of Berenike played an important part in this process. The *Synaxarion* of the Egyptian church and a text about Pesynthios, for instance, provide evidence for a certain Bishop Nabis during the fourth to fifth century (Richter 2002: 142).

Personalities like Moses the Black from Nubia, who lived in Scetis in the fourth or fifth century, are also witnesses for Christian influences in Nubia. In one of Shenoute's homilies, Nubians are mentioned sitting among the congregation in Sohag. It is certainly possible that the monks and hermits of Upper Egypt taught Nubians about their faith at Egypt's southern border (Richter 2002: 143).

In the tumuli of Ballana (420–500), individual objects bearing Christian symbols were discovered. Crosses on vases and lamps show that Christian symbols were known and are evidence for Christians in this region in the fifth century. But the interpretation of these finds should not be too one-sided. A work of art of high quality like a Christian shrine, for instance, did not belong to a private household. Török interpreted this particular find as booty from one of the well-attested raids made by Nubians in Upper Egypt (Török 1995: 92; see the references in Richter 2002: 144f.).[8]

In other places as well, crosses on Christian lamps or tombs are attested. Christian votive lamps were also found in levels which are datable to between 500 and 550, or somewhat earlier (Adams 2000: 102; Edwards 2001: 89–90).

The letter of the Blemmyan king, Phonen, is a problematic source because of difficulties with the language. However, a son of the king was named Moses, which points to a Jewish-Christian tradition (Richter 2002: 146).

Three Coptic letters of the fifth century, found in Qasr Ibrim, offer some important hints of Christianity in the capital. Letter No. 322 is about pepper—it was sent from a monk named Moses to Tantani, an official. On the one hand, the letter documents contacts of monks with Nubia; on the other hand, it seems clear that Tantani was a Christian. This means that Christians lived in Nubia during the fifth century, and that the Christian faith was also acceptable for persons with posts in the administration (Richter 2002: 146–47).

Obviously, in the fifth century the Christian faith was already not only known but also accepted in Nubia, although it remains very difficult to obtain a really satisfactory picture of it since the sources are so limited. Nothing can be said about the percentage of Christians in Nubian society. Archaeologists have tried diligently to uncover churches or house churches datable to before the proselytizing mission in the 540s, but without any success. In Egypt itself the earliest unequivocal evidence is the oldest New Testament papyrus, which dates to the second century, around 125. Bishops are attested at the end of the third century. In the fourth century, churches were built, and by the end of that century the majority of the population was Christian. In Nubia, the first evidence for Christianity dates to the fifth century, and the first churches were built in the sixth.

In the sixth century, an official mission succeeded in converting at least two kingdoms of Nubia to Christianity, a historical event that is confirmed by literary and epigraphic sources. The historical value of the *Church History* written by John of Ephesus can be improved by comparing the source with the so called *Documenta Monophysitica*, a compilation of official documents of the Monophysite church (Van Roey and Allen 1994).

It would be wrong to conclude on the basis of some accurate details in the text that John's report is accurate in its entirety; but the authenticity of several dates and historical events can be demonstrated, so that it is possible to reconstruct how the official Christianization of Nubia came about. One example is John's report about Longinus, the first bishop of Noubadia. According to John, Longinus was enthroned after the death of Patriarch Theodosius in the year 566. Several intrigues resulted in his arrest in Constantinople. Only after three years was he allowed to depart for Nubia. In the *Documenta Monophysitica*, the archive of documents of the Monophysite Church, Longinus is mentioned several times. One document of the collection shows that he was in Constantinople in January 568 and that he was called bishop at that time. The document fits perfectly into the time frame given by John of Ephesus, lending credibility to his account.[9]

To give an idea of John's account, it is useful to summarize the chapters dealing with Nubia. In chapter 6, John tells us "about the barbarous people of the Noubades, and about the cause of their conversion to Christianity." He reports two Nubian missions, the Monophysite one sent out by the empress Theodora, the Melchite one by Justinian. A certain presbyter in Constantinople, Julian, whose idea it was to convert the pagans in Nubia, was the leader of the successful Monophysite mission.

In chapter 7 we are informed "about the arrival of Julian and his companions in the country of the Noubades, how they were received and the other things they did with God's help." Julianus baptized the king, his noblemen, and other people. They were instructed to refuse the king's ambassador, who arrived later. At some time between the years 536 and 548, Julianus stayed two years in Nubia, supported by Bishop Theodore of Philae.

In the next chapter we are told that Longinus became bishop of the Noubades after the death of Pope Theodosius. For three years he was imprisoned in the capital, and after that he traveled to Nubia around the year 570.

Chapter 9 tells us that Longinus was in Nubia for six years. Then he had to travel to Alexandria because of some intrigues. On his way, in Philae, he met Bishop Theodore, who was too old to travel at this time.

In summary, the account of John of Ephesus in combination with other literary, epigraphic, and archaeological sources gives important data for the events in the sixth century (see timetable in Richter 2002: 194–96). The priest Julianus stayed for two years in Nubia (first mission) between the years 536 and 548. He returned to Constantinople before 548. It is likely that in 544 the inscription of Dendur was made, marking Christianity as the official religion in Noubadia. After the return of the priest Julianus to Constantinople, Bishop Theodore of Philae stayed in Nubia for three years. The first bishop of Noubadia, Longinus, was enthroned in the year 566 and traveled to Nubia around 569.

No church on Nubian ground can be dated with certainty before the middle of the sixth century. The church that seems to be the oldest is the Taharqa temple church in Qasr Ibrim, which its excavator, Adams, places in the first half of the sixth century, but which for various reasons is better assigned to the middle of that century (Richter 2002: 160f.). It is likely that a bishopric was established in the seventh century in Qasr Ibrim. The same dating can be found for the other capitals. In Faras (or Pachoras), the bishopric was established in the 620s, but the Mud Church was built in the mid-sixth century.

This agreement of all literary sources of the sixth century with the archaeological results shows that, at this time, the kingdom of Noubadia converted to Christianity. The inscription of Dendur shows that King Eirpanome sent people of his court to attend the transformation of the temple of Dendur into a Christian church. It is the first official Christian document from Nubia and states that from this time on Christianity was the state religion of Noubadia. Without doubt there was a connection with the temple of Philae since Bishop Theodore of Philae, who consecrated the church in the Isis temple of Philae, is mentioned in the inscription of Dendur as the person who brought Christianity to Noubadia.

Sources for the Christianization of Makuria are much rarer. In his chronicle, John of Biclar mentions the middle kingdom as a Christian country in the years 569 and 573 (see in detail Godlewski 2004: 55ff.; Richter 2002: 183). The fact that John of Ephesus narrated a Monophysite mission to Noubadia and Alodia, but didn't mention Makuria, led to the assumption that a competing Melchite mission sent out by the Byzantine court reached Makuria. Also the different style of church architecture in Makuria, which is "much more Byzantine in character than any structure known from northern Nubia" (Godlewski 2004: 55), was interpreted as evidence for a direct connection between the middle kingdom and Byzantium. In its capital, Old Dongola, the three oldest churches can be dated to the second half of the sixth century. The establishment of a bishopric took place at the latest in the seventh century, but presumably already existed in the sixth.

The main source for the Christianization of the southern kingdom, Alodia, is chapters 49 to 51 of the *Church History* of John of Ephesus. Chapter 49 narrates: "The beginning of the conversion to Christianity of the people whom the Greeks call Alodaei and whom we think to be Ethiopians," and chapter 50 tells about "the delegation sent by the Alexandrians to the Alodaei." Chapter 51 is a "narrative of Longinus' entering the Alodian country and how he converted them with gladness and baptized them." In the next two chapters John adds letters as documents concerning the stories reported. The situation of the sources differs from the northern kingdom. Archaeological investigations in Soba and other places recovered some churches which cannot be dated with certainty, but are not earlier than the seventh century. In this area the Christian influence seemed not so strong as in the north and had not reached some areas even in the medieval period (Edwards 2001: 92, 95).

Notes

1   See the overview with references in Richter 2002: 14f.
2   For the research history in general, see Adams 1977: 1–98; Säve-Söderbergh 1987; Török 1997: 7–27.
3   See my forthcoming article, "Recent Research in Christian Nubia (2004–2008)," in *The Acts of the Tenth International Congress of Coptic Studies, Rome, 17–22 September 2012.*
4   See the pleading of Scholz 2003 and Dijkstra 2008 for an earlier and stronger Christianization of Nubia.
5   Dijkstra dates the event, after Gillet 1993, to approximately the first half of the fifth century.
6   See the complete listing in Richter 2002: 139–48: chapter 6, "Zeugnisse für das Christentum vor den 40-er Jahren des 6. Jh."
7   See Richter 2002: 141; Scholz (2003) defends the opinion of his thesis once more, that the story is a historical witness for the early Christianization of Nubia.
8   Edwards reminds us of the opinion of Kirwan, that the items "actually relate to converts or potential converts albeit still being buried with pagan rites" (Edwards 2001: 91).
9   See the evidence for Longinus as a historical person in Richter 2002: 102–108.

7 A Foreshadowing of the Desert Spirituality in Ancient Nubia and Upper Egypt

Ashraf Alexandre Sadek

THE EMERGENCE OF HERMITS and anchorites in the Egyptian deserts during the third and fourth centuries is a major event in the history of mankind. How can it be explained? Some political and social reasons have been offered (see, for example, Regnaud 1990: 42), yet it is also necessary to study the possible link between this phenomenon and the ancient pharaonic civilization.

We shall endeavor here to find out what the ancient Egyptians' relation with the desert was and how this link, associated with the biblical idea of the desert, may have prepared the birth of the Christian 'desert spirituality' that developed in the monastic movement.

The Desert of the Pharaohs
A Place of Suffering and Trial
In some versions of the famous Osirian mysteries, the desert appears as the place of dwelling of Seth, 'the Red God,' linked to Upper Egypt. This god is mainly represented in the crowning ceremonies of the Old and Middle Kingdoms (Erman 1937: 363; Yoyotte 1959; Velde 1967).[1] In Egyptian mythology, this god was chased away by Osiris from the 'black earth' of the valley to the 'red earth' of the desert as a punishment. This, of course, goes with the negative image of the desert as an unknown place of danger and death. The lack of roads made it a place where one could easily get

lost and meet dangerous animals such as hyenas, snakes, scorpions, jackals, and other scavengers. Rebels and asocial people roamed the desert, and could take caravans and travelers by surprise.[2] Hunger and thirst could also bring travelers to their death. Since arable land was a precious commodity in Egypt, the desert became the place for locating necropolises. To this day, the desert remains, for the Egyptians of the Nile Valley or the Delta, a frightening place that should be avoided.

However, this negative image is only one aspect of the desert. Seth was not just an evil god: he was also the one who protected both the borders of the country and the treasures held in the ground of Egypt, the minerals.

A Place for Hiding a Treasure

Indeed, the desert of the pharaohs was very rich. It held precious and semi-precious stones such as amethyst, cornelian, turquoise, and the like; metals such as gold and copper; and building stones such as limestone, sandstone, alabaster, granite, basalt, schist, and so on. All those materials played a fundamental part in the pharaohs' glory. Thus, huge expeditions were regularly organized to the mines and quarries in the desert (Sadek 1980: 16–19). The workmen had to leave the mildness of the green valley to enter into the mysterious and hostile wilderness of the desert. The Wadi Hudi documents (Nubia) mention an expedition of 1,510 men; some expeditions were much bigger.[3] Army officers directed them. The terminology used for the designation of the workmen is rather interesting: *nakht*, 'the strong troops'; *khepesh*, 'the strong (or 'solid') men' (there were about a thousand of these in the above-mentioned expedition); *'wty*, 'the brave ones' (three hundred in the same expedition). These expeditions were indeed dangerous and difficult, and they testify to the extremely organized Egyptian political strength.

Could we possibly see in these trips the foreshadowing of an initiatory trial, in which strong and brave men—certainly physically but probably also mentally and spiritually, as shown by the prayers left by the members of these expeditions[4]—left their ordinary lives in quest of a treasure hidden in the desert?

A Place for Meeting with God

Four different words were used in Ancient Egyptian to denote the desert:

– *khaset* means 'the mountain' or (depending on the context) 'the foreign country'

- *deshret* means 'the red ground'
- *semyt* is used for 'the necropolis,' as well as desert and mountainous regions
- *akhet* is the ideogram of the horizon, represented by a valley between two mountains: 'the horizon is in the desert'

The identification of desert with mountain is an essential aspect for understanding desert spirituality. Indeed, we know the importance of the mountain in biblical symbolism: it is the place of the elevation of the soul and of meeting with God. The identification of the desert with the mountain is a geographical reality in Egypt. Even now, the Egyptians use the same Arabic word, *gebel,* to speak of a mountain and of the desert; interestingly enough, the Coptic word for 'mountain' can also mean 'monastery.'[5] In ancient Egyptian theology, as in the Bible, a mystical meaning is linked to the mountain. The Theban mountain is the most typical example of this representation: it was venerated as the dwelling-place of the goddess Meretseger, whose name means 'Silence Lover.' Some stelae from Dayr al-Medina and Dayr al-Bahari bear prayers dedicated to this holy mountain, as shown in the following examples:

I recite a hymn, she [Meretseger] listens to my call so that I do
  justice on earth . . .
I had been an ignorant man with a pure heart who did not know
  good from evil.
I used to commit the sin of disobedience against the Peak [Meretseger] and she punished me.
I was in her hand night and day.
I was sitting on the brick like [a woman] who gives birth;
I implored for the breeze, and it did not come to me;
I bowed to the Peak of the West, great in power,
And to every god and goddess.
I shall tell the great and the small who are in the crew: Mind
  the Peak,
Because there is a lion in it. The Peak strikes with the blow of a
  ferocious lion.
She goes after whoever disturbs her . . .
I implored my mistress
And I found her coming to me as a pleasant wind.

She was kind to me after having shown her hand to me,
She came back to me with kindness.
She made me forget the pain which was in my heart;
Now the Peak of the West is propitious if one implores her.
  (Sadek 1988: 123)

O Great Peak of the West, in this her name
of Ma'at, daughter of Ra', residing in the Sacred territory, over-
    look (forgive), do not reject me!
Grant [me] abundance [for] my lifetime upon earth,
As I follow you every day,
As you [can] read in every book.
May you grant ascents, indeed, while [I] am here,
Dwelling with those who are alive.
He acts as one who speaks the truth.
Made by the scribe Huy. (Sadek 1984: 79)

These texts, and many others, obviously allow us to speak of a 'desert spirituality' in ancient Egypt.

A Place Leading to Eternal Life

As we have already mentioned, ancient Egyptian necropolises were located
in the desert, frequently in the west where the god-sun sets, taking with
him the deceased for their long underworld journey toward the light.
Thus, the desert appears, in ancient Egyptian thought, as the place of death
and burial. However, it is also the way to the mysterious trip from death to
eternal life. The importance of the desert as an initiation place is obvious
by the above descriptions: place of struggle against evil; place of death; also,
for those who dare enter it, the place where a hidden treasure is waiting for
the brave ones, a place where they may be able to meet God, and find the
door opening onto eternity.

The Biblical Image of the Desert

The desert serves a fundamental function in biblical contexts; above all, it is
the place where prophets, such as Moses and Elijah, met God (notably, on a
mountain)[6] and where the people of God were educated during forty years
of trial during the Exodus.[7] In the New Testament, John the Baptist, the
last prophet, stayed in the desert for years before his manifestation to Israel:

his desert is a place for asceticism and purification, in view of renewal and conversion (Matt 3:1–12; Mark 1:1–8; Luke 3:1–2).

The traditions of the journey of the Holy Family to Egypt, especially in Coptic texts (Homilies), focus largely on the trials faced by Mary in the desert: tiredness, thirst, hunger, and attacks by robbers show the desert once more as a place where one can only rely on God's help to survive; yet it was blessed by the presence of the Holy Child and His Mother.[8]

In Jesus's life, the desert is a place of suffering and privation, where evil is at work and fights with the human soul (Matt 4:1–11; Mark 1:12–13; Luke 4:1–13); yet it is also the place where Jesus retires to rest, with his disciples or in solitude, and to get in touch with his Father through prayer (Luke 6:12; 9:10).

Consequently, there are no contradictions between the desert of the ancient Egyptians and the biblical desert; what is new and revolutionary in the New Testament is the desire expressed by God to get in touch with man and to allow him into His intimacy, the same intimacy that exists between the Father and the Son in the Holy Trinity. Responding to this desire of God's is the scope of Christian monasticism.

The Anchorites' Desert

The desert is so closely linked with the Egyptian hermits and anchorites that the first of them were called 'Desert Fathers.' Palladius may have been the first to write this expression, at the beginning of the sixth century. The history of Egyptian monasticism is first a story of an exodus into the desert. The process followed by Antony, as reported by his biographer Athanasius the Great, is particularly interesting in showing the Egyptian specificity of this vocation. After hearing God's call for total surrender, Antony went to live in a tomb, a place that, for an Egyptian, was full of meanings. He then entered, materially and spiritually, the 'inner desert' or the 'inner mountain,' in order to seek for 'the buried treasure'; there he had to fight against temptation. Again, this attitude recalls that the desert meant, for the Egyptians, a place hiding a treasure that could only be found by the brave, ready to fight to conquer it (St. Athanasius, *Vita S. Antonii*, chapter 47).

Conclusion

As a conclusion to this analysis, it appears that Christian spirituality, when grafted onto the Egyptian mentality regarding the desert as a place of suffering and death, hiding the secret of eternal life, developed this concept in a new way. Thus, for the early monks and continuing to the present, the desert became a privileged place of encounter with God and a way to achieve Christian holiness.

Obviously, the concept of desert is far from being the only explanation for the birth of Christian monasticism in Egypt: the importance of religion both in political organization and in daily life certainly played a very important role. The texts produced by popular religion show the existence of a true pre-Christian mystical spirituality in ancient Egypt (Sadek 1988: 204–21; Quaegebeur 1977: 129–43); it would be most interesting to trace the link between the Egyptian concept of *maat* (justice and truthfulness before the god) and the Christian concept of 'holiness' and the monastic attitude of 'truthfulness.' The so-called *Book of the Dead* also contains germs of what would become the Christian, and more specifically the monastic, asceticism. It should also be mentioned that there existed in pharaonic Egypt communities of ascetics, which, to a certain extent, could be considered as pre-monastic communities (de Cenival 1972). Finally, a most interesting parallel may be drawn between the ancient Egyptian 'temple' as an institution and the Coptic cenobitic monastery, in terms of both organization and function. Like the Egyptian temple, the monastery played a spiritual, social, political, and cultural part in the history and civilization of the country. It actually stood in place of the Egyptian temple, which was a 'national conservatory.' Let us just mention as an example the role played by monasteries in the conservation of the Coptic language.

Generally speaking, it may thus be said that Egyptian monasticism appears as the fruit of the fertilization of pre-Christian mysticism, either official or underlying, by Christian biblical spirituality. Thus, the mark of ancient Egypt is visible in the way Egyptians interpreted, in the anchorite and cenobitic movements, the evangelical call for holiness.

Notes

1   Papyrus Sallier (British Museum), iv, 9, 4–6.
2   Former prisoners were sent to Rhinocolura, modern al-Arish in the Sinai, after their noses were cut off: cf. Carrez-Maratray 1998.
3   Up to 19,000 in Wadi Hammamat in year 38 of Sesostris III; cf. Goyon 1957: n. 63.
4   Sadek 1980: doc. 14:14 (Amun); 19:2 and 20:4 (Osiris); 16:3, 17:3, 22:45, 24:4, 25:3 (Hathor); 22:4 (Satis), etc.
5   As pointed out by Davies (2008: 115).

6   For example, Hosea 2:14; I Kings 17:1–25; II Kings 1 and 2; Exodus 15:22–26; Exodus 19; Numbers 21:6–9.

7   Exod. 1:31–42; Josh. 5:6; Amos 2:10. See also Kitchen 2003: 478—this book is very interesting for the dating of Exodus and the chronology of Israel—and Sadek 1993: 9–11.

8   In *The Vision of Theophilus*, the *Homily of Zacharias of Sakha*, *The Homily on the Rock*, *The Homilies of Cyriacus of Bahnasa*; cf. Sadek and Sadek 2011: 189–92.

8 Contested Frontiers: Southern Egypt and Northern Nubia, AD 300–1500
The Evidence of the Inscriptions

Jacques van der Vliet

Introduction: Frontiers and Beyond

Aswan traditionally represents Egypt's southern frontier. This was already the case in pharaonic times, if not in reality, at least symbolically.[1] The very notion of a frontier implies the notion of discontinuity. Frontiers may mark and even create differences. On this side of the border things are normal, but beyond things are different—or that is what we expect. Yet frontiers are also zones of passage: places of contact where we get to experience the differences, negatively or positively, and where we are forced to react accordingly. Frontiers, which may seem static and eternal at first sight, can acquire a dynamic aspect and come to foster processes of change, for example, linguistic change or cultural change.

Such processes of change are not to be conceived simply as the mechanical outcome of contact. Instead they depend on a wide variety of stimuli, going all the way from a liberal exchange to a strict refusal of contact, and from borrowing to the assertion, or even creation, of distinct identities on either side of the boundary line. Political frontiers, for example, draw seemingly abrupt and clear boundary lines, but at the same time create networks to maintain and—at once—transgress these lines, facilitating specific modes of passage that may become institutionalized in time.

Cultural, linguistic, and religious boundaries are less easy to grasp, even though they may partly or wholly coincide with political ones. They are,

moreover, constantly open to redefinition and may reflect not only changing political and economic circumstances, but also react to shifts within the
social networks that are the bearers of religious or linguistic identity. Frontiers are not merely the end of something and the beginning of something
else, but zones of contact where identities are defined and redefined within
a given spatial setting.

The Aswan region, and in particular Elephantine Island at the northern end of the cataract zone, have for many centuries been the southern
frontier of Egypt. Here, Egypt ends and Africa begins. For many centuries,
though not always, this has been a political frontier, dividing two nations.
Hence its great military importance during some periods of history. Its
status as a linguistic and cultural boundary zone is much less clearly defined.
For example, not only in remote antiquity but even today, Nubian is also
spoken north of the cataract. In ancient and medieval times, Egyptian—in
all its historical forms, from hieroglyphic to Coptic—was used as a written language along the whole of the Middle Nile, as is Arabic today. The
same applies to its role as a religious boundary. For several centuries, Aswan
marked a frontier between Christianity and traditional religion, and later
between Islam and Christianity, but at the same time both religions were
found north and south of the cataract region.

Actually, we are not dealing with one static frontier but with various
contested frontiers: a zone where political, linguistic, and religious identities are negotiated and articulated. Part of this ongoing process is reflected
in inscriptions. Inscriptions are, in fact, privileged means to express these
shifting identities. As written text, inscriptions are linguistic utterances,
vehicles of the forms and values of a chosen language. They are also public
utterances. As a rule they were visibly exposed and primarily meant to be
seen, even by those who could not read them. Finally, they are strongly
formalized. They use the specific codes of the social group that produced
them and—inversely—these codes serve to define and reproduce these
very groups. Better than any other genre of documents, therefore, inscriptions reflect the dynamics of a frontier zone. They mark the theater where
the various social groups act out their identity and assert their authority.

The remainder of this essay will be devoted to a chronological discussion of three groups of selected inscriptions that cover a thousand years of
Christianity in the broader Aswan region. Although occasionally reference
will be made to Meroitic and Arabic inscriptions, the bulk of these texts
are in Greek and Sahidic Coptic, representing the written codes of the elite

groups that produced them. The principal vernacular of the region, Nubian, is practically absent from the written record. The first group of inscriptions illustrates the spread of Christianity and the assertion of Christian institutions on both sides of the cataract in late antiquity. The second group shows the cataract region as a frontier where the world of Islam confronted Christian Africa, represented politically by the Kingdom of Makuria. Finally, some later medieval inscriptions are witnesses to the cracking of the 'Nubian dam' that had been constructed in the seventh century.

Traditional Religion and the Rise of Christianity (298–639)
Kalabsha and Tafa: Political Turmoil and Religious Change
The impressive temple of Kalabsha (Talmis), one of the religious centers of Roman Nubia, preserves a series of inscriptions that reflect on a local scale some of the epochal historical events of late antiquity. Most but not all of these are in Greek and thus bear witness to the strong Hellenization of northern Nubia (the Dodekaschoinos) in this period. One of them, inscribed in Greek in the *pronaos* of the temple, dates from the middle of the third century (248–49). It is a rendering in stone of a decree by "the *strategos* of Omboi and Elephantine," a certain Besarion surnamed Ammonios, to the effect that "all pigs be driven out of the temple of the village of Talmis . . . so that the holy rites may take place in the customary way" (Eide et al. 1998: no. 248). Besarion, a military man, had issued this decree on behalf of the high priest of all Egypt, Myron, who resided at Alexandria.

The priests of the temple of Kalabsha, a renowned cult center of the local god Mandulis, must have been offended by the number of pigs (unclean animals for them, but not for the local villagers who owned the pigs) walking around in the temple area. They were now authorized to chase them from the temple and publicized this authorization on one of the temple walls. The text shows that the region of Kalabsha lay under the military authority of the *strategos* of Omboi (Kom Ombo) and the spiritual authority of the high priest of Alexandria, two Roman officials. Kalabsha was part of the empire and northern Nubia was firmly embedded in the religious and political institutions of Roman Egypt.

Another inscription, still to be seen in the same temple, is the long inscription of Kharamadoye (Eide et al. 1998: no. 300). Its precise date is unknown but it must belong to the fourth or even the early fifth century. Significantly, it is not in Greek but in Meroitic. As the Meroitic language is still imperfectly understood, its contents remain largely obscure, but

Kharamadoye was apparently a king, a *qore* in Meroitic. The inscription reflects a well-known fact: in 298 Diocletian had withdrawn the southern frontier of Egypt to its traditional place, the Aswan region, more precisely, Philae. The Dodekaschoinos, the Roman buffer zone in northernmost Nubia, had become part of the Meroitic empire. It was ruled by governors and, from some time after the fall of the Meroitic empire, around the middle of the fourth century, by apparently independent kings who were buried near Qustul and Ballana, in the neighborhood of Abu Simbel (see Török 2009: 515–30).

As far as the political situation in Lower Nubia after the withdrawal of Roman control and the subsequent fall of Meroe can be judged, it was characterized by great unrest, usually associated with the rivalry between two competing ethnic groups, the Noubades and the Blemmyes. Greek graffiti at Kalabsha mention obscure kings who have been interpreted as Blemmye chieftains, acting as patrons of local cults and their priests (Eide et al. 1998: nos. 310–11). They suggest that at least some of the Blemmyes had settled in the Nile Valley and had become integrated into the Hellenized framework of Lower Nubian society that had been part of Roman Egypt for over three centuries.

This process of acculturation is illustrated even more clearly by a Greek inscription in the temple of Tafa (Taphis) that belongs to the same general period, the late fourth and fifth centuries (Eide et al. 1998: no. 312). It records that a Blemmye *klinarchos* (president) of a *synodos* (a pagan cultic society) had restored the temple hall, called—with an Egyptian word—a *chant*. The persons mentioned bear Blemmye names with an admixture of Egyptian elements. A longer and even more difficult Greek inscription from the temple of Kalabsha, which mentions a fifth-century *phylarchos* (tribal chief) Phonen, also shows the continuity of both traditional Egypto-Nubian cults and traditional Hellenistic-Egyptian social institutions under Blemmye rule (Eide et al. 1998: no. 313).

Blemmye rule in post-Roman Nubia may have been ephemeral only. The Blemmyes were ousted very soon by the Noubades, who probably were the native inhabitants of the Middle Nile Valley, inheriting Meroitic authority in this part of Nubia. The best-known witness to the Noubadian takeover is the triumphal inscription of Silko on the west wall of the forecourt of the temple of Kalabsha (Eide et al. 1998: no. 317). Here Silko, "king of the Noubades and all the Ethiopians," proclaims his victory over the Blemmyes. The inscription is no longer in Meroitic, but in Greek.

Reading this rather pompous text reveals a striking phenomenon. It contains phrases such as "God granted me victory" and, referring to the king's prowess, "I am a lion in the lower regions and a bear in the upper regions." Bears are foreign to both Nubia and Egypt and, in fact, this is the language of the Greek Bible.

Whether or not Silko was a Christian or whether he merely employed a Christian or Jewish scribe are moot points that are hardly important. Silko's monumental inscription announces a profound change of cultural and religious paradigm. The language of the Greco-Egyptian cult societies was replaced by the language of the Bible. It illustrates how finally Christianity came to Lower Nubia: not through the efforts of heroic missionaries, but by a gradual process of acculturation in which religion may not even have been a central concern. The new rulers of post-Roman Nubia adopted cultural models from the empire in order to strengthen their position within Nubian society. The symbolic power afforded by these cultural alliances was no less real than that provided by their political alliances.

The final outcome of this process within the domain of religion can be observed again in Kalabsha. Two Coptic inscriptions incised by a single hand on the temple front, on the left-hand pylon, read: "I, Paul, the priest, prayed here for the first time" and "I, Paul, the priest, set up the Cross here for the first time" (Richter 2002: 162–63). These two very similar texts signal the conversion of the Kalabsha temple into a church, presumably in the middle or the second half of the sixth century. The script and the nature of the texts strongly suggests that they are contemporaneous with the better known inscription that commemorates the conversion of the temple of Dendur during the episcopacy of Bishop Theodore of Philae (ca. 525–after 577). They are written in Sahidic Coptic, but show dialectal forms that are attested in particular in southernmost Egypt (Roquet 1978). The priest Paul was definitely a local man.

Overviewing the entire group of inscriptions from Kalabsha, two remarks must be made. First, the inscriptions from Kalabsha are important witnesses to the major historical events of the period: the integration of northern Nubia into the administrative, religious, and military structures of Roman Egypt; its return to Meroitic authority under the reign of Diocletian; the political instability of the region concomitant with the long-term persistence of local social and religious structures; and finally the gradual adoption of new cultural models, among them a new religion, Christianity. Secondly, in spite of the occasional appearance of a Meroitic king or

an Alexandrian high priest, and the decisive intervention of the emperor
Diocletian, they reflect primarily local issues, from the Nubians' fondness
for pig raising to the priest Paul's conversion of the temple into a church.

Bishop Theodore and Philae as a Symbol of Religious Change

Theodore of Philae, bishop for many years in the sixth century, is known
from literary sources as well as from a considerable number of inscriptions.
One of these, already mentioned, commemorates in Sahidic Coptic the
conversion of the temple of Dendur into a church (Eide et al. 1998: no.
330; Dijkstra 2008: 299–302). It begins:

> By the will of God and the order of King Eirpanome and the eager
> student of the word of God, Joseph, the exarch of Talmis [Kalabsha],
> and as we received the Cross from Theodore the bishop of Philae,
> I, Abraham, the most humble priest, set up the Cross on the day on
> which the foundations of this church were laid

and a date follows (for which, see Ochała 2011).

As in Kalabsha, a priest inaugurated the new church and exactly the
same formula is used to express this event in both places ("I, so-and-so, set
up the Cross"). The Dendur inscription, however, in addition spells out the
patronage of the political and religious authorities of the moment: a Noubadian king with a clearly indigenous name, Eirpanome; a local military
commander, Joseph, based at Kalabsha, whose piety is particularly praised;
Theodore, the bishop of Philae; and various civil officials. Apparently there
was not yet a Nubian hierarchy of bishops in place. The temples of Kalabsha and Dendur were converted by priests, in Dendur and plausibly also in
Kalabsha, under the supervision of the bishop of Philae, the frontier town
between Byzantine Egypt and the Noubadian kingdom. Theodore acted
as the patron of the official Christianization of northern Nubia, together
with a Nubian king, Eirpanome, about whom nothing is known beyond
his name, but who was most likely a Christian, too.

Philae, the see of Theodore, was both a frontier town and a religious
center. As an ancient center of pilgrimage it had attracted for centuries
pilgrims from south and north who came to visit the shrine of Isis and
other gods of the traditional Egyptian religion (Rutherford 1998). From
the north, these were Greeks and Romans in addition to Egyptians; from
the south, Meroites, sometimes from Meroe itself, altogether an immense

area. These pilgrims left a variety of inscriptions, mostly graffiti, in various languages: Greek, Latin, Demotic Egyptian, and Meroitic (Dijkstra 2008: 175–92). The Demotic scribal tradition in Philae, closely associated with the local priesthood, petered out around the middle of the fifth century; the last pagan inscription in Greek on Philae dates from about the same time (456–67). The fate of the traditional cults after this period is uncertain. Yet it took over seventy years before one of the generals of the emperor Justinian, the famous Narses, closed down the temples of Philae, around 535–37.

The latter date is usually taken to be the end of the traditional cults within Egypt, followed by a massive conversion of Philae's temples into churches. The evidence of the various Greek inscriptions left by Bishop Theodore in the great temple of Isis is taken as the expression of a decisive victory over a deeply rooted paganism, most eloquently summarized in one of them: "The Cross has prevailed (and) it always prevails" (Bernand 1969: no. 201). This picture has rightly been modified in recent publications, in particular by Jitse Dijkstra's monograph *Philae and the End of Ancient Egyptian Religion* (2008). Dijkstra correctly observed that the pagan cults in Philae had been moribund for a considerable time before Justinian and that Christianity was installed on the island far earlier than hitherto believed. In fact, bishops of Philae are known from the middle of the fourth century onwards. The Christian communities already had churches of their own and hardly needed the ancient temples for this purpose. The transition was a process at once more gradual and more complex than has usually been supposed, and much less a single dramatic event culminating in the conversion of the great temple of Isis into a church devoted to St. Stephen.

Yet the evidence of the inscriptions remains quite impressive. Not only Theodore but also an earlier bishop, Daniel, active around the middle of the fifth century, left a considerable number of inscriptions, all in Greek (Daniel: Bernand 1969: nos. 194–95; Theodore: Bernand 1969: nos. 200–204, 216; name of bishop lost: Bernand 1969, nos. 220–21, 227). Whereas some of these inscriptions are connected with the conversion of the temple of Isis into the church of St. Stephen (Bernand 1969: nos. 200–204), most others record episcopal involvement in civil building activity on Philae. Actually, from no other place in Egypt do we have so many inscriptions left by bishops. In order to understand this considerable epigraphic activity we have to keep in mind that Philae was a place of symbolic value on either side of the political frontier and had religious as well as military importance. It was moreover dominated by the impressive temple buildings of traditional religion, themselves heavily inscribed with monumental texts in various languages. Understood within this context, the inscriptions left by bishops Daniel, Theodore, and possibly others articulated the new Christian identity of the place and were a means of appropriating the symbolically important landscape of Philae.

In particular, the role of Theodore must have been of crucial importance. From various sources, including historical and church-historical ones, we know that he took a prominent part in the ecclesiastical life of his time, far beyond the boundaries of his diocese. He had the advantage of a long episcopacy, lasting over fifty years, and was clearly held in high regard by military and civil authorities in both Egypt and Nubia. Also, presumably in his time, the early history of the diocese of Philae was codified in a wonderful text that survives in Sahidic Coptic and is now known as the *Life of Aaron*. This collection of edifying stories relates how even the very first bishops of Philae had successfully combated traditional religion, encouraged monasticism, and showed pastoral care for the pagan Nubians.[2] This is precisely what Theodore did after them and what the inscriptions from both Nubia and Philae itself underscore (Dijkstra 2008: 324–33).

Christianity and Islam: A Precarious Balance (639–1173)
War, More War, and Peace: The Years up to the Baqt (652)

Very little is known about the political and military situation in Aswan following the Arab invasion of Egypt in the end of 639 (Bruning, forthcoming). Whereas Alexandria surrendered to the conquerors in November 641, they had to face unprecedented resistance at Egypt's southern frontier. According to a later literary source, Aswan was conquered by the Arabs only in 651–52 (Ibn Hawqal, quoted in Vantini 1975: 153), apparently following an earlier occupation. South of Aswan, the earlier Noubadian kingdom had shortly before become integrated into the powerful Christian state of Makuria, which had its center in the Dongola reach, between the Third and Fourth Nile Cataracts. In a historically important battle near Dongola, the Makurian infantry succeeded in decisively checking the Arab advance in this part of Africa, putting up what has been called the 'Nubian dam' (Ayalon 1989). For this liminal region, a long period of turmoil came to an end only when in the summer of 652 the famous Baqt, a bilateral peace treaty between Muslim-ruled Egypt and the Makurian kingdom, was concluded.

A beautiful inscription discovered in Dongola, the Makurian capital, in 2004 can perhaps be linked to these events (Jakobielski and Van der Vliet

2011). It contains the long eulogy of a "former bishop" of Aswan, Joseph, who had died in Dongola in 668, some sixteen years after the definitive reconquest of Aswan by the Arabs. The text is bilingual. Whereas Greek is used for the formulaic parts, the Sahidic Coptic body of the text contains a prose poem that is unique in the epigraphy of the Nile Valley on account of its rhetorical structure and panegyrical style. The inscription is of special interest, moreover, as it is the earliest precisely dated document found in Christian Dongola so far, and the earliest dated Coptic funerary inscription from Nubia. Since the focus of the text is on the bishop's spiritual and pastoral merits, it does not go into biographical or historical details. Thus it does not explain why this bishop of Aswan had come to end his days in Dongola, even though it emphasizes his status as a foreigner in the Makurian capital. Indeed, however highly Joseph may have been esteemed in his new homeland, where apparently he had lived and worked for some time, he did not occupy any other formal position than that of a "former bishop" of Aswan. This picture suggests that Joseph may have been a refugee who had fled the ongoing violence in Aswan or, perhaps more likely, an exile who as a public personality had sided with the Christian Makurians and was therefore unable to return to his see after 652. A more precise answer can only be expected from the discovery of further sources on Aswan's fate in the eventful years between 639 and 652.

Building a Frontier: Stronghold Aswan and the 'Castle of Philae'

As a result of more than ten years of struggle in and around the Aswan region, Aswan had developed into a major garrison town and administrative center of the new Islamic regime, second only to the new capital of Fustat. From the following centuries, hundreds of Muslim funerary stelae in Arabic have been preserved, a number that is again equaled only in Fustat (Su'ad Mahir Muhammad 1977; 'Abd al-Tawab et al. 1977–86). Aswan's newly gained prominence offers an example of a contested political frontier favoring the growth of new centers of power and new identities. A somewhat forgotten Coptic inscription, dated to 25 February of the year 693, explicitly attests to activity connected with the improvement of infrastructure around Aswan. It formally thanks "the wholly praiseworthy Amir Abu'l-Azz" for improving the road between Aswan and Kom Ombo, "so that men and animals travel on the road comfortably" (Mallon 1911–12: 132*–34*). Earlier Greek inscriptions from the sixth and seventh centuries attest to a similar concern for local infrastructure and record the involvement of the high military, civil, and ecclesiastical officials representing the Christian empire.[3] Now—merely forty years after the pacification of the region—a Coptic inscription shows a Muslim official with an Arabic name to be in charge of the work.

On the Nubian side of the frontier, too, its newly acquired importance became apparent in intensified political and infrastructural activity. In the reign of the Makurian king Mercurius, around 700, whose piety earned him the surname of "the New Constantine" (Evetts 1910: 140), new churches were inaugurated in the northern Nubian towns of Faras and Tafa (Taphis), foundations commemorated by inscriptions in Greek and Coptic (Faras: Łajtar and Twardecki 2003: no. 101; Van der Vliet 2003: no. 1; Tafa: Maspero 1910). Perhaps around the same time or somewhat later, a new office was created, that of eparch of Noubadia. Residing in Qasr Ibrim, the capital of the former kingdom of Noubadia, this was a royal deputy whose main function consisted of overseeing and regulating the diplomatic and commercial contacts with Islamic Egypt (Godlewski, forthcoming).

A dossier from the middle of the eighth century, consisting of one Arabic letter and several Coptic ones and found at Qasr Ibrim, gives us a fascinating glimpse of these contacts (Arabic letter: Hinds and Sakkout 1981; Coptic letters: publication forthcoming by J.L. Hagen, Leiden). They involved not only the eparch of Noubadia, but also various other agents, among whom was a permanent representative of the Nubian kingdom at the office of the Muslim governor in Aswan. More importantly, these documents show that the contacts between the two parties were not limited to matters pertaining to the Baqt and its conditions. The frontier at Aswan was not a closed one and allowed a variety of contacts, from military alliances to conflicts over commercial interests.

Meanwhile the actual frontier remained where it had been in the Byzantine period, at Philae or—more precisely—a set of military strongholds on the east bank near Philae (Gascoigne and Rose 2010). Until well into medieval times, the Makurian kings claimed that their authority extended over all the Nubians from Tilimauara, an unknown locality in the south, "up to the *kastron* (castle) of Pilak (Philae)" in the north (Crum 1905: no. 449; cf. Plumley 1981). Corresponding to "the *kastron* of Pilak," we find on the Nubian side "the *kastron* of the Moors." It is known from a late antique Greek papyrus and was tentatively identified by Adam Łajtar with an ancient fortress-like building on the east bank, opposite Bigeh, about 1.5 kilometers south of Philae. According to medieval sources, this was the northernmost stronghold of the Nubian kings (Łajtar 1997).

An interesting Greek inscription from the east bank near Philae probably dates from the Byzantine period, and underscores the liminal character
of this frontier zone. It records a foundation, perhaps by an *actuarius* (admin-
istrator) of the *kastron* of Philae, and contains this prayer: "Lord God protect
me, the master of this house, and those who live in it, and deliver us from
the craftiness of the devil" (Bernand 1989: no. 239). The exact relationship
of the inscription with the *kastron* of Philae remains to be established, but it
was clearly meant to avert one of the inherent dangers of any liminal zone:
attacks not only by visible foes, but also by invisible ones.

An Ecclesiastical Stronghold: The Monastery of St. Hatre

With the growth of Islamic Aswan, it seems as if the main center of Christian life in Aswan shifts to the west bank. The impressive site of St. Hatre
becomes our main source of documents for the post-conquest period
(Monneret de Villard 1927b). These include numerous inscriptions, in particular the *dipinti* and graffiti in the church and other monastic buildings,
and the hundreds of Coptic epitaphs that have been published by Henri
Munier (1930–31; Hasitzka 1993–2006: 1: nos. 498–675). The monastery
was apparently a center of supra-regional importance. Several of the monks
were Nubians *(Noubas)*, whereas others came from far away places such as
Pemje (Oxyrhynchos) in Middle Egypt. From a certain period onwards
the monastery may have served as a residence for bishops. Two epitaphs
mention bishops and a Coptic dedicatory inscription from the monastery
records a pious foundation by Abraham, bishop of Aswan and Elephantine,
bequeathing half of its income for "the poor of Aswan [and Elephantine]"
(De Morgan 1894: 139, n. 1; cf. Crum 1902a: no. 8322).

The presence of Nubians among the inhabitants of the Monastery of St.
Hatre raises the question of the contacts between the respective Christian
communities on either side of the frontier after the Arab conquest. In spite of
a clearly drawn frontier, demarcated by fortresses, separating a Muslim state in
the north and a Christian one in the south, contacts were apparently varied
and lively. The Coptic tombstones of Nubians in St. Hatre are balanced by
Arabic tombstones of Muslims living in Lower Nubia, mostly from Fatimid
times. One of these even uses the Egyptian (Coptic) calendar that was current in medieval Nubia (Nigm ed Din Mohammed Sherif 1964: 249).

During the entire Fatimid period, the Makurian kingdom held a strong
military and political position in the region. At various periods, Christians
in medieval Egypt looked to Nubia for patronage in times of conflict with

the Muslim authorities. Such patronage is attested for the Aswan region as well. A commemorative *dipinto* in Coptic on one of the walls of the monastery church of St. Hatre dates the death of a monk, Peter, to 19 April 962 "in year 1 of King Zachari (Zacharias)," one of several Makurian kings of this name (Dijkstra and Van der Vliet 2003). Did King Zacharias have real authority over the Aswan region or is this merely the nostalgia of a monk who dreamed of living under a Christian king? In any case, such a dream must have seemed at least reasonably realistic at the time.

The Years of Decline (1173–1500)
The Fall of Qasr Ibrim and Its Echoes
The tenth and eleventh centuries were the period of the greatest political power and prosperity of the Makurian kingdom. Its decline is usually taken to set in with the conquest of Qasr Ibrim by Shams al-Dawla, the brother of Salah al-Din (Saladin), in 1173. The impact of this event was considerable and its echoes can be found in both Christian and Muslim authors, but also in a contemporary inscription from Aswan. In the ancient tombs hewn in the mountain of Qubbat al-Hawa, on the west bank, a church and monastic dwellings had been installed. One of the hermitages contains a Coptic *dipinto*, probably written by a monk, who, from his elevated position, had seen the armies march by. The text runs:

> On this very day, the 22nd of Tobe, the 1st of the moon, (year) 889 of the Era of the Martyrs (17 January 1173). It happened during the reign of the Turks over the entire land of Egypt, while our father Amba Markos was archbishop of the city of Alexandria and in the days also of Theodore, bishop of the city of Aswan, that the Turks [came south?]. They went up to Prim (Qasr Ibrim) and captured it on the 7th of Tobe. They seized everybody (?) who was inside and came (back) and sold them together with [. . .]. (T.S. Richter in Edel 2008: 515)

This is a rather matter-of-fact and neat eyewitness account of what was apparently quite a shocking event: Shams al-Dawla ("the Turks") returning with his booty to Aswan after a campaign of only a few weeks. The fall of Qasr Ibrim must have dealt a fatal blow to any Christian hopes for support from the south to counter the effects of Muslim rule.

The inscription was clearly written by someone who felt himself to be an Egyptian Christian, but Nubian influence is perhaps discernible in the use of a moon date, which was widespread in contemporaneous inscriptions from Nubia. Quite likely, medieval Christians from the Aswan region looked to Christian Nubia not only for patronage, but also as a cultural model, at least in some respects.

Other inscriptions from the same area likewise suggest that Nubian scribal habits were occasionally followed. This is the case of the commemorative *dipinto* dated to year one of King Zacharias at St. Hatre, quoted above. At Qubbat al-Hawa another instance can be found in a bilingual inscription recently published by Renate Dekker. The dedicatory inscription of the Church of St. Severus of 11 March 1180 opens with the same kind of garbled Greek formulae that are found in Nubian graffiti hundreds of kilometers farther to the south. It then continues in Coptic to record the consecration of the church and its baptismal font by a bishop of Aswan, Severos, and the sponsoring of this event by a certain David from the city of Hermonthis, in the Theban region (Dekker 2008: 32–34). In view of the date (only a few years after the fall of Qasr Ibrim) one may wonder whether there was any connection between the military expedition of Shams al-Dawla and the renovation of this church, which may have been damaged by marauding troops.

King Kudanbes and his Retinue

If the neat account of the return of the victorious Shams al-Dawla to Aswan may be called a pathetic document, this is all the more true for the last inscription to be discussed here. It is again situated in the church of St. Hatre. In its latter days, the monastery apparently functioned as a kind of caravanserai giving shelter to travelers and pilgrims, including Muslims from abroad making the Hajj, who left ample traces in the form of both painted and engraved inscriptions in various languages. Thus, in April 1322, a certain Kartolaos left a long inscription in a highly obscure form of Nubian Greek, near the sanctuary of the monastery church, "on the front of the left jamb of the apse" (Griffith 1928: 134–45).

Following an invocation of the Archangel Michael, it enumerates what is apparently the retinue of a Nubian king called Koudanpes (Kudanbes). The latter must have visited the monastery church in great pomp, accompanied by a whole series of bishops, priests, and civil dignitaries, with impressive Greek and Latin titles. The scribe expresses his awe upon seeing so many state and church celebrities, but—as far as we can understand the text—he does not state the occasion of the monarch's visit to the monastery.

Fortunately, the historian al-Maqrizi comes to our help here and reveals the sad reality behind Kartolaos's pompous inscription. The events date to the third period of reign of the Mamluk sultan al-Nasir. In 1315, the latter sent an army to Dongola, the capital of Makuria, to install a puppet king on the Nubian throne. King Kudanbes, a usurper who had previously murdered his own brother, fled together with another brother, Abraham, but both were captured and imprisoned in Cairo in July 1317. Meanwhile another usurper, Kanz al-Dawla, attacked al-Nasir's puppet king and seized the Makurian throne for himself. Then the sultan released Kudanbes's brother Abraham and promised him he would release Kudanbes as well if he were to defeat Kanz al-Dawla. Abraham succeeded and Kanz al-Dawla surrendered to Abraham, but the latter died three days later and the Nubians reinstalled Kanz al-Dawla. Thereupon, in 1323, the sultan sent an army to reinstate Kudanbes. The army reached its aim and chased Kanz al-Dawla out, but, as soon as it returned to Egypt, the latter returned and deposed Kudanbes.

As the date of the inscription shows, Kudanbes's visit to the monastery of St. Hatre in Aswan must have marked a stage on his way from his Cairo prison to be reinstated briefly as a king at Dongola in 1323. In spite of all the glorious titles of his retinue, Kudanbes was no more than a puppet of the sultan and, so it seems, one in a series of otherwise inglorious usurpers. Kartolaos's long inscription looks at the facts from an entirely different angle than the Egyptian historian. As a faithful courtier he calls Kudanbes "a king worthy of three hundred years"! As it appeared, his reign was only a prelude to the final disintegration of the Makurian kingdom and the gradual Islamization of its territory in the following centuries.

Conclusions

From a great distance, the past seems orderly. Clear-cut periods are demarcated by successive wars, revolutions, councils, and dynasties. Conflicting nations and religions face each other as solid blocks. Real history is different and far more confusing. It is the history written by normal people who, in spite of everything, succeed in surviving disasters and crossing borders. They sometimes leave behind simple documents such as a tombstone or a letter on papyrus. Only rarely do these enable us to discern some of their motives and ambitions. The region of Aswan, situated on the borderline between Egypt and Africa, is one of those rare centers where we can observe not merely the clash of empires and civilizations, but also the ways in which societies reacted to these events and gave shape to their existence. A very small part of all this is reflected in inscriptions, but for the history of Christianity on either side of Egypt's southern frontier, this is by no means the least important part.

Notes

1   For a recent discussion of this frontier in antiquity, see Török 2009: esp. 7–22.
2   A rather inadequate edition of the text is Budge 1915: 432–95; a new edition is being prepared by J. Dijkstra and J. van der Vliet.
3   For example, at Kom Ombo (?): Gascou 1994; Aswan: Bernand 1989: nos. 235–37; Philae: Bernand 1969: nos. 194–95, 216–28; probably also Bernand 1989: no. 239, discussed below.

9 The Veneration of Saints in Aswan and Nubia

Youhanna Nessim Youssef

Introduction

The *Synaxarion*, as we have it now, was compiled in Lower Egypt. It includes only a few saints from Aswan and its region. In this article I will mention some of the saints venerated in the region of Aswan and Nubia.

There are three approaches to address this subject:

- The study of the inscriptions and the other material that mention saints.
- The region is very poor in these (Papaconstantinou 2001a: 304).[1]
- The study of the names of the bishops and the clergy.
- The study of the churches and monasteries in the area.

With regard to the saints mentioned in the work of Abu Salih in his chapter on Nubia (fol. 94a–102a), I have two remarks. The first is that there are very few names of churches mentioned in this section. Secondly, setting aside the Virgin Mary and the Archangel Michael, we find that all the saints are of Egyptian origin and also etymologically Coptic. The following is the list of church names mentioned:

- St. Michael (94b, fol. 100b, 101a)
- Virgin Mary (fol. 96a, 101a, 101b)
- St. Onophrius (fol. 98a)

- St. Hatre (fol. 101b, 102a)
- St. Antony (102a)
- St. Menas (101b)
- St. Psate (102a)

This paucity of names is reflected in a paucity of documents (Papaconstantinou 2001a: 304).

The Churches of Nubia

In an earlier study, C. Detlef Müller compiled a list of the names of the churches and monasteries in Nubia according to the excavations carried out there (Müller 1978). The following is the list of the holy figures and saints venerated in the region, with the number of churches dedicated to each:[2]

Trinity	Holy Trinity	2
	Jesus	9
Angels	Four Creatures	5
	24 Elders	2
	Michael	10
	Gabriel	4
	Raphael	3
	Litharkuel	1
Biblical saints	Mary	9
	Apostles	1
	Andrew	2
	James	1
	John	3
	Mark	1
	Peter	4
	Stephen	2
	Thomas	1
	Three Youths	1
Martyrs	George	2
	Colluthos	1
	Kyriakos	1
	Menas	3
	Mer(curi)us	3
	Philotheus	2
	Theodore	1

Monks	Abba Kyr(i)os	1
	Shenoute	1
Bishops	Severus	1
	Epimachus	1
Other	Cross	2

On the basis of the data listed above, I would like to make the following remarks:

1. The biblical saints and heavenly creatures are very well represented in this table while monks and bishops are comparatively rare.

2. The Virgin Mary (like Jesus) is mentioned nine times. The reason is clear. During the evangelization of Nubia, the Chalcedonian and anti-Chaldedonian factions vied to be the first there. The anti-Chalcedonian faction arrived first in the northern and southern kingdoms of Nubia (see below). This group accused the Chalcedonians of being Nestorians. Hence, the invocation of the name of the Virgin Mary as the Mother of God (Theotokos) is a good pledge of 'orthodoxy.' It was at that time also that the problem of Julianism arose. Also the sixth century was the time of creation of new monasteries in Scetis bearing the name of the Virgin Mary, such as Dayr al-Baramus (Evelyn-White 1932: 232–35), which, like other monasteries of the valley, came under the control of the Gaianite faction among the monks. The Severan followers of Theodosius, who had to leave their monastery sometime between 535 and 580, proceeded to establish a monastery dedicated to the Virgin as a counterpart to their original monastery (Cody 1991a: 789–94). The same could be said for the monastery of Dayr al-Suryan at Wadi al-Natrun (Cody 1991b: 876–81), which was established for those monks of the neighboring monastery of Dayr Anba Bishoi who were doctrinal partisans of Severus of Antioch. In the first decades after 518, the opposing party, which subscribed to the Christological views of Julian of Halicarnassus, had gained control of the four original monasteries. Each was then duplicated by a new and separate monastery dedicated to the Theotokos (Mother of God), to which those members of the community who were doctrinal followers of Severus moved. Hence the mention of Mary the Mother of God is directed against both Chalcedonians and Julianists in Nubia.

3. The Archangel Michael is the most popular in the above list. In Coptic thought, the Archangel Michael is the guardian angel. The keeps of the monasteries have a chapel named after him as a protector of the monastery.[3]

This role of the protector is highlighted in Coptic liturgical books;[4] hence in the book of the *Antiphonarion* (Gabra 1996: 37–52; 1998: 49–68) we read:

> You are with them in all their pains, consoling them by Christ.
> Hail to you, Michael the Archangel, the servant of all the saints.
> (O'Leary 1926–28: 58–59)

The *Book of the Glorifications* also mentions:

> The Archangel Michael was with the Apostles until they made the inhabited world return to the knowledge of the truth.
> The Holy Archangel Michael was with the martyrs until they were crowned with the imperishable crown of martyrdom.
> The Holy Archangel Michael was with the cross-bearers[5] until they accomplished their life in the desolate mountains. (al-Muharraqi 1972: 102–103)

In a doxology found in a manuscript in the Coptic Patriarchate collection, we find:

> We welcome you today, O Michael, the comforter of the saints, who takes their requests to God. (al-Suriani 1984b, 1: 164)

In the Coptic Martyrdoms, the Archangel Michael appears to heal the martyr from wounds and afflictions, and finally to take his soul to heaven (Müller 1959a: 90–95). The struggle of a bishop in exile is hence compared to the suffering of martyrdom (Youssef 2006a: 645–56). The invocation of the archangel becomes a need for the protection of the southern borders of Egypt. Even today, the cathedral of Aswan is named after the Archangel Michael.

4. The role of Archangel Gabriel is linked to the annunciation to the Virgin Mary (see above).

5. The veneration of the Archangel Raphael in Alexandria, according to a homily attributed to Cyril of Alexandria, is linked to the arrival of the Emperor Theodosius II at this city (Coquin 1994: 25–56; 1997: 9–58). As the kings of Nubia, such as Mercurius, considered themselves 'the new Constantine' (Seybold 1962: 183), the same could be said for Theodosius, as we will see in the veneration of Apa Kyrios (below).

6. I do not have any explanation for Litharkuel. So far I have not found his name mentioned elsewhere and I do not have any explanation; it could be derived from a pre-Christian local deity!

7. Nearly half of the Apostles are mentioned by their individual names (that is, Andrew, Peter, Thomas, James, and John), and once the Apostles are mentioned as a group. To this list we can also add Mark and Stephen. The veneration of the Apostles is a justification for the Nubian Church as it is not recognized as one of the Apostolic seats (such as Antioch, Alexandria, Rome, Ephesus, and to certain extent Jerusalem and Constantinople). In this group we find the four first Apostles, Peter, Andrew, John, and James. All the saints in this group are attested in Greek and Coptic papyri and inscriptions. However, Thomas does not occur in these documents. It seems that the mention of Thomas is related to his role as a preacher in India. This toponym can fit all races between Ethiopia and India (Datema 1985: 57). Mark is traditionally considered the founder of the Coptic Church. Hence his mention indicates that the Nubian Church follows the Coptic Church.

8. In the Annals of Sa'id ibn al-Bitriq (Eutychius) (876–939), the Chalcedonian patriarch of Alexandria, we find a list of the prominent martyrs: "In the days of both Diocletian and Maximian thousands of martyrs died; they tortured Saint George in all sorts of ways and put him to death in Palestine although he was of the Cappadocian nation, and these two killed Saint Menas, Saint Victor, Vincent, Epimachus and Mercurius"[6] (Evetts and Cheikho 1906, 1: 116; Breydy 1985: 62 §177). This list corresponds to the martyrs commemorated in Nubia with the addition of Philotheus and Colluthos.

9. It is important to note that only two bishops are mentioned. One of them is Severus of Antioch (see below).

10. While the great monks, such as Antony, Paul, Macarius, and Pachomius, who were painted in a monastery at the time of Benjamin in the seventh century (Müller 1956: 313–40; 1959b: 323–47), are absent from our list, Apa Kyrios, or Cyrus, is mentioned.[7] The explanation is that this saint was the brother of Emperor Theodosius. Theodosius is considered an 'orthodox' (anti-Chalcedonian) ruler. The Nubian royal family may also have had a saint among its members.

11. Shenoute is the second monk venerated in Nubia. His name is always linked to his heroic activity at the Council of Ephesus and against Nestorius (Leipoldt 1906: 128–30). Samuel Moawad's study demonstrates

clearly how Shenoute backed Cyril at the Council of Ephesus and how he was inspired by the writings of this saint (Moawad 2008). This action is still commemorated in the Coptic Church (Youssef 2008a). It is because of his 'orthodoxy' that St. Shenoute is commemorated in Nubia.

12. The name of Epimachus is difficult to identify. There is a martyr from Pelusium commemorated on 14 Bashans (O'Leary 1937b: 131). However, a stele from Nubia has been found, dating from around the eighth century and with an inscription in Coptic that reads: "On this day the commemoration of the blessed Epimachus, the third day of Paoni [Baounah]" (van Esbroeck 1991). In order to identify a saint, we need to know the date and the place of his commemoration (Delehaye 1934: 13–14, 17). Although the dates do not correspond, this saint could still possibly be identified as Epimachus, bishop of Pelusium. He is mentioned in the biography of the Patriarch Khael (744–67):

> Now I desire to relate another miracle, shown forth by the Father Epimachus, the bishop. One day he was teaching his people in the city of Al-Faramâ, and exhorting them to avoid heretics, and never to associate with them in anything. And behold, a priest of the Chalcedonians appeared before him to tempt him with guile; and the bishop delivered a long discourse, at the end of which the priest said to him: "I believe in thy creed and confess it." But the bishop Epimachus took holy oil from the body of the holy Severus, the patriarch, and anointed the face of the heretical priest, saying to him: "If thou mockest the Lord, let his power appear in thee!" And immediately a spirit of an unclean devil leapt upon him. . . .
>
> Then the bishop gave orders that his flock should never have a stranger as sponsor, but only members of their own family or their parents. And there were there some heretics, who would not obey him; but God requited them speedily, so that everyone marvelled at the doctrines of the Lord. (Seybold 1962a: 211–13)

The biographer was John I, who was a monk and deacon from the close circles of the patriarch Khael I and who wrote the longest biography in the *History of the Patriarchs* (den Heijer 1989: 145–46). This episode shows his anti-Chalcedonian attitude. It also explains the inclusion of Epimachus among the list of saints venerated in Nubia. We are also told that this Epimachus was a hegumen of the Monastery of Saint Macarius and abbot of a monastery near Tinnis who suffered from the persecution of an emir: "Epimachus was a saint and became worthy to become bishop" (Seybold 1962a: 166).

The biography also narrates the role of the king of Nubia, 'the new Constantine,' Mercurius (Seybold 1962a:183). His successor was an 'orthodox.'

The biography of Khael I narrates the miracle that took place in the Monastery of St. Shenoute (the White Monastery), when the governor of Egypt wanted to enter the monastery with his concubine (Seybold 1962a: 163–64).[8]

Conclusion

Our study of the venerated saints in Lower Nubia leads us to conclude:

- The biblical saints are very well represented, while bishops and monks are only represented by two examples.
- Most of the saints are chosen for their 'orthodoxy.'
- There is special veneration for St. Mark, the founder of the Coptic Church, and St. Thomas, the preacher for India in the larger sense of the term.
- The Archangel Michael is the protector of the kingdom of Nubia.

Part 2: Severus of Antioch and the Area South of Egypt

In a previous paper, I highlighted the relationship between Severus of Antioch and Scetis (Youssef 2006c). In this paper I will focus on the relationship between Severus of Antioch and the southern of regions of Egypt and beyond, that is, Aswan, Nubia, and Ethiopia.

The Biographies of Severus of Antioch

There are four ancient biographies of Severus of Antioch:

- The biography attributed to his old friend Zacharias Scholasticus, written in AD 512–18 and narrating his life up to AD 512.
- John, abbot of the Monastery of Beith-Aphthonia, wrote the complete *Life of Severus of Antioch*.
- We have also a Coptic (Goodspeed and Crum 1908: 578 [10]–585 [17]; Till 1935: 188–200; 1936: 141–43; Munier 1916: 52–53; Orlandi 1968: 351–405), Arabic (Youssef 2004: [1–153]), and Ethiopian (Goodspeed and Crum 1908: 591 [23]–718 [150]) biography attributed to Athanasius of Antioch.[9]

• The *Homily on Blessed Mar Severus, Patriarch of Antioch* by George,
Bishop of the Arabs (McVey 1993).

In addition to this, the Sahidic Coptic homily on St. Leontius by Severus
of Antioch contains an autobiographical section (Garitte 1966). However,
in none of these biographies do we find any mention of the region of
southern Egypt.

Severus of Antioch in Egypt

In a previous article, W.E. Crum attracted the attention of the scholarly
world to the veneration of Severus of Antioch in the region of Thebes,
as he published inscriptions from the tomb of Mery in Abd al-Qurna
and the tomb of Daga in western Thebes (Crum 1922–23). This article
was followed by two studies on the same subject. The first was written by
O'Leary, wherein he studied the presence of Severus in the region of Asyut
and Lower Egypt (O'Leary 1952). The second study was by Anneke van
der Meer, where she repeated the same information concerning the veneration of Severus of Antioch in the region of Asyut (Rifeh) and Sakha, in
addition to what Crum described in western Thebes (Van der Meer 1996).

Severus of Antioch and Ethiopia

As Pauline Allen mentioned, our first sources of information about the
life of Severus are his own letters as well as his homilies (Allen and Haywards 2004: 4), hence we find information about his own life in a letter of
Severus of Antioch to Theodore bishop of Olbe concerning the rebaptism
of a person in case of doubt as to the validity of his or her original baptism.
This letter may be dated during his patriarchate, 513–18. He wrote:

> I remember that in the holy monastery of father Romanus of saintly
> memory also, which is situated in Palestine, that a certain monk, who
> by race was an *Ethiopian* [present author's emphasis], after he had for
> a long time communicated in the sacred mysteries, since he was also
> counted in the order of those who had taken upon them the solitary
> life, upon seeing certain persons baptised there thinking that he had
> seen a strange sight, secretly confessed to one of the brothers that he
> had not been admitted to the divine laver. And the man who was at
> that time archimandrite of the . . ." (Brooks 1904, 2: 422–23 [transla-
> tion], 477–78 [text])

From this text we can see that during the life of Severus in Gaza, there was already an "Ethiopian monk"—we should keep in mind that this does not necessarily mean the actual Ethiopia, but any country south of Egypt, such as Eritrea, Somalia, Ethiopia, or Sudan.

We know that Severus after his baptism went first to the Monastery of Peter the Iberian near Gaza in about AD 490. From the monastery of Peter, Severus graduated to the solitary life in the desert of Eleutheropolis, where his health suffered so badly from the rigors of asceticism that he was taken in by the abbot of the Monastery of Romanus and nursed back to health. Hence we can see that this event took place by the end of the fifth century; that is, Severus was already in contact with a monk from south of Egypt by that time.

Evidence for the Veneration of Severus of Antioch in the Region of Aswan and Nubia

1. The *Homily on Claudius of Antioch*: In a homily falsely ascribed to Severus of Antioch about the discovery of the relics of Claudius of Antioch, we find that Severus of Antioch left the Monastery of St. Moses in Abydos and went to the cataract region. Then he returned back north to the Monastery of St. Pachomius (Godron 1970: [78] 20). This homily can be dated to the seventh century (Youssef 2002).

2. The *dipinto* by David from Armant, dated 13 March AD 1180: This *dipinto* shows that there was a church of Severus of Antioch and also a bishop Severus:

> I have paid for the consecration of this new church, which our father and bishop, Lord Abba Severus, has established. He consecrated it and the baptismal font on this very day, Paremhat 17, (the year of the) Martyrs 896. He consecrated it in the name of the patriarch Severus. Lord, reward me with his holy blessing. Amen. (Dekker 2008)

Abu Salih the Armenian, while talking about Qift (Coptus), mentioned the way to 'Idab where there is a church named after Severus (Evetts and Butler 1893: fol. 103a, 130 [text], 280 [translation]).

3. There was a church in Lower Nubia named after Severus of Antioch in the twelfth century (Müller 1978).

4. In the late fifteenth century, John, bishop of Asyut, Manfalut, and Abu Tig (Youssef 2008b), mentioned a story concerning a meeting between

Severus and the bishop of Nubia, Nicomedes (Youssef 2006b: 44–47). It is important to mention that during his time Nubia started a slow process of Islamization (Adams 1991d).

> 44 Listen then O people who love Christ—at His mention worship and glory are due—so that I might inform you about the miracle which took place by (the hand of) our holy, honoured and great father Abba Severus, on the mountain of Abba Moses which is in the quarry of al-Balyanā,[10] which is on the mountain of Ebot. It is* extremely wonderful and we should not overlook it. It happened in the time of Abba Moses that there was excessive inflation in the land of Upper-Egypt, and it lasted for three consecutive years. Our father the holy Abba Severus arrived at the monastery of Abba Moses at the end of these three years to visit Abba Moses and by coincidence he arrived at the same time as *Nicomedes, the bishop of Nubia* [present author's emphasis].[11] The abovementioned fathers assembled together—by the will of the exalted God—who reveals His wonders through His saints. While these fathers were assembled together, namely the master, father and patriarch, our father Abba Severus, with the honoured bishop Abba Nicomedes, and the father, the holy God-fearing Abba Moses.

It is important to highlight that this meeting took place after the visit of the Coptic Patriarch Theodosius I—the disciple of Severus of Antioch.

Why Was Severus Venerated in the South of Egypt?

To answer this question, we should return to the beginning of the evangelization of Nubia.

The sixth century saw the confrontation between Chalcedonians and anti-Chalcedonians. In this difficult atmosphere, we find Julian the priest[12] who accompanied the patriarch Theodosius I in his exile in Constantinople, and through him had become imbued with a zeal to convert the Nubians. This story is mentioned in the *Ecclesiastical History* of John of Ephesus (Adams 1977: 441–42; Gadallah 1959; Monneret de Villard 1938: 61–64;Vantini 1981: 38–40).The empress Theodora helped him in his mission by giving him some money and preventing the envoy of Justinian (her husband) from accomplishing his own mission. Julian remained in Noubadia for two years, after which his missionary efforts were carried on by Theodore, bishop of Philae (Dijkstra 2008: 271–333).

The final conversion of Noubadia was completed by Longinus between 569 and 575 (Adams 1991b). According to his contemporary, the historian John of Ephesus, Longinus was an Alexandrian who became a member of the anti-Chalcedonian Church of Antioch, and was subsequently dispatched to Constantinople as an envoy of Patriarch Paul of Antioch. He was apparently detained in Constantinople throughout the reign of Justinian, and subsequently under Justin was imprisoned for a time for his anti-Chalcedonian sympathies. Escaping from prison, he returned to Egypt in the year 567 and was thereupon ordered by the patriarch Theodosius I to undertake missionary work in the northern Nubian kingdom of Noubadia. Longinus evidently found a great deal still to do, for he remained in Noubadia for six years. In 575 Longinus returned to Alexandria to assist in the election of a new anti-Chalcedonian patriarch. He became embroiled in a dispute between Syrian and Egyptian claimants and, having backed the wrong party, was forced into exile for several years on the Arabian Peninsula. In 580 he returned once more to Noubadia, and shortly afterward proceeded onward to the southern Nubian kingdom of Alodia, whose king had previously sent him an invitation. Longinus was not able to travel directly up the Nile from Noubadia to Alodia because of the opposition of the kingdom of Makuria which lay between and which had apparently adopted the Melchite (Chalcedonian) Christian confession. As a result, the missionary was forced to travel through the Eastern Desert, in the company of a Beja camel caravan. After considerable hardships he arrived in Alodia, where he was met by a royal deputation and brought directly to the king. According to John of Ephesus, the mission was a complete success, and the conversion of the whole kingdom was soon accomplished. Longinus then sent a report of his success to the king of Noubadia, with instructions that it should be forwarded to Alexandria (Adams 1991c).

It is clear that the conversion of Philae (Aswan) and Nubia took place during the sixth century when the misunderstanding between Chalcedonians and non-Chalcedonians was at its height. The first patriarch who gave his approval for this mission was Theodosius I,[13] the spiritual heir of Severus of Antioch. His followers (such as Jacob Baradee, Paul of Antioch, and so on) (Grillmeier and Hainthaler 1996: 53) often designated him the 'ecumenical patriarch' and meant by this his universal responsibility for the Church. His theology is clearly Severian.

All the manuscripts of the *Synaxarion* (Forget 1954: 192–94) narrate for the day of 28 Ba'una the story about Theodosius taken from the *History of the Patriarchs* (Seybold 1962b: 89–95 [text]). This biography does not mention the mission to Nubia and Philae.

Conclusion
Despite the absence of any mention of the region of southern Egypt, and especially south of Thebes, in all the biographies and the works[14] of Severus of Antioch (as at his time this region was not yet evangelized), the veneration of Severus of Antioch flourished from the second half of the sixth century up to the fifteenth century. This is apparent from the following evidence:

1. The consecration of a church named after him in 1185 in Qubbat al-Hawa.
2. There was a church in Nubia also named after him.
3. A homily of one of the bishops of Asyut praising Severus of Antioch mentions a bishop of Nubia, Nicomedes. This bishop is not attested elsewhere. As a result, the cult of Severus of Antioch became linked to Nubia in the popular mentality.

This veneration of Severus in Aswan and Nubia is easily understood for these reasons:

1. The first person who initiated the mission to Nubia was the spiritual heir of Severus, Theodosius.
2. The first missionaries to Nubia were also anti-Chalcedonian orthodox: Julian the Evangelist, Theodore of Philae, and Longinus.

There are some opinions based on the testimony of Eutychius (Saʿid ibn al-Bitriq) that the kingdom of Makuria (south of Noubadia and north of Alodia) was converted by the Melchites, but became anti-Chalcedonian during the interval between 637 and 731, when there was no Melchite patriarch in Alexandria. Even so, it is certain that it became anti-Chalcedonian by the end of the seventh century, owing its Christian faith to the spiritual heir of Severus of Antioch.

By the middle of the fifteenth century, Christianity had disappeared from Nubia. However the memory of the Christianization of Nubia was always linked to Severus of Antioch, hence the mention of Nicomedes, bishop of Nubia, in the homily on Severus by John, bishop of Asyut,

Manfalut, and Abu Tig. The name of Nicomedes could be a misreading and misinterpretation of the name of a bishop of Nubia called Nabis, who lived some time between the seventh and tenth centuries (Muyser 1944: especially 137–38; Feldalto 1984: especially 312).

Notes

1   See Jacques Van Der Vliet's article in this volume for more details on the inscriptions coming from this region.
2   See Papconstantinou 2001 for the following: George, pp. 69–72; Colluthos, pp. 122–28; Kyriakos, pp. 132–34; Menas, pp. 146–54; Mercurius, pp 145–46; Philotheus, pp. 202–203; Theodore, pp. 97–100; Apostles, pp. 56–58; Andrew, p. 50; James, pp. 102–103; John, pp. 115–16; Mark, pp. 141–43; Peter, pp. 175–76; Stephen, pp. 194–95; Abba Kyrios, pp. 135–36; Shenoute, pp. 185–86; Severus, pp. 188–90; Epimachos pp. 79–80.
3   Cf. Evelyn-White 1932: 73–81, 140, 178, 233; Meinardus 1977: 208, 213, 217, 223, 381, 499, except for the monastery of St. Paul.
4   For these books, see Malak 1964: 1–35; Zanetti 1995b: 65–94.
5   For this title, see Youssef 1994: 61–67.
6   For this author, see Breydy 1983: 1–12.
7   For the complete text see Budge 1914: 126–36. For a list of the fragments see Vojtenko 2008.
8   See also Coquin 1991: 835; van Esbroeck 1991.
9   For these biographies, see Bardy 1941.
10 City on the west bank of the Nile, ten kilometers from Abydos.
11 Otherwise unknown. The mention of a bishop for Nubia for that time, which may come from the lost *Life* of Moses of Abydos, to which §47 alludes, seems totally anachronistic.
12 Adams 1991a.
13 For the works of this author, see Orlandi 1971.
14 Or at least those that survived and have come down to us.

10 Dayr al-Kubbaniya
Review of the Documentation on the 'Isisberg' Monastery

Renate Dekker

THIS CONTRIBUTION WILL FOCUS on the monastery known under the names 'Isisberg' Monastery, Dayr al-Shaykha, and Dayr al-Kubbaniya, which is located to the northwest of Aswan along the riverside. It was partly excavated in 1911 (Junker 1922), but it is presently covered by sand again. Recent photographs offer a view of the monastic site in its present state and show the remains of the largest building, which has been described but not excavated. With permission of the Geological Survey of Norway (NGU) I publish these photographs and also review the available documentation on the monastery.[1]

The Names of the Monastery

Since 2004, the Aswan west bank has been extensively surveyed by the QuarryScapes Project, which is coordinated by the Geological Survey of Norway. This international research project aims to document, characterize, and conserve ancient quarry landscapes in the eastern Mediterranean, and one of the case-study areas is the west bank of Aswan, from Wadi Kubbaniya in the north to the Old Aswan Dam in the south (Bloxam, Heldal, and Storemyr 2007: 2–3).[2] The research team also records archaeological remains, ranging from the Middle Palaeolithic tool sites (240,000–10,000 years ago) to the monastic sites, including the "Isisberg" Monastery (Bloxam 2007: 39–46; Storemyr 2007: 30, fig. 7). This monastery is located about ten

Fig. 10.1. View from the north (courtesy of Storemyr, NGU)

kilometers to the north of Aswan, and about 1.5 kilometers south of the Aswan bridge.[3] It was built on the site of a Ptolemaic temple that was dedicated to Khnum and other deities (Junker 1922: 9–11, 13).

Since the original name of the monastery is unknown, scholars refer to it by various names that are derived from nearby localities. Hermann Junker, who excavated part of the site in February 1910, called it "Das Kloster am Isisberg" ('Monastery of the Mountain of Isis'), after a nearby settlement, Isieion Oros, or 'Mountain of Isis,' which is mentioned on a fourth-century (?) Greek ostracon from the site. The place name 'Esaiao,' which occurs in two Coptic graffiti in the monastic church, supposedly is an abbreviated Copic form (Junker 1922: 3, 8–9, 47–48).[4] The civil settlement, which has not been localized, apparently takes its name from the actual "Mountain of Isis," the hill to the south of the monastery (fig. 10.1).

The modern name of this hill is Gebel Shiha (de Morgan 1894: 202), meaning "the Mountain of the Matron," and the monastery used to be referred to as al-Shehah or Dayr al-Shaykha (Junker 1922: 7).[5] Nowadays, it is usually called Dayr al-Kubbaniya, after a nearby village, but Kubbaniya is also the name of a wadi (De Morgan 1894: 202; Coquin and Martin 1991a: 815; Grossmann 1991b: 815).

The Monastic Site

The monastery is located on a narrow strip of land between the western desert plateau and the Nile. In the past it was best accessible by boat, but

Fig. 10.2. View from the east (courtesy of Storemyr, NGU)

nowadays there is an asphalt road directly on the west side. The site is marked by two high mud-brick walls at about thirty meters' distance from one another, which used to be 1.5 meters thick and almost six meters high (fig. 10.2). They formed the north and south walls of an oblong building that has been described but still remains unpublished (De Morgan 1894: 202; Junker 1922: 60–61). Because of a lack of time and means, Junker decided not to excavate it.

The complex measured 37.5 meters in length and about the same in width, and consisted of at least four buildings, including the church at the center (fig. 10.3). The mud-brick building constructed against the north wall of the church included at least a vestibule leading to the church, a refectory, and a storage room. To the south of the church, and separated from it by a corridor, was another mud-brick building

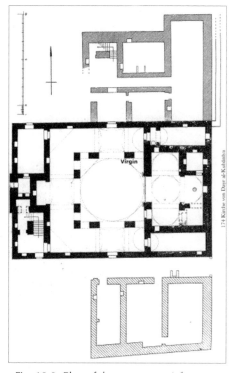

Fig. 10.3. Plan of the monastery (after Grossmann 2002: fig. 174)

that consisted of three rooms and presumably accommodated guests. According to Junker, the extensive western building housed the monks, but his hypothesis needs to be validated (Junker 1922: 57–61, pl. 5).

One of the photographs made for the QuarryScapes Project shows a mud-brick building, seen from the south. Judging from what is visible, it is located in the northern section of the site, but its plan does not correspond with that of the northern building (fig. 10.4). Could it be part of the residential building?

Junker expected that the monastic complex would also include courtyards, workshops, enclosure walls, and a cemetery. Apparently, he had a *koinobium* in mind, a monastery with communal facilities like Dayr Anba Hadra (Monastery of St. Hatre), but on a smaller scale. The compact and regular arrangement of the published buildings suggests that the complex was planned and did not develop organically. However, as part of the material remains are unexamined, it is too early to draw conclusions on the organization of the monastery.

The monastic nature of the site is confirmed by the presence of didactic inscriptions in the room to the northwest of the church, which were

Fig. 10.4. View from the south (courtesy of Storemyr, NGU)

intended to edify monks. The texts include biblical passages or sayings by monastic fathers starting with "an elder said . . ." or "a brother asked an elder. . . ." One text reads: "It befits the monk to keep in mind the remembrance of death, the punishments, the Valley of the Weeping, the sleepless worm, and his meeting with God. Pray for me" (Junker 1922: 45–47).[6]

The Church Building

The church was described by Junker and analyzed by Peter Grossmann, who identified it as an octagon-domed church. He also presented a different reconstruction of the roofing and published a corrected ground plan of the monastery (Junker 1922: 14–44; Grossmann 1982: 54–60, fig. 18; Grossmann 1991b: 815–16; Grossman 2002: 560–62).

The church was a rectangular building, which measured 22.25 x 15.75 meters and about twelve meters in height, but the preserved remains were less than seven meters high. The outer walls were constructed of mud brick on a foundation of dressed stone, whereas the pillars and the inner walls were solidly built of dressed stone, in order to provide sufficient support for the domes and conchs. Stone was also used for the doorways and window frames, but the rest of the building was made from mud brick (Junker 1922: 14–15).

The church was divided into three main sections: the sanctuary, the nave with entrances in the north and south walls, and additional rooms on the west side. The sanctuary was slightly elevated compared to the rest of the building, and its central opening used to be closed off by a wooden screen. Its central part consisted of an altar room and a *khurus*, which were both rectangular in plan, but their roofing used to form a triconch with a small central dome at the center. On either side a long barrel-vaulted room and a smaller chamber were created, in order to use the available space within the rectangular outlines of the building. The small rooms were accessible from the altar room and were probably used to keep liturgical objects, particularly the one on the north side, which displayed three niches. There was no direct connection with the outer rooms, the northern one of which served as a baptistery (Junker 1922: 27–33).

The nave included a square central bay, an ambulatory formed by the two side aisles and a return aisle, and a wide central niche in the west wall. The dome that once roofed the square bay rested on a square substructure with squinches in the corners (resulting in an octagonal base), which was supported by the *khurus* wall and the pillars in the nave. On each side of the substructure there was a wide central arch. The ambulatory was roofed by barrel vaults,

which were interrupted by sail vaults[7] on the axes of the wide arches and connected by diagonally constructed vaults in the corners. The central niche in
the west wall of the nave, opposite the altar room, was rectangular in plan and
barrel-vaulted, in contrast to the semi-circular western niches in the churches
of Dayr Anba Hadra and Dayr Qubbat al-Hawa (Grossmann 1982: 8, fig.
3; Dekker 2008: 22, pl. 2.).[8] Its function is unclear, and no mention is made
of any decoration. To the north and south of it were smaller, round-topped
niches. Above the northern niche was a painted inscription (see below).

Doorways in the northwest and southwest of the nave led to large rooms
in the western section of the church,[9] which were added to make this side of
the church rectangular. They were also accessible from outside. The southern room included a staircase that probably led to the roof,[10] and the space
below it was used for storage. The northern room is the room with the
didactic texts. It led to a small inner room, the function of which is unclear.

It is possible that the monks and laymen used different entrances and
exits. The monks could enter the church through the vestibule of the
northern building and leave by taking the door to the northwestern room,
where they would see the didactic texts, before going outside. Visitors, who
stayed in the building to the south of the church or came from the riverside, may have entered the church through the main entrance on the south
side and left by the door that leads to the southwestern room.

On the outside, the west wall displays a protrusion, which is about as
wide as the western niche and seems to mark it as an important cultic
space, but according to Grossmann this is not the case, for the niche does
not have a clear liturgical function and does not explain such an external
marking (Grossmann 1982: 56, 58; Grossmann 2002: 561). For that reason
he suggested that the exterior of the western section was copied from
another church, but not its interior (Grossmann 1982: 56). My impression, however, is that the protrusion had a practical function and served to
strengthen the west wall, in order to prevent it from collapsing under the
weight of a (now lost) room above the central part of the western section,
which was reached by means of the staircase in the southwest.[11]

Dating the Church

Junker and Grossmann, as well as other scholars, emphasized the similarities between the church of Dayr al-Kubbaniya and that of Dayr
Anba Hadra, and concluded that the two buildings are contemporary,
but they proposed different datings on the basis of typological studies.

Junker considered the Hagia Sophia (finished in AD 537) as the prototype and dated the church to the mid- or late sixth century, but Grossmann referred to the eleventh-century octagon-domed churches in Greece and concluded that the Egyptian examples date to the same century at the earliest (Junker 1922: 23; Grossmann 1982: 60).[12] Ugo Monneret de Villard, who excavated Dayr Anba Hadra in 1924–26, also proposed a late date for both churches, namely the first half of the eleventh century (Monneret de Villard 1927b: 156). C.C. Walters, on the other hand, assumed that they were built in the seventh/eighth century, but "both these churches, in their reconstructed state, probably date to the tenth century" (Walters 1974: 32, 52).

It can be argued that the sixth century is too early, for the church includes a *khurus*, a feature that appears in monastic churches in Egypt from the second half of the seventh century onwards (Grossmann 2002: 71–76). On the other hand, the church of Dayr Anba Hadra already existed in the tenth century, judging from a *dipinto* on the south wall of the northern aisle, which is dated AD 962, and the same may hold for the church of Dayr al-Kubbaniya (Dijkstra and Van der Vliet 2003: 31–39, fig. 1–2).[13]

How can we refine the building history of the church? Being primarily trained as a Coptic papyrologist/epigraphist, I would first look for dated Coptic inscriptions, but none are recorded (Junker 1922: 44–48). I would also like to examine the plasterwork, for the presence of two or more layers can help to establish a relative chronology, but it seems that there was only one layer. Therefore, the dating of the church largely depends on architectural criteria.

It is important to know whether the church has been renovated, as Walters argued. In his view, the pillars in the nave of the church at Dayr Anba Hadra were a late addition, which served to facilitate the placing of the domes over the nave, and the same would have applied to the church at Dayr al-Kubbaniya. According to Junker, there are no indications of this. Rather, the building was destroyed at an unspecified date and never rebuilt (Junker 1927: 11, 24–25). Grossmann, too, described the church as a coherent whole, but remarked that the western section may have been added at a later date, on account of a joint in the north wall (Grossmann 1982: 56, n. 27). It seems as if the church was constructed in two phases: first, the sanctuary and central section were built, whereas the rooms in the west were added shortly afterwards, judging from the regular construction of the wall on either side of the joint.[14]

According to Monneret de Villard, the construction of a dome on a square substructure with triangular squinches in the corners is attested from the tenth century onwards. It first occurs in Islamic buildings in Cairo, and later it is also found in churches in Greece and Italy that date to the early eleventh century (Monneret de Villard 1927b: 61–62, 156). On the basis of this architectural criterion, I propose to date the domed section of the church to the tenth/early eleventh century, but, like Walters, I think that the church was built in the seventh/eighth century.[15]

Wall Painting of the Virgin and a Saint

Junker observed two fragmentary wall paintings on the south sides of the pillars dividing the central nave from the northern aisle, high above ground level and just below the squinches. Only the painting on the eastern pillar was well enough preserved to make a description possible. It depicts the Virgin with Child and a saint at her right-hand side, whose name is written beside his head, but, unfortunately, it is illegible (fig. 10.5). Both standing figures are depicted frontally, the Virgin being slightly taller than the saint. Her face and that of the Child have been deliberately damaged (Junker 1922: 45, 49, pl. 6, fig. 10).

Fig. 10.5. The Virgin and a saint (line drawing: author, 2010)

The Virgin is wearing a long dark tunic and a cloak in a brighter color, which ends in a point at the front. Her head is covered by a *maphorion* and surrounded by a large nimbus. The Child, depicted with curly hair, is clothed in a tunic as well as a pallium. He presumably held a scroll in his left hand, and raised his right hand in blessing. The saint, who seems to be young and beardless, wears a long tunic and a cloak that covers his chest and both shoulders. This garment may identify him as an apostle (see below) or a monk. He does not hold an object, but his right hand, which is lost, was probably raised in blessing (Junker 1922: 49–51).

The Virgin holds the Christ-child in her left arm and gestures toward him with her right hand. As such, she is represented as the *Hodegetria*, meaning "she who points the way." This iconographic type was very common and popular in Byzantine art, particularly the version depicting the Virgin in torso, but is much less attested in Coptic art.[16] Some examples from Egypt show the version of the enthroned Virgin *Hodegetria* (Snelders and Immerzeel 2004: 119–24). The standing *Hodegetria* is rare in Egypt (Snelders and Immerzeel 2004: 122, n. 44), but two other examples are a wall painting in the Monastery of Saint Jeremiah at Saqqara (seventh/eighth century?) and an illumination in a Bohairic manuscript (Vatican Library, MS Copto 1; thirteenth/fourteenth century) (Quibell 1908: pl. LV; Snelders and Immerzeel 2004: 122, n. 44).

According to Junker, the closest parallel for this painting is the wall painting in the apse of the church at Wadi al-Sebua, which depicts the twelve apostles in the same posture and clothing as the saint (date uncertain). In comparison, however, the rendering of the figures in the church at Dayr al-Kubbaniya is more stylized, and therefore points to a later date (Junker 1922: 56–57).

Inscriptions

Junker published ten Coptic inscriptions, which were written in Sahidic, but seem to display some particular spellings which still need to be examined. Also, it would be worthwhile to examine Junker's photographs of the inscriptions, as it may help to improve the readings.

One text is carved above the niche in the northwest section of the nave and includes an invocation of both Jesus Christ and a saint called Apa Colluthos, framed by dotted crosses and lines. Apa Colluthos, a local monastic father or the well-known healer saint from Antinoë (Papaconstantinou 2001a: 122–28), may have been depicted in the niche. At any rate, he was one of the saints venerated in this church (Junker 1922: 45, 57, pl. 4).

The location of two carved Coptic graffiti to the south of this niche also suggests that the northwest section of the nave was considered an important place. One of the graffiti commemorates the birth of the son of an "inhabitant of Esaiao," whereas the other one includes a prayer. In general, the Coptic graffiti are few, but Junker observed some more in the northern building, together with Arabic texts (Junker 1922: 47, 59).

The aforementioned didactic inscriptions were concentrated in the northern room of the western section, particularly on the south wall. It is not stated whether they were carved or written in ink. Some of the texts include biblical citations or reminiscences; three other ones must originate from monastic literature.[17]

Pottery

Hans Demel examined the pottery finds from the church and the northern building, and dated them to the fourth to seventh century.[18] This is not in accord with the late dating of the church. Through the years, much more Coptic pottery has become available for comparison, and it is desirable that the finds from Dayr al-Kubbaniya should be reexamined.

Conclusion

Junker's documentation of Dayr al-Kubbaniya is invaluable for the research on this monastic site, but his early dating, based on the comparative material that was available at the time, is not in agreement with the eleventh-century date proposed by Grossmann. On closer inspection, the church can be dated to the tenth/early eleventh century. As for the paintings, inscriptions, and pottery finds, a more profound reexamination is required to establish their dating and to place them within a wider cultural and social setting. To conclude, I certainly hope that the western section of the site will also be examined and documented.

Notes

1   I warmly thank Tom Heldal, coordinator of the QuarryScapes Project (Geological Survey of Norway), and Per Storemyr of the Archaeology and Conservation Services in Zürich, who is also actively involved with the QuarryScapes Project, for allowing me to publish the recent photographs of Dayr al-Kubbaniya and the map in the present article.

2   For a detailed map of the area, see http://www.quarryscapes.no/text/publications/ QS_del4_MAP1.pdf

3   Junker 1922; Meinardus 1977: 433; Grossmann 1982: 54–60; Coquin and Martin 1991a: 815; Grossmann 1991b: 815–16; Budka 1999: 60–61; Grossmann 2002: 560–62; Kamel and Naguib 2003: 167–70; cf. O'Leary 1923: 233; 1924: 309–10.

4   According to Timm (1984–2007: 2074), the original name of the monastery was "(Ptoou n-) Esaiao," or "Mountain of Isis Monastery." However, the spelling 'Esaiao' recalls the name 'Isaiah.'

5   Cf. Monneret de Villard 1927b: 39; Walters 1974: 19; Grossmann 1982: 54–60; Coquin and Martin 1991a: 815. Junker (1922:7) assumed that the name meant '(grave of) the holy woman,' but as there is no such tomb, he suggested that the domed church may have been mistaken for the tomb of a Muslim saint.

6   Translations by the author.

7   After Grossmann 1982: 59 ("Hängekuppel"); Grossmann 2002: 561 ("Stutzkuppeln");

cf. Monneret de Villard 1927b: 59. Junker, however, reconstructed three small domes (Junker 1922: 38, pl. 1–3).

8   See also the other contributions by the present author in this volume.

9   According to Grossmann, these inner doors could not be used as entrances to the nave, only as exits: cf. Grossmann 1982: 58; Grossmann 2002: 561–62.

10 After Grossmann 1982: 56; Grossmann 2002: 562. According to Junker, however, there was little space for a staircase.

11 See the cross section in Grossmann 1982: 58, fig. 19; Grossmann 2002: fig. 175.

12 On the octagon-domed church in Egypt, see Grossmann 2002: 90–93.

13 See also the present author's contribution on the church of Dayr Anba Hadra in this volume.

14 See the photograph in Junker 1922, pl. 5, fig. 6.

15 See also the chronology of the church at Dayr Anba Hadra by this author in the present volume.

16 See also Junker 1922: 50; Leroy 1974: 108–10, pl. 98.1; Leroy 1975: 52.

17 See Junker 1922: 45–47. The exact sources still need to be identified.

18 See Demel's contribution in Junker 1922: 61–67.

11 The Development of the Church at Dayr Anba Hadra
A Study of the Plasterwork and Dated Inscriptions

Renate Dekker

Situated on the west bank of the Nile near Aswan are the impressive ruins of a monastery that is often called the Monastery of St. Simeon. Inscriptions from the site, however, demonstrate that it was dedicated to Apa Hatre (Anba Hadra), a fourth-century hermit and bishop of Aswan, whose life is described in the Copto-Arabic *Synaxarion* as well as in the unpublished "Life of Hatre" (Monneret de Villard 1927b: 7–9; Timm 1984–2007: 664–67; Coquin and Martin 1991b: 744–45; Dijkstra and Van der Vliet 2003: 31; Gabra 2002: 108–10).[1]

Dayr Anba Hadra is of great importance in the study of Coptic monasticism. The architectural remains attest to the long history of the monastic site, from the sixth/seventh century to about the thirteenth century, and suggest that the complex was well organized (Monneret de Villard 1927b: 10, 154–55; Grossmann 1991c: 745–46 ; Grossmann 2002: 562–65). Other interesting sources are the wall paintings in the church (de Morgan 1894: 133–35; de Bock 1901: pl. 31–32), the Coptic and Arabic inscriptions,[2] the Coptic funerary stelae from the cemetery (Monneret de Villard 1927b: 9, 117–20; Munier 1930–31: 257–300, 433–84; Hasitzka 1993–2006: 1: nos. 498–675), and a small number of Coptic manuscripts, most of them literary, which possibly originate from the monastery (Munier 1923: 210–28, esp. 210 n. 2). Finally, Dayr Anba Hadra is the provenance of a large group of documentary texts on papyrus, parchment, paper, and ostraca, which was found during the excavation of the site by Ugo Monneret de Villard. It was delivered to the Egyptian Museum in Cairo and has so far remained unpublished (Monneret de Villard 1927b: 12).[3] It is to be hoped that this corpus will be rediscovered and published, for it is likely to include much new information on the monastery.

This article examines the development of the church on the basis of internal sources, namely the architecture, the plasterwork, the wall paintings, and dated inscriptions. First I will summarize Monneret de Villard's conclusions on the building history (Monneret de Villard 1927b: 154–55). Then I will describe the plasterwork in the church on the basis of photographs taken by me in 2005 and 2010, and establish *terminus ante quem* dates for each layer. The combination of Monneret de Villard's chronology with these dates will result in a more detailed reconstruction of the history of the church at Dayr Anba Hadra.

The Chronology Established by Monneret de Villard

After having described the architecture, the plasterwork, the wall paintings, and some dated Coptic inscriptions in the church, Monneret de Villard reconstructed the history of the building as follows:

1. The small cave to the northwest of the (later) church was the original cult center on the site. Its walls and ceiling, as well as a rock-hewn wall behind the north wall of the church, are decorated with paintings, which can stylistically be dated to the sixth/ seventh century (Monneret de Villard 1927b: 34–36).

2. The church was built directly at the entrance of the cave and in front of the rock-hewn wall. Eventually, the tomb of the deacon Pesynthios, who died on 14 Barmuda 512 (9 April 796), was constructed against the south wall of the church. Since the church predates the tomb, it must have been built before AD 796 (Monneret de Villard 1927b: 76–78, 155).

3. When the church was rebuilt or thoroughly restored, funerary stelae from the cemetery to the south of the monastery were reused as building material. Since the latest dated stela dates to AM 707 (AD 990–91), the renovation must have taken place after AD 991 (Monneret de Villard 1927b: 31–33, 155; see also Munier 1930–31: no.117; = Hasitzka 1993–2006: no. 615).

4. Three layers of plaster are visible in the church. The deeper the layer, the older it is. The oldest plasterwork was a simple layer of gypsum and in the east apse it was decorated with large painted figures. The second layer was thick and more accurately applied. The paintings of Christ in Majesty and the Twenty-four Elders of the Apocalypse in the east apse were both executed on this layer and can be dated to the twelfth century on the basis of stylistic and technical criteria. The third plaster layer remained undecorated, but is inscribed with graffiti. The oldest dated Coptic graffito was written on 8 Kiyahk 1014 (4 December 1297) (Monneret de Villard 1927b: 29, 48–49, 155).[4]

5. The church originally had two entrances on the east side, which gave access to the side aisles. At a later stage, five rooms were added to the east of the church. Those in the northeast and southeast temporarily served as vestibules, but eventually both entrances were blocked and the southern room was turned into a baptistery (Monneret de Villard 1927b: 33, 154, fig. 11).[5]

On the basis of an architectural study and dated Coptic inscriptions, Monneret de Villard established a fairly precise relative chronology with *terminus ante quem* dates. Although he mentions only one instance of restoration, his observations on the plasterwork and on the development of the eastern rooms indicate that the church was renovated at least twice.

Peter Grossmann also examined the church, but took a different approach by focusing on the typology. He identified it as a combination of a domed oblong church with an octagon-domed church, a type that is mainly attested on the Greek mainland in the eleventh century, and concluded that the building must have been constructed in the first half of the eleventh century at the earliest (Grossmann 1982: 12–13; Grossmann 1991c: 746; Grossmann 2002: 90–93, 564).

Grossmann's dating can only be reconciled with Monneret de Villard's chronology if we assume that the church replaced an earlier building. In that case, the construction of the present church would coincide with the renovation activities during which funerary stelae were reused as building material. However, I do not think that there was an earlier church building.

A Coptic *dipinto* on the south wall of the northern aisle, dated 24 Barmuda 678 (19 April 962), demonstrates that the church already existed in the tenth century (de Morgan 1894: 136 n. 4, 140 n. 1; Dijkstra and Van der

Vliet 2003: 32–35, 39 figs. 1–2 (complete edition); Dijkstra 2008: 62). The text was written on the second plaster layer, which implies that the original plasterwork and the church are even older.

The Plasterwork in the Church

The three plaster layers in the church are best visible on the east wall of the northern part of the *khurus* (fig. 11.1). The original plasterwork (I) consisted of a simple layer of gypsum, fragments of which appear almost everywhere in the church: on the walls of the sanctuary, in the *khurus*, on the west side of the walls dividing the nave from the *khurus*, on the walls and barrel vaults of the side aisles, and on the west wall. The round-topped wall sections in the northwest and southwest of the church, which originally supported sail vaults, also show traces of white plaster and must have been part of this church building in its original state. No dated inscriptions have been observed on this layer.

In the sanctuary this first layer is decorated with a wall painting depicting large standing figures, which are fragmentarily preserved (figs. 11.2 and 11.3). There are traces of four figures on the east wall, two on either side of the niche, and a fifth one on the north wall. They wear red and orange *phelonia* (episcopal vestments), and some of the figures show traces of gospel caskets and yellow nimbi. The garments suggest that the figures represent holy bishops or patriarchs.[6]

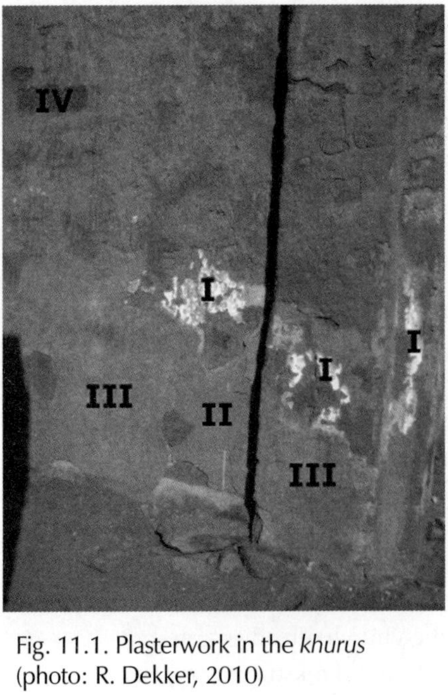

The second layer (II) is grayish-brown mud plaster, fragments of which are preserved on the east wall of the *khurus*, on the walls of the side aisles, and in the secondary rooms on the east side of the church. When these rooms were built, the openings of the doorways leading into the side aisle were reduced in both height and width. At the same time, the semicircular niche in the west wall, which was originally framed by a wide stone arch, was reduced in height and a horizontal layer of stone divided the remaining surface into a conch and a lower section (fig. 11.4).

Fig. 11.1. Plasterwork in the *khurus* (photo: R. Dekker, 2010)

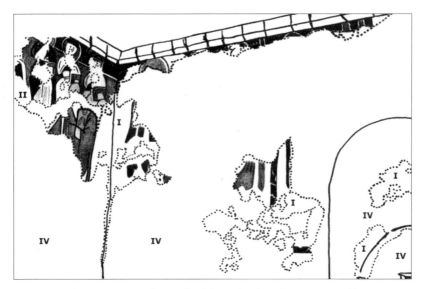

Fig. 11.2. The sanctuary, to the north of the niche (line drawing: R. Dekker, 2010)

Fig. 11.3. The sanctuary, to the south of the niche (line drawing: R Dekker, 2010)

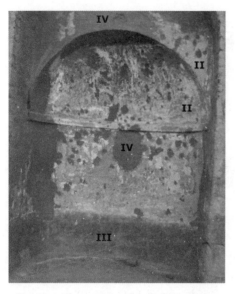

Fig. 11.4. The western niche (photo: R.
Dekker, 2010)

In general, the inscriptions on
this plaster layer were written in red-
brown ink. The oldest dated text is
the above-mentioned *dipinto* dated AD
962. Another dated text is a fragmentary *dipinto* on the west wall of the
room on the east side of the northern
aisle, above the doorway. With some
difficulty I can read the year AM 824,
or AD 1107/1108, on my photographs.[7]
On the basis of these inscriptions, I
conclude that the mud plaster predates
the year AD 962 and was still visible,
that is, not covered by the third plaster
layer, in AD 1107/1108.

The representation of Christ in
Majesty in the conch and that of the
Twenty-four Elders of the Apocalypse
on the walls of the sanctuary were
painted on a layer of gypsum covering the mud plaster, which appears
at the surface in some damaged areas. The same holds for the decoration
of the western niche. The painting of the lower section is destroyed, but
the one in the conch depicts a standing headless figure between two
angels who are bowing in adoration (fig. 11.5). The central figure wears
a yellow tunic and a purple-bluish pallium and raises his right arm, as
if he is making a sign of blessing, while his damaged left hand seems to
hold a gospel casket. Usually, the central figure is identified as the Virgin
Mary (Monneret de Villard 1927b: 65, fig. 73),[8] but I agree with Otto F.
Meinardus that it represents Christ (Meinardus 1977: 444–45). The iconography of Christ standing between two bowing angels is also attested
in a wall painting in the church of the Red Monastery (dated AD 1301?)
(Zibawi 2004: 100).[9]

The third plaster layer (III) is best described as orange and smooth, and
is visible along the bottom of the walls throughout the church, on the sides
of the pillars in the nave, as well as on the low benches along the pillars
and the outer walls of the church. It seems to have been deliberately peeled
from the walls in order to uncover the underlying layers, leaving a border
in the lower zone only. Traces of orange plaster are also preserved in the

Fig. 11.5. Christ flanked by bowing angels (line drawing: R. Dekker, 2005)

small niches in the west wall, on the walls of the secondary room in the southeast, and on the inside and outside of the baptismal font.

The third layer is inscribed with inscriptions, particularly on the east wall of the northern section of the *khurus*. In 1915, Clédat published ten Coptic graffiti and a table with numerals, which were written almost exclusively in black (Clédat 1915: 45–49 [b–g]), but in February 2010, only three graffiti and a fragment of the table were visible on the lower part of the wall, all of them in a sad condition.[10] One of the now lost graffiti was dated 8 Kiyahk 1014, that is, 4 December 1297.[11] To my knowledge, it is the oldest recorded dated inscription on this layer. The latest dated Coptic graffito, which was attested within the doorway of the sanctuary, was written by a visitor in Ba'una 1120, or May/June 1404 (Clédat 1915: 45 [b]).

For the sake of completeness, I also mention the modern red-brown plasterwork (IV) that was applied during the restoration of the church by Monneret de Villard's team, in order to solidify weak sections in the walls, to fill up holes, and to reconstruct the doorways and niches.[12]

The Chronology of the Church

On the basis of Monneret de Villard's chronology, and the results of the study of the plasterwork, the development of the church at Dayr Anba Hadra can be described in five phases.

Fig. 11.6. The 'hidden' cave wall (photo: R. Dekker, 2005)

Phase 1: A Rock-cut Chapel (Sixth/Seventh Century)

When examining my photographs, I get the impression that the decorated cave and the related wall behind the northern church wall are the remnants of a rock-cut oratory or chapel, which was partly demolished during the construction of the church. At the entrance of the cave, almost a quarter of the painted ceiling was destroyed in order to create space for the west wall of the northern aisle of the church (de Morgan 1894: 135 (incomplete); Monneret de Villard 1927b: fig. 65). On the south side of the rock-cut wall, a ridge along the upper part is all that remains of another section of the ceiling (fig. 11.6). Nevertheless, even if the chapel was partly demolished, it was considered important and its remnants remained accessible.

A passage in the north wall leads to a yard and another cave,[13] and predates the decoration of the cave, for the wall painting follows the curved surfaces on both sides of the opening.

The ceiling of the cave is decorated with busts, floral motifs, and geometrical designs. The central bust depicts Christ, judging from the cross within his nimbus, and the remaining seven busts, all equipped with nimbi, may represent apostles.

The cave walls display thirty-six standing figures with nimbi in a single row and more saints are visible on the wall to the east of the passage (de Morgan 1894: 134 (incomplete); Monneret de Villard 1927b: 35–36, fig. 65–69). They form four groups, separated by painted columns:

1. The first two saints wear tunics (blue and orange respectively) and green monastic aprons. Their names are lost, but the first one is

called "Apa."The second figure holds a huge black key. Presumably, these saints represent founding fathers of the monastic community.

2. Four saints wear red, green, orange, and white *phelonia* respectively. Three of them have gray hair and beards and hold a gospel casket. The fourth saint, whose hair and beard are brown, raises his right hand to his mouth. He is depicted as the youngest of the four and, judging from the fragmentary text around his head, which reads "[a]po[st]olos," he probably represents the apostle John. In that case, this group can be identified as the four evangelists.

3. The other thirty saints depicted in the cave wear white garments, except for the first one, a beardless figure with blond hair, who is dressed in a yellow tunic, a shorter white tunic, and a purple cloak. He wears a crown and holds a spear in his left hand while he raises his right hand. At his right-hand side are a yellow shield and a construction with a pointed roof. Possibly, he represents a soldier saint who has received the crown of martyrdom. The rest of the group consists of monks, some of whom are identified as "apa" by fragmentary texts.[14]

4. Six more saints are visible on the wall to the east of the passage, but are partly hidden from view by the north wall of the church.[15] At least two figures hold gospel caskets.

Considering the limited scope of this paper, I must leave a more profound study of the wall paintings for a later occasion.

Phase 2: Construction of the Church (Seventh/Eighth Century)[16]
The church was built before AD 796. The distribution of the oldest plaster layer, a simple layer of gypsum, indicates that at least the sanctuary, the *khurus*, the outer walls (except for the east wall), and the roofing of the side aisles, consisting of barrel vaults and sail vaults, were part of the original building. The pillar bases in the nave, however, do not show traces of early plasterwork. It is, therefore, possible that the pillars and domes over the nave were (re)built at a later stage and do not reflect the original layout of the nave.[17] The church used to have two entrances on the east side, in addition to a third entrance on the north side. The walls of the sanctuary show fragments of a wall painting depicting standing figures who are dressed in liturgical vestments and presumably represent holy (arch)bishops. The original decoration in the conch of the sanctuary is not visible.

Phase 3: First Renovation (Tenth Century)[18]

Before AD 962 the church was renovated. Five rooms were added on the east side of the building, and those to the east of the side aisles came to serve as vestibules. The doorways of the original eastern entrances were reduced in height and width, and the western niche was made smaller as well. Then the walls were covered by grayish-brown mud plaster and partly decorated. The two-zoned composition in the sanctuary depicts Christ in Majesty above and the Twenty-four Elders of the Apocalypse below. The painting in the western niche was also a two-zoned composition, showing Christ between two bowing angels in the conch. The decoration of the lower zone is lost.

Phase 4: Second Renovation (Twelfth/Thirteenth Century)

Between AD 1107/8 and 1297, the church was renovated again. Probably, at this stage, the funerary stelae from the cemetery were reused as building material. The entrances of the vestibules on the east side of the church were closed, the room in the south east was turned into a baptistery, and both the church walls and the pillars in the nave were covered by a smooth layer of orange plaster.

Phase 5: Graffiti near the Sanctuary (Late Thirteenth/Fourteenth Century)

In or before AD 1297, visitors started to write graffiti on the east *khurus* wall, ever closer to the sanctuary. The graffito dated AD 1404 was even written within the doorway to the sanctuary. This phenomenon suggests that the *khurus*, which was intended for clerics only (Grossmann 2002: 71–76, esp 73), was no longer closed off by a wooden screen and that visitors could freely enter it. Apparently, the church was no longer (regularly) used for services.

Conclusion

Elaborating on Monneret de Villard's chronology of the church, this article aims at dating the stages in the building history as precisely as possible by means of a combined study of the plasterwork and the dated Coptic inscriptions that I could localize. The resulting chronology can be refined further by also including dated Arabic inscriptions. The same approach can be applied to the residential building and will help to reconstruct the development of the monastery in general.

In this article, I have briefly discussed the decoration of the chapel and the church and made some new observations on their iconography, but the documentation of the paintings is still incomplete. Another aspect that merits a more profound examination is the original size of the chapel.

Notes

1 On St. Hatre, see Gabra 1988: 91–94; Dijkstra 2008: 54–55.

2 On the Coptic inscriptions, see de Morgan 1894: 136–40 (printed texts and hand copies by U. Bouriant); Clédat 1915: 41–57 (printed texts); Monneret de Villard 1927b: 29 (discussion of some dated inscriptions); Dijkstra and Van der Vliet 2003: 31–39 (complete publication of a *dipinto*). For a particularly interesting timetable, see de Morgan 1894: 137 (nr. 9); Bouriant and Ventre 1900: 575–96; Delattre 2010: 273–86. Only two Arabic graffiti were published, in de Morgan 1894: 138–39.

3 Gawdat Gabra informed me that these textual finds "are not in the Coptic Museum" (personal communication, June 2010).

4 For the graffito, see also Clédat 1915: 48–49 (f. 2). According to Clédat, the year mentioned is 1104 (AD 1388), but the Coptic reads "1014."

5 Cf. Grossmann 1982: 10, pl. 2a; Grossmann 1991c: 746; Grossmann 2002: 565.

6 For illustrations, see de Morgan 1894: 133; Gabra 2002: 11.5.

7 See Clédat 1915: 42, l. 1 (AM 8[. .]) and 11 (AM 82[.]). De Morgan (1894: 140, l. 1) reads AM 821 (AD 1104/1105).

8 Cf. Walters 1974: 312; du Bourguet 1991a: 747; Gabra 2002: 112.

9 Cf. Gabra 2002: 103–104.

10 Clédat 1915: 47 (e: only the red elements of the first column of the table are preserved), 48–49 (e: a Greek *dipinto* that mentions the Nubian king Kudanbes: the first ten lines are almost completely lost), 49 (f. 4: vague traces of the last lines; f. 5: the left side is almost effaced). For the graffito on Kudanbes, see also Griffith 1928: 135 (edition).

11 See note 5.

12 Cf. Monneret de Villard 1927b: 11.

13 Court XXIV and Room XXV in Monneret de Villard 1927b: 67.

14 Two monks were possibly called Moses and Anoup; cf. Monneret de Villard 1927b: 35.

15 For a picture, see Gabra 2002: fig. 11.6.

16 See also Walters 1974: 52.

17 See also Walters 1974: 52 n. 4. For a reconstruction of the layout of the nave, see Grossmann 1982: 8–10, fig. 3.

18 See also Walters 1974: 32.

12 An Updated Plan of the Church at Dayr Qubbat al-Hawa

Renate Dekker

IN A PRELIMINARY STUDY I published a ground plan of the church of Dayr Qubbat al-Hawa based on the discoveries made in 1998 by the Supreme Council of Antiquities (Dekker 2008: 19–36).[1] In February 2010, during the conference in Aswan, the SCA had just resumed the excavation of the church and were about to uncover its sanctuary, which had so far remained hidden below the sand. On the basis of the recent finds and my own research I drew an updated ground plan which shows the layout of the church and its immediate surroundings.[2]

The Monastic Complex

The hill of Qubbat al-Hawa, to the west of Aswan, is honeycombed with ancient rock-cut tombs of local high officials, arranged on four levels (de Morgan 1894: 141ff; Edel 2008).[3] The church is located on the uppermost level, in front of tomb QH 34h, and was part of a monastic settlement, the material remains of which are only partly documented (Grossmann 1985: 339–44; Grossmann 1991: 851–52; Dekker 2008: 19–36).[4]

Dayr Qubbat al-Hawa supposedly started as a settlement of hermits, which centered on the tombs of Khunes and Khui, QH 34h and 34e respectively (Coquin and Martin 1991c: 850; Grossmann 1991d: 851; see also Edel 2008: 474–78, 514–23). In other tombs, Peter Grossmann (1991d: 851) observed systems of basins, new floors, and secondary dividing walls, but the exact size of the settlement still needs to be established. In this respect, it is interesting to note that Coptic ostraca were found not only on the uppermost level (QH 33, 34c), but also on the second one (QH 104, 105, 110), inside the tomb chapels or shafts.[5] These texts are dated to the sixth/seventh century on account of their paleography,[6] and confirm the monastic nature of the early community, for they mention individuals like Apa Joseph, Apa Apollon, and Isaac the novice.[7] A recently discovered wall painting presumably dates to the sixth/seventh century as well.[8]

However, most of the visible remains, including the church and the residential building above QH 34f–g, date to the tenth–twelfth centuries.[9] The Coptic inscriptions in the tombs, particularly the historical text in QH 34f that records the fall of Qasr Ibrim (AD 1173), also point to a later phase of the settlement.[10] By the tenth–twelfth centuries it had developed into a more organized monastery and was headed by an archimandrite[11] or a *hegoumenos* (see below).

The original name of the monastic site is unknown, but it is sometimes called St. George on account of four equestrian saints depicted in QH 34f, three of which are identified as St. George by later graffiti (Coquin and Martin 1991c: 850).[12] The original patron saint of the church is unknown, but after the renovation of AD 1180, the building was dedicated to Severus of Antioch (Dekker 2008: 32–34).

The Church and the Staircase

The church was first examined by Grossmann, who surveyed the site when it was still partly covered by debris (Grossmann 1985: 339–44).[13] On the basis of the visible remains, he localized the church directly in front of QH 34h and reconstructed an octagon-domed church, an oblong building with a square central nave that used to be covered by a dome on an octagonal substructure. Grossmann (1985: 340) remarked that the central part had almost been completely demolished some decades before in order to clear the entrance of QH 34h.[14]

In 1998, the SCA cleared the site from debris and revealed part of a building, wall paintings, and Coptic as well as Arabic inscriptions in the area to the north of Grossmann's reconstructed church, which I examined in my preliminary study of 2008 (fig. 12.1). My adapted plan, created by adding the discovered constructions to Grossmann's ground plan, seemed to show two partly overlapping churches with a similar layout, for the northern building also displayed the features of an octagon-domed church

Fig. 12.1. View of the church (P. Hossfeld, 2009)

(Dekker 2008: 20–25, fig. 1). At that stage of research, I presented two options: either there were two churches, one of them replacing the other one, or there was just one building with two naves.

During the conference in Aswan, I had the opportunity to visit Dayr Qubbat al-Hawa again and realized that both options raise the same problem: there is a large ancient staircase directly in front of QH 34h which is nowadays used by visitors to reach the tombs on the uppermost level. Grossmann did not indicate it in his reconstruction, but it occupies the central area of the nave, the *khurus* and the altar room of the 'southern church,' that is, the area that was thought to have been demolished when the entrance of the tomb was cleared. The presence of this staircase has major consequences for the reconstruction of the monastic site.

For architectural reasons, it is not practical to build a church with heavy roofing on top of a staircase. In that case, the solid walls that supported the large dome of the nave, the smaller one of the *khurus*, and the semi-dome of the altar room would have stood in the area of the steps. However, even if the staircase had been filled up in order to create a foundation for the church, the risk that the filling might eventually slide down under the pressure of the roofing remained.

Moreover, the staircase was the most direct means to reach the monastic site and would have been blocked by the construction of a church on top if it. In order to enter the 'southern church,' visitors would have had to make a detour.

Finally, the staircase was an important connection between the monastic units in and around tombs QH 34e–g and QH 34h, for its uppermost section was flanked by two smaller staircases. The one on the north side makes two turns of 180° and leads up to the 'northern church,' which apparently used to have an entrance in the (now lost) south wall. The southern one leads up to the area in front of tombs QH 34f–g. The remains of low mud-brick walls on both sides of the uppermost step, which Grossmann interpreted as secondary walls in his reconstructed church, may have been part of a portal. In other words, the group of staircases connected the church on the north side and monastic units on the south side and formed an integral part of the monastic complex. The remains of stone walls to the south of the staircase suggest that there was also an eastern portal.

On the basis of these observations I conclude that there was only one church, previously called the 'northern church,' which was located to the north of the staircase in front of QH 34h. This staircase also gave access to the reused tombs QH 34e–g.

Uncovering the Church
In 1998, an Egyptian team headed by inspector Magdi Abdin (SCA) removed the debris from the church and uncovered almost the entire building: the central nave, the pillars that once supported the dome on the north and west sides, the north and west walls, and the decorated semicircular niche in the west wall. The ground plan made by the SCA, which has so far remained unpublished, also shows a large staircase and an ancient tomb to the west of the church (fig. 12.2).

In January–March 2010, Abdin and his team continued the excavation. At the time of the conference in Aswan, they were removing the uppermost layer of the earthen church floor and had just revealed an earlier floor, about 0.5 meters deeper, in the southern section of the western aisle and in the northern aisle. Because of the removal of the upper layer of the later floor, the paintings in the western niche and on the west wall of the western aisle appeared much higher above ground level.

Later during the season, the team revealed the sanctuary, judging from a photograph sent by Abdin (fig. 12.3). It shows the central nave in the

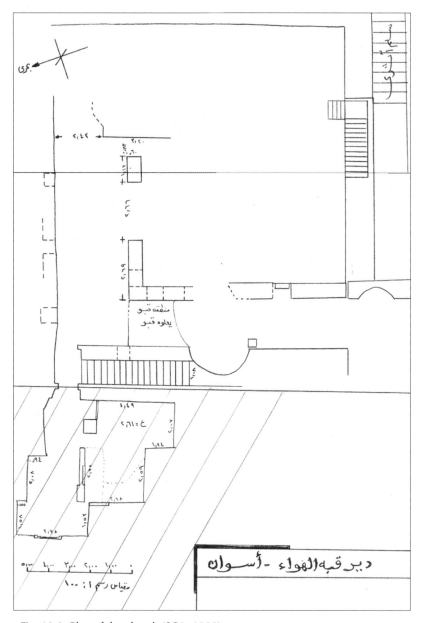

Fig. 12.2. Plan of the church (SCA, 1998)

Fig. 12.3. The sanctuary (M. Abdin, 2010)

foreground, the southern aisle to the right, a *khurus*, the sanctuary, and two
side rooms. Although the remaining walls are low, particularly in the northeast section of the church, the layout of the eastern rooms is well visible.
The southern side room was already included in Grossmann's plan (Grossmann 1985: 344). Abdin also sent photographs of niches that are located in
the area of the sanctuary, but their exact location needs to be established by
another investigation in situ.

A New Ground Plan

On the basis of the plans made by Grossmann and the SCA, the photographs taken by Howard Middleton-Jones and myself in February 2010,
and the ones sent by Abdin, I drew a new ground plan of the church (fig.
12.4). It is a preliminary reconstruction, for I do not have the exact measurements of the sanctuary and the staircase to the south of the church, but
it displays a fairly regular layout.[15]

Basically, the church is an oblong building with a square central nave
that was once surmounted by a dome. The broad northern aisle used to be
covered by two sail vaults, the west one of which is partly preserved. The

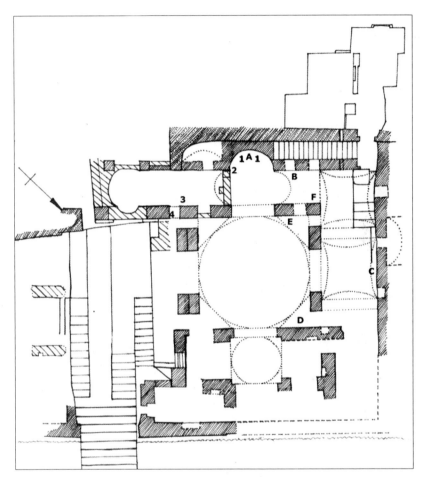

Fig. 12.4. Updated plan of the church (R. Dekker, 2010)

width of the southern aisle is unknown, for the south wall is lost, but the latter possibly stood between the smaller staircases at the entrance of QH 34h. This solution would imply that the northern staircase was integrated into the church building. The northern section of the western aisle is shorter than the southern one and is still covered by a barrel vault. Between the two sections is the semicircular niche with the ascension scene (Dekker 2008: 25–27, pl. 2). As for the sanctuary, the *khurus*, and the partly reconstructed altar room, they are rectangular in plan and were almost certainly roofed by a triconch with a small dome in the center.[16] The church used to

Fig. 12.5. The staircase in the northern aisle (H. Middleton-Jones, 2010)

have a southern entrance that led to the southern aisle and the *khurus*.

In the northwest corner of the church, the SCA recently discovered a staircase on the original floor level, which leads up to the tomb to the west of the church (see below). During my visit, I observed a pavement of regular dressed blocks in front of this staircase and a low bench along the north wall (fig. 12.5).

A rectangular opening in the center of the north wall, about 0.5 meters above the original floor level, gives access to a large vaulted room built against the outer wall of the church. One can also look inside through a small peephole to the left of the opening (Dekker 2008: pls. 1 and 4). Another such vaulted room is found behind the west wall to the south of the semicircular niche. Here, too, there is a peephole, directly above the low entrance. No finds were recorded and the purpose of these rooms is unclear.

There are various niches in the church, including two arched niches in the north wall (Dekker 2008: pls. 3–5), and two vaulted recesses with rectangular openings in the northern section of the west wall (Dekker 2008: pls. 2–3.). The northern recess with the broken shelf may have served to keep small items, but, to my knowledge, no finds are reported.[17] Four more niches were discovered in the area of the sanctuary. One is located in the east wall of the southern side room, another one in the north wall of the *khurus*. The other two niches, which I need to localize, are vaulted and inscribed with Coptic inscriptions.

A doorway in the northwest of the church leads to a stone staircase, which runs parallel to the west wall of the building and is still covered by a barrel vault. It once gave access to the stone constructions built high up against the cliff face, but nowadays the connection is broken. The above-mentioned doorway faces the entrance of an ancient rock-cut tomb, which Abdin identified as a hermitage on account of painted crosses on the walls.

An inner wall divides the irregular tomb chapel in two sections, creating a vestibule and a smaller inner room.

The Renovation of the Church

The previous discussion focused on the original layout of the church. In October/November 1179 (Hatur 896), a *hegoumenos*, or monastic superior, wrote a Coptic *dipinto* on a fresh layer of mud plaster on a secondary mud-brick wall at the southern end of the semicircular niche (fig. 12.4, no. 2) (Dekker 2008: 30–32, pl. 9). The church had just been renovated at the initiative of Bishop Severus, who, according to a Coptic *dipinto* dated 3 March 1180 (17 Baramhat 896), "established" "this new church" and consecrated it together with its baptismal tank on the stated date (fig. 12.4, no. 3) (Dekker 2008: 32–34, pl. 10).

During the renovation, the walls were covered with mud plaster that is best visible in the southern section of the western aisle. This space was turned into a room with a semicircular mud-brick extension on the south side, which partly blocked the entrance of QH 34h, and a low mud-brick wall on the north side, which is preserved up to its original height, judging from the fairly intact plaster on top.[18] On the east side, the spaces between the pillars were closed by means of mud-brick walls, except for the central opening, which became a doorway. This room possibly served as a baptistery, considering its semicircular plan and the reference to a baptismal tank in the above-mentioned dedicatory inscription, which was executed in this very same room.

After the renovation, the floor level inside the newly created room remained low. The same may have applied to the rest of the church, but eventually a new earthen floor was laid, about 0.5 meters above the original floor, which covered the staircase in the northwest corner of the church. At the entrance of the church, a new staircase was built over the original one, and at the south end of the *khurus*, a rectangular area was paved with bricks (fig. 12.2). This staircase was recently removed in order to reveal the original staircase (fig. 12.4).

History of the Church Building

The following reconstruction of the history of the church is based on the combined study of the architecture, the plaster layers, the wall paintings, and dated inscriptions that are mainly written in Coptic. The examination of the plasterwork is particularly useful for establishing a relative chronology: the deeper the layer, the older it is. The dated inscriptions written on or carved through a plaster layer help to propose an approximate dating for that layer as well as for the wall paintings executed on it. Also, a different building material, joints between walls, and the absence of an older plaster layer indicate that a construction is a later addition.

In the tenth or eleventh century, a church was constructed at the bottom of the cliff, slightly to the north of the entrance of QH 34h, which incorporated two rock-cut pillars of the entrance hall of the tomb. The church was not built directly against the cliff face, but slightly to the west, leaving enough space for the semicircular niche in the west wall, a broad stone staircase on the north side, and a vaulted room on the south side. The walls and the lower sections of the pillars in the church were mainly built of stone and the roofing of mud bricks, but fired bricks were used in the arches and the upper parts of the rounded niches. After the construction, the interior of the church was whitewashed and decorated with wall paintings. An Ascension scene was represented in the semicircular niche, and on the west wall, to the north of this niche, a saint, four monks, and a priest were depicted, supposedly the patron saint, whose identity is unknown, and the benefactors of the church (Dekker 2008: 25–29, pls. 2 and 6). The proposed dating of the church to the tenth/eleventh century is based on a comparison with the wall paintings from the cathedral at Faras (tenth century) and the one in the central apse of the church at Dayr Anba Hadra (tenth century).[19]

On 3 January 1125 (8 Tuba 841), Abu Yakub visited the church and carved two Coptic graffiti through the Ascension scene (fig. 12.4, no. 1) (Dekker 2008: 29–30, pls. 7–8).[20] Other visitors also left graffiti, in Coptic, Greek, or Arabic.

Shortly before October/November 1179, the church was renovated at the initiative of Bishop Severus. The southern section of the western aisle was elongated (?) and closed by mud-brick walls in order to create a room that possibly served as a baptistery. It must be noted, however, that the baptismal tank has not been localized. During the renovation, the interior of the church was covered by a layer of mud plaster and appears to have remained undecorated. In March 1180, Bishop Severus consecrated the church and dedicated it to his namesake, Patriarch Severus of Antioch, who was not necessarily the original patron saint.

Again, people visited the church and left their Coptic and Arabic graffiti on the walls or pillars. Another late development was the creation of a new floor, about 0.5 meters above the original one, a new staircase at the entrance of the church, and a brick pavement.

When the church was no longer used for liturgical services, sand and rubble gradually filled its interior and the floor level rose. This accounts for the location of Arabic graffiti on the level of the vaults. In AD 1745 (AH 1158), Isma'il ibn al-Hajj Sulaymi carved an Arabic graffito on the west side of the barrel vault in the northwest section of the church (Dekker 2008: pl. 6).[21]

Conclusions

The recent excavation of the church at Dayr Qubbat al-Hawa by the SCA and another visit to the site made it possible to draw an updated ground plan and to answer the question that I left unanswered in my preliminary study of 2008: was the church a large building with two naves, or should we distinguish two churches, one of which is more recent?

The updated plan demonstrates that there was one single church, previously called the 'northern church.' Instead of the 'southern church' (reconstructed by Grossmann), there was a large ancient staircase which was integrated into the monastic complex and formed a connection between the church and QH 34e–g, tombs that were certainly reused by monks.

Recently, the sanctuary of the church was cleared of debris and its original floor uncovered. Other new finds include two vaulted rooms, to the north and west of the building, and various low niches in the sanctuary, some of them inscribed with Coptic inscriptions.

In my previous study, I concluded that the church was renovated shortly before the end of AD 1179, because of a dated Coptic inscription that was written on later plasterwork. Another examination of the site helped to establish the nature of the renovation: the southern section of the western aisle was turned into a room, which possibly became a baptistery, and a layer of mud plaster was applied on the walls and pillars of the church.

Questions that still need to be answered relate to the identity of the original patron saint of the church, the purpose of the vaulted rooms and niches, and the significance of the church and Dayr Qubbat al-Hawa in general for the Aswan region.

Appendix: The Decoration and Inscriptions in the Church of Dayr Qubbat al-Hawa[22]

In my preliminary study of 2008 I published two wall paintings and four dated Coptic inscriptions in the church of Dayr Qubbat al-Hawa which were essential for the reconstruction of the history of the building (Dekker

2008: 25–34). On closer inspection, it turns out that there are some more (fragmentary) murals in the church and that the locations of two inscriptions are incorrectly indicated in my plan. The recent excavation of the SCA also yielded new finds. This appendix will present an overview of the wall paintings and some particularly interesting inscriptions, the locations of which are indicated in the updated plan (fig. 12.1) of the main article.

The Decoration of the Church

The following list starts with the original wall paintings of the church (A–E) which were executed on whitewash in the tenth/eleventh century.[23] The figurative graffito F, however, is painted on a later layer of mud plaster and postdates the renovation of the church in ad 1179. As for the recently discovered wall painting G, I propose a dating to the sixth/seventh century, as I will explain below.[24]

A. The Ascension scene

This two-zoned composition is located in the semicircular niche in the west wall (Gabra 2002: 107, figs. 10.2–4; Dekker 2008: 25–27, pls. 2–3). The upper zone displays a *mandorla* with the bust of Christ carried by six angels in flight, flanked by two slender figures in white tunics which are fragmentarily preserved and were previously unnoticed. They are standing on a brown base line and are turned toward the central scene, judging from their waving garments, the bare foot of the figure on the left-hand side, and the right hand of the other figure. Considering their prominent position in the upper zone, they could be angels adoring Christ.[25]

The Virgin and the apostles are depicted in the lower section, within a red frame. They are standing in a sandy environment, indicated by a yellow background that reaches up to their knees. Two apostles hold a book and apparently represent the evangelists Matthew and John.

B. The patron saint and benefactors

Four monks, a priest, and a saint are depicted on the west wall of the northern section of the western aisle (Gabra 2002: 107, figs. 10.5–6; Dekker 2008: 27–29, pls. 2 and 6). The painting is particularly interesting because of the rectangular nimbi surrounding the heads of the monks and the priest, an iconographical feature that is generally attested for benefactors of a church or chapel (Jastrzębowska 1994: 350; Dekker 2008: 27). The identity of the saint is unknown, but his archaic garments (a white tunic and a white pallium) and his book seem to point in the direction of an apostle, an evangelist, or a church father. Presumably, he represents the patron saint of the church.

C. A priest, a monk, and a third figure
On the north wall, below the high window in the central bay, traces of three figures are visible (fig. A12.1). The one on the left-hand side is dressed in a white, ankle-length garment without folds and has bare feet. The slightly taller figure on the right side wears a monastic tunic, like those worn by the monks of painting B, considering the V-shaped folds below the knees. Presumably, his

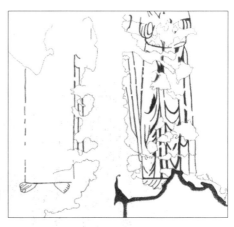

Fig. 12.6. Painting of three figures [C] (R. Dekker, 2010)

tunic was brown, but only the outlines (bluish with a little red) remain. This figure also has bare feet and raises his hands in prayer. Judging from the clothing, these figures represent a priest and a monk. Their postures and their difference in size, as well as the rendering of their garments and feet, strongly recall painting B. On closer inspection, there is a third figure in the damaged area between them. On both sides of the damage one can see the blue outlines and diagonal folds of a wide cloak.

D. A tall figure and three smaller ones
Vague traces of four figures are preserved on the northern section of the wall between the nave and the *khurus*. The one on the north side is tall and wears a blue cloak. His head is lost, but he seems to have a long white beard. The other figures, merely bluish shades, are about half as high, creating the impression that they represent (holy) children or youths.

E. Two more monks
The east side of the pillar nearest to the north end of the western niche displays traces of another wall painting, executed on the stone substructure just below the beginning of the vaults, on the right side (fig. A12.2). Despite its fragmentary state, it shows two standing figures clothed in bluish garments with two sections of V-shaped folds and vertical folds in between. The clothes are rendered in the same way as the monastic tunics

Fig. 12.7. Painting of two monks [E]
(R. Dekker, 2010)

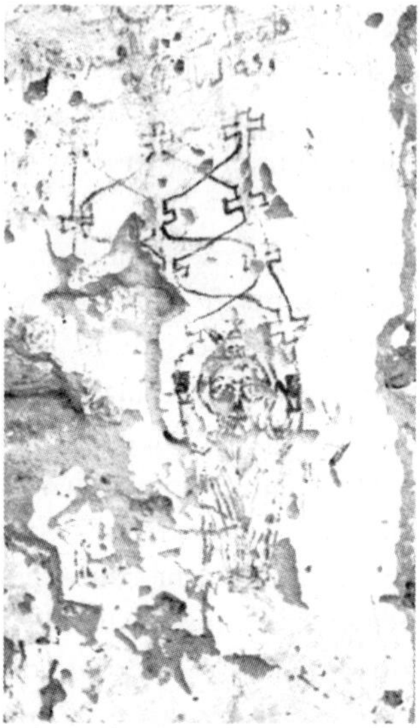

Fig. 12.8. Figurative graffito
[F] of a praying monk
(P. Hossfeld, 2009)

in paintings B and C, which strongly suggests that the figures represent monks. They seem to stand on either side of a pole, indicated by two vertical lines.

F. A praying figure

On the west side of the pillar in the northwest corner of the nave, a visitor painted a praying figure (representing himself?) that may belong to the Arabic graffito just above it, which is also executed in brown ink (fig. A12.3).[26] The figure has a long pointed beard and is clothed in a long tunic with long sleeves, the diagonal folds of which tend inward. His face seems to be enclosed by a hood and on his disproportionately large head is a hat with a high rim (at least on the sides) and a cross on top of it. The figure raises his hands in prayer on either side of his head, while standing next to a low object that looks like a vessel or table with a semicircular outline on a narrow standard, and below a construction consisting of interconnected crosses, arranged in four rows.

The hood and tunic suggest that the figure is a monk, but the hat points in the direction of a cleric of high rank. The construction of crosses

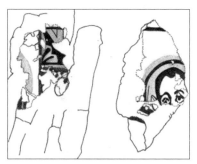

Fig. 12.9. Recently discovered painting [G] (M. Abdin, 2010)

Fig. 12.10. Painting [G]
(R. Dekker, 2010)

serves to indicate a close relationship between the man and the vessel-like
object next to him. It could represent the roof of a church (with highly
stylized domes) in order to create the impression that the praying man is
standing in a sacred space next to a liturgical or sacral object, or it may be
simply a decorative device.

G. A saint next to a pillar
In April 2010, Magdi Abdin sent me photographs of a fragmentary wall
painting that was found among the debris covering the church (figs.
A12.4–5).[27] It is painted on a mud-brick support and its colors are still
remarkably bright. One of the fragments displays the upper part of a head
with a circular nimbus. The other one, which is partly covered by a later
layer of white plaster, shows the outer edge of another nimbus and part of
a column with a capital. A diagonal notched line indicates that the capital
was decorated with stylized quatrefoils.

The artist's palette was limited to yellow, red, and blue. The outlines
of the saint's head are executed with a mixture of red and blue, whereas
those of the column are red. Yellow is used for the nimbi and the capital.
The colors used, the drop-shaped head of the saint, and the rendering of
the capital strongly recall the figures and columns depicted in the cave at
Dayr Anba Hadra, which are stylistically dated to the sixth/seventh century
(Monneret de Villard 1927b: 36).[28] This striking parallel strongly suggests
that the wall painting from Qubbat al-Hawa is roughly contemporary. If so,
this late antique painting must have come from an earlier church building,
and eventually it was covered by white plaster.[29]

The Inscriptions in the Church

Most inscriptions in the church are written in Coptic or Arabic, but there are also some Greek texts, either singular or as part of a bilingual inscription. Sofia Torallas Tovar (Consejo Superior de Investigaciones Científicas [CSIC], Madrid), specializing in Greek and Coptic papyrology and epigraphy, Amalia Zomeño, Arabist (CSIC), and myself, a Coptologist (Leiden University), are preparing an edition of the inscriptions in the church.

In the following overview, I will discuss and localize a selected number of inscriptions, including some that have already been published as well as a recently discovered Coptic text.

1. Two graffiti by Abu Yakub (Dekker 2008: 29–30, pls. 7–8)

Various visitors left their Coptic, Arabic, or Greek graffiti in the semicircular niche in the west wall of the church. They did not intend to destroy the wall painting, but through this practice they hoped to remain present in the church and to partake of its *baraka* (Van der Vliet 2004: 191).

The oldest known dated inscriptions in the church are the two identical Coptic graffiti which Abu Jakub, son of Peter, carved through the Ascension scene on 8 Tuba 841 (3 January 1125). They contain only the name and filiation of the visitor and the date of his visit. Other Coptic graffiti, written in ink or carved, also include a prayer. The phrases "Remember me with benevolence, when You enter Your Kingdom" (Luke 23:42) or simply "Remember me with benevolence" are frequently attested.

2. *Dipinto* by a monastic superior[30]

At the southern end of the western niche, a monastic superior wrote a *dipinto*, a formal inscription, in brown ink. It was executed in Hatur 896 (October/November 1179), presumably in order to commemorate the renovation of the church. The preserved lines include his partly lost name and title *(hegoumenos)*, a prayer, and a date. In my preliminary study, I suggested the name be read as 'Laz[aro]s,' but a photograph made by the SCA in 1998 shows that the 'z' is not correct. For the time being, I propose that it be read as 'La[. . .]s' or even 'La[. . .]e.'

3. *Dipinto* by David from Armant (Dekker 2008: 32–34, pl. 10)

The *dipinto* commemorating the consecration of the renovated church is not located on the north wall, as I stated in my preliminary study, but on the east wall of the room that was created in the southwest, above the doorway.

It was probably part of a bilingual inscription, the Coptic text being written above the left corner and the Arabic one above the right corner. The Coptic text was written, or dictated, by David of Armant, who paid for the consecration of the church, and states that Bishop Severus "established it," consecrated the building and its baptismal tank on 17 Baramhat 896 (3 March 1180), and dedicated it to Patriarch Severus (of Antioch).

4. Greco-Arabic graffito
On the south side within this doorway is a bilingual Greek–Arabic inscription, which was almost completely preserved in 1985 when Peter Grossmann published René-Georges Coquin's reading of the Greek part (Grossmann 1985: 340, n. 7). Presently, the first half of the inscription is lost. The text is written in brown ink and consists of three lines in Greek followed by three lines in Arabic. The Greek text includes a prayer; the Arabic text still needs to be examined.

5. *Dipinto* mentioning superiors
Among the debris, possibly in the southwest section of the church,[31] Abdin's team found fragments of a large Coptic *dipinto* on a collapsed mud-brick wall (fig. A12.6). It was written in brown ink on white plaster in regular upright uncials that recall the script of literary manuscripts from

,Fig. 12.11. Recently discovered *dipinto* [5] (M. Abdin, 2010)

Esna–Edfu (ca. AD 1000).[32] The two largest fragments comprise the lower part of the text, judging from a rim below the last line. The *dipinto* seems to commemorate important individuals, including monastic superiors, for the title *hegoumenos* is mentioned twice.

Conclusions

This appendix was aimed at registering and localizing the wall paintings in the church as well as some inscriptions in order to complement and correct—where necessary—my article of 2008, but it is still a preliminary overview. There is still much to be done to complete the documentation and study of the wall paintings. As for the inscriptions, Sofia Torallas Tovar, Amalia Zomeño, and I are jointly working on an epigraphic survey in order to publish the Coptic, Greek, and Arabic texts, which will hopefully reveal new information on the history of the church at Dayr Qubbat al-Hawa.

Notes

1 For the finds of 1998, see Gabra 2002: 107; Kamel and Naguib 2003: 170–77; Gabra 2004: 1074–75.

2 I warmly thank Magdi Abdin, director of the Islamic and Christian monuments of Aswan (SCA), for giving me permission to publish the church. I am also indebted to Father Abullif and Atef Naguib who sent me photographs taken in 1998, and to Peter Hossfeld of VCS Productions, who shared his high-resolution photographs (made in May 2009). Yves Auberger made many valuable suggestions. Finally, I thank Howard Middleton-Jones, Joost Hagen, and James Taylor for their assistance during our investigation of the site on 4 February 2010.

3 For the distribution of the tombs, see "Proyecto Qubbet el-Hawa (Asuán, Egipto)" at the website of the University of Jaén (Spain). http://www.ujaen.es/investiga/qubbetelhawa/historia.php.

4 Cf. Coquin and Martin 1991c: 850–51; Timm 1984–2007: 2160–61; Gabra 2002: 105–107.

5 Sofia Torallas Tovar (CSIC, Madrid) examined the ostraca from QH 33, while Sebastian Richter (Leipzig) published those from QH 104, 105, and 110 in Edel 2008: 451, 455, 1548–49, 1552, 1572–73, 1765, 1567, 1774–77, 1780–81.

6 Richter confidently dates the ostraca examined by him to the sixth/seventh century, and Torallas Tovar proposes a sixth-century date for those from QH 33 (personal communication in both cases).

7 See Richter's readings in Edel 2008: 1548–49, 1765.

8 See the appendix.

9 For the residential building, see Monneret de Villard 1927b: 16–18, fig. 2; Grossmann 1991d: 852.

10 See Richter's edition of the text in Edel 2008: 514–17, with further references, as well as Jacques van der Vliet's chapter in this volume.

11 See Richter's reading of a Coptic inscription in QH 34e in Edel 2008: 476–77: "Abba Mouses, the most humble archimandrite [of this monasteri]on." This reconstruction justifies the term 'monastery' for the later settlement.

12 For the figurative graffiti, see Edel 2008: 518, 521–22.

13 Cf. Grossmann 1991d: 851.

14 He implicitly referred to the excavation by the Bonner Ägyptologischen Seminars (1959–81); cf. Edel 1985: 55; Edel 2008.

15 For the letters and numerals, see the appendix.

16 Compare the roofing of the churches of Dayr Anba Hadra and Dayr al-Kubbaniya in Grossmann 1982: 7–13, fig. 3; 54–60, fig. 18; Grossmann 2002: 560–65, figs. 174 and 177.

17 On niches, see Grossmann 2002: 184–88.

18 The threshold is partly visible in Dekker 2008: pl. 9.

19 See the author's contribution on this subject in this volume.

20 See also the appendix.

21 Reading by the Arabist Amalia Zomeño (CSIC, Madrid).

22 I warmly thank Magdi Abdin (SCA), Peter Hossfeld (VCS Productions, Switzerland), and Howard Middleton-Jones (Swansea University) for allowing me to make use of their photographs.

23 See the main article; cf. Dekker 2008: 27, 29–30, 34.

24 The wall painting was discovered after my visit to the site.

25 Angels adoring Christ are, for instance, depicted in the western niche at Dayr Anba Hadra (tenth century) and in the Chapel of the Virgin in the Church of St. Mercurius in Dayr Abu Sayfayn (Old Cairo; twelfth century); cf. the author's contribution on Dayr Anba Hadra in the present volume; Leroy 1975: pls. VIa–b.

26 The Arabic graffiti are examined by the Arabist Amalia Zomeño (CSIC, Madrid).

27 The findspot was not mentioned.

28 Cf. de Morgan 1894: 134 (line drawing). See also the author's contribution on Dayr Anba Hadra in the present volume.

29 According to Grossmann (1991d: 851), an earlier church was built in the pillared hall of QH 34h, on account of traces of walls and "the beginning of vaults of a central hanging dome over the altar chamber"; cf. Grossmann 1985: 340. During my visit, I saw a rectangular stone elevation against the north wall of the hall, which is reached from the south by means of some steps and is enclosed by mud-brick walls. If the hall served as a church, the altar would have been located on top of the elevation, but, in that case, the sanctuary would be in the north, instead of in the east. Judging from the plasterwork on the south wall of the hall, the roofing between the pillars consisted of a barrel vault which was also directed north–south.

30 Dekker 2008: 30–32 (no. 2), fig. 1 (incorrectly indicated by 'no. 3'), pl. 9; cf. Gabra 2002: 107, fig. 10.7.

31 The findspot was not mentioned, but the photograph shows a slightly concave wall with mud-brick plasterwork.

32 See, for instance, Budge 1913: pl. LIII.

13 The Christian Wall Paintings from the Temple of Isis at Aswan Revisited

Jitse H.F. Dijkstra and
Gertrud J.M. van Loon

Introduction[1]

Ancient Syene is almost completely covered by the southern part of modern Aswan ('Old Aswan'), which makes archaeological excavation of the site difficult. As a result, only two ancient monuments have been preserved, the temple of Domitian and the temple of Isis. In the 1980s and 1990s successful surveys in the area around the Isis temple led to the creation, in the year 2000, of a joint project of the Swiss Institute of Architectural and Archaeological Research on Ancient Egypt and the Supreme Council of Antiquities. [2] This project, under supervision of Cornelius von Pilgrim, the director of the Swiss Institute, constitutes the first systematic excavations ever to take place in Aswan. Apart from excavating the small plots of land surrounding the temples of Isis and Domitian (fig. 13.1, Areas 1 and 3), several emergency excavations have been conducted whenever the occasion arose after building activities in this densely populated part of Aswan had revealed ancient remains. Thus far, no fewer than sixty-five sites have been explored and three preliminary reports covering the first six seasons (2000–2006) have been published (von Pilgrim, Bruhn, and Kelany 2004; von Pilgrim, Bruhn, Dijkstra, and Wininger 2006; von Pilgrim, Keller, Martin-Kilcher, el-Amin, and Müller 2008).

In the first four seasons the activities of the Swiss–Egyptian mission concentrated in large part on the excavation of the mud-brick houses dating to

137

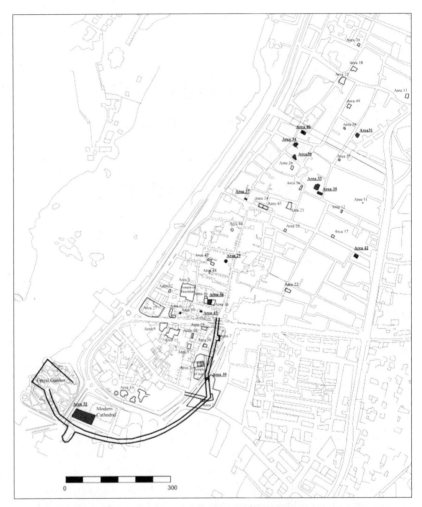

Fig. 13.1. Topographical map with areas investigated during the first six campaigns of the Swiss–Egyptian mission (von Pilgrim, Keller, Martin-Kilcher, el-Amin, and Müller 2008: fig. 1)

the first to eleventh centuries AD around the temple of Isis (fig. 13.1, Area 1) (von Pilgrim, Bruhn, and Kelany 2004: 127–34; von Pilgrim, Bruhn, Dijkstra, and Wininger 2006: 238–51, 272–77). The excavations revived an interest in this temple, which lies buried deep in the middle of the ancient houses (fig. 13.2). The temple of Isis, a small but completely preserved Ptolemaic temple, was discovered in 1871 by engineers working on a railroad

Fig. 13.2. The temple of Isis at Aswan (© G.J.M. van Loon, February 2010)

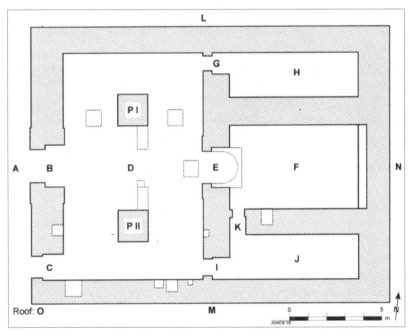

Fig. 13.3. Key map to the temple of Isis at Aswan with a tentative reconstruction
of (parts of) the church (von Pilgrim, Bruhn, Dijkstra, and Wininger 2006: fig. 7)

from Aswan to Shellal (on the east bank of the Nile at Philae). Following its discovery, some plans and copies of reliefs were published at the end of the nineteenth century (Mariette and Maspero 1889: 6 (pls. 22–26); de Morgan et al. 1894: 47–57), but nothing much happened until an Italian team under the supervision of Edda Bresciani started work on the temple a century later, in 1971. The resulting publication, which appeared in 1978, contains, in the first place, an edition of the hieroglyphic reliefs of the temple and the decorated blocks of other buildings found in the surrounding area that were dumped here (Bresciani and Pernigotti 1978). But the Italian team also published several textual and figural graffiti from the temple's walls, and a useful map of the building (which served as the basis for fig. 13.3).[3] The temple as it stands today actually consists only of its nucleus (the *naos*), that is, three chapels for cult statues (fig. 13.3, nos. H, F, J) with a small hall in front of it (the pillared hall, D) containing two square pillars (PI and PII) (Bresciani in Bresciani and Pernigotti 1978: 17).

A first inventory in 2001 by the first author of this article revealed that the publication of the graffiti by the Italian team was far from exhaustive. As a result, a separate project was started, the Isis Temple Graffiti Project, which was aimed at publishing all graffiti (352 in total, both figures and texts) from the temple.[4] From the study of the graffiti it soon became clear that they had much to tell about the architectural history of the building, especially its reuse as a church in Christian times. The Italian team had already found traces of the reuse of the temple as a church, such as Christian graffiti, hacked-away reliefs, certain adaptations in the pavement, wall niches, and, especially, two Christian wall paintings on the opposite faces of the northern and southern pillars (PI–II).[5] On the basis of these features they surmised that the church was built in the pillared hall and that the altar of the church stood in front of the entrance to the main sanctuary (E), which was closed off with an apsidal niche (Bresciani in Bresciani and Pernigotti 1978: 38–41 [pls. XXVII–XXVIII]).[6] As this reconstruction was only assumed but not proven by a systematic study, in 2002–2003 a meticulous analysis was made of the graffiti and other architectural features of the building. In addition to confirming Bresciani's hypothesis that the church was located in the pillared hall (D), this study has resulted in a tentative reconstruction of several essential parts of the church (indicated in fig. 13.3) and the establishment of different phases of reuse of the building in Late Antiquity and later times (Dijkstra in von Pilgrim, Bruhn, Dijkstra, and Wininger 2006: 228–38).

Despite this detailed study, two issues regarding the church have thus far remained open: When was the temple dedicated as a church? And to whom was it dedicated? Both questions have been addressed by Bresciani on the basis of the Christian wall paintings the Italian team discovered. She dated the paintings to the sixth century AD and identified an enthroned figure on the northern pillar as the Virgin Mary. Therefore, she thought it "highly probable" that the church was dedicated to the Virgin.[7] Since it lies beyond the expertise of the first author to properly assess these statements in the light of the ample comparative material now available, he asked the second author to take a closer look at the paintings. The present article—a preliminary version of which, focusing on art historical aspects, was presented by the second author at the International Symposium on Early Christianity and Monasticism: Aswan and Nubia—is the result of our collaborative efforts.[8] In the following we shall start with a description of the wall paintings. We shall then try to interpret the composition. The subsequent section discusses the scenes in the larger setting of the church interior by comparing it to the decorative program of contemporary church interiors known so far. This discussion will lead to a reassessment of the date of the wall paintings and, as a consequence, of the foundation of the church. In the final section we shall come back to the question of whether the church could have been dedicated to the Virgin Mary. We shall argue that both of Bresciani's statements need to be treated with caution.

The Wall Paintings

The wall paintings were located on the south face of the northern pillar and the north face of the southern pillar (fig. 13.3, nos. PI and PII). The earlier investigators of the temple did not notice the paintings, which suggests that the traces were probably already very faint from the beginning.[9] When the Italian team discovered them in 1971 they had become barely visible and for this reason they took photographs on infrared film. Cristina Guidotti then made copies of the originals *in situ* and, with the help of the infrared photographs, compiled drawings that documented everything she could see:[10] one color drawing of the south face of the northern pillar and one black-and-white and one color drawing of the north face of the southern pillar (Bresciani and Pernigotti 1978: 40 [pls. XXVII–XXVIII]). These drawings are all we have to evaluate the paintings, since the originals are now lost. Most likely, the murals were painted on a layer of plaster or on whitewash, although this is not mentioned in the Italian description. Plain plaster or any other decoration has not been found.

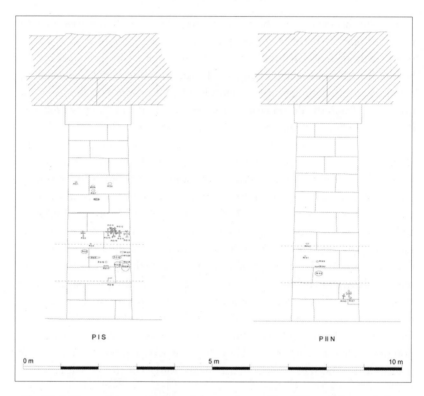

Fig. 13.4. Plans of the south face of the northern pillar (PIS) and the north face of the southern pillar (PIIN) with the graffiti and the (approximate) position of the wall paintings

According to the description by Bresciani, the paintings were both located around one meter above the pavement and were 0.95 meters in height.[11] Unfortunately, she does not tell us whether the paintings covered the whole width of the pillar or just a portion of it.[12] If we take the approximate range she gives from the bottom (1 meter above the pavement) to the top of the scenes (1.95 meters above the pavement), and compare this position with the graffiti on the same pillar faces, the following observations can made (fig. 13.4). On the south face of the northern pillar (PIS) a series of crosses can be seen, incised just above the paintings.[13] The crosses show that the paintings on the pillars were restricted to the strip indicated by Bresciani. Some of the crosses, especially the cluster of more elaborate crosses to the right, might have belonged, like the wall paintings, to the

Fig. 13.5. Wall painting on the south face of the northern pillar (Bresciani and Pernigotti 1978: pl. XXVII).

original decoration of the church. In the area where the paintings were located, several demotic graffiti (indicated in the drawing as ellipses) can be found dating to the Greco-Roman period, which are much effaced, no doubt because of the surface treatment for the Christian paintings.[14] On the north face of the southern pillar (PIIN), a similar pattern emerges, though the graffiti are fewer in number here. Two crosses are found, in this case below the wall paintings, while four demotic graffiti, again very fragmentary, are in the area of the paintings.[15]

When we take a closer look at these paintings, on the south face of the northern pillar (fig. 13.5), a female figure (according to the Italian description), seated on a throne decorated with gemstones, has been depicted in the center. The face and the drapery of the figure, from knee-height down, have been preserved. On either side of the seated figure, three standing saints have been painted. The colors used are white, blue, red, and black. Part of the red frame (with a corner) can be seen below. The description also speaks of a hand of the seated figure, but there is no hand visible in the drawing. In addition, it can be noted that the seated figure and four of the six standing persons (and presumably all of them) are wearing shoes; the standing persons are wearing a basic ankle-length garment, covered with a draped upper garment. The preserved face of the seated figure

Fig. 13.6. Wall painting on the north face of the southern pillar (Bresciani and Pernigotti 1978: pl. XXVIII).

shows no traces of a nimbus. The Italian team has interpreted this person as the Virgin Mary, most probably with her child on her lap, surrounded by standing saints.[16]

The painting on the north face of the southern pillar (fig. 13.6) contains a series of four standing, bearded saints with, at the far right, according to the Italian team, an angel. Also here, part of the red frame has been preserved. In addition, the standing figures seem to wear a nimbus, although they are of various sizes. Their set of clothes looks like a basic ankle-length garment and a draped upper garment, with shoes. While these figures have been depicted frontally, the so-called angel seems to have been depicted in a three-quarter pose.

Interpretation of the Wall Paintings

To start with the painting on the south face of the northern pillar, the person in the center is sitting on a high-backed throne or a stool. The back of this piece of furniture has not been preserved but both types were used to depict seated persons of high rank. The Virgin Mary is a good option for such a seated figure. However, there are more persons who can be

Fig. 13.7. Bawit, Chapel III, north wall: David in King Saul's armor (Clédat 1904–1906: pl. XVII).

portrayed on a throne or stool. Since the interpretation of the central figure in this fragmentary composition is not unambiguous, we shall therefore consider all the options.

Apart from the Virgin Mary and Christ, kings or commanders can also be depicted on a throne or stool. The latter are often shown sitting on a high-backed throne, a stool, or a folding chair. Although in most examples they are depicted in three-quarter pose, like King Herod in a painting in the quarry church of Dayr Abu Hinnis (sixth–seventh century, sitting on a stool) (Clédat 1902: 49 and pl. I; Zibawi 2003: figs. 55, 58–59; van Loon and Delattre 2006: 123–24, figs. 1–4 and pl. V), King Saul represented at Bawit (Chapel III) is sitting on a high-backed throne decorated with gem-stones (sixth–eighth century?) (Clédat 1904–1906: 20, fig. 12, pls. XII-A and XVII; Zibawi 2003: fig. 82). He is dressed in an ankle-length, dark-red draped garment, with shoes (fig. 13.7).[17] Kings or commanders occur mainly in narrative scenes, and although the remains of the central figure from Aswan bear a strong resemblance to King Saul at Bawit, a narrative scene on the northern pillar is unlikely.

This leaves us with Mary and Christ. According to the Italian team, arguments for the identification of the seated figure as Mary are the shape of the face (especially the shading), and the position of the left knee and the hand (not visible), which support the idea of a child on her lap.[18] The face, beardless and round, might indeed indicate a woman; there are, on the other hand, also a number of examples of an enthroned, beardless Christ. For example, a beardless Christ enthroned among archangels and saints can be found in Dayr Abu Maqar (*haykal* of Benjamin, west wall, ninth century) (Leroy 1982: diagram A and pls. I–III), and in an exceptional image of Christ and Mary seated together on a throne in Bawit and surrounded by saints (Chapel LIX, east wall, eighth–ninth century?) (Clédat 1999: 175–76 and photographs 153–55). Double compositions of Christ enthroned in niches in several other rooms in this monastery also show a young beardless Christ (Chapels XVII and XXVI: Clédat 1904–1906: 75–76 and pls. XL–XLIV, 136–37 and pls. XC–XCI; Zibawi 2003: figs. 86 and 87). The color of the garment, dark red, is generally used for both Mary and Christ. The position of the knees, somewhat apart so as to carry a child, might point in the direction of the Virgin. But this pose is also quite common for seated male figures, including the aforementioned examples of King Saul and Christ Enthroned. A positive point for the identification of the figure as Mary is the fact that she wears shoes. The Virgin is never depicted barefoot or wearing sandals whereas Christ most often has sandals.

Considering the evidence and comparisons, the pendulum seems to swing toward Mary rather than Christ as an interpretation of the central figure of the painting on the northern pillar. If the figure represents Mary, she would almost certainly carry her son. Furthermore, the child would have been quite high in her arms. For if he were sitting on her knees, the feet of the Christ Child would still have been visible and the drawing gives no indication of feet.[19] While holding her child high in her arms, the feet could rest on her knee, as in a textile preserved in the Cleveland Museum of Art;[20] she could be nursing, as in the majestic composition in the north conch of the Church of Anba Bishai near Sohag (seventh–eighth century; fig. 13.8) (Laferrière 2008; 26–28 and pl. IV; Bolman 2006a: pls. 1 and 5; Bolman 2008, with earlier literature), or holding a *clipeus* with the image of her son, as can be seen in Chapel XXVIII at Bawit (fig. 13.9) (Clédat 1904–1906: pls. XCVI-b and XCVIII). Furthermore, in the examples discussed (whether Mary or Christ Enthroned) it is clear that more often than not archangels are part of the composition. They flank the enthroned

Fig. 13.8. Sohag, Red Monastery, Church of Anba Bishai, northern conch of the sanctuary (Laferrière 2008: pl. IV).

Fig. 13.9. Bawit, Chapel XVIII, niche in east wall: the Virgin Mary accompanied by archangels (Clédat 1904–1906: pl. XCVI-B).

figure (which is always the focal point of the image) or stand among the saints. In the painting on the north pillar it is impossible to distinguish wings, but, in all probability, angels were also included in this design.[21]

To turn to the south pillar, the three standing saints that can be detected are most probably bearded, hence they are male. They might be monks, but too little has been left to identify them. Some lines at the far left indicate a fourth saint and the figure in three-quarter pose at the far right might be an angel. Rows of standing saints or (saintly) monks are extremely common in churches as well as in monastic buildings in Egypt: for example, in churches, cells, and utility buildings in the Monastery of Apa Apollo at Bawit[22] and the Monastery of Apa Jeremiah at Saqqara,[23] at the quarry church of Wadi Sarga (Doresse 2000: 2[ii]: figs. 31–35, 36b–d, 39, 41),[24] and in the side aisles of the church at Karm al-Ahbariya.[25] In a monastic environment, the series of standing figures often contain a large number of monks. Monks and saints usually carry objects like a book, a censer, a key, a staff, or a scroll, or are depicted in praying position, their hands at chest height or as *orantes*, with arms outstretched. The figures are painted side by side or are separated by trees, plants, or columns. They are usually dressed in a tunic and pallium, or one or two tunics with a shawl or cape. Some compositions show a certain hierarchy or rhythm, for example in Room 40 at Bawit: a frieze of the Archangel Uriel, symmetrically flanked by saints (northern wall) (Maspero and Drioton 1931–43: pls. XLVIIb, XLVIII–L).[26] An often reproduced (fragmentary) painting from Saqqara, now in Cairo (Coptic Museum), shows Apollo in the *orans* position between St. Macarius and Apa Amoun, both holding a book. To the left of St. Macarius, St. Onophrius has been painted, also in the *orans* position.[27] The complete arrangement is unknown. In Dayr Abu Hinnis, a monk, monastic saints, perhaps a bishop, and physician saints flank St. John the Baptist (Zibawi 2003: figs. 64–65; van Loon and Delattre 2004; van Loon and Delattre 2005).

It has been proposed that the saints shown in the painting from Aswan be identified as Victor (the few lines at the far left), Shenoute, Antony, and Pachomius, with the angel reading from Pachomius's *Rule* (MacCoull 1990: 154–55). This identification is not based on any evidence, however: the iconography does not give any clue as to the identity of the saints and, as far as we know, no comparative composition exists.[28] The only thing that can be said is that we are dealing here with standing, most probably male, saints. Whether they were monastic saints, or whether an angel was included, can no longer be ascertained.

The Wall Paintings as Part of a Decorative Program

The fragments of the two paintings on the pillars are the only remains of painted decoration in this church.[29] Compared to the decorative programs known from excavations or still extant in church buildings in Egypt, it is almost certain that these murals were part of a more extended iconographical program. Decorative programs of the eastern part of a church prior to about AD 1000 have seldom survived in Egypt. In northern Nubia, on the other hand, early apse compositions, which are modeled on the Egyptian double composition of Christ Enthroned (upper register) and the Virgin surrounded by apostles (lower register), are better preserved (Godlewski 1992: 289–91).[30]

For example, the churches at Naga al-Oqba (seventh century), Wadi al-Sebua (seventh–eighth century), and the central church at Abdalla Nirqi (end of the seventh century?) contained fragments of such a double composition, with representations of the Virgin in the lower register. The sections preserved show her standing or enthroned; it is not always clear whether she is carrying her son. From the beginning of the eighth century dates the apse composition of the Cathedral of Paulos at Faras (Pachoras), this time in three registers (Godlewski 1992: 287, 289–91, fig. 15, 296–98).[31] Although the Virgin appears in these apse designs, her significance is to underline both Christ's divinity and humanity. Christ, King in past, present, and future (as visualized in the upper register), has become man: "Your radiance rests on my knees, the throne of your Majesty is held in my arms."[32] From Faras Cathedral we also have an interesting design from the same, eighth-century phase of decoration in the eastern end of the north aisle, to the left of the apse: still visible were the Virgin, holding her son high in her left arm, with an angel on the left-hand side and Saint John the Evangelist on the right-hand side. Probably there were more persons depicted.[33]

The few examples from Egypt are all monastic churches; the church at Aswan, by contrast, is part of an urban setting, as are some of the Nubian examples mentioned above (Abdalla Nirqi, Faras).[34] Nevertheless, the primary function of these church buildings, the celebration of the Eucharist, is the same. Although details may differ, the basic decorative scheme of the eastern part, in which the Eucharist takes place, can therefore also be expected to be similar. Since decorative programs of contemporary secular churches from Egypt are missing, we shall compare the position of the paintings in the Aswan church with two well-studied monastic examples, the Church of Anba Bishai (the Red Monastery) near Sohag and the

Church of the Virgin in Dayr al-Suryan (Wadi al-Natrun). In these monasteries, churches and decoration are on a much larger and grander scale.
However, there are still some interesting parallels to be noted.

The eastern triconch of the Red Monastery church shows an enthroned,
nursing Virgin, surrounded by prophets and saints in the northern semi-
dome. In the southern semi-dome, Christ is enthroned among John the
Baptist, John's father Zachariah, and the evangelists, while the eastern
semi-dome was also decorated with Christ Enthroned (very fragmentarily
preserved). These paintings are now dated to the seventh–eighth century.[35]
In the Church of the Virgin in Dayr al-Suryan, there is no image left in
the eastern part of the church (the altar room has been rebuilt and decorated with stucco work, dating to the tenth century) (Immerzeel 2008). In
the *khurus*, the southern semi-dome is covered with a later layer of plaster
and subsequent murals. The most recent layer of the northern semi-dome
was removed a few years ago and an Epiphany scene has come to light:
the Virgin Mary Enthroned, holding a *clipeus* with her son, surrounded
by angels, the Magi, and shepherds (Innemée 2011). The western semi-
dome holds an Annunciation scene, the Virgin and the archangel Gabriel
surrounded by four prophets. The latter paintings are at present dated to
the eighth century.[36] From the surviving examples of sanctuary designs
it appears that the Virgin Mary and Child are often found, apart from in
compositions in the eastern apsidal niche or apse, in the northern part
of the sanctuary. In these examples, the Virgin is enthroned, nursing,[37] or
showing her son who is sitting in her arm or depicted in a *clipeus*. This
investigation strengthens the identification of Mary as the enthroned figure
on the northern pillar at Aswan.

The comparative material adduced thus far to aid in the interpretation of the fragmentary scenes from the Isis temple at Aswan enables us
to come to a reassessment of the date of these paintings, which Bresciani
placed in the sixth century. She based this date on the shape of the eyes
and mouth of the central figure of the painting on the northern pillar and
the face of the saints in the painting on the southern pillar.[38] These elements cannot be taken, however, as indications of a sixth-century date:
stylistic features are notoriously unreliable in dating paintings in Christian
Egypt (van Loon in Gabra and van Loon 2007: 35). A date in this century
is acceptable, but so is the seventh, eighth, or ninth century. On the basis of
the fragments preserved on the pillars, no more specific date can therefore
be given than between the sixth and ninth centuries. Assuming that these

murals belonged to the original decoration of the church, the date of its foundation should also be placed within this timeframe.[39]

A Church Dedicated to the Virgin Mary?

With the establishment of the date of the dedication of the church inside the temple of Isis in the sixth–ninth centuries, the remaining question to be answered in this section is to whom the church was dedicated. Based on her identification of the enthroned figure as the Virgin, Bresciani assumed that the church was also dedicated to her by pointing to the cultic continuity from the veneration of the divine mother, Isis, to the Mother of God, Mary.[40] In an article published in 1990, this information was combined with two papyri (dated to 585 and 586) from the Patermouthis archive, which mention an "Isakos son of Taeion, archdeacon of (the church of) the Holy Mary of Syene." According to the author, "[t]he Church of the Holy Mary must be the Ptolemaic temple of Isis."[41] The identification of the Church of the Holy Mary in the papyri with the church inside the temple of Isis has been generally accepted by subsequent scholars (MacCoull 1990: 154; Porten 1996: 525 n. 16; Richter 2002: 138). However, on several occasions the first author of the present article has expressed his doubts about these inferences on the basis of a single wall painting (Dijkstra 2007b: 195–96, and 2008: 75 and 99 n. 64).[42] A look at the available comparative material from elsewhere in Egypt demonstrates that a wall painting of Mary does indeed not necessarily make a church of the Virgin.

The example of the enthroned, nursing Mary from the Church of Anba Bishai in the Red Monastery mentioned in the previous section shows an elaborate composition with the Virgin Mary in the center (fig. 13.8). However, she is not depicted in her own right but as part of the iconographical program of the sanctuary: Mary was instrumental in Christ's incarnation, which is emphasized by the prophets surrounding her. Another example of the previous section is the Church of the Virgin at Dayr al-Suryan in the Wadi al-Natrun. This church, dedicated to Mary and built in the seventh century, was part of "The Monastery of the Mother of God of Anba Bishoi," a double monastery of the still existing neighboring Monastery of Anba Bishoi,[43] and has preserved an iconographical program in which the Virgin takes a prominent place. Nursing her son, she has been painted on a half column to the right of the entrance to the central altar room; Enthroned with child, an Epiphany scene with Magi and shepherds, she can be found in the northern half-dome *(khurus)*; and an Annunciation scene with prophets has been painted in the western half-dome.[44] Mary is represented in her role as Mother of God; within this framework, however, she holds a central position. But not all churches dedicated to the Virgin Mary hold paintings of her, as is witnessed by the quarry church of Dayr al-Ganadla, near Asyut, which probably dates to the sixth century. The original eastern part of this church has disappeared, but the first layer of decoration in the entire church, including its ceiling, consists of decorative motifs and is aniconic (Buschhausen and Khorshid 1998; van Loon in Gabra and van Loon 2007: 266–73).[45]

These *comparanda* show that a wall painting representing an enthroned Mary cannot be decisive in determining to whom the church in the temple of Isis was dedicated. Also in this case, the painting was undoubtedly part of the iconographical program of the sanctuary. Consequently, the identification of the Church of the Holy Mary of Syene from the papyri as the church in the Isis temple must also remain open.

Examples such as these therefore remind us to be cautious in assuming a cultic continuity in late antique Egypt on the basis of too little evidence. Another case in point is the Church of the Virgin Mary at Philae, situated on the famous temple island four kilometers farther south. "[T]he Holy Virgin Mary Theotokos" is attested in two undated Greek building inscriptions from the island.[46] A third building inscription, this one in Coptic and dating to 752, has been found near the so-called West Church and mentions "the *topos* of the lady of us all, the Holy Theotokos Mary, on Philae."[47] The epithets used for Mary, "our lady" and "Theotokos," have recently been compared with much earlier epithets used for Isis on the same island to prove that a 'cult adoption' took place at Philae.[48] The only reason why the temple of Isis itself was not turned into a church of the Virgin Mary was that the temple was still functioning when the church was dedicated.[49] However, this argumentation is not supported by any evidence, as it is problematic to combine the common, eighth-century terminology of Mary with the much earlier epithets for Isis.[50] We should therefore be cautious in assuming a continuity of cultic practice from Isis to Mary.

Conclusion

In summary, the church built in the temple of Isis yields a rare example, however fragmentary, of decoration in an urban church in late antique to early Islamic Egypt. In all probability, the Virgin and Child surrounded by saints, and most likely angels, have been depicted on the northern pillar.

Four saints and an unidentified person are represented on the southern pillar. Considering the date of these murals, nothing more specific can be said than that they date to between the sixth and ninth centuries. There is no evidence that this church was dedicated to the Virgin, or that it is the Church of the Holy Mary mentioned in the Patermouthis archive. For the questions of the role of the Virgin in church decoration and the cult of the Virgin Mary in Egypt, especially before the year 1000, this subject will need much more research before anything further can be said.[51]

Notes

1   We would like to thank Sabrina Higgins and Justin Kroesen for comments on an earlier version of this article.

2   For the surveys, see Jaritz and Rodziewicz 1994 and 1996.

3   Hieroglyphic-demotic graffiti: Bresciani in Bresciani and Pernigotti 1978: 124–43 (nos. 1–43). Greek graffiti: D. Foraboschi in Bresciani and Pernigotti 1978: 144–45 (nos. 1–2; a third, undecipherable text did not receive a number). Coptic graffiti: Pernigotti in Bresciani and Pernigotti 1978: 146 (nos. 1–8). Figural graffiti: Bresciani in Bresciani and Pernigotti 1978: 34–39. Map: Bresciani and Pernigotti 1978: pl.VI.

4   Dijkstra 2012. This study contains a detailed description and documentation (in the form of a drawing or photograph) of each graffito, as well as introductions to the different groups of graffiti, and a general introduction that will place this (in large part) new body of material in a wider context.

5   Bresciani in Bresciani and Pernigotti 1978: 39: "Ma certamente gli elementi più interessanti, archeologicamente, della cristianizzazione dell'antico tempio come chiesa cristiana, sone le vestigia di affreschi sulle due facce centrali, contrapposte, dei pilastri della sala."

6   Cf. Grossmann 1995: 181–201 at 194, who seems to take over Bresciani's hypothesis, yet remarks that the church was built in "das Allerheiligste des Tempels," that is, the main sanctuary of the temple.

7   Bresciani in Bresciani and Pernigotti 1978: 39–41 (pls. XXVII–XXVIII). Quote on p. 41: "altamente probabile."

8   This article has been published under a different title ("A Church Dedicated to the Virgin Mary in the Temple of Isis at Aswan?") in ECA 7 (2010): 1–16. We would like to thank the editors of the journal for permission to reproduce our text, with some slight adaptations, in this volume.

9   Cf. Bresciani in Bresciani and Pernigotti 1978: 40.

10   Bresciani in Bresciani and Pernigotti 1978: 39: "L'aiuto di una serie di foto all'infrarosso, eseguite da F. Gabrielli nel 1971, è stato assai grande per individuare particolari non chiari all'esame visivo diretto; la pazienza di M. Cristina Guidotti, che ha eseguito i disegni sugli originali, ha permesso di documentare l'umanamente documentabile."

11   Bresciani and Pernigotti 1978: 39: "a 1 m. circa dal pavimento. L'altezza delle scene sono di circa 0,95 m." It is unclear how the wall paintings fit in with the screen wall that is assumed to have been in between the pillars (fig. 13.3; see Dijkstra in von Pilgrim, Bruhn, Dijkstra, and Wininger 2006: 233, and Dijkstra 2008: 104).

Most likely the wall was not higher than one meter, as in many sanctuary barriers in Egyptian churches from this period (Grossmann 2002: 122–25; Bolman 2006b: 76–80), and the wall paintings would have been visible above it.

12   The drawings have no scale.

13   PIS 2, 10–5 (catalogue nos. 125–31 in Dijkstra 2012). Farther up on the wall are five modern graffiti (PIS 1, 6–9 [nos. 344–48]).

14   PIS 3–5, 16–17, 19–24 (nos. 234–44). PIS 18 (no. 174) is an unidentified figure.

15   Crosses: PIIN 6–7 (nos. 132–33). Demotic graffiti: PIIN 1, 3–5 (nos. 252, 254–56), cf. PIIN 2 (no. 253), which seems to be just above the painting and is more legible.

16   Bresciani in Bresciani and Pernigotti 1978: 41: "La figura centrale del pilastro nord è certamente una Madonna."

17   In three textile roundels, a king or commander is depicted in three-quarter pose, seated on a stool. One portrays Herod in the Massacre of the Innocents (Athens, Greek Folk Museum, inv. no. 1382, sixth–seventh century; Apostolaki 1932: 151–52, no. 1382 and fig. 119); the cycle of scenes in the other two roundels remains unclear (Riggisberg, Abegg-Stiftung, inv. no. 589a, eighth–tenth century, Schrenk 2004: 335–37: no. 154; Manchester, Whitworth Art Gallery, inv. no. T.8441a, Schrenk 2004: 337, photograph). In the latter two textiles, the person on the throne is dressed in a long dark-red tunic. Herod in the roundel and in Dayr Abu Hinnis is dressed in a military uniform. For the interpretation of the scenes in the Riggisberg and Manchester roundels, see van Loon 2008.

18   Bresciani in Bresciani and Pernigotti 1978: 41: "il contorno del viso,—l'ombreggiatura—, è segnato con un tretto spesso del pennello; poco resta del velo sulla testa; manca purtroppo tutta la parte centrale della pittura, ma dalla posizione del ginocchio sinistro e da quella della mano, su può forse avanzare l'ipotesi che la Madonna sorregesse un piccolo Gesù."

19   See, for example, a relief in the Coptic Museum (inv. no. 8006, sixth–seventh century, Gabra and Eaton-Krauss 2007: 111, no. 73) and paintings found in the Monastery of Apa Jeremiah at Saqqara (Quibell 1908: 64 and pls. XL–XLI; Quibell 1912: 23 and pls. XXI-A and XXIII-B).

20   Cleveland Museum of Art, inv. no. 67.144, sixth century (photograph in Bolman 2002: fig. 3.5).

21   In a domestic context, a fragmentary painting of Mary and child on a gemmed throne accompanied by archangels and an unidentified figure has been reconstructed on the northern wall of the courtyard of House D at Kom al-Dikka (Alexandria), which has been dated by the excavators to the first half of the sixth century (Rodziewicz 1984: 194–204 [figs. 226–36]; the reconstruction of the scene [fig. 236] can also be found in McKenzie 2007: 238, fig. 406).

22   Clédat 1904–1906; Clédat 1916; Maspero and Drioton 1931–43; Clédat 1999. Church of the Archangel Michael (formerly called the North Church): Clédat 1999: photos 196, 198–99; Bénazeth, forthcoming. Despite this abundant documentation, the series of saints have not been specifically studied.

23   For example in Cell A, north wall (Quibell 1908: 64 and pl. XLIV) and Cell F, east wall, niche (Quibell 1908: pls. LIV–LVI); Room 728, north wall (Quibell 1909: 16–17, pls. VI and XIV-3), Room 1764, north wall (Quibell 1912: 4 and pl. VII) and Room 1772 N ('refectory'), north wall (Quibell 1912: pl. X).

24 The famous painting of Saints Cosmas and Damian and their brothers from Wadi Sarga (now in London, BM EA 73139) is said to have come from a "villa about two miles north of Wadi Sarga" (Dalton 1916: 35).

25 Fragments testify to rows of standing saints among plant motifs and animals. Inscriptions identify Cosmas, Dan(iel), (Ma)ria, and Anr . . . (Witte-Orr 2010: 96, 99, fig. 19 and pl. 32c–d).

26 There was a similar composition in Chapel 1/southwest, east wall (Palanque 1906: 9–10 and pls. X–XII). Another example has been found in Chapel LVI, west wall: seven monks, two equestrian saints, a female saint in *orans* position, two equestrian saints; north wall: monk with staff, monk in *orans* position, four monks with staff, monk in *orans* position, two monks with staff (Clédat 1999: 156–59, photos 135–41, 144–45).

27 Cell A, north wall (Quibell 1908: 64 and pl. XLIV; Rassart-Debergh and Debergh 1981: 187–92; Wietheger 1992: 58–60, 74; Zibawi 2003: fig. 96).

28 Cf. Dijkstra 2008: 99 n. 64, who calls this identification "dubious."

29 The reliefs on both sides of the entrance to the main sanctuary (fig. 13.3, no. E) were hammered out, probably in order to contain wall paintings, but no traces of this decoration have been preserved: Dijkstra in von Pilgrim, Bruhn, Dijkstra, and Wininger 2006: 231, 237; Dijkstra 2008: 104, 106.

30 With many thanks to Magdalena Łaptaś and Dobrochna Zielińska for their bibliographical help.

31 In the church at Debeira only a fragment of the upper register survives, which belongs to Christ enthroned surrounded by the four living creatures (Godlewski 1992: 289).

32 Van Loon in Gabra and van Loon 2007: 32, with earlier literature; quote from a poem on Mary, in which she sings to her son, attributed to Ephraim the Syrian (d. 373) (Brock 1984: 60).

33 Godlewski 1992: 298 and fig. 28, who claims that the Virgin was standing. However, only part of the mural had survived and the position of the Virgin is not clear; she might just as easily be sitting. According to Godlewski, "It would appear that an identical composition was to be found in the same spot of the Abu Oda church." This painting has not been further studied and has disappeared.

34 For the other Nubian churches the context is not clear, but they were definitely not part of a monastery. There is no evidence that the churches of Naga al-Oqba and Wadi al-Sebua (Monneret de Villard 1935: 78–80 and fig. 66; 84–89 and figs. 71–72) were part of a settlement, though they were probably connected to local communities. Many thanks to Wlodzimierz Godlewski for this information.

35 Laferrière 2008: 22–32 and pls. III–IV; most recently Bolman 2008, with earlier literature.

36 Reports of ongoing research in the church under supervision of Karel C. Innemée (Leiden University) are published in the online journal *Hugoye* (http://syrcom. cua.edu/hugoye), with earlier literature. A series of photographs and a video of the discovery can be viewed at the website of the monastery: http://www.st-mary-alsourian.com/Monuments.

37 For the nursing Virgin, see Bolman 2005.

38 Bresciani in Bresciani and Pernigotti 1978: 41: "la forma degli occhi, quella della

bocca della Madonna richiamano una datazione al VI secolo, come anche il volto dei santi sul pilastro sud." It should be noted that in a footnote (n. 93) she points out the fragmentary nature of the paintings.

39 This date seems to be in agreement with two graffiti on the inside of the main entrance on the northern wall (fig. 13.3, no. B) left by a certain Kosma, which is only attested as a personal name from the sixth century onwards. For more details, see the entry for these graffiti (BN 2–3 [nos. 302–303]) in Dijkstra 2012.

40 Bresciani and Pernotti 1978: 41: "è altamente probabile, anche, che la chiesa, impiantata nel tempio di Isi madre divina di Horo, sia stata dedicata alla Madre di Dio, confermando la continuità religiosa, nell'ambiente de Assuan, tra Isi pagana e la Madre divina del cristianesimo."

41 Husson 1990: 132, referring to *P.Lond.* V 1731.45 and *P.Münch.* I 11.77; add the fragment listed under *P.Lond.* V 1850, which mentions a "priest of (the church of) the Holy Mary." For the Patermouthis archive, a bilingual family archive from Aswan that consists of papyri in Greek and Coptic ranging in date from 493 to 613, see Dijkstra 2007b, with references.

42 Cf. Papaconstantinou 2000: 90, who already remarks, "Cette hypothèse paraît à première vue fragile, car la Vierge est constamment représentée dans les églises coptes, sans en être pour autant la dédicataire," but still follows the identification proposed by Bresciani.

43 In the sixth century, the Gaianite Heresy caused rifts in the monastic communities in the Wadi al-Natrun. Monks opposed to the teachings of the Gaianites, who denied the Incarnation and thereby the role of the Virgin Mary as the Mother of God, built new monasteries dedicated to the Mother of God (van Rompay in Innemée and van Rompay 1998: 181–82).

44 A later addition (tenth century) is the representation of the Dormition and Triumph of the Virgin in the *khurus* (Innemée and Youssef 2007).

45 The walls are partly covered with a later layer of plaster with figurative paintings. Unfortunately, it is not known how old this dedication to the Virgin is. For the Nubian examples mentioned earlier, it is not known to whom these churches were dedicated.

46 *I.Philae* II 220.5–6, 221.4–5 (restored), not included in Papaconstantinou 2000.

47 Richter 2002: 128–35 (lines 6–8) for an improved text (cf. *SB Kopt.* I 302); Dijkstra 2008: 320 for an improved translation.

48 Richter 2002: 125–26, 135–36, esp. 135: "die Inschrift der Westkirche zeigt, daß auf der Insel Philae eine Kultadaption stattfand"; followed by Grossmann 2002: 465; Hahn 2008: 231.

49 See for this idea already Baumeister 1986: 187–88.

50 For a detailed refutation of Richter's arguments, see Dijkstra and van Ginkel 2004: 236. See also Van der Vliet 2005: 202 and Dijkstra 2008: 321–22.

51 The study by Papaconstantinou 2000 collects evidence for at least twenty-one churches dedicated to the Virgin Mary in Egypt from papyri and inscriptions. However, a comparable study of the material remains of the cult of Mary is still lacking. Sabrina Higgins, a student of the first author, is currently writing a PhD thesis on this topic.

14 Monastic Life in Makuria

Włodzimierz Godlewski

AFTER THE INCORPORATION of Noubadia at the end of the sixth century and the conclusion in 652 of a treaty (Baqt) at Dongola between Qalidurut, the king of Makuria, and Abdullahi abu Sarh, the governor of Egypt, the kingdom of Makuria comprised the river valley and adjoining territories between Aswan in the north and the Fifth Cataract on the Nile in the south. In the second half of the seventh century, the kingdom of Makuria was already a fully established state with an efficient administration and well-trained army, and with morale running high, fed effectively by the fettered Arab expansion. The peace treaty with the Arab governor of Egypt (caliphate) determined the common border in the region of Aswan for what turned out to be 520 years and guaranteed free trade between the neighboring countries.

Makurian policy toward Constantinople in the early years of the second half of the sixth century had already laid the foundations for the organization of the Makurian church, presumably with a metropolitan in Dongola. There is no doubt that the Christianization of Makuria was inspired by the royal court, but the course it took, as well as its social acceptance, escapes us because of insufficient sources.

The monasteries in Makuria presumably appeared in already organized form as part of the developing church administration. The anchorites' role in spreading Christianity in Nubia, raised in earlier studies, is poorly

Fig. 14.1. Apa Amone. Cathedral of Paulos, Pachoras (Faras) (Archive PCMA)

documented and unlikely. For the eremite movement to develop, it needs to be socially accepted and economically sustained, two factors hardly to be expected in Nubia before official Christianization. But on the walls of Pachoras (Faras) Cathedral have been preserved representations of the holy anchorites: Apa Amone (Michałowski 1974a: 113–16), Abba Onophrius (Michałowski 1967: 152–53, pl.74–75), and Abba Aaron (Michałowski 1974a: 154–56; Łukaszewicz 1982) (fig. 14.1). While the sources are still insufficient, it seems likely that monasticism in Makuria, and also in the kingdom of Noubadia in the sixth century, appeared in an already developed institutional form. Consequently, Makuria may be an interesting area for recognizing relatively early monastic complexes of the sixth to seventh centuries.

Archaeological findings have proved highly controversial, with the discoverers being overly eager to interpret as monasteries any larger structures or even single rooms with fragmentarily preserved inscriptions and wall paintings on the plastered walls. The list of suggested monasteries from the area of Makuria, and its northern province of Noubadia in particular, is relatively long in consequence, but almost entirely wrong or at least not very likely in the best of cases. W.Y. Adams was the first to bring attention to this point, recognizing as satisfactorily documented only the monastic complexes at Ghazali, Qasr al-Wizz, and al-Rahmal (Adams 1977: 478).

Newer studies by P. Jeute (1994) and J. Anderson (1999) also take into account the recent discoveries at Dongola—the monasteries on Kom D and Kom H—and at Hambukol. The monastery on Kom H, presumably the biggest in Dongola, has been identified by S. Jakobielski as the Monastery of the Holy Trinity (Jakobielski 2008). It was probably actually dedicated to Antony the Great as suggested by the funerary stela of the archbishop Georgios, who was earlier an archimandrite of this monastery. But the publisher of the text, A. Łajtar, emphasizes that it is not quite without doubt and one cannot say with all certainty that Georgios was the archimandrite of the monastery at Dongola (Łajtar 2002). The complexes on Kom D in Dongola and at Hambukol can quite likely be interpreted as monastic foundations, but the first is much destroyed, while the second still requires considerable effort to uncover it completely and interpret the findings.

The monasteries from Makuria are also present in the written sources, most fully in descriptions of churches and monasteries penned by the Coptic monk Abu al-Makarim (Vantini 1975: 324–25, 331), but also sporadically in the records of Arab historians and geographers describing Nubia. The information provided, however, is insufficient for an attempt to localize these establishments within Makuria. In the Greek and Coptic texts from sites in Makurian territories, monasteries are mentioned only intermittently: Monastery of Maria in Timaeie (Łajtar and Twardecki 2003: 303–309), monastery at Maurage (Jakobielski 1972: 76–78), monastery at Pouko (Kubińska 1974: 38–40; Łajtar and Pluskota 2001: 336–40), Monastery of Antony the Great (Łajtar 2002; Jakobielski 2008: 288–89), Monastery (?) of the Holy Trinity (Łajtar and Pluskota 2001: 340–54; Jakobielski 2008: 288–89).

All the existing evidence from Makuria is quite uniform in character. These monasteries are big, institutionally organized monastic compounds situated in the vicinity of episcopal settlements, indeed in their close neighborhood, near rivers, sometimes on a rocky river bank, but always isolated from the settlements themselves. Few of the monasteries mentioned in the sources are situated in a wadi or oasis. The modest archaeological evidence, interpreted soundly, confirms the conclusions that can be drawn from the written records. The monastery at Ghazali was built in a wadi and the monasteries at Qasr al-Wizz and on Kom H in Dongola were near big administration centers, including the church administration.

No monastic complex has so far been justifiably identified inside a settlement. Suggestions with regard to some of the buildings at Pachoras and Debeira West do not show satisfactory architectural evidence for their interpretation as a monastery—lack of a church, lack of a refectory with household area, or lack of a complex of furnished cells (Godlewski 2006b: 43–44).

Another suggestion that some of the settlements from the Late Period at Batn al-Hagar may have been monasteries is hardly convincing in the face of the absence of confirmation in the form of texts and funerary stelae of the monks.

The most fully investigated and interesting of the structures uncovered so far is the monastery connected with the episcopal seat at Pachoras. Once we skip the insufficiently documented monasteries, whose existence in the vicinity of the cathedral and in the area of the later pottery workshop and on the ruins of the Meroitic 'Western Palace' had been suggested by F. Ll. Griffith, K. Michałowski, and S. Jakobielski, we are left with the romantically named Qasr al-Wizz (Castle of the Geese), perhaps the best preserved at the time of discovery, a complex rising on a rocky river bank north of the town, connected to the nearby hermitage called the Grotto of the Anchorite. It is now under the water of Lake Nasser.

Pachoras: The Anchorite's Grotto (fig. 14.2.1–4)

On 4 December AD 738, the monk Theophilos put the finishing touches to the decoration of his hermitage, as he himself records in a colophon: "I am who has [hath] written these writings on my dwelling-place" (Griffith 1927: 88; Jakobielski 1972: 66). At the beginning of this colophon he described his objectives: "Do the kindness to pray for me charitably, every one who shall dwell in this abode, that God may bring my [life to an] end pleasing to him, and that I may find compassion in the day of my visitation." The Anchorite's Grotto, as F. Ll. Griffith was pleased to call this spot in Pachoras (Faras) (1927: 81–91), which can only be described as a hermitage, is the only well-known monument from the territory of the kingdom of Makuria that is important in its own right, apart from its role in local monastic life, because of the still underestimated recension of the *apophthegmata patrum* preserved inside it.

At the exit of a wadi, in the northwestern bend of the high rocky *gebel* extending west of Pachoras, one of the bishoprics of Makuria and an important center of Makurian (Nubian) administration and culture, there were four rock-cut tombs dating to the New Kingdom period. The third counting from the south, which is the most spacious inside, was turned into a hermitage in the first half of the eighth century, and presumably inhabited by one of the monks from the nearby Qasr al-Wizz monastery, the most important one in all of Pachoras. F. Ll. Griffith described this interior in the following terms:

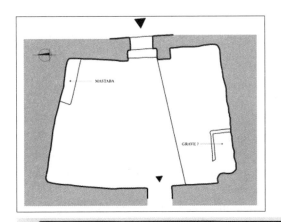

Fig. 14.2. Pachoras. The hermitage of Theophilos; plan and walls with localization of the texts (W. Godlewski and S. Maślak after F. Ll. Griffith 1927)

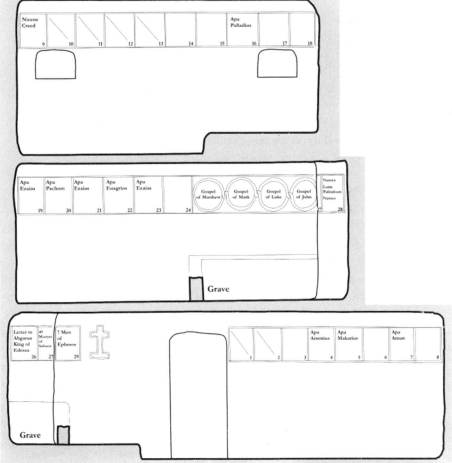

The chamber is of somewhat irregular shape, measuring over four meters from back to front, over five meters along the front wall, and six meters along the back wall. The floor at the south end is twenty centimeters higher than the rest and there is a raised mastaba left in the rock at the northeast corner. At either end of the north wall there appears to have been an oblong niche cut in the rock about 1.2 meters from the ground. That at the west end has been destroyed, the wall surface being much ruined there; at the other end the niche is about thirty centimeters from the east wall and is well preserved. The front wall north of the entrance was very thin, and the upper part has been cut through and afterwards built up with stones and mud, doubling the thickness. The stones along the top of this have been broken out again, but it can be seen that there had been a niche at each end, and lower down in the center a third niche remains complete. . . . In the south-west corner bricks have been laid to form the walls apparently of a grave. To judge by the magic texts written about it, the anchorite may have made the grave his bed during his lifetime. The roof of the chamber is about two meters above the floor. . . . But the most interesting memorial that the hermit has left us is the series of Coptic texts which he painted upon the whitewashed walls in square compartments like the pages of a book greatly magnified. (Griffith 1927: 81–82)

The inscriptions were recorded and copied by Sir J. G. Wilkinson (1835), Canon Weston (1844–46), Professors Sayce and Mahaffy (1895), Dr. Gardiner (1907), and finally by Griffith himself, who is also the author of the fullest publication of 1927. Some of the magic texts had been identified earlier by W. Crum and Pietschmann (Griffith 1927: 82).

The room decoration, on the east wall around the prayer niche as well as on the remaining walls where only Coptic texts were recorded in a regular frame and elaborate composition, is uniform and resembles a codex. There can be little doubt that the idea as well as perhaps the execution, not to mention the funds, must have come from the monk Theophilos. The decoration of the bottom part of the eastern wall and the plaited crosses on either side of a central niche, as well as birds presumably drinking from a vessel in the upper part, are not entirely Nubian in both form and style, and may be described as strongly Coptic-related in character.

The Coptic texts, preserved and recorded only in part, form three distinct groups: the biggest includes twenty-two parables and instructions of the Desert Fathers, obviously constituting a single redaction of the eighth century, a redaction that Theophilos had been in possession of also in codex form, supplemented with the Nicene creed, which he had put on the western wall, north of the entrance to the bedroom. Ending everything is the monk's colophon, which separates the parables from the magical texts that occupy the southwestern corner above the tomb. All the texts that were written here—the incipits of the four Gospels of Matthew, Mark, Luke, and John; the letter of Christ to Abgar, King of Edessa; the list of names of the forty martyrs of Sebaste; the names of the nails of Christ; and a list of the Seven Sleepers of Ephesus—follow the texts from the Coptic *Book of Ritual Power* from the collection in Leiden. Some of them are also recorded in other tombs at Qasr Ibrim, and most fully at Dongola, but the redaction from the hermitage in Pachoras is the earliest in Nubia so far.

It is noteworthy that the saintly monk Theophilos enjoyed the regard of the Makurites, as indicated by numerous graffiti left by pilgrims visiting his tomb and monk's cell for the next few centuries, at least until the eleventh to twelfth centuries. Visitors included church dignitaries (bishops, priests) as well as secular ones, including King Stephanos. Only one graffito, that of the monk Dioscoros, is dated, to AD 933.

Theophilos himself had a strong inner conviction about his religious mission and, presumably because of this, his intention was to leave a monument that would have for the Makurites the same kind of importance as the cell of Nephytios of Paphos for the Byzantine community (twelfth–thirteenth century) (Cormack 1985: 215–51). Theophilos probably decorated his hermitage when he was already at an advanced age, since the texts connected with his tomb feature the same redaction as the texts of the instructions of the Desert Fathers and were probably made at the same time.

It seems the saintly monk did not spend all his time in the cell. There is no domestic equipment in the hermitage, no kitchen or storage place for beverages and food articles. Hence, it may be assumed that Theophilos had spent a large part of his monastic life in the monastery, which was presumably not too far away from his hermitage, and that he depended on this monastery for his livelihood as a hermit. The closest monastery is the Qasr al-Wizz complex, rising on a rocky outcrop of the Nile river bank, closing from the north a plateau on which the city of Pachoras stood with its well-known Cathedral of Paul, erected around AD 707.

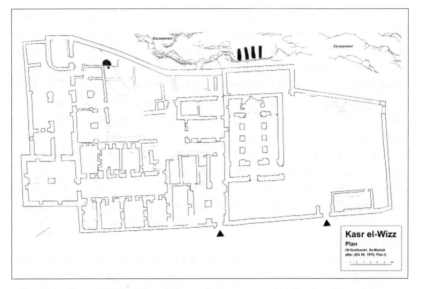

Fig. 14.3. Qasr al-Wizz. Plan of the early monastery (W. Godlewski and S. Maślak after G. Scanlon 1970 and 1972)

Pachoras: Qasr al-Wizz (fig. 14.3)

This site was fully cleared and recorded in 1965 by the Nubian Expedition of the Oriental Institute of the University of Chicago, directed by George T. Scanlon. A preliminary report of the excavations was published in two parts (Scanlon 1970; 1972). G.T. Scanlon had no doubt that the monastery he had uncovered at Qasr al-Wizz was connected with the bishopric at Pachoras.

Scanlon, who was aware of the discoveries made at Faras (Pachoras), where Michałowski believed the early monasteries were situated immediately next to the cathedral, assumed in his interpretation that the Qasr al-Wizz monastery must have functioned at a later date; this is presumably why he considered the already developed (enlarged) church on Qasr al-Wizz as part of a monastic complex and dated the establishment of the monastery to the second half of the ninth century or even the tenth century. Today, the residential structures north of the Cathedral of Paulos are no longer considered monastic. Indeed, even the so-called North Monastery, with a church on the upper floor, was a residence more than anything else. Thus, we cannot—and this has rather become a rule—identify any building within the Pachoras town .complex, whether from

F.Ll. Griffith's or K. Michałowski's excavations, that could have been a monastic establishment.

The location of the church on a high outcrop over the River Nile, far from the settlements, fairly excludes its role as a parish church. Scanlon makes no attempt to explain the function of the early church at Qasr al-Wizz, leaving it as an isolated structure, but because of its undoubtedly early date—he dates it to AD 550–750—he does not link it with the foundation of a monastery.

The Qasr al-Wizz church was a medium-sized three-aisle basilica with narthex and a tripartite eastern end, including an apse with three niches connected with the side rooms and opening toward the nave through a triumphal arch. The architectural decoration found inside it, including the capitals from the arch, the lintels, and the tympana, especially the tympanum with fish from above the entrance to the baptistery, link the monastery church very closely to the Cathedral of Aetios in Pachoras, the latter dated to the 630s (Godlewski 2006b: 33–41). The eastern end of the basilica at Qasr al-Wizz is set firmly in the architectural tradition of Pachoras and the neighborhood. A similar design may be noted in the North and South Churches at Adindan, Debeira West, that is, in the early foundations that are dated to the turn of the sixth century at the latest (Godlewski 1992: 282–84). The plan of the monastic basilica, the absence of a *synthronon* in the apse, and the architectural decoration assigns the building a date in the early seventh century, the time of the erection of the Cathedral of Aetios at Pachoras at the latest (circa AD 630).

There is little reason for the establishment of a church in such an isolated spot. The archaeological assemblage that comes from the excavations here, including both oil lamps from Aswan and locally produced ones, pottery, and metal objects, all indicate the existence of an early settlement in the area around the church. Scanlon mentions early ceramics found in many rooms of the currently excavated monastic complex. Thus, there are no justifiable counter-indications for considering the early basilica at Qasr al-Wizz as a monastery church right from the start and for connecting it with the establishment of the monastic compound as a whole in the first half of the seventh century. This is the date for the church itself, well before the Sassanids' raid on Egypt and their eventual expedition against Noubadia. Apart from the church, the monastic complex comprised a compact storied residential block with a central corridor and two rows of side cells, a refectory, and a household area situated in the immediate vicinity of the refectory and courtyard south of the church. The entire complex, considered by Scanlon as a homogeneous foundation of the ninth/tenth century, may be linked with the early church and dated to the seventh century.

The Qasr al-Wizz monastery is undoubtedly a homogeneous and harmoniously planned complex. In its principal part it clearly follows a functionally developed plan that had already been established in earlier times. Its closest analogy is the Dayr Anba Hadra (Monastery of St. Hatre) complex in Aswan, which is dated to the tenth century (Grossmann 2002: 363–65). The difference in the communication between the church and the residential block and refectory in Aswan is largely due to the monastic architecture being adapted to suit the topography of the two rock-cut terraces on which its stands. There are no parallels among the known early monasteries from Egypt. These monasteries had developed over long periods of time and their architecture reflects enormous complexity and little clarity in their urban arrangement (Wipszycka 2009). Thus, the monastery of Pachoras at Qasr al-Wizz, which dates most probably to the seventh century, is very important for a fuller understanding of the development of monastic architecture in the Valley of the Nile in early medieval times.

The monastery complex (original: 30.5 x 28.5 m; enlarged: 54.5 x 28.5 m) is composed of several units:

1. The western entry block: two rooms—west and east, with entrance to the corridor north–south.
2. The cell block: a long, vaulted corridor (12.5 x 2.8 m) 3.6 m high, with entrances to four vaulted cells on the west and three on the east, and a door into the refectory at the north end. At the south end there was an arched recess (about 0.5 m deep) with the shaft going to the upper story; on its east side there is a light-and-air shaft. Three arched niches are between the doorways in the east wall, which held lamps. The cells were irregular in dimensions and planning, but contained vaulting—inside a small raised platform which went around the cell—and a series of arched niches in the walls.
3. Stairway: entered from the vestibule to the second-floor corridor and cells, most probably eight in number.
4. Vestibule E with a dome, accessed from the courtyard.
5. The refectory: an asymmetrically quadrangular room (5.75 x 7.25 m) with a central pillar (1.1 x 0.75 m) and two pilasters on the

north and south walls. The room was covered by four domes, and
had four windows: two in the north wall and two in the west wall.
On the pavement there were four circular mud-brick benches
(height about 43 cm, width about 35 cm) 1.5–1.8 m in diameter—so five or six monks could be accommodated on each one.
Two entrances, one from the cell block and one from the kitchen.

6. The service area: to the east of the refectory there was a corridor
   with two rooms on its north side with entrances from it, giving
   entry to the south to an open area with two ovens (1.2–1.5 m
   deep) on a raised platform and the latrine (2.9 x 3.1 m) in the
   southeast corner of the monastery.
7. A courtyard with the cellar, hewn into the *gebel* (2.0 x 5.0 m;
   height 2.0–1.5 m).
8. The building attached to the northern wall of the church, most
   probably administrative in function.

Monastery of St. Antony the Great (Kom H) in Dongola

The monastery on Kom H, known also as the Monastery of the Holy Trinity,
stood at the western edge of the city's burial grounds, about 1.5 kilometers
northeast of the Citadel. It was established by one of the first bishops of
Dongola, most likely as early as the beginning of the seventh century. The
dedication to St. Antony the Great is recorded on the stela of Archbishop
Georgios, while the dedication to the Holy Trinity is evidenced in numerous
epigraphic materials from monastic contexts (Jakobielski 2008), but referring
rather to a church, very likely a cathedral. The well-researched monastery
at Pachoras (Qasr al-Wizz), believed to be founded by Bishop Aetios, is a
close parallel to the monastic complex at Dongola and the theory cannot be
excluded that it was actually patterned on it, just as the Cathedral of Aetios
shares many features with the first Cathedral in Dongola.

The Monastery of St. Antony the Great in Dongola consisted of a
church—a three-aisled, domed basilica, a building situated north of the
church, and a complex of cells in the northwestern part of the monastery,
all surrounded by an enclosure wall. The economic base of the monastery
was concentrated in the northwestern part of the complex.

The monastery church (fig. 14.4), which has been explored completely,
proved to be a three-aisled domed basilica of rather long proportions, the
central tower with a wooden dome in the nave resting on four stone pillars
It seems to have been founded in the second half of the sixth century.[1] The

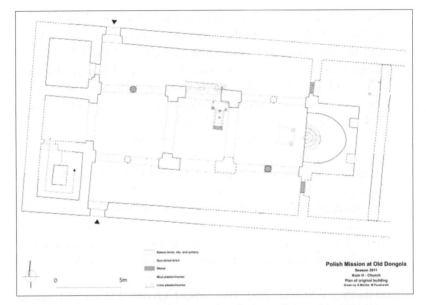

Fig. 14.4. Dongola. Kom H. Monastic Church (S. Maślak, archive PCMA)

apse with *synthronon* and flanking *pastophories* at the east end and the tri-partite western end with a staircase in the southwestern corner, combined with two entrances into the naos, from the north and from the south, were typical of sacral complexes that first became popular in the capital from the second half of the sixth century. The sanctuary occupied the eastern end of the nave, where it was screened off from the rest of the church. The eastern part of the church, behind the apse, was turned into a burial place, similar to the monastery church at Qasr al-Wizz. Graves were also noted in the sanctuary itself, including the tomb of Joseph, bishop of Syene, who died in AD 668. Further research is still needed to permit fuller interpretation of the church and the graves.

To the western wall of the church, at its south corner, was attached structure S, composed originally of two rooms, S.1–2, connected to each other by one entrance at the south wall of S.2 (fig. 14.5). Some later con-structions are also clear, especially in the western part of room S.3. Inside room S.2b there was a bench, and inside room S.1 an altar inside the east-ern niche. In the pavement of S.1 was cut the tomb of a man. The walls of all the rooms of the structure were covered with paintings, over sixty graffiti, and forty-three drawings or scratched designs. It was most likely

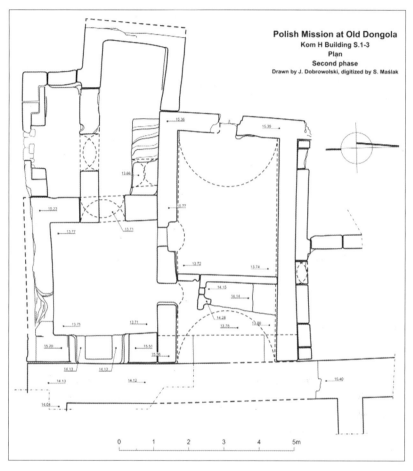

Polish Mission at Old Dongola
Kom H Building S.1-3
Plan
Second phase
Drawn by J. Dobrowolski, digitized by S. Maślak

Fig. 14.5. Dongola. Kom H. Building S, cell and chapel of Anna By (archive PCMA)

the dwelling place of a holy man, probably Anna By, connected to a small oratory, inside which at the end of his life he was buried; his cell was later frequently visited, as signatures indicate (Jakobielski 1993: 306–307, 318, 326, 328–33). It became a commemorative chapel dedicated to Anna By (fig. 14.6), one of the Makurian saints.

The monastery also had an extensive complex of buildings in the northwestern part of the complex, the so-called Northwest Annex, which was already outside the walls and which presumably served the needs of pilgrims and, from the eleventh century, also the bishops of Dongola.

Fig. 14.6. Dongola. Kom H. Building S, graffiti (W. Godlewski, archive PCMA)

Excavated completely, it has been provisionally published. It consisted of a set of rooms of a sacral and administrative nature, repeatedly enlarged, combined with a mausoleum of Dongolan bishops incorporated in the northern part. Its interpretation as a *xenodochion* (a guesthouse for visitors), proposed by B. Żurawski (1999) and supported by S. Jakobielski (2001: 160), needs to be justified more fully in research, but even now it raises serious doubts. Without prejudging any final conclusions on this question, I would like to point out that in connection with the burial place of Archbishop Georgios (d. 1113) and the bishops of the twelfth and thirteenth centuries interred in crypts T.26–T.28, the commemorative function of the northern part of the Northwest Annex appears to be much more evident.

Mausoleum of Bishops (fig. 14.7)

The Northwest Annex of the monastery on Kom H, which is a very complicated structure that underwent repeated rebuilding and enlargement (Jakobielski 2001), incorporates a set of chambers that can be identified as a bishops' mausoleum (Godlewski 2006a). This part, which occupies the northwestern end of the Annex and demonstrates an evident liturgical function, was connected to three funerary crypts (nos. T.26–T.28) containing communal burials. The complex was created by adapting existing architecture (rooms 4, 5, and 7) and adding new units (nos. 1, 2, and 3). From a functional point of view, it was definitely a single complex, but it appears to have been built in two stages at the very least. The chronology of architectural development need not be discussed here in detail, for it does not change the interpretation at all, having bearing only on the dating of particular chambers. The three crypts can be presumed to have been in use simultaneously from at least 1113, the year that Archbishop Georgios died and was interred in the crypt prepared for him (T.28), through the second half of the fourteenth century. The number of burials indicates that the crypts remained in use for about 250 to three hundred years. Some later burials were made in other places or according to the wishes of the individual. Access to all the burial chambers remained easy throughout this time.

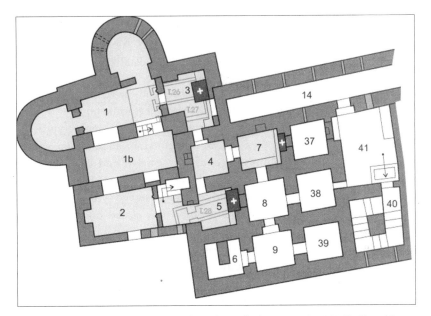

Fig. 14.7. Dongola. Kom H. The chapel over bishops' tombs (W. Godlewski, archive PCMA)

Texts in Greek and Coptic were recorded on the walls of crypt T.28; the long-lived Georgios, archbishop of Dongola, may have also been responsible for their redaction as they are highly unique. They were studied by Adam Łajtar and Jacques van der Vliet in 2010, and the publication is in preparation.

On the western wall, above the entrance to the crypt, the following texts are to be found: introductory invocation (colophon ?) in the form of a short two-line Greek text; the beginning and end of the Gospel of St. Matthew (1:1–2; 28:20); a text in a magical alphabet; twenty-four *nomina sacra* in numerical cryptograms; list of names.

On the northern wall: Gospel of St. Mark; *Oracio Mariae ad Bartos*; list of names; palindrome: *sator-areto-tenet-opera-rotas*.

On the eastern wall: Gospel of St. Luke; *Transitus Mariae* in Coptic.

On the southern wall: Gospel of St. John; Dormition of the Virgin (Euodius of Rome) in Coptic; palindrome.

Chambers 1 and 3 were used undoubtedly as a mausoleum with crypts T.26 and T.27. The eastern of the two rooms (no. 3) acted as a sanctuary with an altar set against the east wall. Room 1 to the west was a kind of naos, separated from the sanctuary by an altar screen, a kind of *templum*, built of brick.

The arched entrance to the sanctuary had relief pilasters in the reveals and a crowning tympanum (Jakobielski and Scholz 2001: pl. XXIII.1–2). An ambo erected of sandstone blocks stood under an arcade to the right of the altar screen. The openings of the funerary shafts leading to the crypts were located inside the naos, in front of the altar screen. The right side of the screen bears the impression of a funerary stela that was removed at some point.

Chambers 2 and 5 constituted a mausoleum connected with crypt T.28. The eastern of the two rooms (no. 5) contained an altar, set up in the blocked passage to a neighboring room. The eastern end of chamber 2 was set apart by an altar screen that had a centrally positioned door with decoration in the form of pilasters and a partly preserved tympanum (Jakobielski and Scholz 2001: pl. XX). The ambo was placed on the left, just beyond the entrance to the sanctuary. Next to it, immured in the east wall, was the funerary stela of Archbishop Georgios.

The only entrance to both commemorative chapels was in the south wall of chamber 2, which acted as a naos.

The two sanctuaries (rooms 3 and 5) communicated through chamber 4 with the *prothesis* furnished with an altar in room 7. Above the altar there was a mural depicting Christ with a chalice and next to the representation the text, in Greek, of five prayers said during the presanctified liturgy (Łajtar 1995).

The key issue is determining the status of the persons interred in the three crypts. In the case of T.28, there is no doubt that it was prepared for Georgios and that the texts of 'Great Power' inscribed on its walls may have been his personal choice. Georgios was a man of exceptional status in the church of Makuria, but presumably also at the royal court, as suggested by the epithets on his funerary stela (Łajtar 2002). In view of his social position, it is less than likely that the other men interred with him in the crypt were not, like him, bishops or archbishops. Crypts T.26 and T.27, which would have to be earlier considering the structural logic of the complex, may have been used as burials for bishops as well. The founder of the crypts and the entire architectural framing for these tombs was likely to have been commemorated in the lost funerary stela that was once immured in the altar screen. It could have been the first archbishop of Makuria, Victor, who is evidenced in the middle of the eleventh century. Just as easily it could have been any other bishop of Dongola in the eleventh century. A similar mausoleum, interring in a single crypt a number of bishops from the eleventh and twelfth centuries, was preserved next to the Cathedral of Petros in Pachoras. There, however, the funerary stelae of all the interred bishops were immured into the wall above the entrance to the crypt, while the three commemorative chapels were definitely more modest in appearance. At Pachoras (Godlewski 2006b: 141–44), as well as at Dongola (Żurawski 1999), tomb equipment included oil lamps, *qullae*, and amphorae. This new form of tomb furnishing appears to concern bishops foremost, as confirmed by the bishops' tombs of the eleventh to fourteenth centuries, located east of the cathedral in Pachoras.

Ghazali

The monastery in Ghazali was built on the rock in Wadi Abu Dom, some sixteen kilometers from where it joins the Nile. The massive wall, in a good state of preservation, some four meters high, enclosed the whole complex and was constructed with large blocks of local schist. The main entrance to the monastery was on the north side, facing the wadi. It was elaborately constructed with an in-turn of the wall on both sides of the gateway and was spanned by an arch built of dressed sandstone blocks. The other four gateways were of simpler construction. One of them leads to the nearest monastic cemetery. The monastery consists of a church, a group of stone-built buildings, and a number of badly preserved mud-brick constructions (Shinnie and Chittick 1961).

The church was built of small blocks of dressed sandstone to the height of about 3.0 meters and red brick in the upper parts of the walls, on the Makurian plan of an elongated three-aisled basilica with a small central dome. The naos was divided by two rows of pillars after the rebuilding of the church, but originally by granite columns. The interior was paved with sandstone slabs. The apse was filled with a *synthronon* and at the eastern part of the nave there was the sanctuary with an altar and screen.

The monastic buildings are located to the west and northwest side of the church. All of them are constructed of rough slabs and blocks of schist, with vaults built of dry mud bricks. The function of the buildings is not known for sure; because of the limited scale of the excavations, they were never finished. The building to the west of the church could be the dormitory. On the north side of it there is a square room with a central pillar, equipped with circular benches. It was recognized as the refectory.

Two well-constructed buildings on both sides of the main entrance were most probably used by visitors to the monastery.

Notes

1 In the 2011 season of the works at Dongola the new investigations of the monastic church clarified its original plan and date of its foundation.

15 Christian Aswan in the Modern Era and the History of Its Cathedral

Metropolitan Hedra

NOWADAYS THE BOUNDARIES of the diocese of Aswan are the same as the governorate. It extends from al-Sebaiya (Edfu) in the north to the city of Abu Simbel in the south. This makes Aswan the second governorate in size in Egypt and the largest diocese in size.

In the past, the governorate of Aswan was divided into several districts, but as for the church, it consisted of six dioceses, many of which disappeared due to political and local factors. In the middle of the fourteenth century, there still existed two bishop's sees: Aswan and Ibrim. Bishop Michael is considered the last bishop of the city of Aswan; he attended the making of Holy Chrism in the Hanging Church in Cairo in the days of Pope John VIII (1300–20). After that the city was totally destroyed and lost its place as the southern border point between the years of 1336 and 1412, due to the struggle between two big tribes, al-Hawarra in Upper Egypt and al-Kenz in Nubia.

During the modern era we find the name of Bishop Gabriel as a bishop of Esna and the borders (Aswan), who participated in the making of Holy Chrism with Pope Peter VII, known as 'al-Gawli,' in 1820.

Then came Bishop Michael, the bishop of Esna and the borders (Aswan), who was born in Luxor. One of his most important accomplishments was the renovation of the Monastery of St. Pachomius in Edfu in 1832. This is the reason that the monastery was known at that time by the name of "Church of Archangel Michael," after Bishop Michael. Another of his accomplishments was building the old church of the Virgin Mary in Aswan city. Also in his time the icon of St. Hatre and his disciple was written by the Jerusalem iconographer, Astasy (Anastasi) al-Rumi, who wrote on it "Lord, recompense in the kingdom of heaven him who toiled."

Bishop Michael was among those who signed the document of ordination for Father David al-Antuni, from the Monastery of St. Antony. In 1854, Father David became Pope Cyril IV and was known as the "Father of Reform."

After the death of Bishop Michael came Bishop Matthaws; he attended the Holy Synod in 1862 that prevented Mark, bishop of al-Buhera, from being nominated to the patriarchate. He died in 1873 and his body was buried next to his predecessor at the Monastery of St. Matthew the Poor, or Dayr al-Fakhuri, near Esna.

Bishop Mark, bishop of Esna and Aswan, stayed in Esna between 1879 and 1919. He was elevated to the rank of metropolitan on 25 October 1896. When he found that the city had lost its importance through the migration of many Coptic families to the city of Luxor because tourists were being drawn there by its important antiquities, he transferred his seat to Luxor in 1919.

Prior to that, in 1889, the cabinet of the Egyptian government decided the following:

1. The abolition of the governorate of Esna and the establishment of a new governorate with the name of 'Governorate of the Border Aswan.'
2. The attachment of Esna to the city of Qena.
3. The governorate of the Border to consist of Edfu with Aswan as a capital of al-Kenuz, 'Nubia.'

In 1895 Bishop Mark started to build a new church in Aswan city in the name of the Virgin Mary. It was completed by the beginning of 1896. The story of the church was reported in *al-Haq* ('Truth') magazine in its 29 February 1896 issue as follows:

The old church was going to fall down and its location wasn't suitable, so the Copts decided to buy a plot of land in order to build the new church on it, but they faced many difficulties that lasted for a long time, as many people claimed that this matter was illegal, as that plot of land had been a cemetery and had been bought for building a house, not a church. With the support of Ali Haydar, new governor of Aswan at that time, the Copts began to build it and they soon were going to finish it. This church is very large, more than 2,000 square cubits. This made Bishop Mark stay more than two months in Aswan in order to finish its building.

In 1901 Bishop Mark established the church of the Virgin Mary in Edfu with the contributions of the wealthy people in the city, under the supervision of Father Paul, the representative of the diocese, and his son Father Mark.

Also worthy of mention is that in 1902 Iqladious Labib, the author of the *Coptic Language Dictionary* and editor of many of the Coptic Church liturgical manuals, visited Aswan with some priests from Edfu and wrote about this visit in the 13 December 1902 issue of *al-Haq* as follows: "Every year the priests of Aswan always celebrate the Holy Mass on the 12th of Kiyahk at the Monastery of St. Hatre (Dayr Anba Hadra), which the foreigners call the Monastery of St. Simeon, commemorating the departure of St. Hatre, who was in Aswan according to the *Lives of the Saints*."

This is considered an important testimony that the Copts of Aswan in the early twentieth century celebrated with prayers the feast of their great saint, St. Hatre, on 12 Kiyahk in a church in his monastery on the western bank of Aswan. Although the monastery is currently under the jurisdiction of the Supreme Council of Antiquities, the Holy Mass is usually performed at the church every year.

On 10 December 1902, at the opening ceremony of the Aswan Dam, Pope Cyril V was one of the invitees. He then appointed Father Bisada Boules as hegumen of the new Church of the Virgin Mary, after he transferred from a church in Girga.

Several years prior to 1913, Bishop Mark had founded a primary and preparatory Coptic school in Aswan; he later established a section for secondary students at the same school. Pope Cyril V visited it in January 1904. He also founded the Church of Archangel Michael in al-Redisiya, near Edfu, and later, in 1918, another church of Archangel Michael was founded in Daraw, Aswan.

After the bishop's seat was transferred from Esna to Luxor, Bishop Mark became responsible for Luxor and Aswan in 1919 and his title was Bishop of Luxor, Esna, and Aswan. He lived in Luxor for fifteen years until his passing on 24 February 1934 after fifty-four years as a bishop.

Several pastoral actions occurred in Aswan during his era, as follows:

1. In 1921, the Church of St. George was founded in Kom Ombo (al-Fabriqua).
2. In 1930, another Church of St. George was founded in Kom Ombo, near the railway station.

Bishop Mark was succeeded by Bishop Basilius in the bishopric of Luxor, Esna, and Aswan. He reigned for eleven years, between October 1936 and October 1947. During the time of Pope Yusab II, Bishop Basilius was elevated to the rank of metropolitan in September 1946. He was known for his honesty and piety, and his love of serving people. He was interested in education, especially the Coptic schools, institutions, associations, and charities, which he used to supervise himself. He also cared about serving the small villages and encouraged Sunday schools. He even used to give lessons in Sunday schools, which the children loved. He was buried next to his predecessor, Bishop Mark, in the Virgin Mary Church in Luxor.

Around 1947, the Church of the Virgin Mary in Edfu was renovated, and in 1948 the foundation for the Archangel Michael church began in the area of Benben in Kom Ombo. However, the Holy Masses did not begin until several years later.

Before it was divided into two dioceses, the last Bishop of Luxor, Esna, and Aswan was Bishop Abraham, between April 1949 and November 1974. He was ordained a bishop during the time of Pope Yusab II, and he used to visit the people of his diocese frequently.

The following are some of his pastoral accomplishments in the diocese:

1. Foundation of the Church of St. George in 1959 in al-Kelh, west of Edfu, which was consecrated later.
2. On 19 January 1960, he celebrated the first Holy Mass in Archangel Michael Church in Benben, which was founded in 1948.
3. On Sunday 30 April 1961, he consecrated St. George Church in al-Kelh, west of Edfu. He also promoted its priest, Father Ghattas Atallah.
4. On 18 March 1962, he consecrated the old building of the English Episcopal church next to the Cataract Hotel in Aswan under the name of the Church of Archangel Michael, according to the owner's wishes, to prevent it from being repossessed.

5. In January 1965, the Church of the Virgin Mary in al-Besiliya, Edfu collapsed and it was rebuilt. He consecrated it in late January 1969.

6. In 1967, St. George's Church began operating in al-Karor near the Aswan Dam, to the south of Aswan, first as an altar, then as a complete church in 1970.

7. On the day of the Assumption of the Virgin Mary, 22 August 1970, the first Mass was conducted in the Church of the Virgin Mary in al-Hurriya, north of Kom Ombo. It is worthy of mention that a blessed man by the name of Lamie Doss did his best to build it, on an area of 1,056 square meters. It was consecrated in 1972.

8. In 1971, the building of St. Mark's Church began as a temporary altar in al-Seil al-Gadid, Aswan. In the same year the building of the Virgin Mary Church began, also as a temporary altar, in al-Nagagra, south of Kom Ombo.

9. In 1972, the Church of the Virgin Mary was founded in Nag al-Fouza, al-Redisiya Bahari, Edfu.

10. On 17 July 1973, a presidential decree was issued to establish both St. Mark's church in al-Seil al-Gadid in Aswan and that of the Virgin Mary in Nag al-Fouza, Edfu.

So, after several churches and altars were built in his time and he ordained many clergymen, Bishop Abraham moved to the Heavenly Glory at the age of sixty-five on the morning of Saturday 23 November 1974, after twenty-six years of serving his people. His body was buried with large crowds in attendance in St. Antony's church.

On the morning of Friday 13 June 1975, Aswan was honored by the visit of Pope Shenouda III, who went to the Church of Archangel Michael, prayed the thanksgiving prayer, and met with priests and members of the church council and its servants to discuss their views on the selection of a new bishop to be ordained. They all agreed on the choice of Father Georgios al-Suriani as bishop of the diocese of Aswan. This was a great turning point in the history of the diocese, as he became the first bishop of Aswan alone, after more than six hundred years of Aswan's being part of a larger diocese that also included Luxor and Esna. The borders of the See of Aswan are now the same as those of the governorate.

On Pentecost Day, 22 June 1975, Bishop Hedra was ordained as the Bishop of Aswan. After the usual spiritual retreat, he arrived in Aswan accompanied by bishops Bishoy, Timothy, and Sarabamoun. He was enthroned there on 8 August 1975.

The new bishop began his ministry with the reconstruction of the Monastery of St. Pachomius in Hagr Edfu in 1976. This occurred after the second blessed visit of Pope Shenouda III to Edfu, in which His Holiness gave his advice about what should be done to revive monastic life there, architecturally and spiritually. The work began in earnest and continued until the Holy Synod recognized the Monastery of St. Pachomius on 26 March 1980, making it the tenth monastery of the Coptic Orthodox Church. On 22 May 1980, at the St. Bishoy Monastery Center in Cairo, Pope Shenouda III changed the titles of the monks residing at the time at the monastery from Anba Bishoy to Pachomi, thus making them officially belong to the Monastery of St. Pachomius.

On 13 November 1988, the first monk from the Monastery of St. Pachomius to be ordained as bishop was appointed by His Holiness Pope Shenouda III as Bishop Tomas of al-Kouseya, Asyut. The second bishop to be ordained from the monastery was Bishop Takla of Dishna.

The following are some of Bishop Hedra's pastoral accomplishments in the new diocese:

1. In 1975, St. George's Church was founded in al-Hagz south (al-Mahamid), Edfu.
2. In 1976, the cornerstone of St. Mark's Church was laid in Aswan in al-Seil al-Gadid.
3. In May 1978, the old Church of the Virgin Mary was renovated in Aswan and services resumed.
4. In 1982, the building of the new Monastery of St. Hatre began next to the ancient one, the area of which was less than the area it occupies today. Many cells were built, with a hermitage, a small church, and a fence surrounding the entire area.
5. On 1 January 1985, the rebuilding of the old church of the Monastery of St. Pachomius in Edfu was completed, retaining all its old characteristics.
6. Many other projects for the rebuilding and expansion of churches in the diocese were carried out. The most recent was a church in Abu Simbel.

The Story of Archangel Michael Cathedral

At the beginning of the twentieth century, Aswan, being a city of little significance, had a small population and only one Coptic Orthodox church, under the name of the Virgin Mary. The Cathedral of the Archangel Michael was at first an Anglican church, with an adjoining villa, built on a land area of about 7,000 square meters. It was built by the British army in the 1920s following its purchase from the Egyptian government by the Anglican Church (or Church of England). After the British army left Egypt, the Episcopal Church decided to sell the church and the land. They contacted the Coptic Charity Association in the city to buy it, seeing that the Coptic Orthodox community outnumbered all the other Christian groups in the city.

15.1 Aswan Cathedral: Somers Clarke memorial (Howard Middleton-Jones)

During the sale negotiations, Mrs. Monira Michael Faltas, a wealthy Copt in Aswan, decided to buy all the church land under the name of the Coptic Orthodox Church, but suddenly, at the contract signing, she registered everything under her own name, and thus she became the outright owner. The contract was registered in 1953 with a low purchase price of LE1,850 because the land was supposed to have been given to the Coptic Church. She kept the land for herself, residing in the villa or priest's residence and closing the church for eight years.

In 1961 she became worried about losing the plot of land, as the official documents stated that this villa was assigned as a house for the priest of the church. Any changes in the conditions would revert the land to the government. Moreover, one of the local officials desired the land. So she asked Bishop Abraham to dedicate the church, but she retained all the management of the church herself, and also kept the priest's house for herself. In the same year a room for making the holy bread was added, as were toilets for the congregation. Then two rooms and a small hall were added to create a bishop's residence. Bishop Abraham consecrated the church under the name of Archangel Michael in 1962. All this new construction led Mrs.

Faltas to sue the church to demolish the newly constructed rooms and to prevent them from controlling the land forever.

The court cases lasted for about a quarter of a century. During this period, the church and the Copts suffered a great deal, especially in 1981 when the sentence was handed down against the church, ordering it to give the land back to the lady and to demolish the new construction. These included the two rooms that became the bishop's residence after 1975 and the baptism room. Many attempts at reconciliation were made before and after the new bishop arrived in 1975, but to no avail.

When the sentence became effective in 1984, the Copts of Aswan protested by staging a sit-in at the church for ten days, praying day and night with daily holy masses until the solution came from heaven: Mrs. Faltas agreed to sell the church, with strict conditions, for LE1,250,000, with all the money to be paid to her within one year. The Church acquiesced to these severe conditions, which were seemingly impossible at the time. The Church had never before collected such a large sum of money in one year; indeed, the diocese's annual income was scarcely LE100,000.

However, during the contract registration process, the lady imposed an additional LE500,000. In addition to this, a sum of LE200,000 was also assessed as a registration fee. Thus the total cost of the purchase was about LE1,950,000. Through God's grace, this enormous sum was collected within one year. Many people contributed to raising this sum of money: His Holiness Pope Shenouda III, some bishops, Copts throughout Egypt, and also emigrant Copts. But the people of Aswan sacrificed the most: some women and children gave jewels, some even gave their wedding jewelry. It was a great joint effort of love, donation, and sacrifice preceded by prayers, tears, Holy Communions, and great efforts by all the priests of the diocese. "The Lord hath done great things for us; whereof we are glad" (Psalm 126:3).

The construction began in 1996 with the demolition of the old church built originally by the British army. A new church, three times as big, was erected in its place according to Coptic architectural conventions, becoming the second largest cathedral in Egypt after that of St. Mark in Anba Ruways in Cairo. On 8 August 2000 the great opening ceremony of the cathedral was held, coinciding with the twenty-fifth anniversary of Bishop Hedra as bishop of Aswan. The first Holy Mass was performed at the cathedral on the morning of Wednesday 9 August 2000, in the presence of their Graces:

15.2. Aswan Cathedral exterior, taken from the River Nile (Howard Middleton-Jones)

15.3 Aswan Cathedral at night (Howard Middleton-Jones)

Bishop Bishoy, secretary of the Holy Synod and bishop of Damietta
and Kafr al-Sheikh
Bishop Benjamin of al-Menoufia
Bishop Sawiris of the Monastery of the Virgin Mary
Bishop Matteos of the Monastery of the Syrians
Bishop Pakhom of Sohag
Bishop Serapion of Los Angeles
Bishop Thomas of al-Kouseya
Bishop Sharobeem of Qena
Bishop Bemen of Qus, Naqada, and the neighboring areas.

On Sunday 19 March 2006 (10 Baramhat AM 1723) the altars and the
baptistery of the new Aswan Cathedral were consecrated by His Holiness
Pope Shenouda III. In attendance on him were thirty-four metropolitans
and bishops along with many monks and priests. He also elevated Bishop
Hedra to the rank of metropolitan. Then he laid the cornerstone for the
new diocese building near the cathedral.

15.4 Aswan Cathedral interior (Howard Middleton-Jones)

15.5 Aswan Cathedral: archangel doors (Howard Middleton-Jones)

16 The Word and the Flesh

Karel C. Innemée

Much has been said and written about Christian painting in Nubia since the discoveries of the 1960s during the UNESCO campaign and the subsequent campaigns in places such as Dongola.

It is remarkable that Christian Nubia is the theme of a conference that has been organized by two Coptic organizations and the Coptic Church. It almost forces us to ask the question: how Coptic was Nubia and can we consider Christian culture in Nubia as an extension of Egyptian Christianity?

In almost all respects, Nubia should be considered separate from Christian Egypt. Politically Makuria and Noubadia (later merged into one state) were independent from Egypt, and linguistically and ethnically Nubia was—and in many respects still is—different as well. In other words, there are numerous elements that define Nubian identity and distinguish it from that of Christian Egypt. When it comes to ecclesiastical hierarchy and dogmatic adherence, the situation is more complex. Nubia was converted to Christianity around the middle of the sixth century, when the schism between Chalcedonians and non-Chalcedonians was already a fact. Initially both confessions existed side by side in Nubia, the kingdom of Makuria being Chalcedonian and Noubadia non-Chalcedonian. After the unification of the two kingdoms in the course of the seventh century, the Nubian Church came under authority of the patriarchate of Alexandria, a somewhat surprising development since the kingdom of Makuria, apparently the dominant partner in the unification,

was originally Chalcedonian in denomination. This must have had consequences for the liturgy celebrated in Nubian churches. Although a complete
Nubian liturgy has not survived, we know that certain parts were in Coptic.

We can consider Christian ritual, and more specifically the liturgy, the
raison d'être for church architecture, and, as a consequence, much of its decoration. This means that in interpreting Nubian mural paintings we should take
into account the contents of the Nubian liturgy, even if our knowledge concerning it is very limited. There is no doubt that Nubian church decoration
is different from Coptic art, in both style and iconography, but by looking for
traces of Coptic influence in it we might be able to detect common elements
in Coptic and Nubian liturgy. A complicating factor is that not all paintings
in a church necessarily have a symbolic connection with the liturgy. Some
paintings have a devotional function and are comparable to icons as objects
of veneration. In some cases this is clear from the stains of soot and oil under
or in the lower part, indicating the use of oil lamps. On the other hand this
does not exclude a liturgical symbolism; images can have a double function.

In spite of its ecclesiastical allegiance to the patriarchate of Alexandria,
Christian Nubia had a culture of its own, both in the religious and in the
profane sense. An important factor in this independence was the fact that
Makuria was an autonomous kingdom, whereas Egypt was part of the
Byzantine Empire and, beginning in AD 642, under Arab Muslim rule. The
conversion of Nubia was a Byzantine initiative, and in spite of the ties with
Alexandria, Nubia never really lost contact with Constantinople. The relationship between state and church in Nubia resembled much more the
situation in Byzantium than in Egypt, and this circumstance had its expression in the arts and rituals at the court in Dongola. The Makurian king and
his court must have looked to the Byzantine court as their great example,
and as a result, both secular and liturgical costumes, as well as ornaments
and official titles, were borrowed from the Byzantine tradition (Frend 1968;
Innemée 1992: 164–66; Innemée 1995b).

From its independent position, Nubia could absorb both Coptic and
Byzantine influences. Much has been said and written about this matter, but
here I would like to discuss it again in the light of church ritual.

Church rituals can be seen as the metaphorical reenactment of a number
of biblical events and ritualized expression of theological dogmas and beliefs.
Most mural paintings in churches are therefore not to be seen primarily as
decoration, but as functional expressions of ideas, a backdrop to and integral
part of the rituals performed in church. That implies that knowledge of these

rituals is necessary to come to a full interpretation of these paintings and, vice versa, these paintings can provide information about rituals performed and celebrated.

In Byzantine church decoration a certain system was developed in the post-iconoclastic era, in accordance with the outcomes of the Second Council of Nicea and patristic ideas about the symbolism of liturgy and church architecture. First of all, one can consider the images a pictorial narrative, showing the believer what he also hears in the readings from the scriptures, mostly the New Testament. Apart from this, according to Otto Demus, the decorative scheme comprises a number of symbolic aspects:

1. In the first place, the church is considered a miniature image of creation, with the dome as an image of heaven and the lower parts of the church as representations of earthly topography.
2. In the second place, the building offers topographical parallels with the holy places in Palestine; in this way the believer can make a symbolic pilgrimage by contemplating the events depicted.
3. Church decoration provides a calendar of the main feasts of the liturgical year. The *dodekaorton*, the series of twelve main feasts, are the core of this calendar, complemented by minor events and the commemoration of the saints (Demus 1948: 15–16). Thus, a painting of the Nativity, for instance, can refer not only to the actual event of the birth of Christ, but also to Bethlehem and the feast of Christmas. These symbolic aspects were clearly elaborated in the Middle Byzantine period, but occurred already in a less elaborated way in the pre-iconoclastic period (Innemée 2000).

Apart from narrative and symbolic functions of the image, we can also distinguish an iconic aspect in certain paintings. In this case the image functions as a substitute for the one depicted, an object of devotion and veneration (Gr. *proskynesis*).

Taking this as a theoretical framework, we can ask ourselves which parts of the framework can be found in Nubian religious painting.

A clear iconographical system, comparable to that of the Middle Byzantine period, has apparently never crystallized in Egypt and Nubia, possibly because iconoclasm and the reactions to it have never affected these regions. Instead, we see the continuation of an informal way of decorating the interior of churches with mural paintings that can be added gradually over a period of time, as in the first layers of paintings in Dayr al-Suryan and in most Nubian churches, while in the cases where an iconographical program was laid out, this program was unique and has not been repeated in other churches. This is the case, for instance, in Dayr Anba Antonius (Monastery of St. Antony).

Central in most churches, both literally and symbolically, is the apse painting. Egypt and Nubia share the so-called double composition, a basic concept with a wide range of variations. In general, it consists of an upper zone in which Christ is represented as a heavenly ruler, while in the lower zone the Virgin Mary stands or sits, flanked by the twelve apostles. Among the earliest examples of such paintings are those in the prayer niches of the monastic complexes of Bawit and Saqqara. Although some of these compositions bear a resemblance to representations of the Ascension, Paul van Moorsel has shown that such an interpretation would be too simple and that the stress lies on a more timeless theme, Christ enthroned in heavenly glory (van Moorsel 1986a). In one of the most famous examples, the niche from cell 6 in Bawit, now in the Coptic Museum in Cairo, we see Christ Enthroned surrounded by flames, wheels, and the four apocalyptic creatures, and flanked by two angels in the upper zone, while in the lower zone the Virgin with Christ on her lap is seated between the twelve apostles and two saints (fig. 16.1). Here, the fact that Christ is depicted twice must exclude an interpretation as an Ascension. What, then, could be an alternative reading of this composition? We can observe the contrast between Christ as a heavenly ruler surrounded by elements that refer to the visions of Ezekiel and St. John and Christ as the child of an earthly mother. This might be read as a reference to the dual nature of Christ. The two parts of the apse can also be characterized as references to 'theophany' and 'incarnation,' two concepts that can be considered complementary to each other. Both have a ritual or symbolic connection with the apse, the central point of the liturgy. If we try to summarize the meaning of the Virgin with Christ on her lap, we can say that it represents the incarnation, the appearance of Christ in the flesh. This is one of the most fundamental points in orthodox theology and is ritually reenacted in the liturgy by the transformation of bread and wine into the material presence of Christ. A representation of the Virgin with Christ on her lap in the apse, be it as a single theme or as part of a double composition, can be taken as a reference to both the dogma of the incarnation and the liturgy that reflects this dogma.[1] The upper part of the double composition of cell 6, as in many other apses in the Nile valley, represents Christ in heavenly glory, surrounded by the four creatures of the Apocalypse and two angels. Flames and wheels

Fig. 16.1. Apse from cell 6 in Bawit (Coptic Museum, Cairo)

appear under the *mandorla* that surrounds Christ. These elements have been
borrowed from the theophanies as described in Isaiah 6:1–4, Ezekiel 1:4–21,
and the Revelation of St. John 4:6–8. The four creatures are not to be seen as
symbols of the four evangelists, but as elements in a visionary representation
of Christ (de Grooth and van Moorsel 1977–78). Christa Ihm calls this type
of apse composition the 'liturgical *maiestas*' because of its reference to the
Trisagion hymn, mentioned in the visions of Isaiah and St. John, and adopted
in several varieties in eastern liturgies (Ihm 1960: 42–51).

The apse of a basilica is traditionally a place of appearance, at first in the
Roman imperial tradition. In this part of the reception hall the emperor was
seated when receiving his guests. In the imperial cult room for Diocletian
in the temple of Luxor, modeled after such reception halls, we see how the
paintings in the apse represent the tetrarchs (Kalavrezou-Maxeiner 1975).
In the earliest Christian apse decorations we see how Christ is represented
as a heavenly ruler, dressed in purple, in a context that is clearly based on
Roman imperial iconography. It is not surprising that this iconography has

not been taken over in Egypt in the post-Chalcedonian period, but that the visionary image was preferred. For this reason we could also call this image a theophany, because it stresses the divine, rather than the imperial, qualities of Christ. In the double composition it complements the lower zone, possibly to express that the apse is not only the place where Christ appears incarnate, but also in his purely divine nature. This belief is illustrated in a story from the *History of the Patriarchs*, where Patriarch Philotheus, at the moment of the consecration of the holy gifts, sees the vault of the apse opening and a hand, apparently the hand of Christ, appearing and making the sign of the cross (van Moorsel 1986b). This aspect of Christ has a visionary character, immaterial and with clear references to the Old Testament prophets. This is not Christ in his human appearance but rather the immaterial Logos, the Word as heard by the prophets. Apart from associating the two parts of the apse with the human and divine natures of Christ, we could also think in a more liturgical direction and see them as expressions of the way that Christ manifests himself in the two consecutive parts of the liturgy: the Word and the Flesh (or bread and wine).

In the sanctuary, these aspects of the appearance of Christ are most dominantly represented, but not here exclusively. According to the Byzantine rite, bread and wine are prepared in the northern *pastoforion* (side room) or *prothesis*. In Coptic and Nubian churches such a side room is not always present, and, even if it is, it has in many cases been transformed into a side chapel in later periods, suggesting that a *prothesis* is not an indispensable part of a church building. In the Byzantine liturgy there was no special ritual for preparing the holy gifts until the middle of the sixth century. Only then was a special procession introduced, starting from the northern *pastoforion*, going through the northern side aisle and the central nave, and entering the sanctuary. By then the developments of the liturgical traditions of Constantinople and Alexandria had already gone their separate ways. It seems therefore unlikely at first sight that the northern *pastoforion* in the Coptic Church had a function comparable to that of the Byzantine *prothesis*. On the other hand, we have a number of reasons to believe that the northern *pastoforion* in Egypt and Nubia could have had a function in the preparation of the holy gifts. In a paper still in preparation, Adam Łajtar shows how this room in Nubia probably functioned as a *prothesis*, in the sense that the consecrated Eucharistic bread was kept here for the liturgy of the presanctified gifts. But there are reasons to believe that, not only for this specific purpose but also for the preparation of bread and wine, the northern side room had a function. In the church of Dayr al-Baramus, excavated in 2005, a small bakery was found behind the apse, east of the church, and connected to it by a passage leading to the northern *pastoforion*. The location and the small size of this bakery suggest that it was used for the liturgical bread. It must have functioned until the ninth century, when it was destroyed, while the *pastoforion* was turned into a side chapel (Innemée 2005: 65–66). Just outside the *pastoforion*, a deposit of empty wine amphorae was found, another indication that the northern *pastoforion* functioned as a *prothesis*. In the Coptic tradition the bakery for the *kurban* is called *bet lahim*, literally 'house of bread.' This is a symbolic allusion to the name of Bethlehem, the birthplace of Christ. The bakery is thus considered the 'birthplace' of the bread that is to be transformed into the body of Christ during the liturgy. Although the *bet lahim* is, strictly speaking, not a part of the architecture of the church, it fits in the observation of Otto Demus that parts of the church (decoration) can be given a topographical symbolism.

Another indication that the northeastern part of the church was associated with the incarnation of Christ can be found in Dayr al-Suryan. Here, in 2006, a painting of the Epiphany was discovered after detaching the thirteenth-century painting of the Dormition in the northern semi-dome of the *khurus* (fig. 16.2). In the composition of the Epiphany we see clear similarities with prayer niches from Bawit and Saqqara, but what is most striking is the similarity with the iconography of the Epiphany on so-called Monza

Fig. 16.2. Northern semi-dome, Epiphany (Dayr al-Suryan)

ampullae, pilgrims' flasks that contained holy oil from churches and other places in the Holy Land. The representations on these *ampullae* are generally considered miniatures of monumental paintings or mosaics in the churches where the contents of the flask originated; thus, the Epiphany representations probably refer to the apse in the church of the Nativity in Bethlehem. The original apse decoration was lost during the Persian invasion in 614.[2] The painting in Dayr al-Suryan can therefore be seen as a copy of the apse in Bethlehem, underscoring the symbolic connection between this part of the church and the incarnation of Christ. In the terms of Demus, the Epiphany painting has a double function and meaning as part of a cycle of liturgical feasts (it follows the scene of the Annunciation in the western semi-dome if we read the cycle clockwise) and as a reference to holy topography.

Not only in Egypt, but also in Nubia, there are indications that the northeastern parts of the church are symbolically linked to Bethlehem and the incarnation. In the Central Church of Abdalla Nirqi a scene of the Nativity has been painted on the eastern wall of the northern aisle, the wall that separates the northern *pastoforion* from the aisle (fig. 16.3) (van Moorsel, Jacquet, and Schneider 1975: 89–92). Originally this *pastoforion* was accessible from the northern aisle, but this doorway was blocked and a passage to the sanctuary was cut into the wall instead. Jean Jacquet suggests that this modification has to do with a change in liturgy, although he does not offer specifics (van Moorsel, Jacquet, and Schneider 1975: 9, 14–15). The painting of the Nativity dates to the late tenth century; the date of the architectural modification is not known. In Faras, too, the Nativity has been represented on the eastern wall of the northern aisle, both in the cathedral and in the tenth-century church south of the cathedral. When the cathedral was destroyed by fire between 927 and 929, a new church was erected on the south slope of the hill (Jakobielski 1972: 110–12). In this church a Nativity was painted at the eastern side of the northern aisle. Only a fragment of a seated Joseph remains (Michałowski 1974b: 175–76). After the cathedral was rebuilt, a monumental painting of the same theme was made in a similar position, on the wall separating the northern *pastoforion* from the northern aisle (fig. 16.4) (Michałowski 1967: 143–47, pls. 63–69). In both the paintings from Abdalla Nirqi and Faras cathedral a particular detail catches the eye, namely the shape of the manger, which looks like a masonry structure with a small window in it. It was in 1970 that Kurt Weitzman explained this by comparing it to the altar in the Church of the Nativity in Bethlehem and presuming that pilgrims'

Fig. 16.3. Nativity from Abdalla Nirqi, Central Church (Nubian Museum, Aswan)

Fig. 16.4. Nativity from the Cathedral of Faras (National Museum, Khartoum)

memories were the medium by which this iconographical influence was transferred (Weitzmann 1970; 1974). But, as in the case of the Epiphany in Dayr al-Suryan, it was probably more than an iconographical detail—a deliberate choice to draw a parallel between this part of the church and the incarnation of Christ and the *locus sanctum* of Bethlehem.

If there are reasons to believe that the northern *pastoforion* had both a function as a prosthesis and a symbolism expressed in the decoration of that part of the church, it is worth investigating whether something similar can be said for the southern *pastoforion* and/or the southeastern part of the church. In the church of the Virgin in Dayr al-Suryan there is a painted semi-dome in the southern part of the *khurus*, but the painting that should be considered the counterpart to the Epiphany is still covered by the thirteenth-century painting of the Annunciation and Nativity. In 1995 I speculated about a painting of Pentecost being hidden under this later layer, but so far there is no way of telling whether this is the case or not (Innemée 1995a). A comparable situation, a juxtaposition of two semi-domes, exists in the church of the Red Monastery, although here the semi-domes are part of a tetraconch forming

Fig. 16.5. Southern semi-dome, Christ Enthroned between four evangelists (Red Monastery, Sohag)

the *haikal*, and not part of the *khurus*. In
the northern semi-dome the Virgin, breast-
feeding Christ, is seated between four Old
Testament prophets, while in the southern conch Christ is enthroned between
the four evangelists (fig. 16.5). There is no
single way of reading this juxtaposition. We
could consider the prophets in the northern painting as the counterparts of the
evangelists, thus placing personifications of
the Old and New Testament opposite each
other. But if we consider the image of the
Virgin with Christ as the representation
of the Word Incarnate and the Eucharist,[3]
then Christ in the southern conch could
be read as the Logos as manifested in the
gospels, the immaterial Word.

The next question would be whether
a comparable juxtaposition of iconographical themes can be found in Nubian
churches. In the case of the church of
Abdalla Nirqi we notice that on the east-

Fig 16.6. Cross-theophany from
Abdalla Nirqi, Central Church (Nubian
Museum, Aswan)

ern wall in the southern aisle a so-called cross-theophany has been painted,
dated to the same period (end of the tenth century) as the Nativity (van
Moorsel, Jacquet, and Schneider 1975: 111–15). This composition, typical for Nubia, consists of a *crux gemmata* with a medallion of Christ in
the middle and the four creatures of the Apocalypse around it (fig. 16.6).
As in the case of certain Coptic and Nubian apse compositions, there is a
strong visionary aspect in this painting. Frits van der Meer has called this
kind of apse composition the 'theophany of the *Trisagion*,' after the words
'Holy, holy, holy' that the four creatures repeat continuously according to
Isaiah and the Book of Revelation and the liturgical hymn that is based
on it (van der Meer 1938: 251–81). Van Moorsel has adopted this term for
the Nubian cross-theophanies (van Moorsel 1972). The Trisagion hymn is
one of the oldest in the eastern liturgies and is sung just before the reading
from the gospels.[4] This could mean that the cross-theophany was associated with this particular part of the liturgy. In the case of Abdalla Nirqi
we may suppose that the Nativity in the north and the cross-theophany

Fig 16.7. Apse with double
composition (Qubbat al-Hawa)

in the south can be seen in a similar relationship (or contrast) to each other as the
lower and upper parts of a traditional apse
composition, showing Christ in his human
and divine qualities respectively, while at
the same time they represent both aspects
through which Christ appears in the liturgy, the Eucharist and the Word.

In the apse of Qubbat al-Hawa we find a
painting that, as for some other apses, can be
read as an Ascension with the Virgin and the
twelve apostles in the lower zone. But in the
upper zone we see Christ not in full figure
but as a half-figure on a medallion, carried
by angels (fig. 16.7). This medallion has
clear similarities to the ones on the cross-
theophanies, probably with the purpose of
suppressing a too-narrative character of the
painting and making the upper part readable
as a separate theophany image.

In the cathedral of Faras another example of juxtaposed images was to
be found. On the eastern wall of the southern aisle there was a Christ in
majesty, seated on a throne. In his right hand he holds a staff surmounted
by a cross, in his left hand an open book. His pallium is covered with pattern of eyes and lines. Below the throne were two angels venerating a
cross (Michałowski 1974b: 185–89). This painting dates to the same time
as the Nativity on the other side of the church. What makes it even more
interesting is that in a later period (twelfth century?) the lower part of this
composition was painted over by a representation of the Holy Trinity, surrounded by the twelve apostles (Michałowski 1974b: 189–90). The latter
detail seems to be borrowed from the lower zones of apse compositions,
though here they clearly appear in a less earthly context.

If we compare the way that Nubian churches have been decorated
to those in Egypt and the Byzantine reach, we see that in this respect
Nubia shows more Coptic influence. In Middle Byzantine art specific
iconographical schemes have been developed in which the liturgical calendar and the symbolism of the building have functioned as guidelines.
In both Egypt and Nubia a more informal tradition was kept in use in

which, gradually, paintings could be added to the interior, commissioned by subsequent donors. Only in a handful of cases, such as the Red Monastery, the semi-domes in Dayr al-Suryan, and the old church in Dayr Anba Antonius, was a complete or partial iconographical program designed. This might give the impression that mural paintings were applied without much system. A lack of uniformity in the painted decoration of churches makes it more difficult to detect an iconographical scheme, but it does not mean that such a system is totally absent. A large number of paintings may have been applied as individual devotional or commemorative images, such as representations of saints and bishops, but in other cases a connection with the liturgy (or both a devotional character and a liturgical symbolism) may be assumed. Especially in the eastern part of the church, a liturgical symbolism in certain paintings seems likely. Although the compositions differ from case to case, we find repeatedly a juxtaposition of the themes of the Virgin with Christ as a child and Christ as a heavenly ruler. These themes can be associated with the human and divine natures of Christ as well as with the presence of Christ in the Eucharist in word and bread.

Although, formally speaking, the northern *pastoforion* in Coptic churches is not needed as a *prothesis*, because the Coptic liturgy does not have a Great Entrance (the procession in which bread and wine are brought from the *prothesis* to the altar), there are reasons to believe that in certain cases the northern *pastoforion* has functioned as such. In Nubia the situation seems comparable, although we know far less about the Nubian liturgy. The iconography of mural paintings in the northeastern part of certain churches in Egypt and Nubia alludes to this function.

Notes
1 Cyril of Alexandria makes this connection in his Commentary on the Gospel of John VI, 64, Migne PG 73, col. 601C–605A.
2 The painting and an analysis of its iconography have been published in Innemée 2011.
3 And in this case the Eucharistic symbolism may be underscored by the fact that the Virgin is nursing Christ, a connection supposed by Elisabeth Bolman (Bolman 2004).
4 Schulz claims that the Trisagion has a Chalcedonian, anti-Monophysite character (Schulz 1980: 46–47), but since it is also part of the Coptic (St. Basil) and Syrian (St. James) liturgies, this does not seem very convincing.

17 The Ascension Scene in the Apse of the Church at Dayr Qubbat al-Hawa
A Comparative Study

Mary Kupelian

Introduction

This paper is particularly concerned with the dominant scene that appears in the apse composition of the church of Qubbat al-Hawa at Aswan. It carefully examines this scene and compares it with similar surviving scenes found in other apse compositions elsewhere. It challenges the widely held view regarding the classification of such a scene and proves that this scene is either an 'Ascension' scene or a 'Second Coming' scene rather than a 'Christ in Majesty' scene as commonly believed.

The paper also sheds light on the presence of certain significant elements within the scene which are both reserved for and restricted to Ascension scenes, usually located at the western side of the apse. The identification of such elements will remove the confusion that always arises when interpreting Ascension and Christ in Majesty scenes, which are often mistaken for one another. It also argues that decorating the interior of the church was not just for beautifying the walls, but had another function that served both liturgy and architecture as well.

The paper is primarily based on a field study carried out in the church of Qubbat al-Hawa together with four other monasteries: Dayr Anba Hadra, also at Aswan; the Sanctuary of Benjamin at Dayr Abu Maqar and the Church of al-Adra at Dayr al-Suryan, both in Wadi

al-Natrun; and finally the Chapel of al-Adra at Dayr Abu Sayfayn in
Old Cairo. The main points to be discussed in this paper are as follows:

1. A demonstration of the importance of the *haikal* (Arabic word for
   'sanctuary') of the church housing the apse. This is the focus of this
   paper. In this part, some examples of apse compositions comparable
   to the apse at Dayr Qubbat al-Hawa will be shown: the apse in Dayr
   Anba Hadra, the west walls of the Sanctuary of Benjamin at Dayr
   Abu Maqar and of the Church of al-Adra in Dayr al-Suryan in Wadi
   Natrun, and finally the Chapel of al-Adra at Dayr Abu Sayfayn.
2. The significance of apse painting and what the apse reflects will be
   discussed, as well as aspects of the images depicted in the apse and the
   iconography of Ascension scenes compared to Christ in Majesty scenes.
3. Finally, the difficulty in studying apse paintings will be discussed.

The churches will be discussed in geographical order from north to south.

Various Forms of Apse
The apse is a semicircular extension of a rectangular hall embedded within
the eastern wall of the church or chapel.

There are three common forms of apse (Grossmann 1991a; 2002: 118–19):

1. An apsidal niche, mostly found in private chapels and monastic
   churches. A fairly large number of apsidal niches found in Egypt
   are in the private chapels of Bawit and Saqqara.
2. A semi-dome apse found in triconch sanctuaries.
3. An apse with a flat wall, which is frequently found in cave churches
   as well as in churches with irregular plans.

The paintings depicted in the *haikal* are directly connected to the
function of this part of the church. The apse paintings only contain representations of the most holy characters, mainly Christ, the Virgin, angels, and
apostles, and scenes imagined as taking place in heaven or where heaven is
the source or the aim of the action depicted.

Aspects of Images Used in Decorating Churches
It is generally agreed that New Testament themes that decorate the
churches have three aspects; symbolic, narrative, and iconic. The symbolic

aspect is theological in nature and has a metaphorical meaning related to it and to the liturgy. The narrative aspect is descriptive and in terms of its role is of the same value as the written word or the biblical event it depicts. The third aspect, iconic, is the representation of a sacred person and is used in worship and veneration, that is, there exists a close interaction between the viewer and the painting.

Themes of Apse Painting

The themes of apse paintings are unique both in subject and aspect in that one image might combine more than one aspect. The themes shows stories derived either from the Acts of the Apostles, for example the Ascension of Christ, or from the Book of Revelation of St. John, for example scenes showing Christ Enthroned in Majesty surrounded by the Four Apocalyptic Creatures and the Twenty-four Elders. In contrast, very little is derived from the Epistles, as they do not seem to have inspired the artists. An exception seems to be the Ascension scenes. The apse in Coptic churches—which is the major point in this article—displays different themes inspired by a mixture of sources from the Old and New Testaments, patristic writings, poems, hymns, and glorifications, and is decorated with themes that occur in the liturgy as well. These sources play a major role in the apse, influencing the iconography of its pictorial art. They are among the factors that have influenced the artist and were considered popular themes in decorating the interior of churches. The themes are either depicted in the whole apse in one complete scene, which is regarded as a single composition in which all the elements are represented in one context without a line separating two themes, or are shown as a double composition in two separated images—either divided by a horizontal line or not. Rarely is the apse decorated with triple compositions. There are three famous themes which frequently decorate the apse, namely the Ascension, a mixture of the Ascension and Christ in Majesty, and scenes depicting Christ in Majesty.

Ascension Scenes

The Ascension Scene at Dayr Qubbat al-Hawa

The main argument here will be based on the Ascension scene in the western apse at Dayr Qubbat al-Hawa. It is an important example of a double composition, where the bust of Christ is depicted in the upper register, carried by six angels, while the twelve apostles surrounding the Virgin are in the lower register. In this scene the apostles are depicted next to the Virgin.

The two-register composition in the western apse of the church is painted on white plaster. The upper register depicts a *mandorla* with a bust of Christ. The upper part of the *mandorla* is unfortunately lost, as is most of Christ's face. Only his chin, beard, and part of his yellow nimbus are visible. Christ wears an orange tunic and a blue pallium, and holds a closed book in his left hand while raising his other hand in a gesture of blessing. The *mandorla* is carried by six angels who appear to be in flight, the upper ones being partially destroyed. The angels, who have their faces turned to Christ, are dressed in white tunics and blue pallia. They have red hair and orange wings, and their heads are surrounded with yellow nimbi (fig. 17.1) (Dekker 2008: 25–27).

The second, lower, register depicts the Virgin flanked by the twelve apostles. The frontal figure of the Virgin is much damaged, so it can be hardly seen that she raises both arms up to Christ. She is clothed in a *maphorion*, and has a yellow nimbus. The figures of the apostles are much damaged as well, particularly their faces. They wear white tunics and alternately red and blue pallia. All of them have yellow nimbi. Only two apostles, dressed in blue, are depicted frontally and hold a book, while the others are shown gazing upward to Christ and raise one or both hands.

The depiction of six angels carrying the bust of Christ is a unique detail which up till now has no known parallels in an apse in Egypt. To the north side of this apse there are six saints depicted; five of them have a square nimbus in contrast to the familiar circular nimbus belonging to the sixth saint, who is most probably the patron saint of the church. This can be interpreted as meaning that these five figures were depicted during their lifetime. This is the second remaining scene in the northern church at Dayr Qubbat al-Hawa (fig. 17.2).

It is worth mentioning that no figure with a square halo is encountered in any church in Egypt except here at Dayr Qubbat al-Hawa and in the apse at Dayr Anba Hadra. In addition to this, Chapel LI at Bawit in middle Egypt and a figure in one of the chapels in Saqqara show the two halos, square and circular, together.

The lower register is more evidence that this depiction is of the Ascension because of the attitude of the Virgin, which is unfortunately much damaged so that one can barely see that she raises both arms up to Christ in *orans*. The arms of the apostles are also lifted upwards to Christ, so the relation between the two registers is clear.

Fig. 17.1. The western apse in the northern church at Dayr Qubbat al-Hawa (courtesy of K. Innemée)

Fig. 17.2. The northern wall showing saints with a square halo at Dayr Qubbat al-Hawa (courtesy of K. Innemée)

The Ascension scene was commonly depicted in Coptic wall painting, for example, in:

1. Chapel XLVI in the Monastery of Apa Apollos in Bawit, which dates most probably to the tenth century (Clédat 1999: 86–88).
2. the Sanctuary of Benjamin in Dayr Abu Maqar at Wadi al-Natrun, which most probably goes back to the eleventh century.
3. the western semidome in the nave of the Church of the Virgin in Dayr al-Suryan, Wadi al-Natrun, which dates to the thirteenth century.[1]

Examples of Ascension scenes comparable to the apse in Qubbat al-Hawa

Example 1: The Church of al-Adra, Dayr al-Suryan, Wadi al-Natrun

The Ascension scene in the nave of the Church of al-Adra in Dayr al-Suryan (fig. 17.3) (Innemée 1995: 130–32; 1998: 143) is the most similar example to the apse of the church in Qubbat al-Hawa because

- their location is in the west;
- the movement of the Apostles is clearly visible;
- some of the apostles are pointing upwards;
- they both date to the twelfth/thirteenth century;
- Christ is carried by angels in flying attitude;
- the Book in Christ's hand is closed;
- the Virgin is shown in *orans* attitude;
- the color of the Virgin's tunic is blue;
- the throne is missing in both Ascension scenes.

Fig. 17.3. The Ascension in the western semi-dome of the nave in the Church of al-Adra at Dayr al-Suryan (courtesy of K. Innemée)

The two registers are similar in elements, but different in minor details such as the number of angels and the figure of Christ. In Dayr al-Suryan, the Ascension is the third event in the narrative cycle of the life of Christ. In contrast, in Dayr Qubbat al-Hawa it is still not known whether the apse in the west is part of a cycle or not.

Comparison of Ascension Scenes

Similarities	Differences
• The movement of the Apostles	• The number of the angels and their representation
• Christ is carried by angels	• The horizontal line between two registers
• Book closed	
• The sign of benediction	• The figure of Christ
• Angels in flying attitude	• The position of the Apostles
• The location in the west	
• The *orans* attitude of the Virgin and the apostles	• The nature of the scene, whether part of a narrative cycle or not
• Blue color of the tunic of the Virgin	• An additional two figures flanking the upper register in Dayr Qubbat al-Hawa
• The throne is missing in both Ascension scenes	
• The yellow halo	

Example 2: The Sanctuary of Benjamin, Dayr Abu Maqar, Wadi al-Natrun
The painting at Wadi al-Natrun, in the Sanctuary of Benjamin in Dayr Abu Maqar, is at the western end of the church, like those at Dayr al-Suryan and Qubbat al-Hawa. Thus, all of the Ascension scenes discovered so far are located in the west, which, in turn, supports the argument that these illustrations are of the Ascension and not Christ Enthroned in Majesty.

The Ascension scene here is also located in the west and dates to the twelfth to thirteenth centuries. The Virgin was depicted in *orans* attitude, but unfortunately this part of the composition no longer exists. Now the wall shows only Christ Enthroned between angels and apostles (fig. 17.4) (Evelyn-White 1933: 94–95; Leroy 1982: 18–21).

Fig. 17.4. The Ascension scene, the Sanctuary of Benjamin, Dayr Abu Maqar, in Wadi al-Natrun (after Zibawi 2003: pl. 186)

A Mixture of Ascension and Christ in Majesty: The Chapel of al-Adra in Dayr Abu Sayfayn

It was observed from comparing scenes found in the east that these would show a mixture of the Ascension and Christ Enthroned in Majesty—in contrast to the scenes in the west, which depicted only the Ascension scene, as we have seen in Dayr al-Suryan and Qubbat al-Hawa.

Further proof of this, taken from the example of the chapel of al-Adra in Dayr Abu Sayfayn, is the presence of the Four Creatures of the Apocalypse, which are only depicted in Christ in Majesty. An important observation is that this apse symbolizes, all at the same time, the past by the Ascension, the present by Christ's kingship, reigning over the church, and the future, which is referred to by his second coming. This apse composition is a unique surviving example because it shows the narrative and the symbolic aspects together. The Ascension scene is mixed with the scene of Christ in Majesty. This scene is located in the east and dates to the twelfth to thirteenth centuries (fig. 17.5).

The scene of the Ascension of Christ is depicted as follows:

1. Christ raises his right hand in benediction and in his left hand he holds the gospel, which rests on his thigh.

2. Next to his throne the inscription reads: Immanuel, "God with us," in Hebrew.

3. Two angels are bowing to him in adoration, with the sun and moon above their heads. In the lower register, the Virgin Mary is represented standing with upraised arms in *orans* attitude and surrounded by the apostles.

4. The scene of Christ in Majesty is shown by the depiction of the throne surrounded by the Four Creatures of the Apocalypse on either side.

Christ in Majesty: The Church of Dayr Anba Hadra, Aswan

This example is chosen for two reasons: first, because of the location of Dayr Anba Hadra not far from Dayr Qubbat al-Hawa, and, second, because it has a unique detail— a figure of a priest equipped with a square halo (Ladner 1941: 34). The apse scene

Fig. 17.5. The central apse in the Chapel of al-Adra in Dayr Abu Sayfayn, a mixture of Ascension and Christ in Majesty (after Zibawy 2003, pl. 220)

shows Christ in Majesty and not the Ascension, as proved by the position of the angels and the flames under the *mandorla*. It is depicted in the apse located in the east. It illustrates Christ Enthroned in Majesty surrounded by the *mandorla* with flames at its base. He holds a book on one knee with his left hand while his right hand, raised in benediction, extends beyond the *mandorla*, which is held by two angels. This scene dates to the twelfth to thirteenth centuries (fig. 17.6) (Gabra 2002: 112).

Interpretations of Double Composition

There are many interpretations for the themes of the apse, especially in the case of the double composition. In some cases, the upper register reflects Christ's divine nature in heaven; this is emphasized by the elements represented next to him, for example the Four Creatures of the Apocalypse. The lower register shows Christ's human form on earth, especially when he is depicted being carried by the Virgin. This is explained as follows: the Word in the upper register becomes flesh, "God Incarnate," in the lower register,

Fig. 17.6. Christ Enthroned in Majesty, flanked by two angels, Dayr Anba
Hadra at Aswan (photograph by author)

and the presence of the Apostles and the Virgin may refer to the foundations of the Church (van Moorsel 2000a: 91–93; 1978: 327–31; Innemée
chapter in this volume).

Summary of Ascension Scenes
One can discern a number of distinctive fixed elements within any Ascension scene:

1. Christ and the angels are always present.
2 The angels are depicted either in flying attitude or in adoration,
   in a kneeling position.
3. The Book in Christ's left hand is always closed.
4. The Four Living Creatures of the Apocalypse are never represented in Ascension scenes.
5. The scene is usually divided into two registers, but the horizontal
   line separating the two sections is not always represented.
6. The Virgin in *orans* attitude and apostles are always represented
   in moving attitude; in particular, some of the apostles are shown
   gazing and talking with each other or pointing upwards.
7. Significantly, the Ascension scene is always located in the west.

Furthermore, the themes in the apse are regarded as an independent iconographic unity and they have no direct iconographic relationship with the other sections of the church. The absence of those themes that appear only on the apse from the other sections of the church, such as the nave, provides ample proof that they were designed specifically for the apse. It can also be concluded, then, that such themes are mostly symbolic and rarely narrative. The only narrative themes in the apse are the Ascension of Christ and the Annunciation. The other scenes in the apse, of Christ in Majesty, are symbolic in nature and are connected with the liturgy. They can also reflect the future, as Christ is depicted as He appeared in the visions of the Old Testament prophets Isaiah and Ezekiel, or as he appeared in St. John's Book of Revelation. In other words, the scenes can refer to his Second Coming (Ihm 1960: 48–55; van Moorsel 1978: 325–30).

A single painting can sometimes combine two aspects, the symbolic and the narrative; that is, the aspect can change according to the event celebrated in the church. It can also be concluded that the apse painting is like a mirror, reflecting to the congregation what is happening on the altar: the appearance of the actual presence of Christ, especially during the celebration of the Eucharist, at the moment of the consecration of bread and wine. Christ, during the liturgy, descends to the sanctuary with his angelic hosts. He is the priest performing this action—through the image—referring to the vision of Philotheus (van Moorsel 2000b: 107–108; Innemée chapter in this volume). Therefore, the image in the apse serves as a representation of the person depicted, which means it renders the person actually present. This symbolic presence of Christ is a development from the image of the emperor in the apse of Roman basilicas. This idea of an image both replacing and representing the physical presence of a person goes back to the imperial cult and is derived from the architecture of the royal palace. Instead of the emperor himself being venerated in the reception hall of his royal palace (Roman basilica), his portrait, depicted in the apse of the cult room of temples, was venerated. One can safely say that the church served here as the reception hall of Christ in the same way as the reception hall of the emperor at his palace. The emperor was physically absent from the cult room but was symbolically present through his portrait. The paintings in apses depicting Christ must have had the same meaning, which is the symbolic presence of Christ, his 'Epiphany.'

Difficulties in Studying Apse Paintings

The difficulties the author encountered in studying the apse paintings can be summarized as follows:

1. While the apse is sometimes painted with a single composition, it is very often painted with double compositions. Therefore, there is no fixed rule for its decoration.

2. In the case of a double composition, the relation between the two registers is sometimes clear, as, for example, in an Ascension theme. But in other cases, the relationship between them proved to be vague, especially in the monastic chapels in Bawit where the two registers are decorated with different scenes not directly connected to each other.

3. The incomplete state of preservation of the apse paintings in many Coptic churches created another hindrance. Therefore, the author had to consult written documents as the only source for such paintings.

Notes

1   Now on display in the new museum at the same monastery.

18 The Nubian Marble Object Preserved in Dayr al-Suryan in Wadi al-Natrun

Bishop Martyros

THE FACT THAT THERE is a tray of white marble, on which there are inscriptions in both the Greek and Nubian languages, in the Museum of the Holy Virgin Monastery (Dayr al-Suryan) in Wadi al-Natrun motivated me to conduct research on that tray and get acquainted with the character of King Giorgios whose name is recorded on it. This Nubian tray will be the focus of this paper.

Most of the information about it was obtained from a published work of Hugh Evelyn-White (Evelyn-White 1933). However, the first to discover that tray was Professor Francis Crawford Burkitt (Burkitt 1903), while the first to examine and study it was Professor Francis Llewellyn Griffith (Griffith 1928).

The Description of the Tray
The tray is located at the museum in the Monastery of the Holy Virgin, al-Suryan, in Wadi al-Natrun. The following is the catalog data at the museum:

Piece Number: 1M
Description: A marble tray
Material: White marble
Diameter: 72 cm
Height: 12 cm

Fig. 18.1. Marble tray with the inscription of King Giorgios IV from the Monastery of the Syrians in Wadi al-Natrun

Fig. 18.2. Back of the tray of King Giorgios IV

Thickness: 2–3 cm
Height of the Two Edges of the Base: 5 cm
Thickness of the Edge of the Base: 2 cm
Number of Lines on the Rim of the Tray: 2 lines
Number of the Lines on the Floor of the Tray: 25 lines
Method of Writing: inscription
Language on the Rims of the Tray: Greek
Language on the Floor of the Tray: Nubian
Date: AM 874 (AD 1158)

The Text on the Marble Tray[1]
The Greek Text Inscribed on the Inner and Outer Rims
On the rims of the tray, the written Greek text is translated by Evelyn-White as follows:[2]

> O God of Spirits and of all flesh, who didst set Death at naught and trample down Hades and give life unto the world, give rest unto the soul of Giorgios Thy servant, the King, in a place of light, in a place of refreshment, where pain and grief and sighing are fled away. Every sin committed by him in word or in deed or in thought, do Thou, as gentle and a lover of mankind, forgive, for [?] there is no man [who] shall live[?]." (Evelyn-White 1933: 217)

The Old Nubian Text on the Floor of the Tray
Unfortunately, neither Burkitt, who discovered the tray, nor Griffith, who examined it, published a translation of the Nubian inscriptions.[3] Griffith only said, "The text on the tray includes prayers and supplications for King Giorgios and a brief statement about his biography. He was born in 1106 AD, enthroned in Nubia in 1130 AD and died in 1158 AD at the age of 52" (Griffith 1928: 121–28; see also Welsby 2002: 89 f., 260).

Remarks about the Tray
The following are general remarks that can be made about the tray and its inscriptions:

1. The liturgical text on the rims of the tray is similar to the Coptic liturgical texts, especially the diptych prayers and the absolution prayers for confessors. The Nubians also used to write dates

according to the Coptic calendar, which means the Nubian
church and its Coptic counterpart were closely related.

2. Three crosses are inscribed above the text on the floor of the
   tray; among them are the letters alpha and omega. They are the
   first and last letters of the Greek alphabet, symbolizing the eternity of the Logos. A funerary epitaph of sandstone dating to the
   fourth century was found in Upper Egypt on which the alpha and
   the omega, in addition to the crosses, are inscribed. That epitaph
   is kept at the Greek Museum in Alexandria under the number
   11852.[4] It is notable that in the Aswan Museum there is a round
   pottery tray that looks like the tray being discussed here. It has no
   inscriptions but there is a representation of a tilapia fish (which
   lives in the Nile) on its floor. The fish is hooked.[5] This representation is a common Christian symbol, as we know.

3. It is certain that the diptych prayers used to be read before tombs.
   During those prayers, a lamp, on which the name of the dead
   person was inscribed, used to be lit. This indicates that the funeral
   epitaphs reflected Christian religious thought. Among the most
   common formulas was the Euchologion Mega in the era of Christian prosperity in Nubia (AD 850–1150). That formula includes
   some texts from the diptych prayers. An example of that formula
   is the epitaph of King Giorgios. A similar formula is found on an
   epitaph dating back to AM 902 (AD 1186). Another example of a
   funeral epitaph was the one belonging to the deacon Butrus, who
   was the disciple of Abba Gawargyos, the bishop of Karta. The text
   on that epitaph was written in Greek except for a line and a half
   at the bottom which were written in the Coptic language. That
   epitaph dates back to AM 745 (AD 1029). It includes the following: "O God, give rest to his soul . . . in paradise where there is no
   weeping or sadness or melancholy" (Mileham 1910: 19).

4. The name of King Giorgios was pronounced "Karky" or
   "Georgy." It is known that the Nubian kings and church members used to change their Nubian names to Greek or Coptic
   names, as they believed that their former life changed as a result
   of their belief in Christ. They chose names like Youannas, Zachariah, Solomon, Marcus, Gawargyos, Maria, and Martha.

5. The monks of the monastery at the time of Evelyn-White's
   visit supposed that the tray was used as an altar top. However,

Evelyn-White wrote that the tray may have been intended to hold the *eulogiae*, the unconsecrated loaves of bread, which are distributed to the congregation at the end of the Divine Liturgy (Evelyn-White 1933: 215). That is why it was found in the southern sanctuary of the church of the Holy Virgin in Dayr al-Suryan. It is also probable that the tray was sent to the Nubian monks in the Monastery of Elias for the Abyssinians for the above-mentioned purpose and then transferred to Dayr al-Suryan before AD 1441 (cf. Evelyn-White 1933: 217).

6. It is improbable that that tray was made in Wadi al-Natrun. It may have been made in Nubia and then sent to the Nubian monks there.

Remarks about the Person of King Giorgios

The archaeological information tells us that King Giorgios, mentioned above, is King Giorgios IV (AD 1131–58). He is the son of King Basil (circa AD 1089) and the father of King Moise who was enthroned in the kingdom of Northern Nubia (Noubadia) in AD 1160. This information was obtained from an inscribed text under a wall painting representing the Nativity in the northern aisle of the cathedral, discovered in Faras (Vantini 1970: 221).

Vantini says that King Giorgios IV became a monk and led an ascetic life in one of the monasteries of Wadi al-Natrun. His epitaph was discovered and on it was found a text written in both Arabic and Coptic. It tells us that he was born in AD 1105, became a king in AD 1131, and renounced the throne in order to go to Wadi al-Natrun (Vantini 1970: 233–34, n.7).

It is mentioned that King Giorgios I ruled in AD 856/859/866–87, King Giorgios II in AD 969–1002, King Giorgios III from AD 1079 to before AD 1089, and King Giorgios IV AD 1131–58.

There was an ancient tradition among the Nubian kings. Some of them renounced their thrones in favor of their sons or nephews in order to become monks, leading an ascetic life in one of the monasteries till their death. These kings used to take holy orders. Examples of those kings are King Zachariah (AD 748) and King Solomon (AD 1080). King Giorgios IV followed that custom and lived in one of the monasteries of Wadi al-Natrun. The question is: Which monastery did he live in? The marble tray was found in Dayr al-Suryan; does that mean that he lived there? Maybe he did not, because both Evelyn-White and Otto Meinardus have said that the tray may have been transferred from the Monastery of the Prophet Elias (or the Cell of Bahoot) for the Abyssinians in the area of St. John the

Little when the Nubian monks moved from there to Dayr al-Suryan after its destruction (Evelyn-White 1933: 217; Meinardus 1989: 131).

Scholars disagree about the name of one of the monasteries in the area of St. John the Little in Wadi al-Natrun. Al-Maqrizi called it Anbanoub. Did he mean the monastery of Nubia, that is, which belonged to the Nubians, and he miswrote it? If so, this monastery is the place where King Giorgios IV lived, as that area included monasteries for monks of different nationalities, such as the Armenians, the Abyssinians, and the Syrians. When those monasteries were ruined, the monks moved to the other populated monasteries such as Dayr al-Suryan, which is located three kilometers northeast of the area. They carried with them their valuable objects, including the marble tray for the celebration of the Divine Liturgy.

Another important question is: Did King Giorgios IV die, and was he buried, in Wadi al-Natrun or in Nubia? We hope we will find the answer in archaeological explorations in the future.

King Giorgios is considered the last of the kings of the era of Christian prosperity in Nubia. Michałowski believes that his son, who was officially enthroned in Nubia in AD 1160, allied with the Fatimids against the Ayyubids in AD 1171 (Michałowski 1970). He was defeated, and thereafter Christianity weakened in Nubia, especially when Toran Shah, the brother of Salah al-Din, invaded and ruled Nubia in AD 1173 (Vantini 1970: 95, 102).

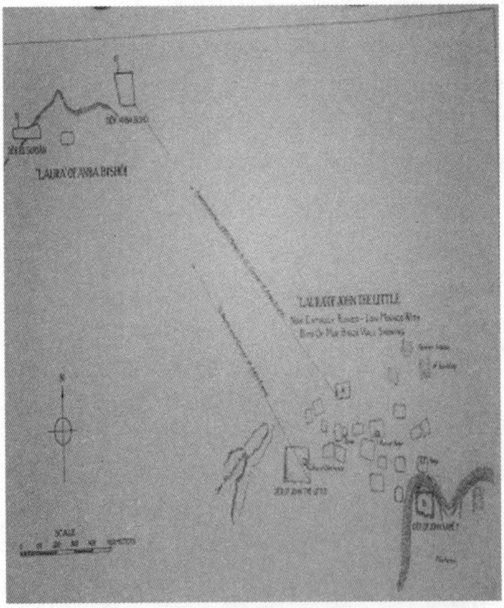

It is notable that King Giorgios IV was at Wadi al-Natrun during the patriarchates of Pope Gabriel II (1131–45), Pope Michael II (1145–46), and Pope John V (1147–66). It is mentioned that the first was a famous merchant, the second was a monk from the "Great Cell" in Wadi al-Natrun, and the third was a monk in the Monastery of St. John the Little in Wadi al-Natrun. This was during the reigns of the Fatimid caliphs al-Amir and al-Hafiz.

Fig. 18.3. The monasteries of the area of St. John the Little, including the Monastery of (Nubians?) and the Monastery of St. Pshoi (Anba Bishoi), as well as Dayr al-Suryan.

This article does not answer the question: Why was that tray, with such an important inscription, found in Dayr al-Suryan, around a thousand kilometers to the north of Nubia? I hope that its content and the photograph of the tray might encourage scholars to study its Old Nubian text and shed a new light on the relationship between Wadi al-Natrun and Nubia, which was perhaps the homeland of the great saint Moses the Black, the first martyr of Wadi al-Natrun (Gabra 1998a: 117, 125).[6]

Notes

1   Throughout this article the name 'George,' mentioned in Evelyn-White 1933 and Vantini 1970, has been replaced with 'Giorgios,' as it is transcribed in Welsby 2002.

2   The full Greek text of the inscription was published in Evelyn-White 1933: 216.

3   Only a few weeks before the final editing of this volume, I became acquainted with Vincent van Gerven Oei's article, "The Old Nubian Memorial for King George" (van Gerven Oei 2011).

4   See also Gabra and Eaton-Krauss 2007: 44 f., no. 28; 46 f., no. 31.

5   For more details on this tray consult Atif Naguib, "Coptic Objects in the Aswan and Nubia Museums," in this volume, fig. 20.4.

6   See also Fr. Bigoul al-Suriany, "Identification of the Monastery of Nubians in Wadi al-Natrun," in this volume.

19 The Digital 3D Virtual Reconstruction of the Monastic Church, Qubbat al-Hawa

Howard Middleton-Jones

IN 2006 A PROPOSAL for a Coptic Multi-media Database was devised, and in the following year the project was developed by collating the maximum amount of available information possible for input into the retrieval system (Middleton-Jones 2010). Although the input and manipulation of this data are extremely time-consuming, it is a critically important process for the ongoing project to build up a comprehensive collection of monastic sites and associated information. This, in turn, will assist in producing a full and succinct record of essential elements for a complete and accurate record of each site, and thus of great advantage for the conservation and ultimate preservation of each site.

The collation and input of information, such as high resolution images and film, bibliographies, excavation reports, and geographical coordinates, to name but a few subject areas, is an ongoing endeavor. However, as the project develops and material comes to light, it is possible to utilize the information to instigate and develop additional research and related cultural heritage projects. One such project that has developed from the dissemination of the data is the virtual-3D reconstruction of a highly vulnerable site, the Church of Qubbat al-Hawa, Elephantine, Aswan.[1]

Dayr Qubbat al-Hawa is located among the ancient Sixth Dynasty tombs of the nobles-governors of Elephantine, on the west bank of the Nile at Aswan. Originally, the monks constructed a hermitage, in about the fourth century, among the tombs of Khunes (Tomb QH 34h), listed as a chancellor, and Khui (Tomb QH 34e), listed as the divine chancellor of the two barques during the Sixth Dynasty reign of Pepi II.

While the original settlement of the monks was mainly centered on this upper level in front of the tombs, Coptic ostraca dating to the sixth century have been found on other levels and also within the shafts of the tombs.

Fig. 19.1. Overall view of the site of Qubbat al-Hawa from the Nile (Peter Hossfeld, VCS, Switzerland)

The current visible standing remains of the church, situated above QH 34, including that of an enclosure wall, date to the tenth and twelfth centuries, corroborated by Coptic inscriptions in the tombs recording the fall of Qasr Ibrim in AD 1173 (Dekker 2008). The monastic site has on occasion been referred to as that associated with St. George, based on the figures of equestrian saints on the walls of a neighboring tomb (QH 34f) and their accompanying texts. Abu al-Makarim, writing in the thirteenth century, also mentions two sites at this location (Evetts and Butler 1895), and it is possible that it may also be associated with the Monastery of St. Antony.

Previous Excavation Work

The site was initially surveyed by Grossmann (Grossmann 1991d) and from that work an octagon-domed church structure was identified and reconstructed. Subsequently, in 1998, the Supreme Council of Antiquities cleared much of the debris on site, revealing further wall additions including Coptic and Arabic inscriptions. In addition, during the excavation process, several wall paintings were revealed, including that on the west wall niche, where a bust of Christ is carried by six angels in flight. Unfortunately, once the debris and sand were removed, so too was the natural protection afforded to the wall paintings. Within a short time, the illustrations began a rapid downward path of decline and erosion due to the rays of the hot sun in the day, cool nights, and blowing sands. Even in the past ten years there has been a noticeable decline, as can be observed in the comparison of photographs taken by Gawdat Gabra in 2001[2] with those of Peter Hossfeld in 2009[3] and myself in 2010,[4] especially of those of the saints in the west wall.

Fig. 19.2. West apse with the bust of Christ and angels (Peter Hossfeld, VCS, Switzerland)

Unfortunately, as far as is known, no published excavation report or record is available of the 1998 excavation, and therefore no photographs are available for comparison.

In 2010, the St. Mark Foundation for Coptic History Studies organized their biannual conference at St. Simeon, Aswan, from where we had the opportunity to visit the site of Qubbat al-Hawa on several occasions. I took this opportunity to take high-resolution photographs of the site accompanied by Renate Dekker, who subsequently discovered additional paintings and inscriptions based on these photographs and the previous high-resolution photographs taken by Peter Hossfeld in the spring of 2009.

While we were attending the conference, further excavation work was undertaken by the SCA under the supervision of Inspector Magdi Abdin, who was also responsible for the earlier 1998 excavations. This excavation and further clearing of the site continued until late March. Based on this work, our high-resolution photographs, and the follow-up research work carried out by Renate Dekker, new interpretations and discoveries from the site were extrapolated.

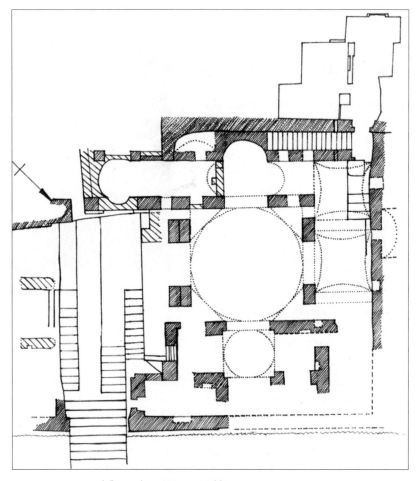

Fig. 19.3. Revised floor plan (Renate Dekker)

It is based on these new discoveries combined with earlier research that our project of a digital 3D reconstruction was initiated and developed. The premise of the project was to utilize the data and information collated from the several site visits, combined with the latest discoveries of Renate Dekker, in order to recreate the site as it appeared the twelfth century. This would also include the wall paintings and inscriptions in situ and ultimately rendered within the walls of the reconstruction, thus displaying the illustrations as one would have observed them at the time of habitation.

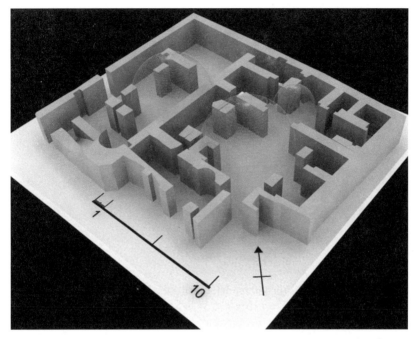

Fig. 19.4. Initial reconstruction model (Peter Hossfeld, VCS, Switzerland)

Equipment

The camera used for the overall project was a Cannon SLR EOS 5D Mark II, with the potential of 21.1 megapixel full-frame CMOS sensor, 14-bit A/D conversion (16,384 colors/each of 3 primary colors), and a wide-range ISO setting of 100–6400. This produces extremely high-resolution photographs for almost any media purpose. In addition, the camera possesses full HD video capture at 1920 x 1080 resolution for up to 4GB per clip with HDMI output for HD viewing of stills and video. The end result is professional media for high-end theater viewing.

On-site measuring was carried out using a Bosch laser distance meter, offering accurate measurements which were incorporated within the three-dimensional modeling. Additional programs and software included Autodesk Photo-modeler, Autodesk 3D MAX 2010, large-range laser 3D scanner, Autodesk 3Ds MAX, and Photoshop CS4 for editing and converting image files. To ensure compatibility of photographic filtering, the recommended Kodak color/grayscale chart 20cm was utilized.

Fig. 19.5. Initial reconstruction model showing the location of the apse with paintings and staircase (Peter Hossfeld, VCS, Switzerland)

Methods

Archaeological sites and features tend to be wholly or partially destroyed, altered, or buried; thus a complete inventory of the material remains is not always possible. However, using reliable and accurate data collection in conjunction with developing methods in virtual-reality technologies and 3D modeling, material remains and architectural elements may be captured, or frozen in time, for the purpose of archaeological and cultural heritage conservation.

Virtual reality (VR) in digital reconstruction of sites and buildings is a tried and tested method of approaching complex datasets, providing useful imagery and direct answers to questions about the construction of a site. In addition, reconstruction in 3D offers a different perception of ancient structures, which may be used for further analysis toward interpretation and an understanding of the past. These methods of digital architecture, and topographical modeling are a useful and developing aid to study and preserve cultural heritage.

Thus, by constructing a digital model of such a site as Qubbat al-Hawa, one may observe not only how the site appeared during its original habitation, with the wall paintings and inscriptions in situ, but how the site was actually constructed. The ultimate aim is to 'capture' the site and to freeze a moment that otherwise may be lost to the ravages of time.

Methods with Floor Plans Available Only

Once the laser measurements were made onsite and stored, providing exact measurements of distances, height, and calculation of volumes, the results were calibrated via the hand-drawn floor plan to a 3D 'scene-in' in Autodesk 3D Max. The items on the drawn plan were then copied into 3Ds MAX and were vectored. The heights of the walls were extruded accordingly.

The lighting of the scene is accomplished by using a so-called "daylight" system within 3Ds MAX; this allows the simulation of sunlight and shadows at any geographical coordinate on earth, at any time of the day and at any point in the year. Details and accuracy are an essential part of the process, requiring qualified operators who are able to provide essential feedback on this process. However, the 3D model is such that it may be modified and expanded to suit the researcher's purposes.

The most comprehensive and accurate reconstructions are based on large-range laser scanners, producing highly accurate data clouds of scanned structures or objects. Based on this method, additional complex reconstructions may be carried out.

An additional method that may be carried out is a 3D reconstruction by photometrical means. This is carried out by using a minimum of three photographs of each chosen area or structure from different viewpoints. Common points in the various photographs are localized and marked in the software. The program image modeler then creates a 3D model. The advantage of this method is that mapping of the 3D object is derived from the photographs themselves.

It is clear that a one-hundred-percent-accurate reconstruction is not always possible due to lack of sufficient information, while some sections need to be interpolated with the help of matter experts. However, the 3D models can give interesting insights and 'what if' scenarios or test the plausibility of assumed constructions. This is of great interest and potential usefulness in cultural heritage programs involving physical conservation work.

Advantages

The advantages of utilizing such methods and tools are many, providing essential information in the areas of cultural heritage, education, museum heritage, archaeological excavations, and conservation and preservation, especially in the field of Coptic art and architecture.

In the field of archaeology, 3D reconstruction modeling allows archaeologists to integrate the various archaeological features and physical contexts to better document the site. In addition, by providing such a program, continued research on such a site may be applied to both on-site and off-site work, such as a desk-based study. The advantage of a desk-based study is that erosion of and human intervention in the site are kept to a minimum, thus maintaining the preservation of the site, and also minimizing the financial expenditures associated with such work.

For the specialists concerned with the conservation and preservation of wall and icon paintings, the 3D modeling and the rendering of high-resolution photographic media will provide essential data in the reconstruction of artistic elements. We have already witnessed this, for example, in the case of the photographic survey of Qubbat al-Hawa, where it allowed Renate Dekker to discover additional inscriptions and artistic elements, hitherto unknown.

The systematic photographic capturing of high-quality images of artistic renderings is an objective process—that is, nothing is forgotten or overlooked by the lens. This model with integrated high-resolution photographic imagery plays an important role in a conservation program.

Currently, there is a rapid move toward historical cultural heritage interpretation, especially within the museum environment, in addition to on-site heritage displays. 3D modeling is an excellent hands-on display method, providing an invaluable tool for education and for promoting public awareness of Coptic heritage.

This modeling and virtual reality method is not restricted to major architectural and archaeological features. It can also be utilized in the reconstruction of individual artifacts such as pots and other daily objects used in antiquity, thereby promoting our understanding of past monastic communal activities.

Conclusion

Many of the Coptic monastic sites distributed throughout Egypt are under constant attack from erosion and pollution, both natural (environmental extremes) and man-made (tourism and vandalism). It is imperative that a program be instigated for these important sites, with their associated unique architectural elements, in order to preserve the Coptic cultural heritage.

One of the main challenges facing these sites is their location. Often situated in isolated desert areas, they are extremely vulnerable to a number of problems, especially natural erosion. While many of these challenges may not be totally overcome, they can be alleviated at least in part by applying these modeling techniques and capturing as much detail as possible, making the framework available for permanent display in the context of heritage management programs.

It is clear that virtual 3D modeling is an invaluable method, not only providing the data and information for developing conservation programs, but also for essential ongoing and future archaeological excavations.

The Qubbat al-Hawa digital reconstruction project is a dynamic and developing undertaking. The methodologies may be applied to similar sites in the future in order to gain important information and knowledge to assist in the preservation of the many diverse and unique Coptic monastic sites.

Notes

1   The author gratefully acknowledges the assistance of Peter Hossfeld of VCS Productions, Switzerland, for his advice and the setting up of the 3D and Virtual Reconstruction software and additional photographic work at the site.
2   Photographs of the saints in the west wall as shown on the jacket of this volume. Gawdat Gabra, 1991.
3   Initial photographic survey of Qubbat al-Hawa using high-resolution imagery. Peter Hossfeld, 2009.
4   Second photographic survey of Qubbat al-Hawa, accompanied by Renate Dekker. Author, 2010.

20 Christian Objects in the Aswan and Nubia Museums

Atif Naguib

THE ARCHAEOLOGICAL SURVEY of lower Nubia (1907–12) was undertaken by the Egyptian government in order to discover and record the historical material that would be lost when the district was submerged by the filling of the old Aswan Dam.

The Ministry of Public Works paid all the expenses of this mission and for the heightening of the dam. In 1912, the ministry also authorized the conversion of one of the largest of the government rest houses, situated on Elephantine Island, into a museum for Nubian antiquities. This is the present-day Aswan Museum. The museum collection includes antiquities and artifacts from Aswan and Nubia, covering all periods up to the Coptic and Islamic periods.

In the early 1960s, when Egypt built the Aswan High Dam, Egyptologists and archaeologists from all over the world responded to UNESCO's appeal to salvage the monuments of Egyptian Nubia before the rising waters of Lake Nasser submerged them forever. More than sixty expeditions ultimately joined the Nubian Rescue Campaign, which resulted in the excavation and recording of hundreds of sites, the recovery of thousands of objects, and the salvage and translocation of a number of important temples to higher ground. Finally, the Nubia Museum was opened in 1997 in Aswan.

The Coptic collections that were transferred from the Coptic Museum in Cairo included tenth-century wall paintings salvaged from the Church of Abdalla Nirqi, and unique objects from Qasr Ibrim and other Christian cities in Nubia.

The most important sites were the Central Church of Abdalla Nirqi and the later Southern Church. The paintings in these two churches were clearly in two different styles. At the time of their discovery one was called 'Byzantine' and it was applied on a thin layer of whitewash, and the other 'Nubian,' which was applied on a thicker layer of so-called Coptic plaster.

The Central Church was built in the middle of the eighth century, when it also received its first paintings of the 'violet style.' The flourishing period was around AD 1000, when the paintings of the 'white style' were applied, partly covering the paintings of the 'violet style.'

Frescos
There are eight frescos now exhibited in the Christian gallery at the Nubia Museum.

1-1. Fresco No. 11495
Theophany with a cross, AD 980–90
196 x 181 cm
Abdalla Nirqi, Nubia Museum

The half-figure of Christ in a small *mandorla*, surrounded by the four living creatures (man, eagle, calf, and lion) with their wings, and a Greek jeweled cross which has been added to the composition. There are many inscriptions, including some next to the founder, on the left. (van Moorsel, Jacquet, and Schneider 1975: 111–12, pl. 78–82)

1-2. Fresco No. 11462
Enthroned *Hodegetria* (date unknown)
110 x 83 cm
Abdalla Nirqi, Nubia Museum

Christ is depicted with red curly hair, two locks of which fall over his forehead. He is dressed in white. His right hand is raised, with three fingers held up. (van Moorsel, Jacquet, and Schneider 1975: 196–207, pl. 88)

1-3. Fresco No. 11471
Virgin *orans* (date unknown)
161 x 87 cm
Abdalla Nirqi, Nubia Museum

The purple color of her clothing makes us think this *orans* is Mary. However, it may possibly be St. Elizabeth. (van Moorsel, Jacquet, and Schneider 1975: 92–93, pl. 72)

1-4. Fresco No. 11466
Archangel with protégé (date unknown)
132 x 107 cm
Abdalla Nirqi, Nubia Museum
The protégé had pink-colored skin, in contrast to the archangel, although the man is portrayed with a full face. He is stretching out both his open hands to the archangel. (van Moorsel, Jacquet, and Schneider 1975: 80–81, pl. 70–74)

1-5. Fresco No. 11469
Traces of two periods (John the Baptist?) (date unknown)
101 x 53 cm
Abdalla Nirqi, Nubia Museum
It is a puzzling painting, not completed all at one time. The oldest part of this fragmentally preserved fresco shows the trunk and shoulders of a male figure. In a later period, however, the top part of this painting was renewed, after a new layer of plaster had first been lavishly applied over the top of the old one. The excavators called the man 'John the Baptist.' (van Moorsel, Jacquet, and Schneider 1975: 124–25, pl. 91)

1-6. Fresco No. 11470
Man seated on a throne (King David the prophet?), tenth century
119 x 91 cm
Abdalla Nirqi, Nubia Museum
He is also depicted in Bawit with this same gray hair, and without a royal crown. Is this sufficient reason to assume that the saint should be identified as King David? (van Moorsel, Jacquet, and Schneider 1975: 193–204, pl. 89)

1-7. Fresco No. 11473
St. John Chrysostom and Petou, about AD 1000
115 x 81 cm
Abdalla Nirqi, Nubia Museum
St. John Chrysostom and Petou. Both shown with full faces. The

inscriptions are to the left of where the saint is standing. (van Moorsel, Jacquet, and Schneider 1975: 117–18, pls. 80, 85)

1-8. Fresco No. 11472
Horseman (fragment), about AD 1000
235 x 123 cm
Abdalla Nirqi, Nubia Museum
    A mounted saint, riding a white horse at a slow pace. Between the legs of the horse the trunk of a naked, bearded man's figure emerges from a storage vessel. The man in the vessel is quoting a liturgical text, "Kyrie eleison." (van Moorsel, Jacquet, and Schneider 1975: 115–16, pls. 83, 87)

Other Objects
2-1. Tombstone No. 6925
11.5 x 9 cm
Sandstone, seventh century
Sakinya (near Toshka), Nubia Museum
    The tombstone bears the name of Iordanes and has eight lines in Greek, reading, "Day of commemoration of Blessed Iordanes: Tobah 13." (Mina 1942: 92, pl. 8)

2-2. Tombstone No. 6968
19 x 11 cm
Sandstone, seventh century
Sakinya, Nubia Museum
    A Greek tombstone bearing the name Kerekou who died in month 6, 13th indiction; it has eight lines. (Mina 1942: 72, pl. 4)

2-3. Architrave lintels No. 2846
135 x 21.5 cm
Sandstone, date unknown
Qasr al-Wizz, Aswan Museum
    A superbly curved and whitewashed architrave lintel with a projecting cornice lay before the western entrance. Though the separate motifs can be individually observed elsewhere in Nubia, the combination herein incorporated seems unique. The tympanum of the extreme motifs reproduces the design of various tombs. The stele has a simple Maltese cross where there would normally only be an inscription. (Scanlon 1970: 37–39, fig. 9)

3. Prayer book No. 6566
16.5 x 17.5 cm
Parchment, date unknown
Qasr al-Wizz, Nubia Museum
Written in Sahidic Coptic and illuminated, complete in seventeen folios. The text was clearly written in black ink on both sides of fifteen leaves and one side of the sixteenth. The decoration was in red, green, and black, sometimes touched with white, and included two crosses of interlace, a three-sided rectilinear frame of interlace, and various zoomorphically rendered capital letters. (Scanlon 1972: 18, pl. 11)

4. Cross No. 11673
9 x 4.5 cm
Wood, date unknown
Gebel Adda, Nubia Museum
Coptic cross of wood, very precise workmanship.

5-1. Censer No. J 90785
8.3 x 11 cm
Bronze, tenth century
Abdalla Nirqi, Nubia Museum
A bronze incense burner with the chains and hook still attached (replaced by a new one at a later time for exhibiting). Pieces of charcoal inside were found when discovered. (van Moorsel, Jacquet, and Schneider 1975: 26, fig. 25)

5-2. Kohl stick No. 2882
12.3 x 1.1 cm
Iron, tenth century
Sabagura, Aswan Museum
Kohl eyeliner has an equilateral cross handle.

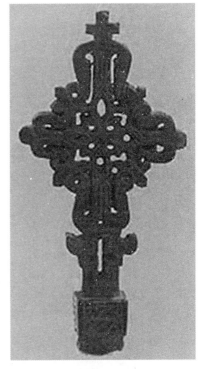

Fig. 20.1. Wooden Coptic cross from Gebel Adda

Fig. 20.2. Kohl stick from Sabagura, tenth century

6-1. Pottery No. 10839
36 x 24 cm
Vase, eighth century
Wadi al-Sebua, Nubia Museum

A large vase with a convex lid surmounted by a cross. The vase is brown ware with a dark brown slip. It is almost cylindrical with a ring base and interior rim, and it is decorated on the surface with geometric and floral patterns in buff paint. (Farid 1967: 74, fig. 17, pl. 8)

6-2. Pottery bowls No. 2515
Large one 10 x 6.5 cm, small ones 7 x 6 cm
Date unknown
Aswan, Aswan Museum

Seven small pottery bowls attached to one another, and fixed to the large bowl in the middle. This vessel was used in the prayer for the anointing of the sick (one of the seven sacraments of the Coptic Church), where seven small lighted wicks are placed in oil and prayers are recited over the oil. Then those in attendance are anointed with the oil with a piece of cotton. The oil is also used later to anoint those who were absent from the service. This vessel is also used in the service following the reading of the Book of the Apocalypse during the Bright Saturday service, part of the Coptic Pascha Week.

6-3. Pottery tray No. 1551
24 cm diameter
Tenth century
Elephantine, Aswan Museum

Large round pottery tray. Its surface is ornamented with floral and plant designs, including a figure of a big fish at the center. It was used for the Holy Bread.

Fig. 20.3. Pottery bowls used in the prayer for the anointing of the sick

Fig. 20.4. Pottery tray from Elephantine decorated with a fish, tenth century

21 Sources for the Study of Late Antique and Early Medieval Hagr Edfu

Elisabeth R. O'Connell

THE LATE ANTIQUE SITE of Hagr Edfu is located in a set of low sandstone hills 2.5 kilometers west of the contemporary town site at Tell Edfu (fig. 21.1). Hagr Edfu's Coptic toponym, *ptoou nTbô*, describes its physical and social relationship to Tell Edfu (*Tbô*). In Coptic, *toou* can mean 'mountain' or 'desert,' and Hagr Edfu rises in the distance on the western horizon,

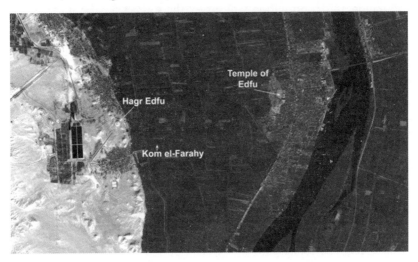

Fig. 21.1. Quickbird satellite image of the Edfu region (© Digital Global)

where it is the most prominent natural feature visible from Tell Edfu. *Toou* can also mean 'cemetery,' and Hagr Edfu was indeed a burial site for the population of Tell Edfu from as early as the Middle Kingdom. A fourth meaning, 'monastery' (Crum 1939: 44–41), is suggested by late antique archaeological remains at the site and, for the early medieval period, proven by toponyms preserved in a corpus of Coptic manuscripts now in the British Library (Gabra 1985; 1991).

Adaptive reuse of earlier pharaonic tombs by Christians was common throughout Egypt in late antiquity and systematic documentation and synthetic study have only recently become common (O'Connell 2007; in press). Like many archaeological sites in Egypt, Hagr Edfu's late antique phase of activity is complicated by its periodic use and reuse up to the present as well as the modern history of official and unofficial excavation (Effland 1999: 22–30). Since 2001, a British Museum expedition directed by W.V. Davies has documented a cluster of three pharaonic tombs and undertaken the mapping of tomb entrances at Hagr Edfu (Davies 2006; 2008; 2009).[1] Since 2007, the mission has systematically recorded late antique remains and other features at the site (Davies and O'Connell 2009; 2011). The resulting combination of archaeological, including papyrological, evidence together with the information from medieval manuscripts from the site provides a welcome opportunity to investigate the character of Christian activity at Hagr Edfu. After a brief introduction to its place in the region, this contribution will survey the sources for the study of the late antique site and suggest possible models with which we might understand the process by which a settlement came to occupy a cemetery.

The Historical and Material Context

In late antiquity, Tell Edfu was the site of the town Apollonos polis in Greek and, as stated above, *Tbô* in Coptic (for variants, see Timm 1984–92: 3:1148–57). From at least the Old Kingdom, the town was the regional administrative capital, benefiting from both the high agricultural yield of the broad alluvial plains of its hinterland and a strategic location at the termini of the roads connecting the Nile Valley to the mines of the Eastern Desert and Red Sea ports and, to the west, the Kharga Oasis (Vernus 1986). The well-preserved Ptolemaic period temple that stands today succeeded an earlier temple also dedicated to Horus of Edfu, and the town continued to be a regional capital into the Roman period when it was garrisoned (Vandorpe and Clarysse 2003; Gascou 1999: 17). The remains of the late antique town stand atop earlier settlement.[2] Seventh- and eighth-century AD documentary papyri excavated in the 1920s demonstrate that the town was the seat of the *pagarch*, who was accountable to the Byzantine *comes et dux* of the Thebaid and, after the Arab conquest of Egypt, the local *amir* (Gascou 1999; Gascoigne 2005). The town was also the seat of a bishop, the first attestation for which dates to the sixth century (Timm 1984–92: 3:1148; Worp 1994: 296). Although the written record indicates that the Persian occupation (AD 617/19–29) was felt in the region (*SB Kopt.* I 36), the Arab conquest does not seem to have had an immediate impact on the daily lives of the town's inhabitants. In the following centuries, the Christian kingdom of Makuria on Egypt's southern border exerted cultural influence and, periodically, political control (Effland 1998; Welsby 2002: 68–77). A significant community of Arabs is evidenced only from the Fatimid period (AD 969–1174), from which time the al-'Amriya mosque, reusing earlier late antique capitals and columns, may date (Gascoigne 2005: 157–59, 186–87).[3] Today, the religious life of the town's sizable Christian minority focuses on the Church of St. Mary, which is under the jurisdiction of the bishop of Aswan (Timm 1979: 94).

British Museum work at Hagr Edfu is beginning to elucidate the archaeology of the site in parallel with the regional capital at Tell Edfu (Bunbury, Graham, and Strutt 2009). By late antiquity, Hagr Edfu had long served as a necropolis for the inhabitants of Edfu. The decoration of an early New Kingdom tomb belonging to a temple official demonstrates that the necropolis was understood as a mound of creation (*i3t*). The site was also the likely location of Behdet, a stopping place on the annual processional route of the cult statues of the divine couple Hathor of Dendera and Horus of Edfu (Davies 2009: 26). By the New Kingdom, hieratic visitors' inscriptions also demonstrate that a neighboring large, well-cut tomb had been reimagined as a temple of Isis (*ḥwt-nṯr*). The discovery of 'Hathor jars' and fragments thereof are indicative of cult practice in the area (Davies and O'Connell 2011: fig. 36). Other ceramics, for example, jars full of embalming equipment (Davies and O'Connell 2011: 105), evidence the continuing use of the necropolis in the first millennium BC. A Roman-period Greek funerary inscription located on the southernmost hill of the necropolis and commemorating Harpocration ('Horus-the-Child'), son of Hierax ('Falcon'), attests the continued prominence of the falcon god Horus, whose cult centered on the temple located at Tell Edfu (Davies and O'Connell 2011).

In late antiquity, many of the earlier rock-cut tombs of the desert escarpment were reused by Christians for habitation. Activity at the site is evidenced by architecture and architectural installations in and around the rock-cut tombs, pottery, Coptic inscriptions, and ostraca (discussed below). Medieval manuscripts copied in the tenth and eleventh centuries and now in the British Library indicate that, at the time, the site was the location of several Christian institutions: a monastery of Mercurius, a *topos* of Aaron and a *topos* of the Archangel Michael (Gabra 1985; Effland 1999: 47–48). The history of the site from the tenth century to the nineteenth century is less well attested (Effland 2004: 16), but a continuous or periodic Christian presence is suggested by a nineteenth-century church built among older mud-brick walls that are visible in twentieth-century photographs (Rustafjaell 1910; cf. Clarke 1912). For much of the twentieth century, and perhaps earlier, the ancient rock-cut tombs on the desert escarpment were reused by the modern Christian population of the region for burial, a practice that was prohibited from 1941 to 1944, but resumed in a limited area thereafter (Fakhry 1947: 47–48). After several seasons' work by Egyptian expeditions in the 1970s, a modern monastery with the nineteenth-century church at its core was dedicated to Pachomius and, in 1980, the complex became the Tenth Official Coptic Orthodox monastery. Around this time, the modern Coptic cemetery was relocated on the open plain to the northwest of Hagr Edfu. Today the modern Monastery of St. Pachomius, Dayr Anba Bakhum, is a popular pilgrimage destination. As a result of this long history of use and reuse, the archaeology of the site is much disturbed, but it nevertheless repays study, adding to the known corpus of ancient necropolises reused in late antiquity.

Archaeology of Late Antique Hagr Edfu

Late antique activity is concentrated on the most prominent of the several hills that constitute Hagr Edfu. To the north, where only coffin-sized chambers were cut, pottery suggests first-millennium BC activity. To the south, where rock-cut tomb entrances are characterized by steeply sloping stepped corridors, pottery suggests use (or reuse) dating from the first to fifth centuries AD. By contrast, the central hill of Hagr Edfu contains relatively large and well-cut tombs that, consequently, were more conducive to habitation.

Near the pinnacle of the hilltop, a sandstone outcrop proved an attractive writing surface throughout antiquity. Whereas modern Arabic inscriptions—

usually containing Christian personal names—are localized on nearby flat surfaces overlooking the modern monastery, ancient activity is evidenced on the worn planes of the outcrop referred to today as 'the rock shelter.' Christian inscriptions share the same surfaces and sometimes partly overlap with earlier, hieroglyphic inscriptions. Christian texts contain *nomina sacra* and personal names such as Apa Dios, Epiphanios, Panoute, Joseph, and Isak.

Below the hilltop, evidence of late antique activity is nearly continuous along the east face of the central hill. Remains of mud-brick architecture—both standing structures and installations making use of earlier rock-cut tombs—cluster in four 'Areas' numbered 1–4 from north to south by the British Museum expedition (fig. 21.2). The most prominent tombs have long been the subject of

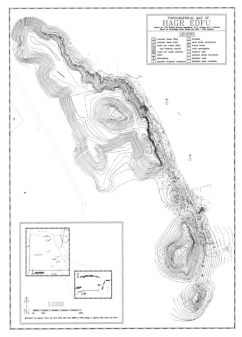

Fig. 21.2. Topographical map of Hagr Edfu (2011) with Areas indicated (F. Jarecki, A. Schmidt, and T. Beckh)

investigation, Egyptological and otherwise, with the result that evidence of later phases of use has largely been cleared away. The resulting spoil heaps contain late antique pottery, as do the mounds created by the foundation trench for the wall of the modern Monastery of St. Pachomius. A surface survey of pottery conducted by D.M. Bailey in 2007 and, since 2008, by T. Beckh, indicates late antique activity dating from the fifth to the ninth centuries AD.

Up to the present, three rock-cut tombs adapted and reused in late antiquity have been investigated by the British Museum team. In each case, the three tombs, located respectively in Areas 2, 3, and 4, were demonstrably 'cleared' before the British Museum began work at the site and very little remains in situ. Nevertheless, a survey of their features is instructive, allowing us to make valuable observations as to the character of activity in late antiquity. One of these tombs (Tomb 2.D) and its immediate environment (Area 2) are described here.

Where the desert escarpment today approaches the northwest corner of the modern monastery wall, a tier of large, well-proportioned tombs is hewn into the rock (fig. 21.3). The ceilings of several of these tombs and others at different elevations have collapsed and most are sanded up, rendering their interiors only partly, if at all, accessible. The courtyards of Tombs 2.A, B, C, and D nevertheless display mud plastering, mud-brick construction, or both. Features carved in stone may also date to the period of Christian activity. For example, Tomb 2.A has a well-worn stairway leading up to the entrance and a bench carved into the south wall of its courtyard; arched niches were hewn into east and north walls of the interior of Tomb 2.B.

Tomb 2.D stands out among the reused tombs in Area 2 because its ceiling, plaster, and decorative program of painted motifs and texts remain relatively intact. The original tomb courtyard is separated from its neighbor to the north by a single-course mud-brick dividing wall. A doorway is cut into the façade on the left and, on the right, there is a low ledge or bench over which is a small round opening that functions as a window and admits a low diffuse light to the interior. The doorway is fitted with a plastered step and door sockets and, above, emplacements for a lintel. Inside the original tomb are two rooms, more or less on an axis. The second room is entered from a doorway cut into the north end of the west wall. This second room has two deep niches extending from its west and south walls (probably originally for burial emplacements). In 2011, removal of windblown sand in the first chamber confirmed that the rock-cut tomb had been 'cleared'

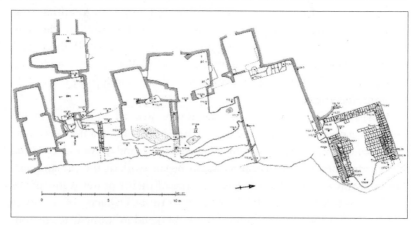

Fig. 21.3. Plan of architecture in Area 2a–b (G. Heindl)

by earlier excavators. Nevertheless, several layers of extant floor indicate multiple phases of plastering consistent with habitation, and future analysis of pottery embedded in these floor layers may suggest dates of occupation. On the walls, a thick mud plaster is coated with a thin layer of white gypsum. The north, west, and south walls are decorated with two crosses on each wall. One cross, located at the east end of the north wall, is painted in black and consists of a knotted design and the others, painted in combinations of red and yellow ochers, are crossed and encircled by vegetal motifs. The crosses on the north and south walls flank Coptic texts framed by triple and double twist guilloche bands also painted in red and yellow ochers. Like the crosses, the texts are today severely damaged and largely illegible, although

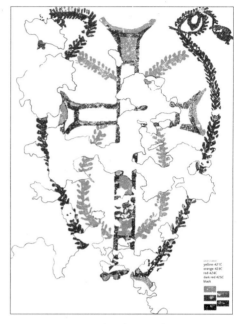

Fig. 21.4. Facsimile of painted cross in Tomb D, Area 2a (E.R. O'Connell and C. Thorne)

the word *pnoute* ('God') is visible in the first line of the painted text on the south wall. Below, a Coptic inscription hastily carved at the east end of the south wall reads *anok Stephanos* ('I am Stephen'), and contrasts with the more deliberate painted program. In the second room of the original rock-cut tomb, a painted cross is located above a large niche in the east wall. It is painted in red and yellow ochers in the same style as the majority of crosses in the first room. Unlike the *dipinti* painted on the white gypsum ground in the first room, this cross is painted directly onto the rock. It is the most complete of the extant crosses (fig. 21.4).

Tomb 2.D is located in a part of the site which today exhibits extensive late antique remains. In addition to reworked rock-cut tombs, the remains of two mud-brick structures stand on successive terraces. At the same elevation as the tier of rock-cut tombs described above, the extant remains of the first mud-brick building measures 4.65 x 5.30 m. Its rubble foundation was built on fill and its east end has collapsed. The entrance is at the west end of the south wall and the three surviving interior walls stand a meter in height. The remains of vaulting bricks along the north wall indicate the roofing method employed and the floor is paved with fired brick tiles measuring 26 x 15 x 3 cm each. Along the interior north and south walls, standing directly on the tiles, are single courses of mud bricks standing on end, which were plastered to serve as benches. The size of the room, floor treatment, and benches suggest a public space, perhaps a church, shrine, or assembly hall.[4] Because the east end is collapsed, there is no indication that the room may have had an apse, a feature which would have provided a more confident identification. To the east and at a lower elevation is a second surviving structure built in multiple phases of construction and, at its greatest extent, measuring approximately 15 x 5 m (not shown on plan). Its function is unclear, but the presence of a large vat may indicate it had storage, processing, or industrial purposes.

Settlement at Hagr Edfu was not centralized, but strung along the terraces of the desert escarpment where the largest and relatively well-cut tombs provided the best spaces to reuse. The development of the settlement was likely ad hoc, expanding as needed. Late antique built structures in and around tombs and modifications to the existing tomb architecture suggest that the tombs were reused for habitation. Such features demonstrate the practical considerations motivating the choice of habitations. The identity of some of the occupants, and perhaps visitors, is suggested by personal names in inscriptions, some of which are mentioned above, and ostraca found at the site.

Fig. 21.5. Ostracon from Area 2a
(J. Rossiter)

Coptic Ostraca from Hagr Edfu

Several Coptic ostraca have been discovered as surface finds in the course of the British Museum expedition's work. Most of the texts are fragmentary, but they contain a handful of personal names and titles, for example, Apa Jakob in an ostracon discovered as a surface find in the second mud-brick structure described above (fig. 21.5). These ostraca join a larger corpus of Coptic and Greek ostraca excavated by an Edfu Inspectorate mission directed by Mohammed Ali in 1980–81 (Gabra 1985: 11–12; 1991; Boud'hors 1999: 4; Blöbaum, in this volume).[5] In the 2009 and 2011 seasons, the BM expedition located these ostraca in the Elkab magazine (Davies and O'Connell 2009; 2011) and, in 2010, A. Blöbaum joined the mission to collate readings made from 1980s photographs provided by G. Gabra (see Blöbaum in this volume).[6] The names found in the texts demonstrate the presence of Christian men at the site. Familial and respectful forms of address (for example, 'father,' 'brother,' 'your holy father,' 'apa') and, much less frequently, ecclesiastical titles ('priest' and 'bishop'), suggest a clerical or monastic milieu.[7] One sherd found in Area 4 breaks just after the word topos, where one would expect to find a name, for example, 'the topos of x,' but, as yet, ostraca from Hagr Edfu do not provide a late antique name for an institution at the site.

Tell Edfu Papyri and Ostraca

Contemporary Greek, Coptic, and Arabic papyri and ostraca excavated at Tell Edfu and dating to late antiquity do not, so far, attest the toponym ptoou nTbô or any of the institutions known from the medieval manuscripts mentioned in the introduction and discussed further below.[8] Greek and Coptic documents from the sixth/seventh century mention 'the church (ekklesia) of Apollon' and several monasteries (Timm 1984–92: 3:1148–57). Saints' shrines attested in seventh- and eighth-century Tell Edfu papyri include the oikos of holy Agnaton, the topos of holy Colluthos, and [the topos?] of holy Stephanos and holy Kyriakos (Papaconstantinou 2001b: 304). Among these toponyms, it is worthwhile to highlight two possible candidates. First, the oikos of Agnaton, which is specified to be 'on the periphery (ekperi) of the town of Apollon,' would have been located precisely where one would expect a martyrium (Gascou 1999: 18): in a cemetery. Second, given that the façade of the largest and best-cut of the ancient Egyptian tombs at Hagr Edfu bears an inscription naming Apa Colluthos, the topos of Colluthos may also be of interest.

Medieval Manuscripts

The toponyms for Hagr Edfu are virtually assured for the medieval period. The findspot of an important corpus of Coptic manuscripts, now in the British Library, has long been identified as Hagr Edfu (P.Lond.Copt. II: xxvii–xxx; Gabra 1985). In an unconfirmed account, a paid informant told one buyer that they had been discovered at the corner of ruined walls near the nineteenth-century church at the site (Rustafjaell 1910: 3–6; P.Lond.Copt. II: xxix). In any case, the shared physical characteristics of the

Fig. 21.6. Frontispiece of the Martyrdom of St. Mercurius (*P.Lond.Copt.* II 130)

manuscripts, their tenth- and eleventh-century dates, and the fact that they all came onto the antiquities market at about the same time suggest that at least a majority came from a single source (*P.Lond.Copt.* II: xxvii). The best evidence for their attribution is the content of the manuscripts themselves.

A majority of the codices bear colophons that provide combinations of the following data: the name and location of the copyist, the date and occasion of the copying, and the recipient for whom the book was copied. Twelve colophons name Esna as the place of production and eight name institutions in Edfu or in the Mountain of Edfu, *ptoou nTbô*, as recipients (Gabra 1985; *P.Lond.Copt.* II: xxvi). Further, they provide the names of up to three Christian *topoi* located in the Mountain of Edfu. A monastery (*monasterion*), church (*ekklesia*), or saint's shrine (*topos*) dedicated to St. Mercurius is the recipient institution in six colophons (fig. 21.6).[9] On analogy with other well-known institutions (for example, the Monastery of Phoibammon at Dayr al-Bahari), it is likely that the three different designations refer to the same place—that is, a monastery containing a church and a *topos*, in this case, a saint's shrine dedicated to Saint Mercurius and perhaps housing his relics (cf. Papaconstantinou 2001b: 271–78). Two other *topoi* known from the manuscripts were dedicated to St. Aaron, the bishop of Philae, and the Archangel Michael, the latter of which is also specified as located in *ptoou nTbô*.[10]

Conclusion

One cannot assume that the toponyms or even the function of the site known for the medieval period would have been the same as in late antiquity. The principal dedication of institutions could change over time. Nevertheless, the material culture on site does suggest the presence of a pre-medieval Christian foundation, the precise character of which must remain hypothetical. Among the range of possibilities, two are particularly attractive. The location of the settlement in a necropolis may signal a process whereby the tomb of a prominent Christian became the locus of a saint's cult administered by monks, as was often the case by the end of the sixth century (Papaconstantinou 2007: 353–56). Alternatively, as suggested by monastic literary sources in particular, the rock-cut tombs of the desert escarpment may have provided shelter to a local holy man (or, much less likely, woman) who later attracted disciples, in time becoming the locus of a monastery which, by the medieval period at least, also housed a saint's relics.

As throughout the later Roman Empire, the collapse of the distinctions of spaces reserved for the living and the dead is one of the defining features of the transition from the Roman to medieval worlds, when, on the one hand, cemeteries containing funerary basilicas, *martyria*, or both, became the focus of settlements, most famously at Rome, and, on the other hand, burial *ad sanctum* became desirable in churches located in already-existing cities and towns. Thus, late antique settlements such as the one at Hagr Edfu demonstrate a shift in the use of space both common throughout wider Christendom and, given the reuse of rock-cut tombs located on the desert escarpment of the Nile Valley, specifically Egyptian.

Acknowledgments

For their comments and suggestions, I thank A. Blöbaum, W.V. Davies, A. Gascoigne, P. Grossmann, T.M. Hickey, and A. Papaconstantinou. All errors of fact and judgment remain my own. Edited papyri and other papyrological resources are cited according to the conventions in Oates, Willis, Sosin, Bagnall, Cowey, Depauw, Wilfong, and Worp 2011.

Notes

1 The British Museum Expedition is grateful to the Supreme Council for Antiquities, the members of the Permanent Committee, and the chief inspector of Edfu, Zenan Noubi Abdel Salam, for permission to work at Hagr Edfu. I thank the Edfu inspectors with whom I have worked since 2007: Zenan Noubi Abdel Salam (2007), Suzie Sameir Labib (2008), Ramadan Hassan Ahmed (2009 and 2011), and Osama Ismail Ahmed (2010).

2 For the bibliography of excavation reports for the French and Franco-Polish missions to Tell Edfu in the 1920s and 1930s, see Timm 1984–92: 3:1154–55. For new work, see, for example, Möller 2005.

3 For the possibility that this mosque was one of several erected in Upper Egypt

between 1077 and 1082 to commemorate victories over Bedouin tribes, see Gascoigne 2005, and, for the wider political context, Sanders 1998 and Welsby 2002: 68–77. For modern Muslim tribal identity in the Edfu region, see H.C. Korsholm Nielsen 2004.

4 For churches of this size that happen also to be located in ancient Egyptian necropolises, see Qurnat Mar'i (Castel 1979: fig 1) and Saqqara (Smith, Davies, and Frazer 2006: fig. 4). I thank P. Grossmann for ongoing discussion concerning the identification of this structure.

5 G. Gabra, personal communication, 2007.

6 Special thanks are due to Ramadan Hassan Ahmed, the inspector of the Elkab Magazine, who located these ostraca and facilitated access and study.

7 For a discussion of distinctions between family and spiritual family designations in documentary texts, see O'Connell 2007: 265.

8 For an overview of Greek and Coptic Tell Edfu text editions, see Gascou 1999: 13–16 and Boud'hors 1999. For new text editions, see Bacot 2009. For Arabic papyri from Tell Edfu dating to the ninth and tenth centuries, see P.Cair.Arab. 1.48, 56; 5.299, 339, 6.372, and, for additional edited documents, Sijpesteijn 2007: 12–13.

9 For St. Mercurius, see Papaconstantinou 2001b: 145–46.

10 For St. Aaron, see Papaconstantinou 2001b: 145–46 and Dijkstra 2008. For Michael, see Papaconstantinou 2001b: 154–59.

22 Christianity in Kom Ombo

Adel F. Sadek

Introduction

Kom Ombo[1] lies on the eastern bank of the Nile between Mount al-Silsila and Aswan. It was an important trade stop for caravans between Sudan and Egypt. The most important monument is the double-celled temple from the Ptolemaic period dedicated to the crocodile god Sobek and the falcon god Haroeris (Horus) (Grossmann 1991e). The old town of Omboi vanished and became a mound called Kom Ombo; the word *kom* in Arabic means 'mound.' A new city by the same name arose at the beginning of the twentieth century, bordering the old site.

Fig. 22.1. Ombos viewed from the Nile (Morgan, Bouriant, Legrain, and Jéquier 1895)

249

The History of Christianity in Kom Ombo

In the history of the Christian kingdom of Nubia, Christianity made the First Cataract the starting point for the spread of the new faith upriver (MacCoull 1990: 151). We are informed by a Paschal letter of Athanasius of Alexandria, dating to AD 347, that Syene had a bishop by then (Timm 1984–92: 1:222–35).

Already by the mid-fifth century, Bishop Appion attested to churches on Philae as well as to the threatening presence of the pagan Nubians who continued to worship in the temple of Isis on the island. Justinian ordered the closure of the temple between 535 and 537, putting an end to the coexistence of both pagan and Christian cultic use of the building (MacCoull 1990: 153; Munier 1938: 47). With funds provided by the fifth-century bishop of Philae, Daniel, the island of Philae was repaired and, in the sixth century, the Isis temple complex on the island was transformed into two Christian sanctuaries dedicated to St. Stephen and the Holy Cross, under the leadership of the sixth-century bishop, Theodore (Nautin 1967).

We do not know when Christianity began in Kom Ombo[2] or how it ended, apart from some disconnected information. From a Paschal letter by Patriarch Theophilos XXIII (AD 385–412) we know that bishop Verres replaced the deceased Sylvanus (Munier 1943: 12). Another bishop of the city participated in the consecration of a building or guest house of the church in the sixth to seventh century, as mentioned in an inscription on a memorial tablet (Hall 1905: 1–2, pls. I and II, no. 1196).[3] A priest called Serenus from Omboi served as an arbiter in a document dating to the fifth century in the Patermouthis archive (MacCoull 1990: 156).[4] From Kom Ombo itself, a tax receipt on an ostracon refers to Mena the monk, son of Doretheus, who paid a sum as tax for his community (Crum 1902b: 36, nos. 407 and 408).

The name of Omboi is mentioned in a document dated AD 567, which is a petition by the councilors of Omboi to the governor of the Thebaid. In this petition, the councilors accuse a person of "renewing the sanctuaries" for a group of Blemmyes and of raiding with them the fertile lands around Omboi (Dijkstra 2004). This may refer to Omboi as a nome capital and may mean that the nome still consisted of the traditional first Upper Egyptian nome, including the towns in the area of the First Cataract, forty kilometers south of Omboi, that is, Syene, Elephantine, and Philae. Hence the councilors of Omboi would have been responsible for this whole area (Dijkstra and Worp 2006: 183). In the sixth century, Omboi is listed among

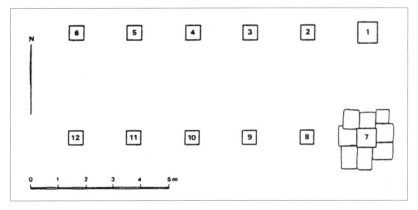

Fig. 22.2. Plan of the column bases forming the church in the Ptolemaic temple at Kom Ombo (Jones 1992)

the eleven most important towns of the eparchy of the Upper Thebaid; moreover, Omboi had an episcopal see from at least AD 402 onwards (Dijkstra and Worp 2006: 187; Worp 1994).

Archaeological Findings

In the area of the Ptolemaic temple, and within its enclosure wall, some pedestals of columns were found to the northwest of the temple building (Barsanti 1915: 168–76). Barsanti, who restored the temple, reports twelve column bases, a carved capital, and a single column shaft. All this masonry is of sandstone and is generally referred to as a church (fig. 22.2) (Jones 1992: 97). East of this stands a single dwelling house of the early Christian period in which Barsanti found a basket containing metal liturgical objects belonging to the church (Barsanti 1915: 174).

Altar Instruments

The patriarch or a bishop must consecrate the liturgical instruments of the Coptic Church, as well as everything worn or used during the services, as part of the general process of consecration.[5]

Chalices

Barsanti found two chalices made of copper (Bénazeth 2004: 1160, 1166, Coptic Museum nos. 5146 and 50850) and another of glass (Barsanti 1915: 176). The use of glass chalices is mentioned frequently in the history of church in different situations (Muyser 1937). These two copper chalices show that the community was not rich, so they were made of copper instead of gold or silver. The two copper chalices were probably used only at the major feasts, and the glass one was used in the daily services. In the *History of the Patriarchs* during the patriarchate of Alexander II, we read:

> O brethren, you have seen how we have been robbed of all the property of the church, even of the cups in which the Pure Blood is offered; so that we have been forced to make chalices of glass and patens of wood instead of the gold and silver vessels, because Kurrah has robbed us of them. (Evetts 1910: 61 [315]–62 [316])

It seems that the Copts faced this problem regularly, for the Coptic Church still has a special rite for filling the chalice if it is ever found empty due to a crack or any other accident.[6]

One of the copper chalices is characterized by the presence of two hands (Bénazeth 2001: no. 318). There are two inscriptions, one of Alpha, referring to Christ (Rev. 22:13), and the other is part of the name of the church, starting with "Apa" (fig. 22.3). The second part is not clear, as the inscription is in bad condition, so we do not have the complete form of the name. The remaining letters do not direct us to any known saint, so perhaps this was a local saint. The other chalice is very simple (Bénazeth 2001: no. 319) and resembles the ordinary chalices shown in depictions of the sacrament that appear in paintings.[7] No traces of gilding can be detected, unlike on some other liturgical instruments found in Luxor (Messiha 1992: 130).

Fig. 22.3. Copper chalice with inscriptions from Kom Ombo (Bénazeth 2001: no. 318)

Processional crosses

Two processional crosses of copper were also found (Bénazeth 2001: nos. 316 and 317), which implies that Christians used to make processions in the area, perhaps around the temple, such as is attested later in the rite of the procession of the Feast of the Cross[8] and on Palm Sunday (Viaud

1967–68; Youssef 2007). There is also another iron cross from Kom Ombo which was not discovered by Barsanti (fig. 22.4).

The use of these crosses remains debatable: while some assume that they were used as functional processional crosses, others opt to view them simply as part of the chandelier. It is very surprising that the Greek inscription on the iron cross invokes "God the Helper" without mentioning the name of the church or that of the donor(s) (Bénazeth 2001: no. 217).

Paten

One of the liturgical instruments is the copper paten used during the Eucharist and found in Kom Ombo by Barsanti. There is no inscription on the paten showing the name of the church or the donor (Bénazeth 2001: no. 320).

Other Finds from the Site of Kom Ombo
Chandelier

The form of the copper chandelier can be compared with the chandeliers used in Egypt to this day (fig. 22.5). There are holes for glass vessels containing oil, a shape widespread in this area.[9] The archaeological context, as well as the crosses of the ornamentation, lead us to believe that this chandelier belongs to a church; however, no inscription of dedication has survived (Bénazeth 2001: no.187).

The metal objects of Kom Ombo would probably have been made by the same atelier that produced the portable altars of Luxor, only a few kilometers from Kom Ombo (Messiha 1992). The chandelier of

Fig. 22.4. Iron cross with inscriptions from Kom Ombo (Bénazeth 2001: no. 217)

Fig. 22.5. Copper chandelier ornamented with crosses, with places to hold oil lamps (Bénazeth 2001: no. 187)

Fig. 22.6. Wooden weight box with carved cross on the cover (Strzygowski 1904: no. 8815)

Kom Ombo resembles to a great extent a copper chandelier from Edfu that has six places to fix glass vessels of oil (Bénazeth 1992: 164, AF 1329).

Weight box in wood

The site of Kom Ombo also produced an empty weight box in wood, which has places to put different weights and a small scale (Strzygowski 1904: 142, no. 8815).[10] Its cover is ornamented with a carved cross; the sign of the cross or some symbols and sentences of invocation found on a box refer to its legal approval (fig. 22.6). It was one of the duties of a bishop in late antique Egypt to check the weights and approve them for use (Rutschowscaya 1979: 4).

Oil lamp

An oil lamp in copper was found at the site of Kom Ombo. This was discovered with the other liturgical instruments (see above), such as the chalice and the paten. Although an oil lamp could be for both liturgical and non-liturgical use, the archaeological context makes us incline to a liturgical use. The canons of the church, such as the *Didascalia* or the *Canon of Hippolytus*, insist that the church should have lights as a symbol of heaven. Abraham of Hermonthis in the sixth century received many undertakings from priests and deacons to keep the lamps of the church lit (Crum 1902b: nos. 41 and 45). There are also some rites of the Coptic Church where light plays an important role, such as the rite of unction of the sick[11] (Gabra, Pearson, Swanson, and Youssef 2008: 261–62) or the reading of the Apocalypse during Bright Saturday (Burmester 1967: 293). In Coptic literature we encounter healing miracles that use the oil put in front of the relics of the saints (Godron 1991).

Conclusion

Despite the lack of documents coming from Kom Ombo, we can assume that Christianity started there at least in the fourth century. Several names of its bishops are mentioned in different documents and archaeological finds. Some of the names of the clergy have also come down to us to add to our knowledge. The archaeological finds in Kom Ombo demonstrate liturgical activities, most probably associated with the activities of pilgrimages in nearby areas.[12]

This short paper makes no pretension of delivering a detailed study of the presence of Christianity in Kom Ombo. It gives an overview of the Christian community before the Arab Conquest and in the first centuries thereafter.

Notes

1   Since the Old Kingdom, Elephantine had been regarded as the traditional capital of the first Upper Egyptian nome. In the third or second century BC, Omboi became the metropolis of the nome and, at least from the reign of Vespasian until the end of the second century AD, Omboi was the capital.

2   Timm 1984–92: 3:1468–70.

3   The memorial tablet mentioned other names of officials, such as Gabriel the duke of the Thebaid and Phoibammon the chancellor. This reflects a well-established city with a bishop and churches with a guest house, considered by the authorities as a public place.

4   The archive of Patermouthis, son of Menas, contains fifty documents, in both Greek and Coptic, divided between the collections of London (British Library) and Munich (Bayerische Staatsbibliothek). The archive ranges over a time span of 120 years (Farber and Porten 1986).

5   Liturgical instruments include paten, chalice, spoon, chalice ark, Gospel casket, censer, fan, incense box, cruet, manual cross, processional cross, Eucharistic bread basket, basin and ewer, and a small vessel for conveying the sacraments to the sick (Burmester 1967: 23–29; Gabra, Pearson, Swanson, and Youssef 2008: 166–67).

6   This rite is still used if some accident befalls the chalice that causes its contents to disappear through breakage or if water, vinegar, or oil has been poured into it by mistake (cf. al-Masry 1940; Burmester 1967: 88).

7   In Bawit where David appears filling a chalice (Clédat 1916: fig. 25 and pl. IX); in the hands of the Twenty-four Elders in the Sanctuary of Benjamin in Dayr Abu Maqar (Leroy 1982: figs. 2 and 3, pls. 8–18); also to some extent it resembles the chalices in the hands of the Twenty-four Elders and the chalice presented by Melchizedek to Abraham in the paintings of the sanctuary of the Monastery of St. Antony (van Moorsel 1995: pls. 14, 16).

8   The Coptic Church celebrates the Feast of the Cross on 17 Tut (27 September) and 10 Baramhat (19 March). The first date commemorates the discovery of the Holy Cross by Queen Helena, the mother of Constantine the Great, in the fourth century. The second date commemorates the recovery of the Holy Cross from the Persians by the Roman emperor Heraclius in the seventh century (Gabra, Pearson, Swanson, and Youssef 2008: 140).

9   One chandelier of the same shape comes from the nearby area of Edfu, and two others from an unknown area (Bénazeth 1992: 164, AF 1329; 166–67, E 11711 and

E 11699).

10 Weight boxes generally contain a delicate hand scale (Rutschowscaya 1979: 3, fig.
    6), used for weighing precious metals or medicine. The symbol of the scale has a
    very important meaning in ancient Egyptian literature and religion. It also appears
    in the hand of the symbol of justice on the wall of graves of al-Bagawat, the early
    Christian necropolis in Kharga Oasis (Fakhry 1951: 74, fig. 66, pl. XXII).

11 One of the seven sacraments in the Coptic Church, the ceremony is performed
    before the sanctuary screen. A lampstand holds seven unlit lamps. As the priest
    begins to read each of the seven prayers for the sick, he lights one of the lamps
    (Burmester 1967: 144).

12 The commemoration of saints in the vicinity is well known, such as the pilgrimage
    of St. Mercurius (1 August) in the village of Higazah south of Qus, of St. Theodore
    in Luxor (24 January), and of St. Ammonios the martyr and bishop of Esna (23
    December) (Viaud 1979: 61–62).

23 Identification of the Monastery of the Nubians in Wadi al-Natrun

Fr. Bigoul al-Suriany

Introduction

Christianity was introduced into Nubia by the sixth century. By the eighth century, the whole of Nubia had become Christian. It would be safe to assume that the Nubians shared with their neighbors, the Egyptian Christians from Upper Egypt, the various aspects of the non-Chalcedonian faith, including saints and worship practices.

When the Arabs invaded Egypt, by the mid-seventh century, they tried unsuccessfully to continue into Nubia. However, a treaty (Baqt) was imposed on Nubia by which the Nubians would supply the Muslim authority in Egypt with a number of slaves in exchange for other goods needed in Nubia (den Heijer 1989: 57, note 203). Thereafter, some Copts and Syrian refugees went to live in Nubia. This cultural exchange strengthened the link between the Copts and the Nubians.

The Christian presence of Nubia became apparent by the tenth to eleventh centuries; not only did the Nubian king become the protector of the Pope of Alexandria, but he also obtained the authority to establish a monastery in Scetis (Wadi al-Natrun).[1] The Islamization of Nubia proceeded gradually and by the fourteenth century Christianity no longer existed in the entire area (Adams 1991d).

This paper will establish the existence of Nubians in Scetis, and identify the patron saint of this monastery.

Surveys of the Monasteries in Wadi al-Natrun

Medieval historical studies have brought to us many surveys of the famous religious places in Egypt. Some of them still survive. Abu al-Makarim, a Coptic historian from the twelfth century, in his survey stated that the monasteries of Wadi al-Natrun at that time numbered seven: "St. Macarius, the Syrians, St. Bishoi, St. John Kame, Lady Baramous, St. Moses, and St. John the Little" (al-Suriani 1984a: fol. 64b–73b.)[2] Omar Tosson, in his study *Wadi al'Natrun*, mentioned that Ibn Fadl Allah al-Imari, a Muslim historian during the thirteenth century, had visited the desert of Scetis in AD 1299 and mentioned only the number of seven monasteries without giving more details about the patron saints or the inhabitants of these monasteries (Tosson 1935: 65).

Next is the famous historian of the fifteenth century, the Muslim historian al-Maqrizi, who was able to survey the area as well. Despite the fact that the number of the monasteries mentioned in the previous surveys was seven, he stated:

> The monastery of St. Macarius, the elder, a famous monastery among them and near it lays four ruined monasteries. This was formerly the monastery of the pious monks, and a Patriarch was not recognized by them until they had made him take his seat in this monastery, after he had sat upon the throne in Alexandria. It is said that there were 1,500 monks here, but now there are few. There are three saints named Macarius: the greatest who was abbot of this monastery, St. Macarius of Alexandria, and St. Macarius the bishop; and their bones are kept in three hollow pieces of wood, and are visited by the Christians. Here is also the letter written by 'Amr Ibn al-'As to the monks of Wadi Habib, about the treasure ship of the northern districts, as it has been related to me by one who had heard it from a man who had seen it there. St. Macarius the elder received the monastic rule from Antony, the first among them who wore the monk's cap and the Askim, which is a band of leather with which the monks alone gird themselves, and upon which there is a cross. He met Antony on the eastern mountain-range, where the monastery of Al'Arabah is, and remained for some time with him; and then Antony clothed him with the monastic habit and bid him go to Wadi al-Natrun and there take up his abode....The monastery of St. John the Dwarf is said to have been built during the reign of Constantine the son of Helena. This

St. John possessed notable qualities, and was one of the most famous monks. The circumstances of this monastery were very favourable, and many monks lived there; but now only three monks are left there. The monastery of John Kama, and the monastery of Elias, which belonged to the Abyssinians; both of these are destroyed, because worms injured their wood-work, so that they fell to pieces. The Abyssinians then went to the monastery of the Virgin of St. John the Dwarf which is a small monastery near that of St. John the Dwarf. Near these monasteries stands that of St. Anub, now likewise destroyed. St. Anub was a native of Samannud, and was put to death at the beginning of Islam, and his body is placed in a house at Samannud. The monastery of the Armenians near these monasteries was destroyed. In their neighbourhood stands also the monastery of Bu Bisha'i, greatly revered among them, because Bisha'i was one of the monks who belonged to the class of Macarius and John the Dwarf. It is a very large monastery. A monastery opposite to that of Bu Bisha'i formerly belonged to the Jacobites but for 300 years was in the possession of the Syrian monks, and is now in their hands. The place where these monasteries are is called Birkat al-Adyirah (lake of the monasteries). The monastery of the Virgin Baramous, dedicated to the name of the Virgin Mary; there are some monks. Opposite to it stands the monastery of Moses or Abu Moses the Black also called Baramous; this monastery is dedicated to the Virgin of Baramous, so that Baramous is the name of the monastery. A story is told of it as follows: Maximus and Domitius were the sons of the emperor of the Romans, and had a teacher called Arsenius. The teacher took himself from the land of the Romans to Egypt, crossed this desert of Shihat, adopted the monastic life, and remained there till he died. He was an excellent man, and both the aforesaid sons of the emperor came to him during his life, and became monks at his hands. When they died their father sent and had the church of Baramous built in their names. St. Moses the Black was a bold robber, who had murdered 100 men; then he adopted Christianity, became a monk, and wrote many books. He is one of those who kept the forty days' fast entirely without food, and he was a Berber by race. (al-Maqrizi 1892, vol. 2: 508–509)

While al-Maqrizi was clear about the Armenian monastery, the monastery of Anub is not identified. There was one monk with some brothers whose name was Anub, a contemporary of St. John the Little and St. Pshoi (Evelyn-White 1932: 369, 398, 400, 402, 406–407). However, his existence as a patron saint is not attested by the list mentioned in the *History of the Patriarchs*. Al-Maqrizi's testimony refers to St. Anub, the martyr of Samannud from the fourth century, while no other evidence confirms this attribution. The only possibility is a misreading of Anub to An-Nub or al-Nub (= the Nubians, like the Syrians in al-Suryan or as-Suryan). This hypothesis is plausible as the presence of Nubians is well attested. Therefore, as the existence of the Monastery of the Nubians is not attested by al-Maqrizi, we may expect that he was relying on other sources that confused the name of Abanub with the Monastery of the Nubians.

Lastly, during the first half of the twentieth century, two surveys were carried out on the monasteries and *manshopias*[3] in Wadi al-Natrun. The first was done by Evelyn-White, a western archaeologist on a mission from the New York Metropolitan Museum of Art, and the other was done by Prince Omar Tosson. Evelyn-White visited the area of the monasteries during the second decade of the twentieth century.[4] He discussed in his book the Nubian objects that are in al-Suryan Monastery, with a good report about their background, but neglected to mention the existence of the Nubian inhabitants (Evelyn White 1932: 2:400). Shortly after, Prince Omar Tosson visited the monasteries during the 1930s, and mentioned a site for the Nubian monastery (Tosson 1935: 65).

Sources of the History of the Church

Having traced the outlines of Nubian history, I will now discuss the different sources related to the monasteries of Wadi al-Natrun in order to identify the presence of Nubians. In particular we will investigate the following two biographies found in the *History of the Patriarchs* of the Coptic Church:

1. The life of Pope Cyril II, the sixty-seventh patriarch (1076–90)
2. The life of Pope Gabriel IV, the eighty-sixth patriarch (1370–78)

In AD 1088, Mawhub ibn Mansur ibn al-Mufarrij (den Heijer 1989: 81–115), the Alexandrian deacon, mentioned in his biography of Pope Cyril II that there were seven monasteries in Wadi al-Natrun: "St. Macarius, St. John the Little, the Syrians, St. Bishoi, St. John Kame, el-Baramous, and St. Moses" (Evelyn-White 1932: 2:360). Also in that biography there is a list of the relics that the author had seen. This list informs us indirectly about the monasteries that existed in Scetis at that time (Atiya, 'Abd al-Masih, Khs-Burmester, and Khater 1959: 358 [translation]):

> The Three Abba Macari, the forty-nine Martyrs, St. Zeno: St.
>   Macarius Monastery
> St. Bishoi and St. Paul of Tamoh: St. Bishoi Monastery
> St. John the Little: St. John the Little Monastery
> St. John Kame: St. John Kame Monastery
> St. Moses the Black: St. Moses Monastery
> St. James the Persian and the finger of St. Severus: The Syrian
>   Monastery
> Tomb of Mother Hilaria and St. Ptoleme: not identified

Hence, the monastery of the Nubians, if it existed at that time, did not possess any relics of a patron saint.

According to the history of Pope Gabriel IV (1370–78), he consecrated a bishop for Faras in Nubia in AD 1372, named Timothy, but nothing is mentioned about his roots (Plumley 1975: 4). Also, in 1374, in the description of the *Rites of the Concoction of the Myron by Pope Gabriel IV* by Bishop Athanasius of Qus, it is mentioned that Pope Gabriel and his group of bishops visited the monasteries of the area during his stay, but without mentioning the name of the Nubian monastery.

> And after that he intended to visit the rest of the monasteries. The monks of the monastery of Abba John (Yuhnes) came to him—among them the priest Peter (Butrus) the abbot of the above mentioned monastery and Simon (Sim'an) his brother. He rode with the bishops and the recitation continued in front of him with psalis from Saint Macarius to the vicinity of Abba John. The monks of the mentioned monastery came out to welcome him with the Abyssinian monks and the Armenian monks with censers and gospels and crosses.
>
> When he drew near the monastery he recited the absolution near the tombs and entered the monastery. When he reached the door of the church he sat and his feet were washed according to the custom and he entered to the church and he prayed the ninth hour and went to the cell prepared for him and every one of the monks went to the cell prepared. . . . When it was sunset, the father, lord patriarch came to the church with the bishops and he celebrated the

prayer with Anba John bishop of Abu Tig. When it was the matins of
Wednesday, the fourth day of the glorious resurrection, the 10th of
Baramudah, he came to the church and celebrated the Eucharist and
concelebrated with Anba Michael of Sammanud. Having dismissed
the church, he visited *niri* [the cells] of the Ethiopians and the Armenians. He rode with the bishops to the monastery of Anba Bishoi.
The monks of this monastery and the Syrians and Abyssinians welcomed him as usual. He entered the monastery of Anba Bishoi and
prayed the sixth hour and after that he rode towards the monastery
of Baramus. He was welcomed by the monks of this monastery and
the monks of Lady Baramus as usual and he entered the monastery
of Baramus and prayed the ninth hour and offered the incense and
concelebrated with its compiler Athanasius of Qus. He went out
from Baramus towards Lady Baramus and they prayed the sunset
and concelebrated with Anba Samuel of Esna. When it was Thurs-
day the fifth day of the glorious resurrection which is the 11th of
Baramudah, he entered the church and prayed the third hour and
concelebrated with Anba Michel of Sammanud. Having finished the
service he rode with the bishops to the monastery al-Syrian and
was welcomed by the monks of al-Syrian and Anba Bishoi as usual.
He entered to the church of al-Syrian and prayed the sixth hour
and after that he rode with the bishops to the monastery of John
Kama and was welcomed by the monks of this monastery and also
the Abyssinians and Armenian monks and he entered the monastery
of Abba Kama and prayed the ninth hour and after that he rode
towards the monastery of Anba Macarius and it was the sunset when
he reached the angelic road. He got blessed by the relics of the saints
and went up to the cell prepared for him and all the bishops did so.
(Youssef and Zanetti: forthcoming)

Now, it is very problematic to match the content of the surveys with
that of the *History of the Patriarchs*. But, nonetheless, it seems that not all
the monasteries or monastic communities were visited by the patriarchs
(as when Pope Johannes ibn al-Masry visited the monasteries of Wadi al-
Natrun).[5] In some other biographies the patriarchs visited some secondary
monasteries and big *manshopia*s (such as the Abba Zakaria monastery, Ibgig,
and the Tinishti'nri [the great cell] *manshopia*s) (al-Suriani and Daoud 1989:
71, 153),[6] and they also spent some time there. As mentioned previously,

there were no relics of a patron saint of the Nubians, though the presence of the Nubians is well attested in the surveys.

Hagiographical Evidence from the Library of al–Suryan Monastery

Throughout history, monasteries, especially in the Coptic Church, have had an important role as conservators. In following the evolution of the cult of the patron saint of the monastery of the Nubians, the study of the liturgical texts from this library is of great importance. One of the best examples of the cult of a saint in Wadi al-Natrun is the veneration of St. Pesynthios, bishop of Coptus in the sixth century (Gabra 1984). He is depicted in the wall paintings of the church of Dayr al-Suryan dated to around 800 (Innemée and van Rompay 2002) and his cult survived for a long time, as the last attestation is a doxology of St. Pesynthios in MS 389 lit. "Psalmody," dated 1 Tut AM 1597 (AD 1880).

Youhanna Nessim Youssef demonstrated clearly that the *Doxology of Elijah* was mainly intended to be said during the visit of the patriarch to the Monastery of the Armenians (Youssef 2005). A doxology from MS 453 lit. "Doxologies," datable to the eighteenth century, provides the names of the fathers of monasticism. Among them we can read the name of Aba Onophrius, the anchorite who was mentioned by Abu al-Makarim as a saint venerated in Nubia (al-Suriani 1984a: 3: fol. 98a, p. 183). Also, there is the life of St. Onophrius, datable to the fourteenth century, which is the only copy of this biography in the monasteries of Wadi al-Natrun.[7] Amazingly enough, according to W.E. Crum, Pesynthios delivered a homily praising Onophrius.[8]

Conclusion

From the observations above, we can conclude the following:

- Probably this monastery was named after St. Onophrius the anchorite, as he was commemorated in Nubia.
- No relics were recorded as found in this monastery, as this saint died and was buried in his cave in the inner desert, which is attested by his biography.
- The MSS collection of al-Suryan monastery helped in attesting the veneration of St. Onophrius, which indicates that he was considered as a patron saint in one of the monasteries of Scetis.

Based on the above conclusions, it can be argued that that the Monastery of the Nubians was dedicated to St. Onophrius.

Notes

1   Den Heijer 1989: 209 mentions the story of a Nubian monk who met the patriarch Zacharias and was thrown to the lions during the persecution of al-Hakim.
2   This book survives in a single manuscript divided into two collections. For specific studies, see al-Suriani 1990: 78; for codicology and composition, Zanetti 1995a: 85–133; for authorship and influence, den Heijer 1993: 209–19; for social study of the Delta, Martin 1997: 181–99; 1998: 45–49; 2000: 83–92; 2004: 313–20; Youssef 1998–99: 45–54.
3   A technical term meaning a group of cells usually surrounding the cell of an elder.
4   Evelyn-White 1932: 3:vii. "This statement is the more interesting since Nubian inscription shows unmistakably there were Nubian monks in the valley."
5   Library of the Monastery of al-Suryan, MS 275 Homilies, fol. 176b.
6   Cf. Moawad 2006.
7   Library of the Monastery of al-Suryan, MS 299 Homilies, fol. 230a.
8   This homily was ascribed to him by W.E. Crum, London, British Library, MS Oriental 6800.

24 Monneret de Villard (1881–1954) and Nubia

Fr. Awad Wadi

THE FIRST SCHOLAR to write about Monneret de Villard (hereafter referred to as MdV) was Giorgio Levi Della Vida (1954). The text was included in a volume edited by Ugo Scarpocchi (1954), with a bibliography of MdV divided into four groups: Egypt, Nubia, Ethiopia, and "Varia." Giorgio Levi Della Vida then provided further information about MdV's personality and produced an additional bibliography (Levi Della Vida 1955). Ernest Kühnel republished this bibliography with an introduction two years later (Kühnel 1957). In 1987 a complete bibliography appeared with 197 titles of books and articles published between 1904 and 1966 (Piemontese 1987).

The Coptic Encyclopedia only devotes a few lines to MdV, and only lists two of his titles in the bibliography (Atiya 1991). The *Encyclopaedia Aethiopica*, on the other hand, is very generous toward MdV, dedicating two pages to him with a very rich bibliography (Fiaccadori 2007).

Ugo Monneret de Villard was of French origin. His family left their home in Burgundy for Italy during the French Revolution. He was born in Milan in 1881—on 16 February according to Levi Della Vita (Scarpocchi 1954: 33) or on 16 January according to G. Fiaccadori (2007: 1004) and E. Kühnel (1957: 627). He completed his studies as an engineer in the Politecnico in Milan in 1904, received his doctorate in 1908, and began to teach medieval architecture. He did so until 1908 according to Levi Della Vita (*Corriere della Sera*, 6 November 1954), or until 1924 according to

265

Fiaccadori (2007: 1004). During that period he developed his interest in Oriental art. He started to write in 1904 and his first studies were on Italian art and architecture. After more than fifty books and articles, he embarked on the study of Egyptian archaeology in 1921, in the second volume of the new review, *Aegyptus*. He was to write for this review until 1940. Between 1921 and 1928 he directed the first archaeological mission in Egypt and, between 1929 and 1934, the first expedition in Nubia financed by the Italian Foreign Ministry. In 1937 he worked in Ethiopia. In 1940 he left Milan for Rome and in the academic year 1943–44 he taught Christian archaeology at the University of Rome. In 1950 he received the national prize of the Accademia Nazionale dei Lincei. He died in the night of 4 November 1954 at the age of seventy-four. He was a member of the Accademia Nazionale dei Lincei and the Institut d'Égypte, and was a corresponding member of the Institut de France. He was an architect, an archaeologist, a historian, and an epigrapher all in one (Levi Della Vida 1955: 172; Kühnel 1957: 627; Fiaccadori 2007: 1004).

MdV's works on Christian Egypt and Nubia can be divided into three groups: various studies on Egypt (monasteries and churches); studies on Aswan; and studies on Nubia. Where Ancient Nubia is concerned, he produced some articles and a book about the pre-Christian period. Here, however, I shall only refer to his work on Christian Nubia.

MdV worked in Nubia from 1929 to 1934. But he began to write about the Nubian question well before 1929—in 1925 there appeared his first article on a Greek text in 'Anibah in Nubia, in which he gave the text without any translation or commentary (MdV 1925: 250). In the course of his archaeological expeditions, in 1931, he published three articles on his work (MdV 1931a; 1931b; 1931c). A further article appeared in 1932, the second part of which is on the Melchite Nubian church (MdV 1932), and in 1933 he published his first book, *Le iscrizioni del cimitero di Sakinya, Nubia*. Sakinya is near Toshka. MdV only spent ten days in the Christian cemetery there, in January 1933. After an introduction (MdV 1933: i–viii), he gives the texts of 222 epigraphs (1–23), followed by the indices (24–28), with nine tables at the end. The first fifty-nine epigraphs are in Greek. As MdV writes at the end of the introduction: "Lascio ai filologi ed agli epigrafisti lo studio di questi e tanti altri problemi che possono essere sollevati dallo studio di queste iscrizioni: io mi sono limitato a mettere a loro disposizione il più rapidamente possibile il materiale per ogni futura indagine." With these words MdV wanted to say that he was neither a philologist nor an epigraphist.[1]

In 1934 MdV published a new article about the bishops of Nubia (MdV 1934). The starting point is chapter 10 in the *Histoire de l'Eglise d'Alexandrie* by Vansleb (1672: 29–30). There were seven ecclesiastic provinces in the kingdom of Dongola, and MdV identified the names of the bishops in these provinces.

Within a year of the completion of MdV's archaeological mission in Nubia, the first two volumes on the expedition appeared. The first volume contains the text (MdV 1935). In the introduction (pp. iii–xvi), the author tells how the western world first heard about Nubia. He lists the earlier works on Nubia and the important dates in its modern history: 1898, the construction of the Aswan dam; and 1907–12, the heightening of the dam. At the end of the introduction he mentions some of the difficulties he faced: he had neither enough time nor money, and no access to any good libraries. The introduction is followed by a long bibliography (pp. xvii–xxxix). We then have a description of the Christian area in Nubia from Shallal in the north to Saqadi in the south. For some places MdV relies on earlier information, since, in his own time, all traces of antiquity had disappeared. But in many cases we have his own original description. Some cities had more than one church. In Philae there were six. MdV gives the names of nine bishops (pp. 5–10). There were also many churches in Faras (pp. 188–97), but in some places he could not enter because they had been converted into mosques or were used as houses. The number of churches and cemeteries described by MdV is enormous, but he only identified a small number of monasteries. He does not provide translations for any of his texts. New excavations complemented his work on some sites, for example in Faras[2] and in Abdalla Nirqi (1964). However, we only know of many other places from his work, since the sites have now disappeared forever.

The second volume contains the first hundred tables. The third and fourth volumes were only published much later, in 1957, after the death of the author (MdV 1957). In the introduction to the third volume, bearing the date 1951, the author says that he was obliged to reduce a great deal of his work and acknowledges that it is incomplete, "incompletezza che se in parte dipende dalla mia insufficiente preparazione, principalmente però è dovuta all'esiguità del materiale librario a mia disposizione in Italia." The book contains ten chapters. The first three, which occupy half of the volume, are about the construction of the churches (MdV 1957, vol. 3: 1–52). The third chapter, about the churches in the pharaonic temples, is very short, but very important (pp. 51–52). MdV initially states that all the temples, with the exception of the two temples of Abu Simbel, were partly used as churches. He then blames the first Egyptologists for destroying these buildings without having studied them. He quotes Maspero as an example of archaeologists who criticize the perceived defacement of ancient sites as "l'œuvre de méchants Coptes." In fact, the Nubian Christians only destroyed a single temple in Philae in order to build a new church.

The fifth chapter on monasteries (MdV 1957, vol. 3: 61–62) is also important. MdV only saw the traces of monasteries in the following places: Naga' al-Sheima, Sheima Amalika, Amada, al-Ramal, Geziret Tet, and Dayr al-Bollor. The fourth volume contains the plates CI–CCIII. Some are in color.

In the years 1936–37, MdV published three articles about Nubian Christian questions.

In 1938 appeared the announced *Storia della Nubia Cristiana* (MdV 1938). It is not merely a history; it a study of the geography, the civil and ecclesiastical history, and the organization of the state and the church in Nubia.

From this history (pp. 30–31), we know that, in the third century, there were Christians in Nubia, even before the area was Christianized in the sixth century. From the fourth century there were bishops in Philae: Macedonius, Mark, Isaac, and Pseleusius (p. 44). Philae was a place of encounter between Egyptian and Nubian.

The Christianization of Nubia began in the sixth century, after the closing of the pagan temple of Isis in Philae in 542–45. This is the subject of the fifth and sixth chapters (pp. 53–70). The author mentions two theories about this question. According to John of Ephesus the first missionaries were commissioned by the empress Theodora, wife of Justinian, under the guidance of the priest Julian from the Coptic Church. MdV does not give great credence to John of Ephesus, and from the study of the epigraphs and the liturgy arrives at the conviction that the first missionaries were Melchites sent out by the emperor Justinian (p. 61). But this church disappeared from Nubia when Egypt was without a Melchite patriarch for about one hundred years, from 637 to 731 (p. 62). This theory is also corroborated by the testimony of the historian John of Biclar (p. 66).

The first struggles between Christian Nubia and Islamic Egypt began around 641 (pp. 71–78). MdV mentions what Islamic historians wrote about the Baqt, and then he specifies the real meaning of this word (derived from the Latin *pactum*, a pact or covenant) (p. 87).

In the beginning of the eighth century, Nubia became one kingdom under Mercurius, king of Makuria (pp. 79–83). At that time all of Nubia was under the control of the Coptic Church (p. 99).

In the tenth century the Islamic presence in Nubia increased (p. 118). In the Fatimid period (pp. 122–29), the Nubians attacked Egypt and dominated a part of Upper Egypt. After that there were good relations between the Nubians and the Fatimids (p. 129).

About the end of the eleventh century there appeared in Nubia a new tradition in the succession of the kingdom: from maternal uncle to nephew (p. 175). This would be one of the causes of the end of Christian Nubia: as Muslims married Nubian women of the royal house, their children were brought up as Muslims, and these sons rose to the throne when their Nubian maternal uncles died.

In 1172/1173 the brother of Saladin (Salah al-Din) invaded Nubia as far as the city of Qasr Ibrim (Primis) and transformed her cathedral church of the Virgin Mary into a mosque (p. 196). This occupation ended in 1175.

The last chapter (pp. 211–21) of MdV's *Storia* is about the end of Christian Nubia. In the time of Sultan Baybars (1260–77), in 1272/1273, the Nubians attacked Egypt, especially the port of 'Aidhab and Aswan. In 1275/1276 there was internal conflict in Nubia, and Egypt aided Shekandah to depose King David. In 1286 Egypt invaded Nubia, and Dongola fell into their hands. In 1315 there appeared a Muslim king in Nubia, and in 1323 the complete Islamization of Nubia began. The last words of MdV's *Storia* are: "La Nubia Cristiana è finita: il cristianesimo scompare dal centro dell'Africa. L'Islām ha trionfato" (p. 221). It can therefore be said that Christianity began in Nubia with a religious conflict between Empress Theodora and Emperor Justinian (Melchites and anti-Melchites) and ended with a political conflict.

MdV's book also contains a list of the kings of Nubia (p. 223), a chronological summary (pp. 224–26), alphabetical indices (pp. 227–46), and ten maps.

This study (written more than seventy years ago) remains fundamental and indispensable for the knowledge of the history of Nubia. There are only a few newer books about Nubian history.[3] After the *Storia*, MdV wrote three other articles, one in German, in 1937 (the only one in German), the second in 1941, and the last in 1951 as a small summary of the archaeology and history of Nubia (MdV 1951). So ended the activity of the engineer Monneret de Villard as a great archaeologist and historian.

Notes

1   See also Levi Della Vida 1955: 180–81.
2   See Vantini 1970 and the various volumes of the Polish Archaeological Mission.
3   For example: Vantini 1975; 1981; Adams 1977.

25 The Conservation of the Mural Paintings of St. Hatre Monastery

Ashraf Nageh

Introduction

The Monastery of St. Hatre (Dayr Anba Hadra) represents one of the tragic situations of Coptic heritage. Although it was published by Monneret de Villard in 1927 and became well known to scholars and researchers, it does not receive either attention or appropriate protection (Monneret de Villard 1927a). Comparison between the old photos, published in 1927, and the actual situation at the present time gives quite a clear progression of the deterioration of the buildings in general and the wall paintings in particular (fig. 25.1).

Site Geology and Location

The monastery is located on the west bank of Aswan city. This area is covered with silicified sandstone and extends about twelve kilometers square, north to Gebel Gulab and south to Gebel Tangar. It was one of the major sources of this type of stone in the Pharaonic period, especially during the Old and Middle Kingdoms. Harrell mentioned that this area was used as a sandstone quarry during these times (Harrell 1989; Aston, Harrell, and Shaw 2000). However, the study of geology and the ancient quarries in this area indicated that the burials from the Coptic period that were found inscribed with crosses south of the monastery could represent a burial site connected with the nearby monastery of St.

Fig. 25.1 Apse of the main church, in 1927 (above) and in 2010 (below) (Dr. Sami Sabry)

Fig. 25.2 Location of the monastery (Google Earth)

Simeon (known as Dayr Anba Hadra). In general, the topography of the site consists of irregular hills (Yassin, 2006).

The Wall Paintings of St. Hatre Monastery

The remains of the wall paintings in the Monastery of St. Hatre are found in eight locations inside the monastery, five of them on the ground floor

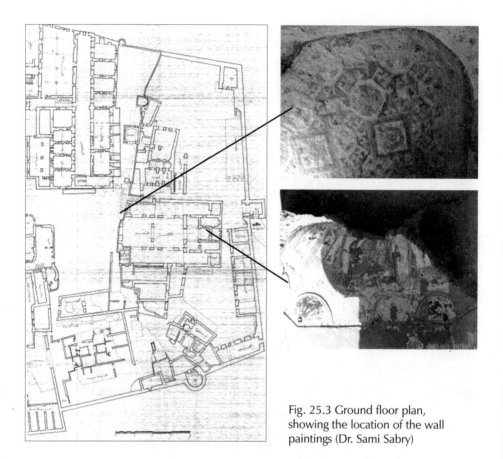

Fig. 25.3 Ground floor plan,
showing the location of the wall
paintings (Dr. Sami Sabry)

and the other three on the first floor. They represent painted figures, and
inscriptions or graffiti. They are as follows.

Ground floor (fig. 25.3)

1. The apse of the church
2. The west niche opposite the apse
3. Inside the rock-cut cave No. XIII (according to the plan of the ground
   floor by Monneret de Villard, 1927a)
4. The south wall in the rock-cut cave No. XXIV (according to the plan
   of Monneret de Villard, 1927a)
5. A separate room near the entrance of the keep

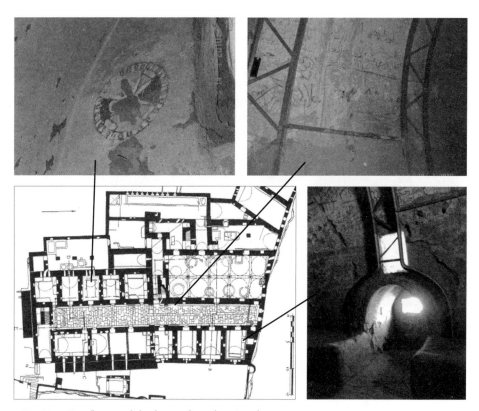

Fig. 25.4 First floor and the keep plan, showing the locations of the wall paintings (Dr. Sami Sabry)

First floor of the keep (fig. 25.4)
1. The main gallery
2. The pilgrims' room
3. A monk's cell

The Structure and Composition of the Mural Paintings

Normally wall paintings are composed of several layers: the support, the preparation layer, the whitewash layer, and the paint layer (Mora, Mora, and Philippot 1984). The support is made of adobe and, in one case, cut rock. It could be presumed that the monastery is built of sandstone because it is

Fig. 25.5 Composition of the wall-painting layers in St. Hatre monastery
(Dr. Sami Sabry)

located among sandstone quarries. However, the silt and clay of the Nile
River were present in abundance on the bank of the river, which encouraged the use of adobe as a building material for the monastery, a material
much better suited to such a hot climate.

The second layer is the preparation layer, which is made of clay to
smooth the surface of the wall. The third layer is the whitewash; in some
cases this is a thick layer, most probably made of lime with sand as a filler.
The last layer is the paint, which consists of limited pigments mixed with
a binder and applied to the painting surface (fig. 25.5). There have been
no technical studies done to investigate the technique of Coptic wall
paintings in general. However, the paintings of St. Hatre present a unique
case for a comparison study between the wall-painting techniques of the
Copts along the Nile Valley and those of Christian Nubia. Identification
of the chemical composition of each layer and its properties can be performed by an analytical process.

It is worth mentioning that superimposed layers were found in a limited number of places, indicating the presence of different layers applied at
different time periods as renovation work was done in the past (fig. 25.6).

Deterioration Factors

Weathering is the natural process whereby building materials decay into smaller particles by a slow, continuous process that affects all substances exposed to the atmosphere (Siegesmund, Weiss, and Vollbrecht 2002). It works together with all the other deterioration factors to damage monumental buildings and objects. In general the weather in Egypt is hot and dry in the summer and damp in winter (http://www.climatetemp.info/egypt/aswan.html).

Rainfall

The rainfall over this district (Aswan) is very limited, as in any desert region. Several years may pass without any rain at all, but when it does occur it may be very heavy and the water then flows as streams or even torrents in the valleys.

Temperature

The daily maximum temperature during the months of June, July, and August is above 40°C and is just below 40°C during the months of May and September. These five months are the hottest months of the year. Desert conditions exist over the district; in the winter it is cold and in the summer it is extremely hot. The difference in temperature between day and night is always great throughout the year.

Wind

The normal wind conditions in Egypt are controlled by various atmospheric factors that occur on a seasonal basis. Depending on the atmospheric circulation in the eastern Mediterranean, including the Egyptian coast, three seasons have been distinguished:

1. The winter season extends from November to March, with a wind speed of 4 knots (7.4 km/hr), coming from all directions, but northerly and northwesterly winds are the most prevalent.
2. The spring season extends from April to May, with an average wind speed of 2 knots (3.7 km/hr). The main direction of the wind ranges between north and northwest, with a small percentage from the northeasterly direction.
3. The summer season extends from June to October. The maximum wind speed is 8.5 knots (15.7 km/hr), occurring in September, while the minimum wind speed is 1.5 knots (2.8 km/hr) in August.

A hot spring wind that blows across the region, known as the sirocco (*khamsin* in Egypt), is an important climatic phenomena in Egypt. The wind forms in small but vigorous low-pressure areas and sweeps across the northern coast of Africa. Higher wind velocity (up to 140 km/hr), accompanied by sand and dust from the deserts, can increase the air temperature suddenly by about 20°C within two hours.

Humidity

Relative humidity (RH) expresses the amount of moisture contained in materials at equilibrium with the environment. This is almost independent of temperature. As relative humidity changes, the object's water content adjusts to the new relative humidity level, creating a new equilibrium. At higher RH, there is more water in the objects. This occurs slowly, depending on the thickness and absorbency of the material. Aswan is one of the driest areas in Egypt. In summer the RH is about 20 percent, while in winter it rises to 48 percent.

Evaluation of the Environmental Conditions

Each factor may represent an ideal measure when considered separately; for example, the RH is ideal in Aswan compared with other places in Egypt. Conversely, the temperature is too high, at around 40°C, for several months of the year. In fact, all the factors combine to produce weathering of the different exposed materials. The wall paintings in St. Hatre Monastery have suffered from environmental factors because of direct exposure to the conditions. The demolition of the church roofing increased the speed of deterioration of the paintings there, and within seventy years the paintings became badly damaged. The indoor paintings are in a better state of conservation. The human factor has combined with these factors and has played an important role in damaging the paintings.

Plan for Conservation
Protection of the Site

The protection of the site should be the first act in the conservation of the wall paintings of St. Hatre Monastery. Providing a roof and doors and closing the openings should be the first step in conservation and restoration of the architecture to allow for the start of proper conservation of these wall paintings.

A Comprehensive Study of the Wall Paintings

The study of wall painting is based mainly on chemical and physical investigation. This requires identification of the composition of the different layers, characterizing their structure and other physical properties. In recent years, the study of the technical characterization of the composition of wall paintings and the physical and chemical changes that occur in paintings due to the weathering processes has become a strategy for the conservation of a historical site and its cultural heritage (Warke, McKinley, and Smith 2006). A full understanding of the structural and material characteristics is required for the practice of conservation. The characteristics of the materials used in restoration work and their compatibility with existing materials should be fully determined. The main objective of analyzing archaeological paintings, as well as most other archaeological materials, is usually to clearly identify the object. This is not, however, the only objective, since the results of chemical analyses often also provide insights into any weathering processes that the object may have undergone, as well as its provenance and chronology.

Sampling

Sampling archaeological materials for analytical purposes may sometimes be the most difficult stage in an analytical procedure, in view of the fact that obtaining a representative sample of some types of materials may be the most difficult step in an entire analytical procedure. Sampling of an important historic building or ancient monument in general, and wall painting in particular, is destructive, but the damage incurred by taking a representative sample must be weighed against the prospective deterioration and loss if unrepresentative sampling were to lead to inappropriate treatment (Jefferson, Hanna, Martin, and Jones 2006). The sample should consist of scales of the painting material, taken from the invisible side of the painting. The sample should not by any means affect or damage the wall paintings.

Conservation work

The term 'art conservation' denotes the maintenance and preservation of works of art and their protection from future damage and deterioration. 'Art restoration,' by contrast, denotes the repair or renovation of artworks that have already sustained injury or decay and the attempted restoration of such objects to something approaching their original undamaged appearance (Henry 2006).

Conservation work on wall paintings includes the fixing of the detached paint and painting layer as the first intervention to stabilize the condition of the paintings. The cleaning performed on paintings will vary according to each painting's nature and the type and condition of the deposits. The consolidation of the different layers will be the last step. Adding varnish may be recommended. Finally, the graffiti in Coptic and Arabic should be preserved as a part of the history of the monument. The edges of the paintings can be preserved by a process of plaster integration.

Abbreviations

AAAHP	*Acta ad archaeologiam et artium historiam pertinentia*
ASAE	*Annales du Service des antiquités de l'Égypte*
BASP	*Bulletin of the American Society of Papyrologists*
BIFAO	*Bulletin de l'Institut français d'archéologie orientale*
BSAC	*Bulletin de la Société d'archéologie copte*
CSCO	Corpus Scriptorum Christianorum Orientalium
ECA	*Eastern Christian Art*
HdO	Handbuch der Orientalistik
IAEG	International Association for Engineering Geology and the Environment
IFAO	Institut français d'archéologie orientale
JARCE	*Journal of the American Research Center in Egypt*
JbAC	*Jahrbuch für Antike und Christentum*
JEA	*Journal of Egyptian Archaeology*
JJP	*Journal of Juristic Papyrology*
LAAA	*Annals of Archaeology and Anthropology, Liverpool*
MDAIK	*Mitteilungen des Deutschen Archäologischen Instituts Kairo*
MIFAO	Mémoires de l'Institut français d'archéologie orientale du Caire

OCA	Orientalia Christiana Analecta
OLA	Orientalia Lovaniensia Analecta
OMRO	*Oudheidkundige Mededelingen uit het Rijksmuseum van Oudheden te Leiden*
RQA	*Römische Quartalschrift für christliche Altertumskunde und Kirchengeschichte*
SASOP	Sudan Antiquities Service Occasional Papers
SKCO	Sprachen und Kulturen des christlichen Orients
VChr	*Vigiliae Christianae*
ZÄS	*Zeitschrift für Ägyptische Sprache und Altertumskunde*
ZPE	*Zeitschrift für Papyrologie und Epigraphik*

Bibliography

'Abbas, I. 1984. *al-Rawd al-mi'tar fi khabar al-aqtar. Mu'jam jughrafi ma'a faharis shamila, ta'lif Muhammad ibn 'Abd al-Mun'im al-Himiari.* 2nd ed. Beirut: Maktabat Libnan.

'Abd al-Hamid, M.M. 1973. *Muruj al-dhahab wa-ma'adin al-jawhar, tasnif al-rahhala al-kabir wa-l-mu'arrikh al-jalil Abi al-Hasan 'Ali ibn al-Husayn ibn 'Ali al-Mas'udi.* 2 vols. 5th ed. Cairo: Dar al-Fikr.

'Abd al-Masih, Y., A.S. Atiya, and A. Burmester. 1948. *History of the Patriarchs of the Egyptian Church, Known as the History of the Holy Church by Sawirus Ibn al-Mukaffa' Bishop of al-Asmunin.* Vol. 2, part 2. Cairo: Société d'archéologie copte.

'Abd al-Tawab, 'A.M., and S. Ory. 1977–86. *Stèles islamiques de la nécropole d'Assouan.* Textes arabes et études islamiques 7. Cairo: IFAO.

Adams, W.Y. 1965. "Architectural Evolution of the Nubian Church, 500–1400 AD." *JARCE* 4, pp. 87–139.

———. 1977. *Nubia: Corridor to Africa.* London: Penguin.

———. 1977. *Nubia: Corridor to Africa.* Princeton, NJ: Princeton University Press.

———. 1991a. "Julian, Evangelist." In A.S. Atiya, ed., *The Coptic Encyclopedia*, vol. 5, p. 1380. New York: Macmillan.

———. 1991b. "Longinus." In A.S. Atiya, ed., *The Coptic Encyclopedia*, vol. 5, pp. 1479–80. New York: Macmillan.

———. 1991c. "Nubia, Evangelization of." In A.S. Atiya, ed., *The Coptic Encyclopedia*, vol. 5, pp. 1801–1802. New York: Macmillan.

———. 1991d. "Nubia, Islamization of." In A.S. Atiya, ed., *The Coptic Encyclopedia*, vol. 6, pp. 1802–1804. New York: Macmillan.

———. 2000. *Meinarti I. The Late Meroitic, Ballana and Transitional Occupation.* Sudan Archaeological Research Society Publication 5. London: Archaeopress.

Allen, P., and C.T.R. Haywards. 2004. *Severus of Antioch*. The Early Church
Fathers. London and New York: Routledge.

Anderson, J. 1999. "Monastic Lifestyles of the Nubia Desert: Seeking the
Mysterious Monks of Makuria." *Sudan & Nubia* 3, pp. 71–83.

Apostolaki, A. 1932. *Τα Κοπτικά Υφάσματα του εν Αθήναις Μουσείου Κοσμητικών
Τεχνών*. Athens: Estia.

Aston, B.G., J.A. Harrell, and I. Shaw. 2000. "Stone." In P.T. Nicholson and I.
Shaw, eds., *Ancient Egyptian Materials and Technology*. Cambridge: Cambridge
University Press.

Athanasius. *Vita S. Antonii*. PG 26, cols. 835–976. English translation: R.T. Meyer,
1950, *The Life of St. Anthony*, London: ACW. French translation: B. Lavaud,
1979, *Vie et conduite de notre Père saint Antoine*, Bégrolles-en-Mauges: Abbaye de
Bellefontaine.

Atiya, A.S. 1991. "Monneret de Villard, Ugo." In A.S. Atiya, ed., *The Coptic
Encyclopedia*, vol. 5, pp. 1668–69. New York: Macmillan.

Atiya, A.S., Y. 'Abd al-Masih, O.H.E. Khs-Burmester, and A. Khater. 1959. *History
of the Patriarchs of the Egyptian Church Known as the History of the Holy Church*.
Vol. 2, part 3. Cairo: Société d'archéologie copte.

Ayalon, D. 1989. "The Nubian Dam." *Jerusalem Studies in Arabic and Islam* 12,
pp. 372–90. Reprinted 1994 in *Islam and the Abode of War: Military Slaves and
Islamic Adversaries*. Collected Studies Series 456, no. 12. Aldershot: Variorum.

Bacot, S. 2006. "Quelques textes relatifs aux measures de vin d'Edfou au VIIᵉ
siècle." In A. Boud'hors, J. Gascou, and D. Vaillancourt, eds., *Études coptes 9,
Onzième journée d'études, Strasbourg, 12–14 juin 2003*, pp. 33–44. Cahiers de la
bibliothèque copte 14. Paris: De Boccard.

———. 2007. "Le vin à Edfou." In S. Marchand and A. Maranjou, eds., *Amphores
d'Égypte de la basse époque à l'époque arabe*, pp. 713–20. Cahiers de la céramique
égyptienne 8.2. Cairo: IFAO.

———. 2008. "Un calendrier liturgique d'Edfou sur ostracon, l'O.EdfouCopt.
Lit. 1." In A. Boud'hors and C. Louis, eds., *Études coptes 10, Douzième journée
d'études, Lyon, 19–21 mai 2005*, pp. 91–101. Cahiers de la bibliothèque copte
6. Paris: De Boccard.

———. 2009. *Ostraca grecs et coptes des fouilles franco-polonaises sur le site de Tell
Edfou. O.EdfouCopte 1–145*. Bibliothèque d'études coptes 19. Cairo: IFAO.

Bagnall, R.S. 1993. *Egypt in Late Antiquity*. Princeton, NJ: Princeton University Press.

Bardy, G. 1941. "Sévère d'Antioche." In *Dictionnaire de théologie catholique*, 14, col.
1988–99. Paris: Beauchesne.

Barsanti, A. 1915. "Rapport sur les travaux de consolidation exécutés a Kom
Ombo." *Annales du Service des antiquités de l'Égypte* 15, pp. 168–76.

Basilios, Archbishop. 1991. "Liturgical Instruments." In A.S. Atiya, ed., *The Coptic
Encyclopedia*, vol. 5, pp. 1469–75. New York: Macmillan.

Basset, R., ed. 1904–29. *Le synaxaire arabe jacobite*. Coptic ed. Patrologia Orientalis
1, 3, 11, 16, 17, 20. Paris: Firmin-Didot.

Baumeister, T. 1986. "Das Stephanuspatrozinium der Kirche im ehemaligen Isis-
Tempel von Philä." *RQA* 81, pp. 187–94.

Bénazeth, D. 1992. *L'art du métal au début de l'ère chrétienne: Musée du Louvre, Catalogue du département des antiquités égyptiennes.* Paris: Éditions de la Réunion des Musées nationaux.

———. 2001. *Catalogue général du Musée copte du Caire. Objets en métal.* Cairo: IFAO.

———. 2004. "Le trésor de Kôm Ombo: Un groupe d'objets liturgiques d'époque byzantine." In M. Immerzeel, J. van der Vliet, M. Kersten, and C. Zoest, eds., *Coptic Studies on the Threshold of a New Millennium: Proceedings of the Seventh International Congress of Coptic Studies, Leiden, August 27–September 2, 2000,* pp. 1159–71. OLA 133. Louvain, Paris, and Dudley, MA: Peeters.

———. Forthcoming. *L'église de l'archange Michel dite l'église nord du monastère de Baouit.* With contributions by Fl. Calament, A. Delattre, and N. Vanthieghem. Cairo: IFAO.

Bernard, A. 1989. *De Thèbes à Syène.* Paris: C.N.R.S.

Bernard, E. 1969. *Les inscriptions grecques et latines de Philae.* Vol. 2, *Haut et Bas Empire.* Paris: C.N.R.S.

Biedenkopf-Ziehner, A. 1983. *Untersuchungen zum koptischen Briefformular unter Berücksichtigung ägyptischer und griechischer Parallelen.* Koptische Studien 1. Würzburg: G. Zauzich.

Bloxam, E. 2007. "A History of Silicified Sandstone Use in Egypt from the Middle Palaeolithic to Roman Period." In E. Bloxam, T. Heldal, and P. Storemyr, eds., *Characterisation of Complex Quarry Landscapes: An Example from the West Bank Quarries, Aswan,* pp. 37–50. http://www.quarryscapes.no/text/publications/QS_del4_Report_LR.pdf.

Bloxam, E., T. Heldal, and P. Storemyr, eds. 2007. *Characterisation of Complex Quarry Landscapes: An Example from the West Bank Quarries, Aswan.* http://www.quarryscapes.no/text/publications/QS_del4_Report_LR.pdf

Bock, W. de. 1901. *Matériaux pour servir à l'archéologie de l'Égypte chrétienne.* St. Petersburg: E. Thiele.

Bolman, E.S., ed. 2002. *Monastic Visions: Wall Paintings in the Monastery of Saint Antony at the Red Sea.* New Haven and London: Yale University Press.

———. 2004. "The Coptic Galaktotrophousa Revisited." In M. Immerzeel, J. van der Vliet, M. Kersten, and C. Zoest, eds., *Coptic Studies on the Threshold of a New Millennium: Proceedings of the Seventh International Congress of Coptic Studies, Leiden, 27 August–2 September 2000,* vol. 2, pp. 1173–84. OLA 133. Louvain, Paris, and Dudley, MA: Peeters.

———. 2005. "The Enigmatic Coptic Galaktotrophousa and the Cult of the Virgin Mary in Egypt." In M. Vassilaki, ed., *Images of the Mother of God: Perceptions of the Theotokos in Byzantium,* pp. 13–19. Aldershot: Ashgate.

———. 2006a. "Late Antique Aesthetics, Chromophobia, and the Red Monastery, Sohag, Egypt." *ECA* 3, pp. 1–24.

———. 2006b. "Veiling Sanctity in Christian Egypt: Visual and Spatial Solutions." In Sh.E.J. Gerstel, ed., *Thresholds of the Sacred: Architectural, Art Historical, Liturgical, and Theological Perspectives on Religious Screens, East and West,* pp. 72–104. Washington D.C: Dumbarton Oaks Research Library and Collection.

————. 2008. "The Red Monastery Conservation Project, 2006 and 2007 Campaigns. Contributing to the Corpus of Late Antique Art." In G. Gabra and H.N.Takla, eds., *Christianity and Monasticism in Upper Egypt*, vol. 1, *Akhmim and Sohag*, pp. 305–17. Cairo: American University in Cairo Press.

Boud'hors, A. 1999. "Réflexions préalables à la publication des textes coptes d'Edfou (Papyrus et Ostraca)." In N. Grimal, ed., *Tell-Edfou soixante ans après: Actes du colloque franco-polonais, Le Caire, 15 octobre 1996*, pp. 1–7. Fouilles Franco-polonaises 4. Cairo: IFAO.

————. 2006. "Paléographie et codicologie coptes: Progrès et perspectives (1996–2004)." In A. Boud'hors and D.Vaillancourt, eds., *Huitième congrès international d'études coptes (Paris 2004) I. Bilans et perspectives 2000–2004*, pp. 95–109. Cahiers de la bibliothèque copte 15. Paris: De Boccard.

Bourguet, P. du. 1991. "Dayr Anbā Hadrā: Art." In A.S. Atiya, ed., *The Coptic Encyclopedia*, vol. 3, p. 747. New York: Macmillan.

Bouriant, U., and A.F.Ventre. 1900. "Sur trois tables horaires coptes." *Mémoires Institut égyptien* 3, pp. 575–96.

Brakke, D. 1995. *Athanasius and the Politics of Asceticism*. Oxford: Clarendon Press.

————. 1998. *Athanasius and Asceticism*. Baltimore: Johns Hopkins University Press.

————. 2006. *Demons and the Making of the Monk: Spiritual Combat in Early Christianity*. Cambridge, MA: Harvard University Press.

Breydy, M. 1983. *Études sur Sa'id ibn Batriq, et ses sources*. CSCO Subsidia 450. Louvain: Secrétariat du CSCO.

————. 1985. *Das Annalenwerk des Eutychios von Alexandrien*. CSCO Arabici 44. Louvain: Secrétariat du CSCO.

Bresciani, E., and S. Pernigotti. 1978. *Assuan. Il tempio tolemaico di Isi/I blocci decorati e iscritti*. Biblioteca di Studi Antichi 16. Pisa: Giardini.

Brock, S. 1984. *The Harp of the Spirit: Eighteen Poems of Saint Ephrem*. 2nd enlarged ed. San Bernardino, CA: Borgo Press.

Brooks, E.W. 1904. *The Sixth Book of the Select Letters of Severus Patriarch of Antioch*. Vol. 2. London: Text and Translation Society.

————. 1935. *Iohannis Ephesini. Historiae ecclesiasticae. Pars tertia*. CSCO 105. Scriptores Syri 54. Louvain: L. Durbecq.

Brune, K.-H. 2005. "Schooldays in the Fayoum in the First Millennium." In G. Gabra, ed., *Christianity and Monasticism in the Fayoum Oasis: Essays from the 2004 International Symposium of the Saint Mark Foundation and the Saint Shenouda the Archimandrite Coptic Society in Honor of Martin Krause*, pp. 33–43. Cairo: American University in Cairo Press.

————. 2007. *Index zu Das christlich-koptische Ägypten in arabischer Zeit (Stefan Timm)*. Wiesbaden: L. Reichert.

————. 2010. "Das Koptische Ägypten. Schulalltag in Ägypten im 1. Jahrtausend n.Chr." *Kemet* 19 (1): 39–44. Berlin: Kemet-Verlag.

Bruning, J. Forthcoming. "Egyptian Control over the Egyptian–Nubian Frontier between AD 600 and 750." In P.M. Sijpesteijn, ed., *Late Antiquity and Early Islam: Authority and Control in the Countryside. Proceedings of the Conference at Leiden University, September 13th–16th 2010*.

Budge, E.A.Wallis, ed. 1913. *Coptic Apocrypha in the Dialect of Upper Egypt.* London: British Museum.

————, ed. 1914. *Coptic Martyrdoms in the Dialect of Upper Egypt.* London: British Museum.

————, ed. 1915. *Miscellaneous Coptic Texts in the Dialect of Upper Egypt.* London: British Museum.

Budka, J. 1999. "Auf den Spuren von Hermann Junker: Das Kloster am Isisberg." *Kemet* 8, no. 3: 61–62.

Bunbury, J., M.A. Graham, and K.D. Strutt. 2009. "Kom el-Farahy: A New Kingdom Island in an Evolving Edfu Floodplain." *British Museum Studies in Ancient Egypt and Sudan* 14, pp. 1–23.

Burkitt, F.C. 1903. "On Some Christian Gravestones from Old Dongola." *Journal of Theological Studies* 4, pp. 585–87.

Burmester, O.H.E. 1967. *The Egyptian or the Coptic Church: A Detailed Description of Her Liturgical Services and the Rites and Ceremonies Observed in the Administration of Her Sacraments.* Textes et Documents 10. Cairo: Publications de la Société d'archéologie copte.

————. 1975. *Koptische Handschriften I.* Verzeichnis der orientalischen Handschriften in Deutschland 21, part 1. Wiesbaden: Steiner.

Buschhausen, H., and F.M. Khorshid. 1998. "Die Malerei zu Deir al-Genadla." In M. Krause and S. Schaten, eds., *ΘΕΜΕΛΙΑ. Spätantike und koptologische Studien Peter Grossmann zum 65. Geburtstag,* pp. 55–67. SKCO 3. Wiesbaden: Reichert.

Campagnano, A., and T. Orlandi. 1984. *Vite di monaci copti.* Collana di Testi Patristici. Rome: Città Nuova.

Carrez-Maratray, J.-Y. 1998. "Le Sinaï des Grecs et des Romains: un passage méconnu de Diodore." In D.Vabelle and Ch. Bonnet, eds., *Le Sinaï durant l'Antiquité et le Moyen Âge. 4000 ans d'histoire pour un désert,* pp. 88–92. Paris: Errance.

Castel, G. 1979. "Étude d'une momie copte." In *Hommages à la mémoire de Serge Sauneron, 1927–1976.* Bibliothèque d'études 82, pp. 121–43. Cairo: IFAO.

Castigione, L., L. Barkóczi, Á. Salamon, G. Hajnóczi, L. Kákosy, L. Török, and V. Pósa, eds. 1964. *The Hungarian Excavation in Egyptian Nubia.* Offprints from the Acta Archaeologica Accademiae Scientiarum Hungaricae 26 (1974) and 27 (1975). Budapest: Academiae Scientiarum Hungaricae.

Cerulli, E., et al. 1970–84. *Opus geographicum.* 9 vols. Naples: Istituto Universitario Orientale di Napoli.

Cheikho, L. 1906. *Eutychii Patriarchae Alexandrini Annales.* CSCO 50, 51; Scriptores Arabici 5, 6. Louvain: L. Durbecq.

Choat, M. 2006. *Belief and Cult in Fourth-Century Papyri.* Studia Antiqua Australiensia 1. Turnhout: Brepols.

————. 2007. "Early Coptic Epistolography." In A. Papaconstantinou, ed., *The Multilingual Experience in Egypt, from the Ptolemies to the Abbasids,* pp. 153–78. Surrey: Ashgate Publishing Limited.

————. 2010. "Epistolary Formulae in Early Coptic Letters." In N. Bosson and A. Boud'hors, eds., *Actes du huitième congrès international d'études coptes, Paris, 28 juin–3 juillet 2004,* vol. 2, pp. 667–78. OLA 163. Louvain, Paris, and Dudley, MA: Peeters.

Clarke, S. 1912. *Christian Antiquities in the Nile Valley: A Contribution towards the Study of the Ancient Churches.* Oxford: Clarendon Press.

Clédat, J. 1902. "Notes archéologiques et philologiques II. Deir Abou-Hennîs." *BIFAO* 2, pp. 44–67.

———. 1904–1906. *Le monastère et la nécropole de Baouît.* Vol. 1, fasc. 1–2. MIFAO 12. Cairo: IFAO.

———. 1915. "Les inscriptions de Saint-Siméon." *Recueil de travaux relatifs au philologie et à l'archéologie égyptiennes et assyriennes* 37, pp. 41–57.

———. 1916. *Le monastère et la nécropole de Baouît.* Vol. 2, fasc. 1. MIFAO 39. Cairo: IFAO.

———. 1999. *Le monastère et la nécropole de Baouit. Notes mises en œuvre et éditées par D. Bénazeth et M.-H. Rutschowscaya avec contributions de A. Boud'hors, R.-G. Coquin et É. Gaillard.* MIFAO 111. Cairo: IFAO.

Cody, A. 1991a. "Dayr al-Baramus." In A.S. Atiya, ed., *The Coptic Encyclopedia,* vol. 3, pp. 789–94. New York: Macmillan.

———. 1991b. "Wadi al-Natrun." In A.S. Atiya, ed., *The Coptic Encyclopedia,* vol. 7, pp. 876–81. New York: Macmillan.

Coquin, R.-G. 1975. "Les inscriptions pariétales des monastères d'Esna: Dayr al-Šuhada–Dayr al-Fahuri." *BIFAO* 75, pp. 241–84.

———. 1984. "Les lettres festales d'Athanase (CPG 2102). Un nouveau complément: le manuscript IFAO, Copte 25." *Orientalia Lovaniensia Periodica* 15, pp. 133–58.

———. 1991. "Dayr Mari Maryam." In A.S. Atiya, ed., *The Coptic Encyclopedia,* vol. 3, p. 835. New York: Macmillan.

———. 1994. "Discours attribué au patriarche Cyrille sur la dédicace de l'Église de Raphael rapportant les propos de son oncle, le patriarche Théophile, version copte." *BSAC* 33, pp. 25–56.

———. 1997. "Discours attribué au patriarche Cyrille sur la dédicace de l'Église de Raphael rapportant les propos de son oncle, le patriarche Théophile, version arabe." *BSAC* 36, pp. 9–58.

Coquin, R.-G., and M. Martin. 1991a. "Dayr al-Kubāniyyah: History." In A.S. Atiya, ed., *The Coptic Encyclopedia,* vol. 3, p. 815. New York: Macmillan.

———. 1991b. "Dayr Anbā Hadrā: History." In A.S. Atiya, ed., *The Coptic Encyclopedia,* vol. 3, pp. 744–45. New York: Macmillan.

———. 1991c. "Dayr Qubbat al-Hawā: History." In A.S. Atiya, ed., *The Coptic Encyclopedia,* vol. 3, pp. 850–51. New York: Macmillan.

Cormack, R. 1985. *Writing in Gold: Byzantine Society and Its Icons.* London: George Philip.

Cribiore, R. 1996. *Writing, Teachers, and Students in Graeco-Roman Egypt.* American Studies in Papyrology 36. Atlanta, GA: Scholars Press.

———. 1999. "Greek and Coptic Education in Late Antique Egypt." In S. Emmel et al., eds., *Ägypten und Nubien in spätantiker und christlicher Zeit. Akten des 6. Internationalen Koptologenkongresses Münster, 20–26 Juli 1996.* Vol. 2, *Schrifttum, Sprache und Gedankenwelt,* pp. 279–86. SKCO 6.2. Wiesbaden: Reichert.

Crum, W.E. 1902a. *Coptic Monuments*. Catalogue général des antiquités égyptiennes du Musée du Caire, nos. 8001–8741. Cairo: Service des antiquités. Reprinted 1975, Osnabrück: Otto Zeller Verlag.

———. 1902b. *Coptic Ostraca from the Collections of the Egypt Exploration Fund, the Cairo Museum and Others. The Text Edited with Translations and Commentaries. With a Contribution by F.E. Brightman*. London: The Egypt Exploration Fund.

———. 1905. *Catalogue of the Coptic Manuscripts in the British Museum*. London: British Museum.

———. 1922–23. "Sévère d'Antioche en Égypte." *Revue de l'Orient Chrétien* 23, pp. 92–104.

———. 1925. "Koptische Zünfte und das Pfeffermonopol." *Zeitschrift für ägyptische Sprache und Altertumskunde* 60, pp. 103–11.

———. 1939. *Coptic Dictionary*. Oxford: Oxford University Press.

Cyril of Alexandria. 1864. *Expositio in Johannis Evangelium* (= J.P. Migne, Patrologia Graeca, vol. 73). Paris: Migne.

Dalton, O.M. 1916. "A Coptic Wall-Painting from Wadi Sarga." *JEA* 3, pp. 35–37.

Datema, C. 1985. "New Evidence for the Encounter between Constantinople and 'India.'" In C. Laga, J.A. Munitz, and L. Van Rompay, eds., *After Chalcedon: Studies in Theology and Church History Offered to Professor A. Van Roey for his Seventieth Birthday*, pp. 57–65. OLA 18. Louvain: Peeters/Departement Oosterse Studies.

Davies, W.V. 2006. "British Museum Epigraphic Expedition Report on the 2005 Season." *Annales du Service des antiquités de l'Égypte* 80, pp. 133–51.

———. 2008. "British Museum Epigraphic Expedition Report on the 2006 Season." *Annales du Service des antiquités de l'Égypte* 82, pp. 39–48.

———. 2009. "La tombe de Sataimaou à Hagar Edfou." *Égypte Afrique & Orient* 53, pp. 25–40.

Davies, W.V., and E.R. O'Connell. 2009. "The British Museum Expedition to Elkab and Hagr Edfu, 2009." *British Museum Studies in Ancient Egypt and Sudan* 14, pp. 51–72. http://www.britishmuseum.org/research/online_journals/bmsaes/issue_14/davies_oconnell.aspx.

———. 2011. "The British Museum Expedition to Elkab and Hagr Edfu, 2010." *British Museum Studies in Ancient Egypt and Sudan* 16, pp. 101–32. http://www.britishmuseum.org/research/online_journals/bmsaes/issue_16/davies_oconnell.aspx.

Davis, S.J. 2008. *Coptic Christology in Practice: Incarnation and Divine Participation in Late Antique and Medieval Egypt*. New York: Oxford University Press.

de Cenival, F. 1972. *Les associations religieuses en Égypte*. Cairo: IFAO.

de Grooth, M., and P. van Moorsel. 1977–78. "The Lion, the Man, the Calf and the Eagle in Early Christian and Coptic Art." *BABesch, Bulletin Antieke Beschaving* 52–53, pp. 233–45.

Dekker, R. 2008. "'New' Discoveries at Dayr Qubbat al-Hawâ, Aswan: Architecture, Wall Paintings and Dates." *ECA* 5, pp. 19–36.

Delattre, A. 2010. "Une curieuse table d'ombres au monastère de Baouît." *Le Muséon* 123, pp. 273–86.

Delehaye, H. 1934. *Cinq leçons sur la méthode hagiographique*. Subsidia Hagiographica 21. Brussels: Société des Bollandistes.

de Morgan, J., U. Bouriant, G. Legrain, and G. Jéquier, eds.1894. *Catalogue des monuments et inscriptions de l'Égypte antique.*Vol. 1.Vienna: Adolphe Holzhausen.

———. 1895. *Catalogue des monuments et inscriptions de l'Égypte Antique*. Haute Égypte.Vol. 2, *Kom Ombos*, part 1.Vienna: Adolphe Holzhausen.

Demus, O. 1948. *Byzantine Mosaic Decoration*. London: Routledge & Kegan Paul.

den Heijer, J. 1989. *Mawhub Ibn Mansur Ibn Mufarrig et l'historiographie copto-arabe*. CSCO 513, Subsidia 83. Louvain: Peeters.

———. 1993. "The Composition of the History of the Churches and Monasteries of Egypt: Some Preliminary Remarks." In D. Johnson, ed., *Acts of the Fifth International Congress of Coptic Studies, Washington, 12–15 August 1992*, vol. 2, part 1, pp. 209–19. Rome: Centro Italiano di Microfiche.

Dijkstra, J.H.F. 2002. "Horus on His Throne: The Holy Falcon of Philae in His Demonic Cage." *Göttinger Miszellen* 189, pp. 7–9.

———. 2004. "A Cult of Isis at Philae after Justinian? Reconsidering *P.Cair.Masp.* I 67004." *ZPE* 146, pp. 137–54.

———. 2007a. "'Une foule immense de moines': The Coptic *Life of Aaron* and the Early Bishops of Philae." In B. Palme, ed., *Akten des 23. internationalen Papyrologenkongresses, Wien, 22.–28. Juli 2001*, pp. 191–97. Papyrologica Vindobonensia 1.Vienna: Österreichische Akademie der Wissenschaften.

———. 2007b. "New Light on the Patermouthis Archive from Excavations at Aswan: When Archaeology and Papyrology Meet." *BASP* 44, pp. 179–209.

———. 2008. *Philae and the End of Ancient Egyptian Religion: A Regional Study of Religious Transformation (298–642 CE)*. OLA 173. Louvain and Paris: Peeters.

———. 2012. *Syene I: The Figural and Textual Graffiti from the Temple of Isis at Aswan*. Beiträge zur ägyptischen Bauforschung und Altertumskunde 18. Darmstadt and Mainz: von Zabern.

Dijkstra, J.H.F., and J. van der Vliet. 2003. "'In Year One of King Zachari': Evidence of a New Nubian King from the Monastery of St. Simeon at Aswan." *Beiträge zur Sudanforschung* 8, pp. 31–39.

Dijkstra, J., and M. van Dijk, eds. 2006. *The Encroaching Desert: Egyptian Hagiography and the Medieval West*. Leiden and Boston: Brill.

Dijkstra, J.H.F., and J.J. van Ginkel. 2004. Review of S.G. Richter, *Studien zur Christianisierung Nubiens* (Wiesbaden: Reichert, SKCO 11). *Le Muséon* 117, pp. 233–37.

Dijkstra, J.H.F., and K.A. Worp. 2006. "The Administrative Position of Omboi and Syene in Late Antiquity." *ZPE* 155, pp. 183–87.

Doresse, J. 2000. *Les anciens monastères coptes de Moyenne-Égypte (du Gebel-et-Teir à Kôm-Ishgaou) d'après l'archéologie et l'hagiographie*. Neges Ebrix, Bulletin de l'Institut d'archéologie yverdonnoise 3–5. Lausanne: Institut d'archéologie yverdonnoise.

Edel, E., A. Edel, B. Kohn, and E. Pusch. 2008. *Die Felsgräbernekropole der Qubbet el-Hawa bei Assuan*. Part 1, vols. 1–3. Munich: F. Schöningh.

Edwards, D.N. 2001. "The Christianisation of Nubia: Some Archeological Pointers." *Sudan & Nubia* 5, pp. 89–96.

Effland, A. 1998. "Zur Geschichte der Kopten im Raum Edfu." *Kemet* 7, pp. 44–48.

————. 1999. "Zur Grabungsgeschichte der archäologischen Stätten zwischen Hager Edfu und Nag' al-Hisaja al-Gharbi." In D. Kurth, ed., *Edfu: Bericht über drei Surveys. Materialien und Studien*, pp. 21–39. Die Inschriften des Tempels von Edfu, Supplement 5. Wiesbaden: Harrassowitz.

————. 2004. "Materialien zu Archäologie und Geschichte des Raumes von Edfu." PhD diss., Universität Hamburg.

Eide, T., T. Hägg, R.H. Pierce, and L. Török. 1998. *Fontes Historiae Nubiorum. Textual Sources for the History of the Middle Nile Region between the Eighth Century BC and the Sixth Century AD.* Vol. 3, *From the First to the Sixth Century AD.* Bergen: University of Bergen, Department of Classics.

Erman, A. 1937. *La religion des Égyptiens.* Paris: Payot.

Evelyn-White, H. 1926, 1932, 1933. *The Monasteries of the Wadi 'n Natrun.* The Metropolitan Museum of Art Egyptian Expedition, Parts 1, 2, 3. New York: The Metropolitan Museum of Art. Reprinted, Arno Press, 1973.

————. 1932. *The Monasteries of the Wadi 'n Natrun.* The Metropolitan Museum of Art, Egyptian Expedition. New York: The Metropolitan Museum.

————. 1933. *The Monasteries of the Wadi 'n Natrun.* Vol. 3, *The Architecture and Archaeology.* New York: Metropolitan Museum of Art Press.

Evetts, B.T.A., ed. 1910. *History of the Patriarchs of the Coptic Church of Alexandria.* Vol. 3, *Agathon to Michael I (766).* Patrologia Orientalis 5, fasc. 1. Paris: Firmin-Didot. Reprinted 1947.

Evetts, B.T.A., and A.J. Butler. 1893/1895. *Churches and Monasteries of Egypt and Some Neighbouring Countries Attributed to Abû Sâlih the Armenian.* Oxford: Clarendon Press.

Evetts, B.T.A., and L. Cheikho, eds. 1906. *Eutychii Patriarchae Alexandrini Annales,* by Sa'id ibn al-Batriq. CSCO Arabici 1. Paris and Beirut: Secrétariat du CSCO.

Faber, J.J., and B. Porten. 1986. "The Patermouthis Archive: A Third Look." *BASP* 23, pp. 81–98.

Fakhry, A. 1947. "A Report on the Inspectorate of Upper Egypt. 4.C. The Cemetery of Hagir Edfu." *Annales du Service des antiquités de l'Égypte* 46, pp. 47–48.

Fakhry, A. 1951. *The Egyptian Deserts: The Necropolis of El-Bagawat in Kharga Oasis.* Cairo: Service des antiquités de l'Égypte.

Farid, S. 1967. "Excavations of the Antiquities Department at El-Sebu." In *Campagne internationale de l'UNESCO pour la sauvegarde des monuments de la Nubie: Fouilles en Nubie (1961–1963),* pp. 61–75. Cairo: Ministère du tourisme et des antiquités, Service des antiquités de l'Égypte.

Feldalto, G. 1984. "Liste vescovili del Patriarcato di Alessandria." *Studia Patavina–Rivista di Scienze religiose* 31, pp. 249–323

Fiaccadori, G. 2007. "Monneret de Villard, Ugo." In S. Uhlig, ed., *Encyclopaedia Aethiopica,* vol. 3, pp. 1004–1006. Wiesbaden: Harrassowitz.

Forget, I. 1954. *Synaxarium Alexandrinum.* CSCO 67, Arabici 3–5. Louvain: Secrétariat du CSCO.

Fournet, J.-L., and J. Gascou. 1998. "Papyrus inédits d'Edfou de la collection de l'IFAO." *BIFAO* 98, pp. 171–96.

Frankfurter, D. 1998. *Religion in Roman Egypt: Assimilation and Resistance.* Princeton, NJ: Princeton University Press.

————. 2006. "Hagiography and the Reconstruction of Local Religion in Late Antiquity." In J. Dijkstra and M. van Dijk, eds., *The Encroaching Desert: Egyptian Hagiography and the Medieval West*, pp. 39–55. Leiden and New York: Brill.

Frend, W.H.C. 1968. "Nubia as an Outpost of Byzantine Cultural Influence." *Byzantinoslavica* 29, pp. 319–26.

Gabra, G. 1984. *Untersuchungen zu den Texten über Pesyntheus, Bischof von Koptos (569–632).* Bonn: R. Habelt.

————. 1985. "Zur Bedeutung des Gebietes von Hagir Edfu für die Koptologie und Nubiologie." *MDAIK* 41, pp. 9–14.

————. 1988. "Hatre (Hīdra), Heiliger und Bischof von Aswan im 4. Jahrhundert." *MDAIK* 44, pp. 91–94.

————. 1991. "Hagir Idfu." In A.S. Atiya, ed., *The Coptic Encyclopedia,* vol. 4, p. 1200. New York: Macmillan.

————. 1996. "Untersuchungen zum Difnar der koptischen Kirche. I: Quellenlage, Forschungsgeschichichte und künftige Aufgaben." *BSAC* 35, pp. 37–52.

Gabra, G. 1998a. "Bemerkungen zu Moses dem Schwarzen." In M. Krause and S. Schaten, eds., *ΘΕΜΕΛΙΑ. Spätantike und koptologische Studien Peter Grossmann zum 65. Geburtstag*, pp. 117–26. Wiesbaden: Reichert.

————. 1998b. "Untersuchungen zum Difnar der koptischen Kirche. II: zur Kompilation." *BSAC* 37, pp. 49–68.

————. 2002. *Coptic Monasteries: Egypt's Monastic Art and Architecture.* Cairo: American University in Cairo Press.

Gabra, G., and M. Eaton-Krauss. 2007. *The Treasures of Coptic Art in the Coptic Museum and Churches of Old Cairo.* Cairo: American University in Cairo Press.

Gabra, G., B.A. Pearson, M.N. Swanson, and Y.N. Youssef, eds. 2008. *Historical Dictionary of the Coptic Church.* Lanham, MD; Toronto; Plymouth, UK: Scarecrow Press.

Gabra, G., and G.J.M. van Loon. 2007. *The Churches of Egypt: From the Holy Family to the Present Day.* Cairo: American University in Cairo Press.

Gadallah, F.A. 1959. "The Egyptian Contribution to Nubian Christianity." *Sudan Notes and Records* 40, pp. 38–43.

Gardner, I., and M. Choat. 2004. "Towards a Palaeography of Fourth Century Documentary Coptic." In M. Immerzeel, J. van der Vliet, M. Kersten, and C. Zoest, eds., *Coptic Studies on the Threshold of a New Millennium: Proceedings of the Seventh International Congress of Coptic Studies, Leiden, 27 August–2 September 2000*, vol. 1, pp. 495–503. OLA 133. Louvain, Paris, and Dudley, MA: Peeters.

Garitte, G. 1966. "Textes hagiographiques orientaux relatifs à Saint Léonce de Tripoli." *Le Muséon: Revue d'études orientales* 79, pp. 357–58 §IV.

Gascoigne, A. 2005. "Dislocation and Continuity in Early Islamic Provincial Urban Centres: The Example of Tell Edfou." *MDAIK* 61, pp. 153–89.

Gascoigne, A.L., and P.J. Rose. 2010. "Fortification, Settlement and Ethnicity in Southern Egypt." In P. Matthiae et al., eds., *Proceedings of the Sixth International Congress on the Archaeology of the Ancient Near East, May 5–10, 2009, "Sapienza"—Università di Roma*, vol. 3, pp. 45–54. Wiesbaden: Harrassowitz.

Gascou, J. 1979. "Papyrus grecs inédits d'Apollônos Anô." In *Hommages à la mémoire de Serge Sauneron 2: Égypte post-pharaonique*, 30–33. Bibliothèque d'étude 82. Cairo: IFAO.

———. 1994. "Deux inscriptions byzantines de Haute-Égypte (réédition de *I. Thèbes–Syène* 169 r° et v°)." *Travaux et mémoires* 12, pp. 323–42.

———. 1999. "Edfou au Bas-Empire, d'après les trouvailles de l'IFAO." In *Tell-Edfou soixante ans après. Actes du colloque franco-polonais, Le Caire, 15 octobre 1996*, pp. 13–20. Fouilles franco-polonaises 4. Cairo: IFAO.

Gillet, A. 1993. "The Date and Circumstances of Olympiodoros of Thebes." *Traditio* 48, pp. 1–29.

Godlewski, W. 1992. "The Early Period of Nubian Art: Middle of Sixth–Beginning of Ninth Centuries." In Ch. Bonnet, ed., *Études nubiennes. Conférence de Genève. Actes du VIIe Congrès international d'études nubiennes, 3–8 septembre 1990*, vol. 1, pp. 277–305. Neuchâtel: Compotronic.

———. 2004. "The Rise of Makuria (Late Fifth–Eighth Cent.)." In T. Kendall, ed., *Nubian Studies 1998: Proceedings of the Ninth Conference of the International Society of Nubian Studies, August 21–26, 1998*, pp. 52–73. Boston: Boston University Department of African-American Studies.

———. 2006a. *Dongola, City of Kings and Bishops.* Warsaw: PCMA. DVD publication.

———. 2006b. *Pachoras: The Cathedrals of Aetios, Paulos and Petros. The Architecture.* PAM Supplement 1. Warsaw: Warsaw University Press.

———. Forthcoming. "A Short Essay on the History of Nobadia from Roman to Mamluk Times." In J.L. Hagen and J. van der Vliet, eds., *Qasr Ibrim, between Egypt and Africa.* Leiden: Nederlands Instituut voor het Nabije Oosten.

Godron, G. 1970. *Textes coptes relatifs à saint Claude d'Antioche.* Patrologia Orientalis 35 fasc. 4 N166. Turnhout: Brepols.

———. 1991. "Healings in Coptic Literature." In A.S. Atiya, ed., *The Coptic Encyclopedia*, vol. 4, pp. 1212–14. New York: Macmillan.

Goehring, J.E. 2005. "The Dark Side of Landscape: Ideology and Power in the Christian Myth of the Desert." In D.B. Martin and P.C. Miller, eds., *The Cultural Turn in Late Ancient Studies: Gender, Asceticism, and Historiography*, pp. 136–49. Durham, NC: Duke University Press.

Goodspeed, E., and W.E. Crum. 1908. *The Conflict of Severus Patriarch of Antioch by Athanasius.* Patrologia Orientalis 4 fasc. 6. Paris: Firmin-Didot.

Goyon, G. 1957. *Nouvelles inscriptions rupestres du Wadi Hammamat.* Paris: Librairie d'Amérique et d'Orient.

Griffith, F.Ll. 1927. "Oxford Excavations in Nubia." *LAAA* 14, pp. 57–115.

———. 1928. "Christian Documents from Nubia." *Proceedings of the British Academy* 14, pp. 117–46.

Grillmeier, A., and T. Hainthaler. 1996. *Christ in Christian Tradition.* Vol. 2, part 4, translated by O.C. Dean. London: Mowbray; Louisville, KY: Westminster.

Grossmann, P. 1971. "Zur Datierung der frühen Kirchenanlagen aus Faras." *BZ* 64, pp. 330–50.

——. 1982. *Mittelalterliche Langhauskuppelkirchen und verwandte Typen in Oberägypten: Eine Studie zum mittelalterlichen Kirchenbau in Ägypten*. Glückstadt: J.J. Augustin.

——. 1985. "Ein neuer Achtstützenbau im Raum von Aswan in Oberägypten." In P. Kriéger-Posener, ed., *Mélanges Gamal Eddin Mokhtar*, pp. 339–48. Cairo: IFAO.

——. 1991a. "Architectural Elements of the Churches: Apse." In A.S. Atiya, ed., *Coptic Encyclopedia*, vol. 1, pp. 195–96. New York: Macmillan.

——. 1991b. "Dayr al-Kubāniyyah: Architecture." In A.S. Atiya, ed., *The Coptic Encyclopedia*, vol. 3, pp. 815–16. New York: Macmillan.

——. 1991c. "Dayr Anbā Hadrā: Architecture." In A.S. Atiya, ed., *The Coptic Encyclopedia*, vol. 3, pp. 745–46. New York: Macmillan.

——. 1991d. "Dayr Qubbat al-Hawā: Architecture." In A.S. Atiya, ed., *The Coptic Encyclopedia*, vol. 3, pp. 851–52. New York: Macmillan.

——. 1991e. "Kom Ombo." In A.S. Atiya, ed., *The Coptic Encyclopedia*, vol. 5, p. 1418. New York: Macmillan.

——. 1995. "Tempel als Ort des Konflikts in christlicher Zeit." In P. Borgeaud et al., eds., *Le temple, lieu de conflit: Actes du colloque de Cartigny 1991* pp. 181–201. Louvain: Peeters.

——. 2002. *Christliche Architektur in Ägypten*. Handbook of Oriental Studies, section 1: The Near and Middle East 62. Leiden: Brill.

Hahn, J. 2008. "Die Zerstörung der Kulte von Philae. Geschichte und Legende am ersten Nilkatarakt." In J. Hahn, S. Emmel, and U. Gotter, eds., *From Temple to Church: Destruction and Renewal of Local Cultic Topography in Late Antiquity*. Religions in the Graeco-Roman World 163, pp. 203–42. Leiden: Brill.

Hall, H.R. 1905. *Coptic and Greek Texts of the Christian Period from Ostraca, Stelae, etc. in the British Museum*. London: The British Museum.

Harrell, J.A. 1989. "An Inventory of Ancient Egyptian Quarries." *Newsletter of the American Research Center in Egypt* 146, pp. 1–7, plus cover photo. Reprinted, in part, in the *Newsletter of the Association for the Study of Marble and Other Stones in Antiquity*, 1990, vol. 3, no. 2, pp. 3 and 5–8.

Hasitzka, M.R.M. 1990. *Neue Texte und Dokumentation zum Koptisch-Unterricht*. Mitteilungen aus der Papyrussammlung der Österreichischen Nationalbibliothek 18. Vienna: Österreichische Nationalbibliothek.

——, ed. 1993–2006. *Koptisches Sammelbuch*. Mitteilungen aus der Papyrussammlung der Österreichischen Nationalbibliothek, n.s. Vienna: Hollinek; Munich and Leipzig, K.G. Saur.

Henry, A., ed. 2006. *Stone Conservation Principles and Practice*. Shaftesbury: Donhead Publishing.

Heurtel, Ch. 1998. "Reçus coptes d'Edfou." In M. Rassart-Debergh, ed., *Études coptes 5*, pp. 137–51. Cahiers de la bibliothèque copte 10. Paris and Louvain: Peeters.

Hinds, M., and H. Sakkout. 1981. "A Letter from the Governor of Egypt to the King of Nubia and Muqurra concerning Egyptian-Nubian Relations in 141/758." In W. al-Qadi, ed., *Studia arabica et islamica: Festschrift for Ihsân 'Abbâs on His Sixtieth Birthday*, pp. 209–29. Beirut: American University in Beirut Press. Reprinted 1996 in M. Hinds, *Studies in Early Islamic History. Studies in Late Antiquity and Early Islam* 4, pp. 160–87. Princeton, NJ: Darwin Press.

Hussey, J.M. 1966. *The Cambridge Medieval History.* Vol. 4, *The Byzantine Empire: Part 1, Byzantium and Its Neighbours.* Cambridge: Cambridge University Press.

Husson, G. 1990. "Houses in Syene in the Patermouthis Archive." *BASP* 27, pp. 123–37.

Hyvernat, H. 1977. *Les actes des martyrs d'Égypte.* Hildesheim and New York: Georg Olms.

Ihm, C. 1960. *Die Programme der christlichen Apsismalerei vom vierten Jahrhundert bis zur Mitte des achten Jahrhunderts.* Wiesbaden: Franz Steiner.

Immerzeel, M. 2008. "Playing with Light and Shadow: The Stuccoes of Deir al-Surian and Their Historical Context." *ECA* 5, pp. 59–74.

Innemée, K.C. 1992. *Ecclesiastical Dress in the Medieval Near East.* Leiden: Brill.

——. 1995a. "Deir al-Sourian: The Annunciation as Part of a Cycle?" *Cahiers archéologiques* 43, pp. 129–32.

——. 1995b. "Observations on the System of Nubian Church-decoration." *Cahiers de recherches de l'Institut de papyrologie et d'égyptologie de Lille* 17, pp. 279–89.

——. 1998. "The Iconographical Program of Paintings in the Church of al-Adra in Deir al-Surian: Some Preliminary Observations." In M. Krause and S. Schaten, eds., *ΘΕΜΕΛΙΑ: Spätantike und koptologische Studien Peter Grossmann zum 65. Geburtstag.* SKCO 3, pp. 143–53. Wiesbaden: Reichert.

——. 2000. "Topographical Elements in Floor Mosaics in Syria and Jordan." *Essays on Christian Art and Culture in the Middle East* 3, pp. 20–29.

——. 2005. "Excavations at the Site of Deir al-Baramus 2002–2005." *BSAC* 44, pp. 55–68.

——. 2011. "A Newly Discovered Painting of the Epiphany in Deir al-Surian." *Hugoye: Journal of Syriac Studies* 14, no. 1, pp. 63–85.

Innemée, K.C., and L. van Rompay. 1998. "La présence des Syriens dans le Wadi al-Natrun (Égypte). À propos des découvertes récentes de peintures et de textes muraux dans l'Église de la Vierge du Couvent des Syriens." *Parole de l'Orient* 23, pp. 167–202.

——. 2002. "Deir al-Surian (Egypt). New discoveries of 2001–2002." *Hugoye* 5, no. 2. http://syrcom.cua.edu/hugoye/Vol5No2/HV5N2InnemeeVanRompay.html

Innemée, K.C., and Y.N. Youssef. 2007. "Virgins with Censers: A Tenth-century Painting of the Dormition in Deir al-Surian." *BSAC* 46, pp. 71–85.

Jakobielski, S. 1972. *Faras 3: A History of the Bishopric of Pachoras on the Basis of Coptic Inscriptions.* Warsaw: PWN–Éditions scientifiques de Pologne.

——. 1993. "The Report on Salvage Works on Kom H Effected in 1990 Field Season." *Kush* 16, pp. 305–33.

——. 2001. "Das Kloster der Heiligen Dreifaltigkeit: Bauphasen des nordwestlichen Anbaus." In S. Jakobielski and P.O. Scholz, eds., *Dongola-Studien: 35 Jahre polnischer Forschungen im Zentrum des makuritischen Reiches*, pp. 141–68. Warsaw: ZAŚ PAN.

———. 2008. "The Holy Trinity Monastery in Old Dongola." In W. Godlewski, A. Łajtar, and I. Zych, eds., *Between the Cataracts: Proceedings of the Eleventh Conference for Nubian Studies, Warsaw University, 27 August–2 September 2006*. Part 1: *Main Papers*, pp. 283–302. PAM Supplement Series 2.1. Warsaw: Warsaw University Press.

Jakobielski, S., and P.O. Scholz, eds. 2001. *Dongola-Studien: 35 Jahre polnischer Forschungen im Zentrum des makuritischen Reiches*. Warsaw: ZAŚ PAN.

Jakobielski, S., and J. van der Vliet. 2011. "From Aswan to Dongola: The Epitaph of Bishop Joseph (died AD 668)." In A. Łajtar and J. van der Vliet, eds., *Nubian Voices: Studies in Christian Nubian Culture. JJP* Supplement 15, pp. 15–35. Warsaw: Warsaw University.

Jaritz, H., and M. Rodziewicz. 1994. "Syene: Review of the Urban Remains and Its Pottery." *MDAIK* 50, pp. 115–41.

———. 1996. "Syene: Investigation of the Urban Remains in the Vicinity of the Temple of Isis (II)." *MDAIK* 52, pp. 233–49.

Jastrzębowska, E. 1994. "Encore sur la quadrature du nimbe." In A.R. Veganzones, ed., *Historiam pictura refert*, pp. 347–59. Vatican City: Pontificio Instituto di Archeologia Cristiana.

Jefferson, D., S. Hanna, B. Martin, and D.M. Jones. 2006. *Identifying and Sourcing Stone for Historic Building Repair: An Approach to Determining and Obtaining Compatible Replacement Stone*. Technical Advice Note. Swindon: English Heritage.

Jeute, P. 1994. "Monasteries in Nubia: An Open Issue." *Nubica* 3, no. 1, pp. 59–97.

Johnson, D. 1980. *A Panegyric on Macarius Bishop of Tkôw Attributed to Dioscorus of Alexandria*. CSCO 415, 416; Scriptores Coptici 41 (text), 42 (translation). Louvain: Secrétariat du CSCO.

Jones, M. 1992. "An Unusual Foundation Deposit at Kom Ombo." *BSAC* 31, pp. 97–107.

Junker, H. 1922. *Das Kloster am Isisberg. Bericht über die Grabungen der Akademie der Wissenschaften in Wien bei El-Kubanieh, Winter 1910–1911*. Vienna: Akademie der Wissenschaften.

Kalavrezou-Maxeiner, I. 1975. "The Imperial Chamber at Luxor." *Dumbarton Oaks Papers* 29, pp. 225–51.

Kamel, N., and A. Naguib. 2003. *Tarikh al-masihiya wa 'atharuha fi Aswan wa-l-Nuba*. Cairo: 3Jo Group.

Kitchen, K. 2003. *On the Reliability of the Old Testament*. Cambridge: Eerdmans.

Korsholm Nielsen, H.C. 2004. "Tribal Identity and Politics in Aswan Governorate." In N. Hopkins and R. Saad, eds., *Upper Egypt: Identity and Change*. Cairo: American University in Cairo Press.

Kubińska, J. 1974. *Faras 4: Inscriptions grecques chrétiennes*. Warsaw: Éditions scientifiques de Pologne.

Krause, M. 1975. "Die Formulare der christlichen Grabsteine Nubiens." In K. Michałowski, ed., *Nubia: Récentes recherches*, pp. 76–82. Warsaw: Musée national.

———. 1981. "Das christliche Alexandrien und seine Beziehungen zum koptischen Ägypten." In N. Hinske, ed., *Alexandrien: Kulturbegegnung dreier*

Jahrtausende im Schmelztiegel einer mediterranen Großstadt, pp. 53–62. Aegyptiaca Treverensia 1. Mainz: Philipp von Zabern.

Kruit, N., and K.A. Worp. 2002. "A Seventh-century List of Jars from Edfou." *BASP* 39, pp. 47–56.

Kühnel, E. 1957. "In Memoriam Ugo Monneret de Villard, 1881–1954." *Ars Orientalis: The Arts of Islam and the East* 2, pp. 627–32. Ann Arbor: University of Michigan.

Ladner, G. 1941. "The So-called Square Nimbus." *Mediaeval Studies* 3, pp. 15–45.

Laferrière, P.-H. 2008. *La bible murale dans les sanctuaires coptes.* MIFAO 127. Cairo: IFAO.

Łajtar, A. 1995. "Greek Inscriptions from the Monastery on Kom H at Old Dongola." In M. Starowieyski, ed., *The Spirituality of Ancient Monasticism,* pp. 51–55. Krakow: Wydawnictwo Benedyktynow.

————. 1997. "Τὸ κάστρον τῶν Μαύρων τὸ πλησίον Φίλων. Der dritte Adam über *P.Haun.* II 26." *JJP* 27, pp. 43–54.

————. 2002. "Georgios, Archbishop of Dongola (+1113) and His Epitaph." In *Studies Presented to Benedetto Bravo and Ewa Wipszycka by Their Disciples. JJP* Supplement 1, pp. 159–92. Warsaw: Raphael Taubenschlag Foundation.

Łajtar, A., and K. Pluskota. 2001. "Inscribed Vessels from the Monastery of the Holy Trinity at Old Dongola." In S. Jakobielski and P.O. Scholz, eds., *Dongola-Studien: 35 Jahre polnischer Forschungen im Zentrum des makuritischen Reiches,* pp. 335–55. Warsaw: ZAŚ PAN.

Łajtar, A., and A. Twardecki. 2003. *Catalogue des inscriptions grecques du Musée National de Varsovie. JJP* Supplement 2. Warsaw: Warsaw University, Raphael Taubenschlag Foundation.

Layton, B. 1985. "Towards a New Coptic Palaeography." In T. Orlandi and F. Wisse, eds., *Acts of the Second International Congress of Coptic Studies, Rome, 22–26 September 1980,* pp. 149–158. Rome: C.I.M.

————. 1987. *Catalogue of Coptic Literary Manuscripts in the British Library Acquired since the Year 1906.* London: British Library.

Leipoldt, J. 1906. *Sinuthii Archimandritae Vitae et Opera Omnia.* CSCO, Coptici 2. Reprint 1954. Louvain: Secrétariat du CSCO.

Leroy, J. 1974. *Les manuscrits coptes et coptes-arabes illustrés.* Paris: P. Geuthner.

————. 1975. *Les peintures des couvents du désert d'Esna.* Cairo: IFAO.

————. 1982. *Les peintures des couvents du Ouadi Natrun.* La peinture murale chez les coptes 2. MIFAO 101. Cairo: IFAO.

Levi Della Vida, G. 1955. "Ugo Monneret de Villard, 1881–1954." *Rivista degli Studi Orientali, Roma* 30, pp. 172–88.

Łukaszewicz, A. 1982. "En marge d'une image de l'anachorète Aaron dans la cathédrale de Faras." *Nubia Christiana* 1, pp. 192–211.

————. 1990. "Some Remarks on the Iconography of Anchorites from the Faras Cathedral." *Nubica* 1/2, pp. 549–56.

————. 1999. "Le papyrus Edfou 8 soixante ans après." In *Tell-Edfou soixante ans après. Actes du colloque franco-polonais, Le Caire, 15 octobre 1996,* pp. 29–35. Fouilles franco-polonaises 4. Cairo: IFAO.

MacCoull, L.S.B. 1988. "The Coptic Papyri from Apollonos Anô." In *Proceedings of the Eighteenth International Congress of Papyrology, Athens, 25–31 May 1986*, pp. 141–60. Reprinted in *Coptic Perspectives on Late Antiquity* 11. Norfolk: Galliard.

MacCoull, L.S.B. 1990. "Christianity at Syene/Elephantine/Philae." *BASP* 27, pp. 151–62.

Malak, H. 1964. "Les livres liturgiques de l'église copte." *Mélanges Eugène Tisserant*, 3, Studi e Testi 233, pp. 1–35. Vatican City: Biblioteca Apostolica Vaticana.

Mallon, A. 1911–12. "Coptica." *Mélanges de la Faculté orientale (Université Saint-Joseph, Beyrouth)* 5, pp. 121*–34*.

al-Maqrizi, T. 1892. *al-Mawaiz wa al-I'tibar fi thikr al-Khitat wa al-Athar*. Vol. 2. Cairo (Bulaq): Government Press.

———. 1895. "Account of the Monasteries and Churches of the Christians in Egypt." In B.T.A. Evetts, *The Churches and Monasteries of Egypt*. Oxford: Clarendon.

Mariette, A., and G. Maspero. 1889. *Monuments divers recueillis en Égypte et en Nubie*. Paris: Franck.

Martin, A. 1996. *Athanase d'Alexandrie et l'église d'Égypte au IVe siècle (328–373)*. Rome: École française de Rome.

Martin, J. 2001. *Spätantike und Völkerwanderung*. 4th ed. Oldenbourg Grundriss der Geschichte 4. Munich: Oldenbourg.

Martin, M. 1997. "Le Delta chrétien à la fin du XII° siècle." *Orientalia Christiana Periodica* 63, pp. 181–99.

———. 1998. "Alexandrie chrétienne à la fin du XII° siècle d'après Abu l-Makarim" In C. Décobert and J.Y. Empereur, eds., *Alexandrie médiévale*, vol. 1, pp. 45–49. Études alexandrines 3. Cairo : IFAO.

———. 2000. "Chrétiens et musulmans à la fin du XII° siècle." *Valeur et distance: Identités et sociétés en Egypte*, pp. 83–92. Paris: Maison méditerranéenne des sciences de l'homme.

———. 2004. "Dévotions populaires au Caire à la fin du XIIe siècle." In U. Zanetti and E. Lucchesi, eds., *Aegyptus Christiana: Mélanges d'hagiographie égyptienne et orientale dédiés à la mémoire du P. Paul Devos Bollandiste*. Cahiers d'orientalisme 25, pp. 313–20. Geneva: Patrick Cramer.

Maspero, J. 1910. "Le roi Mercure à Tâfah." *Annales du Service des antiquités de l'Égypte* 10, pp. 17–20.

Maspero, J., and É. Drioton. 1931–43. *Fouilles exécutées à Baouît par Jean Maspero. Notes mises en ordre et éditées par Étienne Drioton*. MIFAO 59. Cairo: IFAO.

al-Masry, H.I. 1940. "The Rite of the Filling of the Chalice." *BSAC* 6, pp. 77–90.

Mathäus, B. 1985. *al-Difnar: Qibti-Arabi*. Beni Soueif: Anba Ruweis.

McKenzie, J.S. 2007. *The Architecture of Alexandria and Egypt, c. 300 BC to AD 700*. New Haven, CT: Pelican.

McVey, K.E. 1993. *George, Bishop of the Arabs: A Homily on Blessed Mar Severus Patriarch of Antioch*. CSCO, Syri 216. Louvain: Secrétariat du CSCO.

Meinardus, O.F.A. 1977. *Christian Egypt, Ancient and Modern*. 2nd rev. ed. Cairo: American University in Cairo Press.

———. 1989. *Monks and Monasteries of the Egyptian Deserts*. Cairo: American University in Cairo Press.

————. 1999. *Two Thousand Years of Coptic Christianity*. Cairo: American University in Cairo Press.

————. 2002. *Monks and Monasteries of the Egyptian Deserts*. Cairo: American University in Cairo Press.

————. 2006. *Monks and Monasteries of the Egyptian Desert*. Rev. ed. Cairo: American University in Cairo Press.

Mekhaiel, N. 2008. "Shenoute as Reflected in the *Vita* and the *Difnar*." In G. Gabra and H.N. Takla, eds., *Christianity and Monasticism in Upper Egypt*, vol. 1, *Akhmim and Sohag*, pp. 99–106. Cairo: American University in Cairo Press.

————. 2009a. *Untersuchungen zur Entstehung und Überlieferungsgeschichte des koptischen Difnars anhand der Hymnen der letzten vier Monate des koptischen Jahres*. Münster: Aschendorff Verlag.

————. 2009b. "Wichtige Personen der koptischen Kirche des 4. Jahrhunderts im Spiegel des Difnars." *Hallesche Beiträge zur Orientwissenschaft* 43 (7). Halle/Saale: Druckerei der Martin-Luther-Universität Halle Wittenberg.

Messiha, H. 1992. "Portable Altars—Luxor Treasure (1893)." *BSAC* 31, pp. 129–34 and pls. XVII–XIX.

Meurice, C. 2006. "Découverte et premières études des peintures du monastère de Saint-Siméon à Assouan." In A. Boud'hors, J. Gascou, and D. Vaillancourt, eds., *Études coptes 9: Onzième journée d'études, Strasbourg 12–14 juin 2003*, pp. 291–302, pl. 6. Paris: De Boccard.

Michałowski, K. 1967. *Faras: Die Kathedrale aus dem Wüstensand*. Einsiedeln, Zurich, and Cologne: Benziger Verlag.

————. 1970. "Open Problems of Nubian Art and Culture in the Light of the Discoveries at Faras." In E. Dinkler, ed., *Kunst und Geschichte Nubiens in christlicher Zeit*, pp. 11–28. Recklinghausen: Aurel Bongers.

————. 1974a. *Faras: Wall Paintings in the Collection of the National Museum in Warsaw*. Warsaw: Wydawnictwo Artystyczno-Graficzne.

————. 1974b. *Faras: Die Wandbilder in den Sammlungen des Nationalmuseums zu Warschau*. Warsaw and Dresden: Wydawnictwo Artystyczno-Graficzne, VEB Verlag der Kunst.

Middleton-Jones, H. 2010. "The Coptic Monasteries Multi-media Database Project." In G. Gabra and H.N. Takla, eds., *Christianity and Monasticism in Upper Egypt*, Vol. 2, *Nag Hammadi–Esna*, pp. 245–51. Cairo: American University in Cairo Press.

Migne, J.-P. 1857. *Patrologia Graeca*. Vol. 26. Paris.

Mileham, G.S. 1910. *Churches in Lower Nubia*. Philadelphia: University Museum.

Mina, T. 1942. *Inscriptions coptes et grecques de Nubie*. Cairo: Société d'archéologie copte.

Mitchell, W.J.T. 1994. *Landscape and Power*. Chicago: University of Chicago Press.

Moawad, S. 2006. "Zur Originalität der Yusab von Fuwah zugeschriebenen Patriarchengeschichte." *Le Museon* 119, pp. 255–70.

————. 2008. "The Relationship of St. Shenoute of Atripe with His Contemporary Patriarchs of Alexandria." In G. Gabra and H.N. Takla, eds., *Christianity and Monasticism in Upper Egypt*, vol. 1, pp. 107–19. Cairo: American University in Cairo Press.

————. 2010. *Untersuchungen zum Panegyrikos auf Makarios von Tkōou und zu seiner Überlieferung.* SKCO 18. Wiesbaden: L. Reichert.

Möller, N. 2005. "Les nouvelles découvertes de Tell Edfou." *Bulletin de la Société française d'égyptologie* 164, pp. 29–46.

Monneret de Villard, U. 1925. "Iscrizioni di 'Anibah." *Aegyptus* 6, p. 250.

————. 1927a. *Description générale du monastère de S. Siméon à Aswân.* Milan: Tipografia e Libreria Pont. e Arcivescovile San Giuseppe.

————. 1927b. *Il monastero di S. Simeone presso Aswân.* Vol. 1, *Descrizione archeologica.* Milano: Tipografia e libreria pontificia arcivescovile s. Giuseppe.

————. 1931a. "L'esplorazione della Nubia medioevale." *Bollettino Assocciazione Internazionale Studi Meditterranei* 2, no. 3, pp. 19–23.

————. 1931b. "La missione per lo studio dei monumenti cristiani della Nubia e i suoi lavori del 1930–31." *Aegyptus* 11, pp. 514–15.

————. 1931c. "Rapporto preliminare dei lavori della missione per lo studio dei monumenti christiani della Nubia 1930–31." *ASAE* 31, pp. 7–18.

————. 1932. "Note nubiane. 1. Articula (Plin., N.H., VI, 184); 2. La chiesa melkita di Nubia." *Aegyptus* 12, pp. 305–16.

————. 1933. *Le iscrizioni del cimitero di Sakinya, Nubia.* Cairo: IFAO.

————. 1934. "I vescovi giacobiti della Nubia." MIFAO 67, *Mélanges Maspero* 2, *Orient grec, roman et byzantine*, fasc. 1, pp. 57–66. Cairo: IFAO.

————. 1935. *La Nubia Medioevale.* Vol. 1, *Inventario dei monumenti.* Service des antiquités de l'Egypte, Mission archéologique de Nubie, 1929–1934. Cairo: IFAO.

————. 1938. *Storia della Nubia Cristiana.* OCA 118. Rome: Pontifical Institute for Oriental Studies.

————. 1948–54. "Nubia." *Enciclopedia Cattolica* 8, col. 1985–87. Vatican City: Enciclopedia Cattolica.

————. 1957. *La Nubia Medioevale.* Vols. 3 and 4: *Origine e sviluppo delle forme monumentali.* Service des antiquités de l'Egypte, Mission archéologique de Nubie, 1929–1934. Cairo: IFAO.

Mora, P., L. Mora, and P. Philippot. 1984. *Conservation of Wall Paintings.* London: Butterworth.

Mossakowska, M. 1999. "Les ostraca et les papyrus d'Edfou dans les collections polonaises." In *Tell-Edfou soixante ans après. Actes du colloque franco-polonais, Le Caire, 15 octobre 1996*, pp. 49–53. Fouilles franco-polonaises 4. Cairo: IFAO.

al-Muharraqi, A.A. 1972. ⲡⲓϫⲱⲙ ⲛ̄ⲧⲉ ⲛⲓⲛ5ϭⲟⲑ ⲉⲑⲟⲩⲁⲃ ⲛ̄5ⲡⲁⲣ5ⲉⲛⲟⲥ ⲛⲓⲁⲅⲅⲉⲗⲟⲥ ⲛⲓⲁⲡⲟⲥⲧⲟⲗⲟⲥ ⲛⲓⲙⲁⲣⲧⲟⲣⲟⲥ ⲛⲉⲙ ⲛⲏⲉ5ⲟⲟⲩⲁⲃ (The Book of the Holy Glorifications of the Virgin, the Angels, the Apostles, the Martyrs, and the Saints). Cairo: self-published.

Müller, C.D.G. 1956. "Benjamin I Patriarch von Alexandrien." *Le Muséon: Revue d'études orientales* 69, pp. 313–40.

————. 1959a. *Die Engellehre der koptischen Kirche: Untersuchungen zur Geschichte der christlichen Frömmigkeit in Ägypten.* Wiesbaden: O. Harrassowitz.

————. 1959b. "Neues über Benjamin I, 38 Agathon 39 Patriarchen von Alexandrien." *Le Muséon: Revue d'études orientales* 72, pp. 323–47.

————. 1978. "Grundzüge der Frömmigkeit in der nubischen Kirche." In J.

Leclant and J.Vercoutter, eds., *Études nubiennes*, pp. 209–24. Cairo: IFAO.

Munier, H. 1916. *Manuscrits coptes. Catalogue général des antiquités égyptiennes du Musée du Caire*. Cairo: IFAO.

————. 1923. "Mélanges de littérature copte 3: Manuscrits coptes sa'idiques d'Assouan." *Annales du Service des antiquités de l'Égypte* 23, pp. 210–28.

————. 1930–31. "Les stèles coptes du monastère de Saint-Siméon à Assouan." *Aegyptus* 11, pp. 257–300, 433–84.

————. 1938. "Le christianisme à Philae." BSAC 4, pp. 37–49.

————. 1943. *Recueil des listes épiscopales de l'Église copte.* Textes et Documents 2. Cairo: Publications de la Société d'archéologie copte.

Muyser, J. 1937. "Des vases eucharistiques en verre." *BSAC* 3, pp. 9–28.

————. 1944. "Contribution à l'étude des listes épiscopales de l'Église copte." *BSAC* 10, pp. 116–76.

Naguib, A. 2009. " 'Alaqat al-kanisah al-qibtiyah bi-l-Nuba min al-qarn al-rabi' wa-hatta al-qarn al-khamis 'ashr" (The Coptic Church and Nubia: Relationship from the Fourth to the Fifteenth Century). PhD diss., Coptic Studies Institute, Cairo.

el-Naqlouny, A. 2010. "Indexing of Manuscripts for the Churches of Naqada and Qus." In Gawdat Gabra and Hany N.Takla, eds., *Christianity and Monasticism in Upper Egypt,* Vol. 2, *Nag Hammadi and Esna*, pp. 105–20. Cairo: American University in Cairo Press.

Nautin, P. 1967. "La conversion du temple de Philae en église chrétienne." *Cahiers archéologiques* 17, pp. 1–43.

Nigm ed Din Mohammed Sherif. 1964. "The Arabic Inscriptions from Meinarti." *Kush* 12, pp. 249–50.

Oates, J., W. Willis, J. Sosin, R. Bagnall, J. Cowey, M. Depauw, T. Wilfong, and K.A. Worp. 2011. *Checklist of Greek, Latin, Demotic and Coptic Papyri, Ostraca and Tablets.* http://scriptorium.lib.duke.edu/papyrus/texts/clist.html

Ochała, G. 2011. "The Date of the Dendur Foundation Inscription Reconsidered." *BASP* 48, pp. 217–24.

O'Connell, E.R. 2007. "Transforming Monumental Landscapes in Late Antique Egypt." In K. Sessa, ed., *Holy Households: Domestic Space, Property, and Power*, in *Journal of Early Christian Studies* 15, pp. 239–74.

————. In press. "The Discovery of Christian Egypt: From Manuscript Hunters toward an Archaeology of Late Antiquity." In G. Gabra, ed., *Coptic Civilization*. Cairo: American University in Cairo Press.

O'Leary, De L. 1923. "Review of H. Junker and H. Demel." *Journal of Egyptian Archaeology* 9, pp. 233.

————. 1924. "Review of H. Junker and H. Demel." *Journal of the Royal Asiatic Society* 56, pp. 309–10.

————. 1926–28. *The Difnar of the Coptic Church from the Manuscript in the John Rylands Library with the Fragments of a Difnar Recently Discovered at the Dêr Abu Makar in the Wadî Natrun*. London: Luzac and Co.

————. 1937a. *The Saints of Egypt*. London: Society for Promoting Christian Knowledge.

————. 1937b. *The Saints of Egypt, an Alphabetical Compendium of Martyrs, Patriarchs and Sainted Ascetes in the Coptic Calendar*. Reprinted 1974. London and New York: Society for Promoting Christian Knowledge.

————. 1952. "Severus of Antioch in Egypt." *Aegyptus, raccolta di scritti in onore di Girolamo Vitelli II*, 32, pp. 425–36.

Opitz, H.-G. 1935–41. *Athanasius Werke*. Vol. 2.1, *Die Apologien*. Berlin: De Gruyter.

Orlandi, T. 1968. "Un Codice Copto del 'Monastero Bianco' Economii de Severo di Antiochia, Marco Evangelista, Atanasio Di Alessandria." *Le Muséon: Revue d'études orientales* 81, pp. 351–405.

————. 1971. "Teodosio d'Alessandria nella letteratura copta." *Giornale Italiano di Filologia* 23, pp. 175–85.

Palanque, Ch. 1906. "Rapport sur les recherches effectuées à Baouit en 1903." *BIFAO* 5, pp. 1–21.

Palladius. 1904. *Lausiac History*. Edited by C. Butler. Texts and Studies 6, Cambridge. Vol. 1, *Prolegomena*; vol. 2, *Introduction and Text*. English translation: R.T. Meyer, 1965, *The Lausiac History*, London: ACW.

Palme, A. 1986. "Corrigenda zu einigen Ostraka aus Edfou." *ZPE* 64, pp. 91–95.

Papaconstantinou, A. 2000. "Les sanctuaires de la Vierge dans l'Égypte byzantine et omeyyade: L'apport des textes documentaires." *JJP* 30, pp. 81–94.

————. 2001a. *Le culte des saints en Égypte des Byzantins aux Abbasides: L'apport des inscriptions et des papyrus grecs et coptes*. Paris: CNRS.

————. 2001b. *Le culte des saints en Égypte des Byzantins aux Abbassides: L'apport des sources papyrologiques et épigraphiques grecques et coptes*. Le monde byzantin. Paris: CNRS Editions.

————. 2006. "Historiography, Hagiography, and the Making of the Coptic 'Church of the Martyrs' in Early Islamic Egypt." *Dumbarton Oaks Papers* 60, pp. 65–86.

————. 2007. "The Cult of Saints: A Haven of Continuity in a Changing World?" In R. Bagnall, ed., *Egypt in the Byzantine World*, 300–700, pp. 350–67. Cambridge: Cambridge University Press.

Payne Smith, R. 1860. *The Third Part of the Ecclesiastical History of John Bishop of Ephesus, Now First Translated from the Original Syriac*. Oxford: Oxford University Press.

Piemontese, A.M. 1987. "Bibliografia delle opere di Ugo Monneret de Villard, 1881–1954." *Rivista degli Studi Orientali* 58, pp. 1–12.

Plumley, J.M. 1981. "A Coptic Precursor of a Medieval Nubian Protocol." *Sudan Texts Bulletin* 3, pp. 5–8.

Plumley, M. 1975. *The Scroll of Bishop Timoteos*. London: Egypt Exploration Society.

Porten, B., ed. 1996. *The Elephantine Papyri in English: Three Millennia of Cross-Cultural Continuity and Change*. Documenta et monumenta orientis antiqui 22. Leiden: Brill.

Quaegebeur, J. 1977. "Les saints égyptiens pré-chrétiens." *Orientalia Lovaniensia Periodica* 8.

Quibell, J.E. 1908. *Excavations at Saqqara (1906–1907)*.Vol. 2. Cairo: IFAO.
———. 1909. *Excavations at Saqqara (1907–1908)*. Cairo: IFAO.
———. 1912. *Excavations at Saqqara (1908–1909, 1909–10):The Monastery of Apa Jeremias*. Cairo: IFAO.
Ramzi, M. 1994. *al-Qamus al-jughrafi li-l-bilad al-misriya min 'ahd qudama' al-misriyin ila sanat 1945*. 2 parts, 6 vols. Cairo: al-Hay'a al-Misriya al-'Amma li-l-Kitab.
Rassart-Debergh, M., and J. Debergh. 1981. "À propos de trois peintures de Saqqara." *AAAHP* 1, pp. 187–205.
Raven, M.J. 1996. "The Temple of Taffeh:A Study of Details." *OMRO* 76, pp. 41–62.
Regnaud, L. 1990. *La vie quotidienne des pères du désert en Égypte au IVe siècle*. Paris: Hachette.
Remondon, R. 1953. *Papyrus grecs d'Apollônos Anô*. Documents de fouilles de l'Institut français d'archéologie orientale du Caire 19. Cairo: IFAO.
Richter, S.G. 2002. *Studien zur Christianisierung Nubiens*. SKCO 11.Wiesbaden: Reichert.
Rodziewicz, M. 1984. *Alexandrie 3: Les habitations romaines tardives d'Alexandrie à la lumière des fouilles polonaises à Kôm el-Dikka*.Warsaw: PWN, Éditions scientifiques de Pologne.
Roquet, G. 1978. "Le morphème *(E)TAH-* et les graffites coptes de Kalabcha." *BIFAO* 78, pp. 533–38.
Russell, N., trans. 1980. *The Lives of the Desert Fathers: The Historia Monachorum in Aegypto*. Kalamazoo, MI: Cistercian.
Rustafjaell, R. 1910. *The Light of Egypt from Recently Discovered Predynastic and Early Christian Records*. London: Kegan Paul, Trench, Trübner.
Rutherford, I. 1998. "Island of the Extremity: Space, Language and Power in the Pilgrimage Traditions of Philae." In D. Frankfurter, ed., *Pilgrimage and Holy Space in Late Antique Egypt*. Religions in the Graeco-Roman World 134, pp. 229–56. Leiden: Brill.
Rutschowscaya, M.H. 1979. "Boîtes à poids d'époque copte." *Revue du Louvre et des Musées de France* 29, no. 1: 1–5.
Sadek, A. 1980. *The Amethyst Mining Inscriptions of Wadi El-Hudi*.Vol. 1. Warminster: Aris and Phillips.
———. 1984. "An Attempt to Translate the Deir el-Bahari Hieratic Inscriptions." *Göttinger Miszellen* 71, no. 1: 67–91.
———. 1988. *Popular Religion in Egypt during the New Kingdom*. Hildesheimer Ägyptologische Beitrage 27. Hildesheim: Pelizaeus Museum.
———. 1993. "L'Égypte, les Hébreux et la Bible." *Le monde copte* 23.
Sadek, A., and B. Sadek. 2011. "Un fleuve d'eau vive." Vol. 1, "Les Sources." *Le monde copte* 34.
Sanders, P.A. 1998. "The Fatimid State, 969–1171." In C.F. Petry, ed., *The Cambridge History of Egypt*.Vol. 1, *Islamic Egypt, 640–1517*, pp. 151–74. Cambridge: University of Cambridge Press.
Säve-Söderbergh, T. 1987. *Temples and Tombs of Ancient Nubia:The International Rescue Campaign at Abu Simbel, Philae and Other Sites*. London and Paris: Thames and Hudson.

Scanlon, G.T. 1970. "Excavations at Kasr el Wizz: A Preliminary Report." *JEA* 56, pp. 29–57.

———. 1972. "Excavations at Kasr el Wizz: A Preliminary Report 2." *JEA* 58, pp. 7–42.

Scarpocchi, U. 1954. "In Memoriam Ugo Monneret de Villard, 1881–1954." *Les cahiers coptes* 7–8, pp. 32–38. Cairo: Institut copte.

Schaff, P., and H. Wace. 1994. *A Selection of Nicene and Post-Nicene Fathers*. 2nd series, 38 vols. Peabody, MA: Hendrickson.

Scholz, P.O. 1988. "Frühchristliche Spuren im Lande des ANHP AIΘIOΨ Historisch-archäologische Betrachtungen zur Apostelgeschichte 8:26–40." PhD diss., University of Bonn.

———. 2003. Review of "Siegfried G. Richter, Studien zur Christianisierung Nubiens (Sprachen und Kulturen des christlichen Orients, Bd. 11, Wiesbaden 2002)." *OrChr* 87, pp. 248–54.

Schrenk, S. 2004. *Textilien des Mittelmeerraumes aus spätantiker bis frühislamischer Zeit*. Fabric analysis by Regina Knaller. Die Textilsammlung der Abegg-Stiftung, vol. 4. Riggisberg: Abegg-Stiftung.

Schulz, H.J. 1980. *Die byzantinische Liturgie*. Trier: Paulinus Verlag.

Seybold, C.F. 1962a. *Severus Ben El-Moqaffaʿ*. Historia Patriarcharum Alexandrinorum CSCO, Arabici 8. Louvain: Secrétariat du CSCO.

———. 1962b. *Severus Ben El-Moqaffaʿ*. Historia Patriarcharum Alexandrinorum CSCO Arabici 9. Louvain: Secrétariat du CSCO.

Shinnie, P., and N. Chittick. 1961. *Ghazali: A Monastery in the Northern Sudan*. SASOP 5. Khartoum: Sudan Antiquities Service.

Siegesmund, S., T. Weiss, and A. Vollbrecht. 2002. "Introduction." In S. Siegesmund and T. Weiss, eds., *Natural Stone, Weathering Phenomena, Conservation Strategies and Case Studies*, pp. 1–7. Geological Society Special Publication 205. London: Geological Society.

Sijpesteijn, P. 2007. "Arabic Papyri and Other Documents from Current Excavations in Egypt (with an Appendix of Arabic Papyri and Some Written Objects in Egyptian Collections." *Al-Bardiyyat: Newsletter of the International Society for Arabic Papyrologists* 2, pp. 10–23.

Simaika, M., and Y. ʿAbd al-Masih. 1939. *Catalogue of the Coptic and Arabic Manuscripts in the Coptic Museum*. Cairo: Publications of the Coptic Museum.

Smith, H.S., S. Davies, and K.J. Frazer. 2006. *The Sacred Animal Necropolis at North Saqqara: The Main Temple Complex, Archaeological Report*. Excavation Memoirs 75. London: Egypt Exploration Society.

Snelders, B., and M. Immerzeel. 2004. "The Thirteenth-Century Flabellum from Deir al-Suryan in the Musée Royal de Mariemont (Morlanwelz, Belgium)." *ECA* 1, pp. 113–39.

Storemyr, P. 2007. "Introduction to Previous Archaeological Research at the West Bank of Aswan." In E. Bloxam, T. Heldal, and P. Storemyr, eds., *Characterisation of Complex Quarry Landscapes: An Example from the West Bank Quarries, Aswan*, pp. 21–36. http://www.quarryscapes.no/text/publications/QS_del4_Report_LR.pdf

Strzygowski, J. 1904. *Koptische Kunst: Catalogue général des antiquités égyptiennes du Musée du Caire.* Vienna: Imprimerie Adolf Holzhausen.

Su'ad Mahir Muhammad. 1977. *Madinat Aswan wa-atharuha fi al-'asr al-islami.* [Cairo: Central Book Organization.]

al-Suriani, S. 1984a. *Tarikh al-kanais wa al-adyurah fi al-qarn al-thani ashr.* Cairo: self-published.

————. 1984b. *Tartib al-Bay'at.* Vol 1. Cairo: Self-published.

————. 1990. "Icônes et iconographie d'après le manuscrit d'Abu el-Makarim, publié en arabe au Caire 1984." *Le monde copte* 18, pp. 78.

al-Suriani, S., and N.K. Daoud. 1989. *Tarikh al-aba' al-batarikah li-Yusab Usquf Fuwwah.* Cairo: self-published.

te Velde, H. 1967. *Seth, God of Confusion: A Study of His Role in Egyptian Mythology.* Leiden: Brill.

Till, W. 1935. *Koptische Heiligen und Martyrerlegenden.* OCA 102. Rome: Pontificio Istituto Orientale.

————. 1936. *Koptische Heiligen und Martyrerlegenden.* OCA 108. Rome: Pontificio Istituto Orientale.

Timm, S. 1979. *Christliche Stätten in Ägypten.* Beiheft zum Tübinger Atlas des Vorderen Orients B36. Wiesbaden: L. Reichert.

————. 1984–92. *Das christlich-koptische Ägypten in arabischer Zeit.* 6 vols. Beiheft zum Tübinger Atlas des Vorderen Orients B41. Wiesbaden: L. Reichert.

————. 1985. *Das christlich-koptische Ägypten in arabischer Zeit.* Tübinger Atlas der Vorderen Orients 41 (3). Wiesbaden: L. Reichert.

Török, L. 1995. "Egyptian Late Antique Art from Nubian Royal Tombs." In C. Moss and K. Kiefer, eds., *Byzantine East, Latin West: Art Historical Studies in Honour of Kurt Weitzmann,* pp. 91–97. Princeton, NJ: Princeton University Press.

————. 1997. *The Kingdom of Kush: Handbook of the Napatan-Meroitic Civilization.* HdO, part 1, vol. 31. Leiden: Brill.

————. 2009. *Between Two Worlds: The Frontier Region between Ancient Nubia and Egypt 3700 BC–AD 500.* Probleme der Ägyptologie 29. Leiden and Boston: Brill.

Tosson, O. 1935. *Wadi al-Natrun wa ad-duyratahu.* Reprint: Cairo: Madbuli Bookshop, 1966.

Valbelle, D., and Ch. Bonnet, eds., 1998. *Le Sinaï durant l'Antiquité et le Moyen Âge: 4000 ans d'histoire pour un désert.* Paris: Errance.

van der Meer, A. 1996. "Het verblijf van Severus van Antiochië in Egypte." *Het Christelijkoosten* 48, pp. 49–72.

van der Meer, F. 1938. *Maiestas Domini.* Rome: Pontificio Istituto di Archeologia Cristiana.

van der Vliet, J. 2003. *Catalogue of the Coptic Inscriptions in the Sudan National Museum at Khartoum (I. Khartoum Copt.).* OLA 121. Louvain: Peeters/ Departement Oosterse Studies.

————. 2004. "History through Inscriptions: Coptic Epigraphy in the Wadi al-Natrun." *Coptica* 3, pp. 187–207. Republished in M.S.A. Mikhail and M. Moussa, eds., *Christianity and Monasticism in Wadi al-Natrun,* pp. 329–49, Cairo: American University in Cairo Press.

————. 2005. Review of S.G. Richter, *Studien zur Christianisierung Nubiens*. Wiesbaden (SKCO 11). *VChr* 59, pp. 219–23.

————. 2006. "Bringing Home the Homeless: Landscape and History in Egyptian Hagiography." In J. Dijkstra and M. van Dijk, eds., *The Encroaching Desert: Egyptian Hagiography and the Medieval West*, pp. 13–37. Leiden and New York: Brill.

Vandorpe, K., and W. Clarysse, eds. 2003. *Edfu: An Egyptian Provincial Capital in the Ptolemaic Period: Brussels, 3 September 2001*. Brussels: Koninklijke Vlaamse Academie van België voor Wetenschappen en Kunsten:Vlaams Kennis- en Cultuurforum.

van Esbroeck, M. 1991. "Epimachus of Pelusium, Saint." In A.S. Atiya, ed., *The Coptic Encyclopedia*, vol. 3, pp. 965–67. New York: Macmillan.

van Gerven Oei, Vincent W.J. 2011. "The Old Nubian Memorial for King George." In Adam Łajtar and Jacques van der Vliet, eds., *Nubian Voices: Studies in Christian Nubian Culture, JJP*, Supplement 15, pp. 225–62. Warsaw: Raphael Taubenschlag Foundation.

van Lantschoot, A. 1929. Recueil des colophons des manuscrits chrétiens d'Égypte 1/1. Louvain: Istas.

van Loon, G.J.M. 2008. Review of S. Schrenk, *Textilien des Mittelmeerraumes aus spätantiker bis frühislamischer Zeit*. Fabric analysis by Regina Knaller. Die Textilsammlung der Abegg-Stiftung, vol. 4 (Riggisberg: Abegg-Stiftung, 2004). *ECA* 5, pp. 147–48.

van Loon, G.J.M., and A. Delattre. 2004. "La frise des saints de l'église rupestre de Deir Abou Hennis." *ECA* 1, pp. 89–112.

————. 2005. "La frise des saints de l'église rupestre de Deir Abou Hennis. Addition et correction." *ECA* 2, p. 167.

————. 2006. "Le cycle de l'enfance du Christ dans l'église rupestre de saint Jean Baptiste à Deir Abou Hennis." In A. Boud'hors, J. Gascou, and D. Vaillancourt, eds., *Études coptes 9. Onzième journée d'études (Strasbourg 12–14 juin 2003)*. Cahiers de la bibliothèque copte 14, pp. 119–34. Paris: De Boccard.

Van Minnen, P. 2006. "Saving History? Egyptian Hagiography in Its Space and Time." In J. Dijkstra and M. van Dijk, eds., *The Encroaching Desert: Egyptian Hagiography and the Medieval West*, pp. 57–91. Leiden and New York: Brill.

van Moorsel, P. 1972. "Die Nubier und das glorreiche Kreuz." *BABesch, Bulletin Antieke Beschaving* 47:125–34.

————. 1978. "The Coptic Apse-composition and Its Living Creatures." *Études nubiennes, colloque de Chantilly, 2–6 juillet 1975*. Bibliothèque d'étude 77, pp. 325–33. Cairo: IFAO.

————. 1986a. "Analepsis? Some Patristic Remarks on a Coptic Double-composition." In O. Feld and U. Peschlow, eds., *Studien zur spätantiken und byzantinischen Kunst Friedrich Wilhelm Deichmann gewidmet* 3. Monographien des Römisch-Germanischen Zentralmuseums, vol. 10, pp. 137–41. Mainz: Habelt Verlag.

————. 1986b. "The Vision of Philotheus (on Apse-decorations)." In M. Krause, ed., *Nubische Studien: Tagungsakten der 5. internationalen Konferenz der International Society for Nubian Studies, Heidelberg, 22–25 September 1982*, pp. 337–40. Mainz am Rhein: Philip von Zabern.

————. 1995. *Les peintures du monastère de Saint-Antoine près de la Mer Rouge*. MIFAO 112. Cairo: IFAO.

————. 2000a. "On Coptic Apse-compositions, among Other Things." In P. van Moorsel, ed., *Called to Egypt: Collected Studies on Paintings in Christian Egypt*, pp. 91–96. Leiden: Nederlands Instituut voor het Nabije Oosten.

————. 2000b. "The Vision of Philotheus (on Apse-decorations)." In P. van Moorsel, ed., *Called to Egypt: Collected Studies on Paintings in Christian Egypt*, pp. 107–14. Leiden: Nederlands Instituut voor het Nabije Oosten.

van Moorsel, P., J. Jacquet, and H. Schneider. 1975. *The Central Church of Abdallah Nirqi*. Leiden: Brill, National Museum of Antiquities.

Van Roey, A., and P. Allen. 1994. *Monophysite Texts of the Sixth Century*. OLA 56. Louvain: Peeters.

Vansleb, J.M. 1672. *Histoire de l'Église d'Alexandrie*. Paris: Clousier & Prome.

Vantini, G. 1970. "The Excavations at Faras: A Contribution to the History of Christian Nubia." *Museum Combonianum* 24, Collana di Studi Africani dei Missionari Comboniani. Bologna: Editrice Negrizia.

————. 1975. *Oriental Sources concerning Nubia*. Collected and translated by G. Vantini. Heidelberg: Heidelberger Akademie der Wissenschaften; Warsaw: Polish Academy of Sciences.

————. 1981. *Christianity in the Sudan*. Bologna: EMI.

Vernus, P. 1986. "Tell Edfu." In W. Helck and E. Otto, eds., *Lexikon der Ägyptologie* 6, pp. 323–31. Wiesbaden: Harrassowitz.

Viaud, G. 1967–68. "La procession des deux Fêtes de la Croix et du Dimanche des Rameaux dans l'église copte." *BSAC* 19, pp. 211–26.

————. 1979. *Les pèlerinages coptes en Égypte: D'après les notes du Qommos Jacob Muysser*. Bibliothèque d'études coptes 15. Cairo: IFAO.

Vivian, T. 1993. *Histories of the Monks of Egypt and The Life of Onnophrius*. Cistercian Studies 140. Kalamazoo, MI: Cistercian Publications.

Vojtenko, A. 2008. "Parents de l'empereur de Byzance dans les déserts d'Égypte: Les Vies d'Apa Cyrus et d'Hilarie la Bienheureuse." In A. Boud'hors and C. Louis, eds., *Études coptes 10, douzième journée d'études (Lyon 19–21 mai 2005)*, pp. 309–18. Cahiers de la bibliothèque copte 16. Paris: De Boccard.

von Pilgrim, C., K.-Chr. Bruhn, J.H.F. Dijkstra, and J. Wininger. 2006. "The Town of Syene: Report on the Third and Fourth Season in Aswan." *MDAIK* 62, pp. 215–77.

von Pilgrim, C., K.-Chr. Bruhn, and A. Kelany. 2004. "The Town of Syene: Preliminary Report on the First and Second Season in Aswan." *MDAIK* 60, pp. 119–48.

von Pilgrim, C., D. Keller, S. Martin-Kilcher, F.M. el-Amin, and W. Müller. 2008. "The Town of Syene: Report on the Fifth and Sixth Season in Aswan." *MDAIK* 64, pp. 307–58.

Walters, C.C. 1974. *Monastic Archaeology in Egypt*. Warminster: Aris & Phillips.

Warke, P.A., J. McKinley, and B.J. Smith. 2006. "Weathering of Building Stone: Approaches to Assessment, Prediction and Modelling." In S.K. Kourkoulis, ed.,

Fracture and Failure of Natural Building Stones: Applications in the Restoration of Ancient Monuments, pp. 313–27. Dordrecht: Springer.

Weitzmann, K. 1970. "Some Remarks on the Sources of the Fresco Paintings in the Cathedral of Faras." In E. Dinkler, ed., *Kunst und Geschichte Nubiens in christlicher Zeit*, p. 331. Recklinghausen: Bongers Verlag.

———. 1974. *Loca Sancta and the Representational Arts of Palestine*. Dumbarton Oaks Papers 28, pp. 35–39. Washington, DC: Dumbarton Oaks.

Welsby, D.E. 2002. *The Medieval Kingdoms of Nubia: Pagans, Christians and Muslims along the Middle Nile*. London: British Museum Press.

Westendorf, W. 1977. *Koptisches Handwörterbuch*. Heidelberg: Universitätsverlag C. Winter. Reprinted 2000.

Wietheger, C. 1992. *Das Jeremias-Kloster zu Saqqara unter besonderer Berücksichtigung der Inschriften*. Arbeiten zum spätantiken und koptischen Ägypten 1. Altenberge: Oros.

Winlock, H.E., and W.E. Crum. 1926. *The Monastery of Epiphanius at Thebes*. 2 vols. New York: Metropolitan Museum.

Winter, E. 1982. "Philae." In W. Helck and E. Otto, eds., *Lexikon der Ägyptologie*, vol. 4, pp. 1022–27. Wiesbaden: Harrassowitz.

Wipszycka, E. 2009. *Moines et communautés monastiques en Égypte (IVe–VIIIe siècles)*. *JJP* Supplement 11. Warsaw: Raphael Taubenschlag Foundation.

Witte-Orr, J. 2010. *Kirche und Wandmalereien am Karm al-Ahbariya. JbAC* Ergänzungsband 36. Münster: Aschendorff.

Worp, K.A. 1994. "A Checklist of Bishops in Byzantine Egypt (A.D. 325–c. 750)." *ZPE* 100, pp. 283–318.

Yaqut al-Hamawi. 1977. *Mu'jam al-buldan*. 5 vols. Beirut: Dar Sadir.

Yassin, M. 2006. "Geological Exploration for the Friendship Project, East Aswan, Egypt." IAEG Paper number 707.

Youssef, Y.N. 1994. "Quelques titres des congrégations des moines coptes." *Göttinger Miszellen* 139, pp. 61–67.

———. 1998–99. "Multiconfessional Churches in Egypt during the Twelfth Century." *Bulletin of Saint Shenouda the Archimandrite Coptic Society* 5, pp. 45–54.

———. 2002. "Coptic Monastic Sites in the Seventh and Eighth Centuries According to a Homily Ascribed to Severus of Antioch." *Coptic Church Review* 23, no. 4, pp. 103–107.

———. 2004. *The Arabic Life of Severus of Antioch Attributed to Athanasius*. Patrologia Orientalis 49 Fasc. 4 N 220 (Pontificio Istituto Orientale–Roma). Turnhout: Brepols.

———. 2005. "A Doxology of St Elijah." *BSAC* 44, pp. 93–104.

———. 2006a. "The Archangel Michael and the Patriarchs in Exile in the Coptic Tradition." In N. Bosson and A. Boud'hors, eds., *Actes du huitième congrès international d'études coptes, Paris, 28 juin–3 juillet, 2004*, pp. 645–56. OLA 163. Louvain, Paris, and Dudley MA: Peeters.

———. 2006b. *A Homily on Severus of Antioch by a Bishop of Assiut*. Patrologia Orientalis 50 Fasc. 1 N 222 (Pontificio Istituto Orientale–Roma). Turnhout: Brepols.

————. 2006c. "Severus of Antioch in Scetis." *Ancient Near Eastern Studies* 43, pp. 141–62.

————. 2007. "Procession of the Cross and Palm Sunday according to a Manuscript from Saint Macarius." *BSAC* 47, pp. 159–68.

————. 2008a. "Bohairic Liturgical Texts Related to St Shenoute." In G. Gabra and H.N. Takla, eds., *Christianity and Monasticism in Upper Egypt*, vol. 1, pp. 179–200. Cairo: American University in Cairo Press.

————. 2008b. "John, Bishop of Assiut, Manfalut and Abu Tig." *Collectanea Christiana Orientalia* 5, pp. 183–99.

Youssef, Y.N., and U. Zanetti. Forthcoming. "The Description of the Rites of the Concoction of the Myron by Pope Gabriel IV by Bishop Athanasius of Qus."

Yoyotte, Jean. 1959. "Déserts." In *Dictionnaire de la civilisation égyptienne*. Paris: Fernand Hazan.

Zanetti, U. 1995a. "Abu l-Makarim et Abu Salih." *BSAC* 34, pp. 85–133.

————. 1995b. "Bohairic Liturgical Manuscripts." *Orientalia Christiana Periodica* 60, pp. 65–94.

Zaynahum, M., and M. al-Sharqawi. 1998. *Al-Mawa'iz wa-l-i'tibar bi-dhikr al-khitat wa-l-athar al-ma'ruf bi-l-khitat al-maqriziya, ta'lif Taqi al-Din Ahmad ibn 'Ali al-Maqrizi*. 3 vols. Cairo: Maktabat Madbuli.

Zibawi, M. 2003. *Images de l'Égypte chrétienne: Iconologie copte*. Paris: Picard.

————. 2004. *Koptische Kunst: Das christliche Ägypten von der Spätantike bis zur Gegenwart*. Milan: Schnell & Steiner.

Żurawski, B. 1999. "Faith Healing, Philanthropy and Commemoration in Late Christian Dongola." In S. Emmel, M. Krause, S.G. Richter, and S. Schaten, eds., *Ägypten und Nubien in spätantiker und christlicher Zeit. Akten des 6. Internationalen Koptologenkongresses Münster, 20–26 Juli 1996*, vol. 1, pp. 423–48. Wiesbaden: Reichert.

————. 2007. "Banganarti 2004/2005." *PAM 17: Reports 2005*, pp. 301–21.

————. 2008. "The Churches of Banganarti, 2002–2006." In W. Godlewski, A. Lajtar, and I. Zych, eds., *Between the Cataracts: Proceedings of the Eleventh Conference for Nubian Studies, Warsaw University, 27 August–2 September 2006*. Part 1: *Main Papers*, pp. 303–20. PAM Supplement Series 2.1. Warsaw: Warsaw University Press.